Stephen A. Douglas

Stephen A. Douglas
*The Political Apprenticeship,
1833–1843*

Reg Ankrom

McFarland & Company, Inc., Publishers
Jefferson, North Carolina

LIBRARY OF CONGRESS CATALOGUING-IN-PUBLICATION DATA

Ankrom, Reg, 1946–
Stephen A. Douglas : the political apprenticeship, 1833–1843 / Reg Ankrom.
    p.   cm.
Includes bibliographical references and index.

ISBN 978-0-7864-9807-9 (softcover : acid free paper) ∞
ISBN 978-1-4766-2044-2 (ebook)

1. Douglas, Stephen A. (Stephen Arnold), 1813–1861.   2. Lincoln, Abraham, 1809–1865—Adversaries.   3. Illinois—Politics and government—To 1865.   4. Presidential candidates—United States—Biography.   5. Legislators—United States—Biography.   6. Legislators—Illinois—Biography.   7. United States. Congress. House—Biography.   8. United States. Congress. Senate—Biography.   I. Title.

E415.9.D73A83 2015   328.73'092—dc23   [B]   2015006784

BRITISH LIBRARY CATALOGUING DATA ARE AVAILABLE

© 2015 Reg Ankrom. All rights reserved

No part of this book may be reproduced or transmitted in any form or by any means, electronic or mechanical, including photocopying or recording, or by any information storage and retrieval system, without permission in writing from the publisher.

Cover image: Original painting of Stephen A. Douglas by Charles Loring Elliot, circa 1840 (courtesy George Buss of Freeport, Illinois)

*McFarland & Company, Inc., Publishers
Box 611, Jefferson, North Carolina 28640
www.mcfarlandpub.com*

For Jane

Contents

Acknowledgments ix
Chronology Through the First Douglas Decade in Illinois xi
Preface 1
Introduction 3

1. Jacksonville, Illinois 5
2. "I have become a Western man" 16
3. Party Democrat Stephen A. Douglas 36
4. Sophisticates and Sophists 43
5. "The *Lord*, and the *Legislature*, and *Gen Jackson*" 53
6. A New Party in Jackson's Image 63
7. "The least man I ever saw" 73
8. The First Douglas-Lincoln Contest 83
9. A Scheme to Capture the Capital 93
10. Convening the Faithful 105
11. The Contest for Miss Mary Ann Todd 123
12. The First Douglas-Lincoln Debates 134
13. Creating a Constitutional Crisis 145
14. The Move to Pack the Court 154
15. Judge Douglas 162
16. Quest for Congress 177
17. Natural Phenomena 186

Epilogue 191
Chapter Notes 193
Bibliography 213
Index 221

Acknowledgments

You are the first person I wish to thank. You chose this book to read, and I am grateful for your willingness to take a chance on me and my subject, Stephen A. Douglas.

Many others deserve thanks, too, particularly those who put up with my turning almost any conversation over the last few years into monologues about Stephen A. Douglas and Abraham Lincoln. My friend Dr. David Costigan, emeritus professor of history at Quincy University, is responsible for that. He is a brilliant teacher of American history and his passion for it rubbed off.

I am grateful for the help of Glenna Schroeder-Lein, manuscripts librarian at the Abraham Lincoln Presidential Library, the place I began researching Stephen Douglas. She was enthusiastic about my project, even as I was uncertain about it. A scholar in her own right, Schroeder-Lien is the author of *Lincoln and Medicine*, a fascinating look at the medical history of the Lincoln family. I also want to thank her colleagues Dr. James Cornelius, Lincoln Library curator, and Roberta Fairburn, images coordinator, for courtesies and much good help.

My friend Beth Lane, who wrote a highly detailed, engaging book, *Lies Told under Oath*, about a murder in Adams County that drew national attention in 1912, kindly read the manuscript. The executive director of the historical society in the community that sent Douglas to Congress in 1843, Lane offered many pointers that I think made the manuscript better. Thanks to Jean Kay, Martha Pappenfoht, and my many historical society friends, whose love for history always inspires.

My interest in Douglas and Lincoln has taken me to several conferences and symposia over the past few years. I have appreciated the kindnesses of so many great scholars and historians—the names Michael Burlingame, Allen Guelzo, Harold Holzer, James Huston, Jennifer Weber, Garry Wills, and Douglas Wilson immediately come to mind—who listened to questions and offered helpful observations and suggestions.

I want to express particular appreciation to my good friend George Arthur Buss of Freeport, Illinois, site of the second Douglas-Lincoln Debate, as the great debates were called in 1858. Holzer has called Buss one of the most authentic and authoritative Lincoln re-enactors around. I believe it. Like Lincoln, Buss is six feet, four inches tall, wears size 14 boots, and is as skinny as if he lived on Lincoln's "homeopathic soup ... made by boiling the shadow of a pigeon that had starved to death." I have not heard Buss err in response to any question put to him about Lincoln. Buss *is* Lincoln.

Buss also happens to be chairman of the Stephen A. Douglas Association of Chicago, whose members gather in dwindling numbers each year at Douglas's Tomb in South Chicago near the anniversary of the senator's death. I was surprised that a man who knew Lincoln so well was so well informed about Douglas.

"You cannot know President Lincoln without knowing Senator Douglas," he said.

Finally, I thank my family. I thank my mother Doloris, who kept her four boys together after polio took her young husband. By her example we learned the values of hard work and love for others. I am grateful that son Jud and daughter Alice never suggested golf as an avocation but encouraged their dad's interest in history, instead. My wife Jane has been my life's greatest blessing. In all things she has been my best listener and teacher.

Chronology Through the First Douglas Decade in Illinois

1813 Birth, Brandon, Vermont, April 23
1833 Arrives in Jacksonville, Illinois, November 14
1834 Licensed to practice law in Illinois, March 4
1835 Elected state's attorney for First Judicial District, February 10
1836 Elected to General Assembly as state representative from Morgan County, August 1
1837 Appointed land register by President Van Buren; moves to Springfield, March 4
1838 Loses race for Congress to John Todd Stuart, August 6
1840 Appointed secretary of state, November 30
1841 Elected associate justice of Illinois Supreme Court and moves to Quincy, March 3
1843 Elected to U.S. House of Representatives, Fifth Congressional District, August 7

"It has been truly said that 'compromise is the essence of politics'; genuine compromises, however, can only be concluded with regard to *measures*, never between principles, that is, between intellectual and moral conceptions which, in their very essence are the opposite poles of an idea."
—Hermann E. von Holst[1]

Preface

Dr. James M. Cornelius, curator of the Abraham Lincoln Presidential Library and Museum, has estimated that there are 18,000 publications about Abraham Lincoln.[1] More is added to the literature on our nation's civil saint almost weekly. As a lover of Lincoln, I say deservedly so.

By comparison, only a handful of works has been written about Lincoln's principal political opponent, Stephen Arnold Douglas, the politician in whose wake Lincoln followed for 26 years. As authoritative Lincoln scholar George Buss of Freeport, Illinois, has said, one must know Douglas to know Lincoln. A Lincoln folklorist, as well as chairman of the Stephen A. Douglas Association, Buss knows the stories of both 19th century giants.

This book covers what I propose was Douglas's ten-year political apprenticeship in Illinois. He arrived in Jacksonville, the seat of Morgan County and the state's most erudite community at the time, in mid–November 1833. Douglas had no intention to stay. He merely wanted to meet the people who had named their town for his boyhood hero, Andrew Jackson. What he found in Jacksonville was his first great challenge, offered, ironically, by John J. Hardin, the shirttail nephew of Jackson antagonist Henry Clay.[2] Hardin in less than two years after his own arrival to Jacksonville from Kentucky had tipped the political scales in Jacksonville and Morgan County from Jackson to Clay. A commanding figure in demeanor, stature, and intellect, Hardin had made Jacksonville the bastion of National Republican politics in Illinois.[3]

Douglas arrived with a single trunk of possessions, including a few books and $1.25. The outgoing 20-year-old Jacksonian found little to have kept him in Jacksonville. Even the city's strongest Jacksonian, Murray McConnel, the city's first lawyer, had little more than advice to offer. Douglas took it. But when it did not work out, he set his own course. And it began in Jacksonville.

For the next ten years, Douglas apprenticed himself in the life, law, and politics of Illinois. Keen observation educated him in how disparate communities, whose residents could as easily ignore laws for which enforcement was lacking, could still get along. The state had been settled from the south up, with southern pioneers crossing at Cairo, Illinois' southernmost town. There the waters of the Ohio and Mississippi rivers met and separated slave states below from free states above. Douglas was himself part of a swelling wave of Easterners who found passage to Illinois on boats on the Ohio River and the Erie Canal. He had few fixed ideas or principles to muddy up the way of getting along with the people he met. His apprenticeship was to prove that flexibility was a better salve than firmness for neighborly ills he encountered, even—maybe more importantly—in politics.

Douglas's migration west reflected both his ambition and impatience to practice law. New York, where he left his family in June 1833, required seven years of classical and legal studies to be licensed for lawyering. He had four years to go when he discovered that Ohio required only one year. In haste he left for Cleveland and quickly obtained a clerkship with one of the city's most prominent law firms. After four days there, an illness confined him to bed for four months, ending the job and nearly his life. A miraculous recovery and learning that Illinois required candidates for the bar to be twenty-one or older, a resident for at least six months, white, male, and have the testimony of two lawyers about his qualification and moral standing, Douglas continued on west.

Douglas reached Jacksonville on the morning of November 14, 1833. Within six weeks, he proclaimed the city "the Paradise of the World" and declared himself a "Western man."

Admitted to the bar, Douglas hung his shingle on the side of the Morgan County courthouse. There was little evidence that he had any law business. Most of the county's other lawyers determined to starve him out of what there was. Business or no business, Douglas did not need to be starved out. He found a calling in politics more interesting.

John Hardin, the rock of Jacksonville culture and politics, was Douglas's first lesson and first test. It was a Hardin challenge that taught Douglas how others might be persuaded to join causes, always his causes, good for them, and good for him. In all causes over the next ten years in Illinois, Douglas successfully learned that to succeed was to manage the processes that won for him both elections and appointments—and the adoration of the majority of his neighbors, who were often astounded by his success. They elected him state's attorney and state representative. They helped him build a Democratic machine and awarded him its leadership. They supported his efforts to wrest control of the office of secretary of state from a lifetime appointee solely to gain the affections of a large new block of voters. He won an appointment from President Martin Van Buren and repaid him by heading his reelection campaign in Illinois—one of only two successful state campaigns—for Van Buren in 1840. Douglas would involve himself in some of the state's greatest controversies, including his outlandish and entirely self-serving reorganization of the judiciary of the state of Illinois. At the age of 27, that effort resulted in his appointment as a justice of the Illinois Supreme Court he reorganized. In August of 1843, his neighbors in Western Illinois elected him to the U.S. House of Representatives. Within days of his arrival in Washington, D.C., his party's leadership recognized the capabilities of the freshman congressman and assigned him the ask of arbitrating a squabble in the House that had all the makings of a constitutional crisis. Douglas resolved it before it bacame a crisis.

Douglas's decade in Illinois had been a successful apprenticeship, preparing him to become the journeyman legislator and statesman that his party, the nation, and the Union would require in the years ahead.

Introduction

THROUGHOUT THE NIGHT OF NOVEMBER 13, 1833, arcs of fire slit the sky over the North American continent. At New Salem, a small village along the Sangamon River in Central Illinois, the fiery display woke the village's citizens. They feared the end of the world had arrived—and most gathered that night outside the village's twelve log cabins. At any moment they expected clouds to form, Jesus Christ to appear, and their resurrection and glorious ascension into Heaven with Him. It did not happen, and the village's citizens for weeks afterward convened meetings to ponder the meaning of the event.[1] One of their neighbors, a rangy and gangling twenty-five-year-old storeowner and postmaster, also witnessed the event but declined to join the gatherings that night or any of the nights that followed. Wholly uninspired by the phenomenon, Abraham Lincoln never attached any meaning to it.[2]

Neither did a twenty-year-old Easterner who that same night was being bounced around in a stagecoach cabin on the Sangamon-Alton Trace Road. Suffering vertigo, Stephen Arnold Douglas was doing all he could to keep from throwing up.[3] Douglas was making his way from Alton to Jacksonville, Illinois, a diversion he had decided to take while migrating toward a still unknown destination in the West. Like Lincoln, Douglas never acknowledged the event above him that night.

To this point in their lives neither Lincoln nor Douglas had given much thought to cosmic forces. Like so many descendants of the American Revolution, which established a nation, and the Second Great Awakening, which launched its democracy, each of these transplants—one perhaps more than the other—believed he had the power to design his own destiny. As their ambitions grew, Douglas and Lincoln made their way along a path of politics, so largely dependent on their personal abilities to win the approbation of their neighbors. Their paths—personal and political—would cross many times in the coming years. Douglas's path would seem to be without obstacle. Each office he acquired in Illinois became a stepping stone to the next. Lincoln's path had seemed promising but then faltered in the Douglas decade in Illinois. Douglas had been learning to control events. Lincoln, as he later acknowledged, seemed to be controlled by them.[4]

Douglas's rise and the way he achieved it amazed many, Lincoln among them. Within the decade after his arrival in Illinois, Douglas engineered his election as a state's attorney, orchestrated his election as a state legislator, and masterminded the creation and his leadership of the state's Democratic Party organization. He won an appointment from President Martin Van Buren to become the federal land register at Springfield. Always with his own purposes, Douglas pulled the wires to persuade Governor Thomas Carlin to appoint him secretary of state, even though Carlin had promised the job to another man.[5] Douglas then organized one of the most brazen efforts in state history to reorganize the Illinois Supreme Court—just to get himself appointed an associate justice. He succeeded. He was twenty-seven years old.[6]

During that same ten-year period, Lincoln established a public service record of four two-year terms in the Illinois General Assembly. He was every bit as ambitious as Douglas, but his political career in the next decades would be limited to two terms as a Springfield township trustee and a single term in Congress (1847–1848). Until he was elected president, Lincoln could only look with a dispirited awareness at Douglas, who had proven himself capable of overcoming every adversity until his power rivaled even that of the president of the United States.[7] Lincoln's envy of the younger Douglas's ascendency seemed to drip from him when in 1856 he wrote: "Twenty-two years ago, Judge Douglas and I first became acquainted; we were both young then—he a trifle younger than I. Even then we were both ambitious, I, perhaps quite as much as he. With me, the race of ambition has been a failure—a flat failure. With him, it has been one of splendid success. His name fills the Nation, and it is not unknown in foreign lands."[8]

Lincoln acknowledged the stellar rise of the diminutive Douglas. The first time he saw Douglas—buttonholing legislators in Vandalia in 1834 to pass two self-serving bills—Lincoln's play on words disparaged the five-foot four-inch Easterner as "the least man I ever saw."[9]

By November 1843 Douglas had become the more astral figure of the two. His star streaked brilliantly over Illinois. A no-less politically ambitious Abraham Lincoln by that time had left the General Assembly—"gloom fairly dripping from him"—and resigned himself to the practice of law in Springfield.[10] Craving public office every bit as much as Douglas did, Lincoln found himself denied the opportunity. In the Democratic organization he had helped create, Douglas saw to that. His Democracy Party reached solidly into every Illinois precinct. Lincoln knew it. When in 1841 a group of Whigs asked Lincoln to run for Illinois governor, he declined. A Whig could not win statewide office in Illinois, Lincoln told them.[11]

In August 1843 Abraham Lincoln, thirty-four years old, and his second law partner Stephen Trigg Logan moved their law office from nearby Hoffman Row to the third floor of the recently built Tinsley Building on the southeast side of the Springfield square. The federal district courtroom was on the floor directly below Lincoln's office and the Illinois State Capitol was just north, across Adams Street. Except for his two-year term in Congress, Lincoln would spend the next seventeen years in Springfield, working from that office and one other nearby, to which he and partner Billy Herndon moved their practice in 1852.[12]

On December 4, 1843, Stephen Arnold Douglas, thirty years old, arrived in Washington, D.C., a newly elected United States congressman from Quincy, Illinois. There Douglas would reach the pinnacle of the American political cosmos on a trajectory whose path he personally had charted. Before he died on June 3, 1861, Douglas, forty-eight years old, had been a three-time presidential candidate within his party and had become the most powerful Democrat in the nation. He had learned the art and science of politics, had figured out how to move measures and men, in his ten-year political apprenticeship in Illinois.

1. Jacksonville, Illinois

IT WAS THE NAME of the Central Illinois town that attracted twenty-year-old traveler Stephen A. Douglas to Jacksonville. He had not decided to stay. He simply wanted to see the place and meet the people who had honored his hero Andrew Jackson. From the time he was a boy in Brandon, Vermont, Douglas had venerated Jackson. At age fourteen Jackson was a volunteer in the American Revolution and had the scars on the fingers of his left hand and forehead left by the sword of a British officer to mark his personal rebellion against an enemy of American liberty. Jackson had been the savior of New Orleans at the end of the War of 1812, America's second war with Great Britain. Jackson had been a teacher, lawyer, congressman, U.S. senator and, to the delight of his young admirer, now in 1833 the president of the United States. Over the next 25 years, Douglas would map a similar path for himself.

In 1825, the same year Morgan County's surveyor laid out the town of Jacksonville in Central Illinois, the Illinois legislature made the community the county seat. It was confirmation that Jacksonville was a community of destiny. Some already were predicting that by the end of the decade Jacksonville would be the site of Illinois' third state capital.[1] Congressman Joseph Duncan, whose speculations in land at the time already ranked him among the state's wealthiest men, was among those speculating on the future of Jacksonville.

As Illinois' only congressman—elected in 1826 to the first of four terms—Duncan could live anywhere in Illinois. He chose to move to Jacksonville in 1830. Confident of Jacksonville's promise, he was completing work on a seventeen-room mansion in the Colonial Georgian style on the city's west side at the time of Douglas's arrival. Duncan named his mansion "Elm Grove," which became the site of many "brilliant dinners and receptions" for leading men of the time. The Duncans' guest lists included Illinois political leaders like John J. Hardin, Orville Hickman Browning, and Abraham Lincoln, and Democrats like John A. McClernand. And Stephen Douglas.[2] In June 1837 Daniel Webster, a Whig statesman of national repute and a friend of Duncan from his days in Congress, honored Jacksonville with a visit of several days of speech making. Duncan honored Webster with barbeques, everyone welcome, in the north pasture behind Elm Grove. Some students of Illinois College thought the introduction of Webster by college president Edward Beecher was a better example of oratory than Webster's.[3]

One of the city's favorite sons was Samuel Drake Lockwood, appreciated for the honor he brought to the city as a 36-year-old associate justice of the four-member Illinois Supreme Court in 1825. Lockwood, too, was confident about the future of Jacksonville. His home was less than a half mile south of Duncan's.

Jacksonville was near the geographic center of Illinois, making it well situated for a population that was growing and spreading northward. Having migrated mainly from the Lower and Upland South, Jacksonville's settlers—who sought to distance themselves from an institution back home that devalued their labor almost as much as that of enslaved black laborers—continued to beckon families and friends to a town whose arms were open to all comers, as long as they were white.[4] Jacksonville did not exclude free blacks, but it segregated them to a section on the southwest side of the city. Residents called it "Africa."[5]

The community was an engine of development. Its commerce was flourishing—a saw mill, flour mill, two carding factories, a cotton factory, a distillery, a tannery, and three brickyards. Its merchants and craftsmen were ready to handle the growing demand for goods and services. At the community's center was a public square around which sixteen stores, six taverns, several shops, and a two-story brick courthouse stood shoulder to shoulder.[6] Jacksonville had five churches, whose sectarian rivalries sometimes divided the community. The most recent was the emergence of the Congregationalist, whose particularly fearless tendencies to abolitionize agitated the community even more than religious prejudices.[7]

A beacon of erudition, Jacksonville in 1826 had one of the state's first common schools, and a group of pioneers that year set out to organize a college. That effort had succeeded with the merger of their work with the plan of a band of Yale Divinity School students to found Illinois College in 1829.[8] The new college occupied a vaunted setting atop a gently sloped drumlin on the community's western side left by the last receding glacier thirteen millennia earlier. The first college building in Illinois crowned the hilltop. It was a two-story Greek Revival structure built in 1830 and named for the college's first president, Edward Beecher.[9] Beecher was the firstborn son of Boston luminary minister Lyman Beecher and one of 11 siblings of the Beecher vine on which abolitionism was to mature so powerfully.

Jacksonville eclipsed nearby Springfield in those attributes that made a place attractive to settlers. A Scottish traveler who had spent three years exploring the American continent in the early 1830s found Jacksonville the most attractive of the communities he had seen anywhere, comparable, he wrote, to the best boroughs of Great Britain.[10] In his book, published the year Douglas began his westward journey, author James Stuart wrote that of all the states and territories he had visited, in the richness of resources, the independence of the people, in settlements, and their successes, there was none to compare to Illinois' Jacksonville.

"Think of Windsor Park," wrote Stuart, "or Strathfieldsaye, or of parks for all the noblemen and wealthy landlords in Britain to be had here at a dollar and a-quarter an acre, in the neighborhood of such rivers, and all consisting of land of the richest soil, and of the most beautiful waving shape and smooth surface, all laid out by the hand of Nature, as English parks are,—the wood far more beautifully."[11]

A contemporary visitor from New England was as lavish in his praise: "You cannot find a village east of the Hudson, of the same number of inhabitants, possessing so many men of literary eminence and moral worth, nor a community of greater refinement in taste and manners."[12]

Not all visitors of the day, however, shared Stuart's enthusiasm for the prairie community. In 1832, the year before Stuart's visit, poet William Cullen Bryant had ventured to Jacksonville for a reunion with his pioneer brothers Arthur and John Howard Bryant, who tilled 80 acres of rich dirt southwest of the community. Bryant would write of his horseback ride into the Illinois wilderness, of sleeping in log houses, eating cornbread and honey, and of a chance meeting with volunteers on their way to the Black Hawk War, not knowing that their captain was Abraham Lincoln. He was impressed enough to write two poems.[13] But the poet found little to like about Jacksonville. He found no "graceful deer," "adventurous bee," that filled the savannas of Illinois with his hum like the sound of an advancing multitude.[14] It did not help that Bryant's introduction to Jacksonville occurred at 11 p.m. when he crossed the threshold of a local tavern in which the lodging available was in an upstairs room filled with seven double beds. By Bryant's account, each of the beds was occupied, some by "brawny, hard-breathing fellows."[15] The innkeeper instructed him to squeeze next to one of them. Only by the intensity of his dissatisfaction with such an arrangement did Bryant manage to get a room and bed of his own.[16] The next morning, before traveling to his brothers' farm—and finding nothing better to do, Bryant wandered around Jacksonville. He judged severely what he saw.

"It is a horridly ugly village," was his assessment, "composed of little shops and dwellings stuck close together around a dingy square, in the middle of which stands the ugliest of possible brick courthouses, with a spire and weather-cock at its top."[17]

Bryant's expectations may have been high. When he passed through Springfield, he gave Jacksonville more credit: "Springfield is ... situated on the edge of a large prairie, on ground somewhat more uneven than Jacksonville, but the houses are not so good, a considerable portion of them being log cabins, and the whole town having an appearance of dirt and discomfort. The night was spent in a filthy tavern."[18]

The look of Jacksonville was one thing about the community that had not changed in the year before Douglas arrived, and he was not as persnickety in his judgment about it. Like Stuart, Douglas found more to like in this town of 2,500. And there was something particularly appealing to his developing personal interest. He saw that "everything which had political ambition behind it pointed to Jacksonville."

"It was the polestar among Illinois cities," Douglas said.[19]

There was enough business in Jacksonville for eleven lawyers, who practiced in the county courthouse's second floor courtroom—although some complained the courtroom was too sparse and small.[20] These professionals occupied offices in the new two-story brick courthouse and in wood-framed buildings along State Street, whose alignment pointed toward the great west. Douglas had made up his mind before he left his family at Canandaigua, New York, that he would practice law. Indeed, it was his reason for leaving.[21]

Douglas was to discover a troublesome irony, although it would prove to be an exquisite one, in the town named for his ideal statesman. Jacksonville in 1833 was *the* bastion of the anti–Jackson Party in Illinois, the party which to Douglas represented everything foreign to the interests of the people. The man presiding was Jacksonville's John J. Hardin, a gentrified lawyer and politician. Hardin learned his lessons in politics from his own father, Martin D. Hardin, who had held several government positions, including a seat in the U.S. Senate from Kentucky.

Hardin was the nephew by marriage of U.S. Senator Henry Clay of Kentucky. Hardin's widowed mother Elizabeth Logan Hardin was married to the senator's brother Porter Clay. This was just too good a coincidence for Douglas, who disdained any unfavorable treatment of his president. Like others of the Jacksonian stripe, Douglas believed Clay had colluded with John Quincy Adams to "cheat" Jackson out of the presidency in 1824. Although Jackson had won the popular vote in the four-way contest for the presidency, he garnered too few electoral votes to make him president outright. In accordance with the Twelfth Amendment, that meant the election would be decided by the members of the U.S. House of Representatives, where Clay as house speaker could be expected to exert considerable influence on the decision. Clay would not be able to use his position to directly advance his own candidacy, however. He had finished fourth in the vote for Electoral College electors. The Twelfth Amendment provided that the names of only the top three finishers—in this case they were Andrew Jackson, John Quincy Adams and William Crawford—would be forwarded to the House. Crawford was out, the victim of a stroke that left him paralyzed and unable to serve. Delegates pledged to Clay, a Westerner like Jackson, at Clay's direction threw their support to Adams. And after the House subsequently elected Adams president, Adams named Clay his secretary of state.

That not only created a firestorm. It also led to the creation of a new national political party.

Morgan County's anti–Jackson strength by 1833 was stunning, a circumstance that Douglas discovered in a personal way when seeking a position to read law. Only two of the county's lawyers were members of Jackson's national Democratic Republican Party. The importance of that shift became apparent to Douglas in looking at the results of the two most recent presidential elections. In 1828, Morgan County voters gave Andrew Jackson their overwhelming support. Jackson took 702 of the 884 votes, or 71 percent, over John Quincy Adams, the standard bearer once again for the National Republican Party, also known now as the Anti-Jackson Party. In 1832 Jackson electors again won Morgan County. But by a significantly smaller margin of 1,226 to 1,003, or 55 percent.[22] Hardin's uncle Henry Clay was Jackson's opponent in this later election.

Jackson's narrower victory over Clay greatly disturbed Morgan County's Jackson men.[23] What made it particularly confusing was that Joseph Duncan, a whole-hog Jackson Democrat, in 1831 had won 74 percent of the vote in Morgan County to be re-elected to Congress. Duncan had beaten a highly respected Southern Illinois judge, Sidney Breese, and former Illinois governor Edward Coles to remain Illinois' representative in Congress. Coles had no chance to win. Elected governor in 1822, he had successfully led a fight to stop an attempt by the southern-dominated state legislature to legalize slavery in Illinois. His election had been a fluke. The electorate's majority—pro-slavery voters—cast 59.6 percent of the vote for pro-slavery candidates. Those candidates, Supreme Court Justices Joseph Phillips and Thomas Browne, had friends in almost equal numbers, who split that vote. Illinois militia commander James Moore took 7.2 percent. It meant that although nearly two thirds of the voters in 1822 supported someone else, Coles won the governor's office with only 33.2 percent of the vote.[24] Ten years later, in 1832, Coles answered the pleas of like-minded anti-slavery friends to become a candidate for Congress. He promised to be faithful to no party but only to those who voted for him.[25] Few did.

John J. Hardin, nephew by marriage of U.S. Senator Henry Clay of Kentucky, had assumed political leadership of Morgan County by the time Stephen A. Douglas arrived on November 14, 1833. Wanting only to see the town of Jacksonville, named for his boyhood hero Andrew Jackson, Douglas decided to stay when he saw opportunity in challenging Hardin for political pre-eminence (courtesy Abraham Lincoln Presidential Library and Museum).

Jacksonville's Democrats were in disarray. Duncan was the cause. He had quietly disavowed his earlier allegiance to the party of Jackson. The president's displeasure with the U.S. Bank, an about-face on patronage, and the veto of a section of the National Road in Kentucky had cost Jackson the affection of Duncan and Democrats like him who once had eagerly supported him. Duncan's support for Jackson never had been uncategorical. Jackson had given Duncan a personal pledge not to fire competent men from federal offices, which Jackson later ignored. Duncan promoted a non-political civil service, even denying his patronage to a brother, James Duncan, who sought appointment as an Indian agent in Jackson's administration.[26]

The president also vetoed the recharter of the U.S. Bank, which greatly troubled Duncan. He believed a national bank through its ability to extend credit, providing the capital his state's businesses needed to expand, was important for commercial health and growth of Illinois, his district.[27] Jackson's assaults on the bank had caused the defection to Clay of a good number of the Democracy's voters in Morgan County.

The president's veto of an appropriation bill for the Kentucky section of the National Road, which was to connect Washington, D.C., to Illinois' capital at Vandalia, sealed Duncan's disaffection with Jackson. Like Duncan, many of Jacksonville's southern settlers had come from Kentucky, and the road was important to them.

Morgan County's votes in 1832 made it clear to Douglas that Clay's adherents owned Morgan County. To a young admirer of the principles of Old Hickory, this could not stand. Douglas would make it his mission to restore Jacksonian Democracy in the community blessed by Jackson's name.

Douglas was part of a swelling tide of immigrants into the old northwest's opening lands. What started as a rivulet of pioneers, hacking their way through trackless trees and head-high, sharp-edged prairie grasses that could cut through a horse's hair and hide, had turned into streams of settlers whose ears still rang with the echoes of stories of rich soil and independence—reward for courage and industry. There was a vast ocean of black dirt yet to yield to cultivation—and to new destinies.

As the stream of pathfinders and pioneers continued, there appeared no end to the opportunity that awaited them in the new country. In Western Illinois a young Kentucky lawyer, himself a recent arrival, took notice of this stream of settlers from the south.

"Our country at present is swarming with travelers," wrote Jacksonville's John Hardin to a friend back in Lexington. "It appears as if the flood gates of Kentucky had broken loose, and her population set free had naturally turned their course to Illinois and Missouri."[28]

The course Hardin noticed, in either case, was northward. Southerners made up the majority of Jacksonville's citizens, most of them settling with the belief that they had gotten away from the troublesome effects of slavery—and blacks.[29] The invention of the cotton gin in 1793 had made the production of short-staple cotton profitable in their native Upland South. As planters moved their slaves and cotton production into the uplands, they managed to take control of local and state governments, the interest always obliging them to protect these peculiar property interests. Free farmers were left with the choice to tolerate such incursions, to try to become slave-holding plantation owners, or to sell out and migrate north. Their practice of agriculture, and for many of them their religion, led them to choose to move.[30]

Douglas found Jacksonville a city in quiet conflict about slavery. The few families that had settled in Morgan with slaves—to comply with the state's constitution, which prohibited slavery, they were referred to as personal or house servants—found themselves subject to anger and ostracism. The great majority of Morgan County's settlers, including most from the South, had been squarely in the no-slavery camp. When a question was to be placed before the state's voters on August 2, 1824, to change the constitution to allow slavery in Illinois, nearly one hundred fifty Morgan men formed the "Morganian Society" to "concentrate public opinion" to resist the call for a referendum. Although the society's resistance was passive, the efforts were effective. Morgan County residents defeated the slavery question by one of the greatest margins in the state. Ninety-one percent, or 432 votes, were cast against the proposition. Only 42 voters supported it.[31] Morgan County's predominantly Southern electorate clearly advocated the prohibition of slavery in Illinois. While there was little sympathy for slave-holding, however, Douglas found even less sympathy for blacks. Jacksonville voters could fiercely fight proposals to bring bondage to Illinois not because of strong sentiment against human bondage but because of its threat to racial homogeneity. Douglas would come to see that the campaign against the peculiar institution only added to a growing sense of anxiety over the question of slavery.[32]

Slavery was not the sole cause of anxiety in Jacksonville. Social, political and religious ideas were driving wedges between settlers there. Cotton state and Eastern and Northern state ideals and traditions contended for preeminence.[33] The conflicts in Jacksonville had been exacerbated by the arrival in 1829 of a group of young men, "The Yale Band," seven recent graduates of the Yale Divinity School at New Haven, Connecticut. Although their mission was to work against what they considered the dark forces of Rome and the Catholic Society of Jesus, the Jesuits, in evangelizing the west,[34] these young graduates of the Yale Divinity School brought with them Eastern abolitionist ideas that put them increasingly at odds with a majority of the people of Jacksonville. Douglas would become aware that even though they had come here to escape slavery, Southerners still could take umbrage at criticisms of the institutions of their native states. Most believed that slavery was best for the Negro.[35] The Yale Band, whose members founded Illinois College in 1829 and the Congregational Church in 1833 in Jacksonville, were outspoken in sermon and declaration against slavery.[36]

The sympathies they brought with them and which they espoused in Jacksonville insulted the honor of the largest demographic group in the Jacksonville area. The Easterners were almost universally anti-slavery. And making matters worse, they also brought with them the causes of new reform movements as advocates of temperance, women's rights, free schools, and free pulpits for an educated ministry.

"Their ideas were poison to most of the southerners," one local historian observed, "and, besides, they were shrewd traders and fluent talkers and these Yankees at once became the objects of the deepest animosities of the southerners ... who thought themselves, in some way, the rightful owners of the region."

The intensity of their opposition to slavery produced an unexpected and unwanted result. These same citizens of the Jacksonville area, who had voted more strongly than nearly anyone else in the state against the introduction of slavery into Illinois in 1824, were nudged into the pro-slavery ranks.[37]

Young men who studied at Illinois College absorbed full-heartedly these anti-slavery sentiments. Billy Herndon, the future law partner of Abraham Lincoln, was one of them. After the murder of the Rev. Elijah P. Lovejoy in Alton in November 1837, Herndon participated in a riotous action on the college's campus. Within ten days after Lovejoy and Illinois College president Edward Beecher led a convention in Alton to organize the state's first anti-slavery society, Lovejoy was martyred by a mob bent on throwing his anti-slavery press into the Mississippi River. Although Herndon's father Archer Herndon, a state senator and owner of the Indian Queen tavern in Springfield, yanked Herndon from the college, Billy Herndon never forgot what he learned about abolition at the college. In the years to come, he would pass along those lessons to law partner Lincoln.

By the time of his arrival in Jacksonville, Douglas found the residents of the community openly split over slavery. He could glean the strains of strong Puritanical thought that had been set down in a community whose roots extended to an equally strong Cavalier tradition. These were, here, immature reflections of great traditions in conflict.

"The Jacksonville Yankees were as advanced in their thought as those in Massachusetts and Connecticut and their southern neighbors were as tenacious in their ideas as were southerners in the Cotton States," a local historian observed. "This peculiar situation, perhaps, existed nowhere else in America.... Certainly in no place in Illinois and probably in no place in the West were antagonistic principles championed by abler groups of men."[38]

Stephen A. Douglas found a powerful new kind of promise in the West. It was freeing. Nature, not neighbor, was the dominant influence, and with the strength to overcome her, the highest levels of freedom and confidence stood before the frontiersman as broad and unlimited as the horizon. Here men had the chance to live out the idealism of Thomas Jefferson's yeoman farmer, unfettered and basking in independence. In each settlement was an American rebirth of freedom. Here one could be Andrew Jackson's common man, where neither neighbor nor entanglement would shackle. Here men shed "knee britches" for long-legged pants of the frontier.

"The early society of the Middle West was not a complex, highly differentiated and organized society," observed early American historian Frederick Jackson Turner in 1893. "Almost every family was a self-sufficing unit, and liberty and equality flourished.... Both native settler and European immigrant saw in this free and competitive movement of the frontier the chance to break the bondage of social rank, and to rise to a higher plane of existence."[39]

Thin at first, layers of civilization began to replace the first wave of pioneers, but individualism and democracy persisted even when a higher social organization succeeded in implanting itself.[40] Jacksonville was one of a growing number of towns in which the ties between the American frontier and American democracy were bound. Its settlers would provide to Douglas numerous models of stout independence and ambition, even though ambition was forced upon some. Kentucky immigrant John J. Hardin revealed a chauvinistic view about who belonged in this new west:

> There are [sic] a certain description of young men who ought never to leave their mothers' apron strings and who know how to conduct themselves when abroad but whine and talk about home as tho' there were no other place decent people could live. These have no business here. Another class with talent and no energy in a short time become dissatisfied—they need the fostering hand of encouragement and flattery and for such there is no place here.... There is still another class, my friend, who are willing to take things as they find them, to think of home as a hallowed spot yet not contrast it with a county six years old and not yet populated.... If there are any such as these in your knowledge give them all encouragement to come here.[41]

There was one class of settler, however, in exceedingly short supply in Jacksonville. It was a scarcity the writer lamented seriously. That was women. An enterprising man, Hardin suggested to his friend, could earn as much as 150 pounds of tobacco in exchange for each head in a cargo of the "fair freight," his quaint euphemism for women.[42]

There were lessons for Douglas to learn in politics in Morgan County. On the one hand, he would see that politics often chose any man who in some way had distinguished himself. Colonel Seymour Kellogg, Morgan County's first settler, was a revered example in the county. Kellogg had been a commissioned officer and veteran of the War of 1812. He and his wife and seven children arrived in the county in 1819 and built a single-room cabin on the north fork of the Mauvaisterre Creek. By the end of the year, nineteen others, including Kellogg's brother Captain Elisha Kellogg, had settled Morgan County's first town, Exeter. The colonel's voluntary leadership was so well appreciated by his neighbors that with the founding of the county they would help elect him the county's first commissioner and shortly afterward a justice of the peace.[43]

The rise to prominence of Douglas's friend and mentor Murray McConnel was similar.[44] McConnel was considered among the most capable of Morgan's professional men. Although McConnel, the first lawyer in Morgan County, had won the approbation of his neighbors for his help with legal matters, it was only with great reluctance that he agreed to accept their desire that he represent them in the Illinois General Assembly at Vandalia for the 1832–34 term.[45] This reluctance was a convention of many men of the South when called upon by friends and neighbors for the honor of public service. Southern statesmen were to be wise and virtuous men, independent of interest. True statesmen did not seek an office. The office sought them. Ambition was the enemy of statesmanship.[46]

Douglas learned in Jacksonville that any man, even the coarse and illiterate, could rise to imminence for a community service that citizens valued. In the months before Douglas reached Jacksonville, cholera spread death in the community. While great fear enveloped the community, local cabinetmaker John Henry organized a team of neighbors to bury the fifty-five citizens the pestilence killed that summer. His appreciative neighbors overlooked Henry's illiteracy to elect him their state representative, later a state senator and—when Abraham Lincoln declined to take the seat of Edward D. Baker, who resigned a year early from the 29th Congress to join fighters in the Mexican War—as their representative in Congress.[47]

Jacksonville's focus on politics was obsessive—and at that time one-sided. Politics elsewhere in Illinois continued to lean toward Jackson's Democracy Party. But anti–Jackson men were the power in Jacksonville when Douglas took up residence there. Hardin, considered the brightest and most powerful anti–Jackson man in the young state, was responsible for that. And he had a reputation for disposing easily with those who opposed him.

"To incur his displeasure was regarded by many as political suicide," one observer wrote.[48]

Hardin was to become Douglas's first great challenge.

The place Douglas had chosen to make his western home, for all its apparent homogeneity, was conflicted over the great issue of slavery. Like the state of Illinois, populated from its southern tip northward, Jacksonville was home to settlers from the uplands of the Carolinas, Kentucky, Tennessee, and Virginia.[49] At the time Illinois achieved statehood in 1818, seventy-five percent of its population was from the South. The balance of the population was mixed, from New England and European countries like England, Germany and Ireland.[50] These were sturdy men. Some were educated. Most were not. Some had wealth. Most did not. While most of the transplants had left the South to get away from slavery, many remained convinced that slavery was a beneficial condition for the inferior Negro.[51]

Jacksonville was a key stop along the route between Louisville, Kentucky, and Palmyra, Missouri, a route heavily traveled by Kentuckians, a good number of them taking to more promising grounds their property, including slaves. Acquisition of two huge landmasses made the difference between these two states separated only by the Mississippi River. Illinois had been part of the Northwest Territory in which slavery had been prohibited. And Missouri had been part of the Louisiana Purchase in which slavery had been sanctioned. Although they considered Illinois good land in which to settle, travelers from Virginia and Kentucky migrated through Illinois and on into Missouri because they could not keep slaves in Illinois.[52] Hardin lamented that fact. Hardin looked at each opportunity as a means for his community—and his political base—to grow. He had witnessed the transients, many of them people of means, passing through Jacksonville with their trains of horses and cattle and some with slaves. A good number of travelers were from his home state on their way directly west from Jacksonville to Missouri. Many who passed through Jacksonville expressed an interest in settling there but hesitated because of the state's ban on slavery.

"We cannot locate in Illinois," one slaveholder wrote, "because you have adopted an anti-slavery constitution, and we cannot hold our property here."[53]

"In nine cases out of ten they remark that if they could bring their negroes here they would go no further [sic]," Hardin wrote to a friend.[54]

Hardin had settled in Jacksonville a few years before Douglas. By his calculation, two-thirds of the community were native Kentuckians, which would work to his advantage. He was from Lexington and had relatives who were powerful state and national leaders.[55] His deceased father Martin Hardin had been Kentucky's secretary of state and a U.S. senator. It was not long before Hardin himself would become one of Illinois' strongest leaders in the practice of law and politics. He was considered fearless, opinionated, and attached to his friends with "hooks of steel." His Morgan County colleague Joseph Gillespie described Hardin as an erect figure of square build with a military bearing that was practiced and intentional. Hardin, in fact, was attracted to the military, an interest that would win him the rank of general in the state militia and ultimately lead him to his death in the Mexican War. A hunting accident that occurred when the breech pin of his rifle exploded into the right side of his face, causing the loss of one of his hazel-colored eyes, left him disfigured.[56]

Hardin had more than a passing interest in state laws related to slavery. When Martin Hardin died in 1823, he left his wife his slave-worked Kentucky plantation—and debts amounting to $50,000. Ignoring recommendations that she sell the estate to pay off the debts, Elizabeth Logan Hardin struggled to make the property productive. Her second husband, Porter Clay, complained to his stepson that the plantation was costing substantially more than it provided. Clay asked Hardin whether he "would consent for the land and negroes to be sold this coming year or not.... Your ma wishes you to speak freely your mind. She thinks it would be a ruinous business to rent out the farm and hire out the negroes."[57]

At about this time, August 1833, John Hardin was involved in the sale of a small family of three Kentucky slaves. He personally bought the fourth member of the family, a boy named Benjamin, euphemistically called a servant under Illinois' indenture law. With the transaction, Hardin broke up the family and broke the will of their deceased owner, his own father, whose wish had been to keep them together. Shortly thereafter, the Hardins obtained an eight-and-a-half-year-old girl named Dolly, who by her mark on an indenture agreement would be required to serve the Hardins until she reached the age of eighteen.[58]

Hardin's sister Lucy Jane and her husband Marcus A. Chinn figured into one of the city's largest stirs over slavery of the time. A surveyor, Chinn had moved to Jacksonville as an employee of the fledgling Northern Cross Railroad. The Chinns brought with them their two slaves Emily and Robert Logan, who learned that by virtue of their residence in the free state of Illinois they were free. The two fled from the Chinn house and took refuge in "Africa," a small enclave of free black men and women on Jacksonville's south side who hid them. Robert was caught outside of Africa, taken to the Illinois River town of Naples, where Hardin had him put on a boat to New Orleans. There Robert Logan was sold and never heard from again.

New England settlers in Jacksonville helped Emily Logan in her pursuit of freedom. Logan challenged the Chinns' ownership in Morgan County court. Because the case had dragged on for more than two years, presiding judge William Thomas ordered the trial moved to Sangamon County, where Edward D. Baker and Ninian W. Edwards represented Logan before Judge Samuel H. Treat. The Sangamon jury ruled for her freedom but allowed only one dollar in damages. It was the Logan case that is credited with spurring Jacksonville abolitionists to establish a local station on the Underground Railroad.[59] Emily Logan remained in Jacksonville the rest of her life.[60]

There was among many Illinoisans a strong distaste for slavery. Yet there was an even stronger distaste for blacks. In learning the history of Illinois, Douglas discovered that although they had rejected an opportunity in 1824 to erect a constitution to permit slavery, whites in Illinois readily countenanced "Black Laws" that would limit their presence among them.

"They [white settlers] were poor and wished to find a spot where their labor would not be degraded by contact with the negro either in freedom or slavery," wrote Yale graduate and Jacksonville émigré Julian Monson Sturtevant about his Jacksonville neighbors of 1830. "They wished to live in a free state, but were determined not to labor with emancipated negroes as their equals before the law. They hated the aristocratic slaveholders, the free negro, and above all persons who were suspected of favoring emancipation."[61]

This disdain for the black race was not merely a matter of a cultural or geographic experience. Sturtevant's Illinois College professorial colleague Jonathan Baldwin Turner, who would champion land grant colleges in Illinois, contended in a scholarly work that blacks of the Equatorial region could not coexist with the Anglo-Saxon, or "Polar" man, as Turner called him:

> They could no more permanently and properly dwell together, than the two zones which bred them could lie in the same latitude. It is indeed possible, in nature or in theory, that the black man might stay in the North long enough to be transformed into a genuine Polar man; but that would take probably thousands of years, and it is not possible, therefore, in history and in fact; or, if so, he would then of course cease to be an Equatorial man, and the richest portion of the globe would be created for nothing, and remain forever a pestilential waste.[62]

Illinois historian Calvin Pease confirms the observations of the Easterners: "Freemen came from slave states because 'it is impossible for free men to thrive by honest labor among slaveholders and slaves. The planter would not tax himself for free schools; but the farmer must suffer from the pilfering of negroes and ride patrol all night while his women shared with the planter's wife the dread of a slave insurrection.'"[63]

Comforted by the opinions of territorial governor Ninian Edwards, who owned slaves, early Illinois slaveholders believed there would be a way around the anti-slavery provisions of the Northwest Ordinance that would permit them to hold onto their human property.[64] The federal census of 1810—eight years before Illinois achieved statehood—disclosed 168 slaves residing in the territory. By the time the territory's convention delegates were framing a constitution for statehood, the number of slaves had increased to 917.[65] Although the number of free blacks also was increasing, they were subject to more restrictive laws. When Douglas arrived in Jacksonville in late 1833, he found ambivalence in the community toward this group of less than 100 blacks. The Easterners supported them with goods and good will. But Douglas could rightly ask if these signs of enlightenment were more than tokens of tolerance. Even in Jacksonville, enlightened men made the arguments that other enlightened Northerners would take up—to reject the idea of slavery but accept the idea of inferiority.[66] They had been segregated in that small Jacksonville ghetto called Africa.[67] There were a few brave souls in Jacksonville, generally shunned themselves, who were fully empathetic to the plight of those confined to Africa. They had begun their own form of protest of maltreatment of blacks by dressing only in woolen clothing. They spurned all clothing made of cotton, the product of Southern slave labor.[68] Douglas could not help but notice this conflict in microcosm created by race and slavery, even in this most enlightened frontier community.

2. "I have become a Western man"

STEPHEN ARNOLD DOUGLAS was born big. Nurse Ann DeForrest, who assisted with the baby's delivery, recorded the boy's weight as fourteen pounds at birth, nearly eleven percent of his weight at maturity.[1] He was born on April 23, 1813, in his mother's bedroom in the family's one and one-half story cottage next to the Baptist Church in Brandon, Vermont. At the approximate center of town the home was a convenient place for his father, a physician, to see patients. The boy Stephen was the son of Dr. Stephen Arnold and Sarah Fisk Douglas, who were married in January 1811. A daughter, Sarah, was the couple's first born on October 29, 1811. The family descended from Scottish stock.

Father Stephen was early in his practice of medicine when apoplexy took his life. At thirty-one years old, the eldest son of Benajah Douglas's nine children was coddling his three-month-old namesake when his body stiffened in the chair. The boy Stephen, not three months old, was fatherless.[2] Neighbor John Adams Conant claimed that he had entered the living room at the moment the doctor suffered the stroke and saw the boy Stephen roll down his father's legs toward the fire in an open fireplace of the Douglas home. Conant would be fond of repeating that he had changed the course of history by rescuing the boy Stephen from the flames.[3] Conant never explained—it does not appear he was ever asked—why a fire was needed in the Douglas home on that Sunday, July 1, 1813.

Douglas, of course, had no recollection of his father but spoke of him with great affection. He gathered his warm feelings for the father he never knew from his father's flattering friends. His father, Douglas was proud to note, was "a man very much beloved by all who knew him."[4]

At the time of Douglas's birth, the country was again at war with Great Britain. Vermonters had done themselves proud in the first war with the British, the American Revolution. From Pawlet, just north of Brandon, in September 1777, five hundred men under Colonel John Brown were sent to attack Fort Ticonderoga, Mount Defiance, and Mount Hope. The heroic stories of Colonel Brown and his Rangers, fatigued by an all-night march and immediately attacking and taking the old French lines at Ticonderoga and Mount Defiance, were well known to Brandon boys like Douglas.[5] It was another Vermonter, Ethan Allen, who had thrilled the nation's first Congress—and proud Brandon's boys—when he and a small force of Green Mountain men overran Fort Ticonderoga in May 1775. The cannon and military stores they captured would figure prominently into General Washington's breaking the British siege at Boston.[6] As a boy Douglas was heir to the stories of battles around the hills and valleys of the Green Mountains during the revolution. Stories of the more ribald kind also won the approval boys' approval.

Allen's admiration for Washington was expressed in a tale that grew out of his visit to Great Britain shortly after the Revolutionary War. To tease Allen, his English host had hung a picture of General Washington over the working section of the host's "Back House," or out-

Stephen Arnold Douglas was born in this home in Brandon, Vermont, on April 23, 1813; his father died here two months later. From here Douglas, his mother, and sister—both named Sarah—moved to his uncle Edward Fisk's farm where he helped with farm chores. At age 15, he left when his uncle reneged on what Douglas believed was a promise to send him to Brandon Academy (courtesy Middlebury College Special Collections and Archives, Middlebury, Vermont).

door privy. When Allen made no mention of his experience on his return from a visit to the Back House, his host asked if he had seen Washington's picture there. Allen acknowledged the picture and said he thought it was an appropriate place for an Englishman to put it. The surprised Briton asked why.

"There is nothing that will make an Englishman shit so quick as the sight of General Washington," said Allen.[7]

Douglas's grandfather Benajah Douglas was a Pennsylvanian and himself a Revolutionary War soldier. He was with Washington at Valley Forge and at Yorktown.[8] Born in December 1760, Benajah Douglas was just a few years older than Andrew Jackson, his grandson's champion. Although he was too young to have a direct connection with soldiers of the War of 1812, Stephen Douglas was raised in a community in which lived men whose torn and mangled limbs and minds reminded their neighbors of the heroism and human costs of the War of Independence. Brandon and the small towns around it had sent thirty-nine young men to that war.[9] And their stories of the British and the war were recited like poetry bred familiar by the repetition of it. The stories were told and retold by the Brandon men who had soldiered in it.

Those who knew Douglas's grandfather predicted the boy would grow into the physique and character of Benajah. They were right. At maturity, Stephen Douglas stood five feet, four inches and weighed 130 pounds. He was barrel-chested and for his height was almost as big in body as any man. Had his shorter-than-average legs been three inches longer, he would have been of above-average height for his day.[10] The editor of the Newburyport, Massachusetts, *Herald-Republican* one day would describe them as "small duck legs." The editor observed that Providence had provided them wisely—since Douglas "would want backbone more than legs in his battle of life."[11]

Douglas had a large head and ample forehead imposed like a cliff over a set of thick eyebrows and a deeply set pair of steel-blue eyes. A fold of skin connected the eyes from tear duct to tear duct. Later in life, a furrow running from this fold almost to his hairline would develop like a straight cut between his eyebrows that would deepen with age and conviction. The bridge of Douglas's nose widened the expanse between his eyes and ended at unusually thick, flared nostrils. The philtrum of his nose spread outward from each nostril, appearing to pull at the top of the arcs of Douglas's finely drawn lips in a way that expressed humor and confidence. Douglas's chin was set like a large oval amid the expanse of a firmly squared jaw. And the short-knotted ties and cravats Douglas preferred created the appearance of a slight double chin.

He would sweep shocks of thick dark hair, often unruly, from the left to the right side of his head, a lock falling occasionally over his left eye, which he would push back and smooth out over his ear. Over the years, he would experiment with hairstyles, having it cut both short and long.

Douglas's complexion was described in a story by the *New York Tribune* as being "red and rowdyish," without explaining the meaning of the latter term, which was more typically used to characterize an individual's personality.[12] On the vertical fold of skin on the left side of Douglas's face was a small, barely noticeable mole. Except for a period in 1857, Douglas was clean-shaven throughout his life.[13]

Grandfather Benajah, who had been a tavern keeper in Saratoga County, New York, arrived in Brandon in 1794, eleven years after its organization.[14] Like many of his neighbors, Benajah Douglas became a small farmer of some merit and an even more successful politician. No forum was off limits for Benajah Douglas's interest in state and town affairs. When Methodist Church circuit steward Gideon Horton formed the first Methodist class in Brandon in August 1798, Benajah Douglas was among its members. He and every one of the other young men in that class became active in Brandon and Vermont politics.[15] Benajah Douglas's neighbors elected him a selectman of Brandon and five times made him their representative to the Vermont General Assembly. By the time of his election to the Vermont legislature, the tone of the state had been cast. Anti-federalists had laid down principles for the state in full accord with the U.S. constitution. Sovereignty rested not in the central government or state government, for that matter, but in *the people*. Vermont led the colonies in casting off the vestiges of aristocracy and class. It abolished property qualifications for suffrage, ending the perception that only property holders had the ability to understand and manage the affairs of government. There was none of the fear that the commercial men around the ports of Massachusetts had about "excesses of democracy." Nor was there any latent desire among the same men to defer or delay the Revolution in the hope that they might regain the full rights of Englishmen under the king.[16] Vermont was fully engaged in Democracy. The state replaced the practice of viva voce voting with the ballot, which would be cast in secret, and held that any voter (women could not vote) was qualified to serve in the state legislature. While most other states would provide in their constitutions for a Senate, whose members represented property—and a more democratic House, Vermont assigned supremacy to democracy itself by providing for only a single house. In this state, the power was concentrated in the branch closest to the people. No further checks and balances were wanted.[17]

Douglas's Vermont had the distinction of being the first state to outlaw adult slavery on July 8, 1777.[18] By the time Douglas was born in 1823, slavery in Vermont had become an abstraction. The first U.S. Census recorded only seventeen slaves in Vermont in 1790. By the 1800 census, slavery there was non-existent.[19]

Benajah Douglas was considered the Demosthenes of Brandon. With a mind that seemed to retain even the most trivial fact, he was able to speak on any subject—and derived great pleasure from doing so. His listeners were just as pleased to hear his orations, which he often studded with embellishments. It was said of Benajah Douglas that he would "add as much spice to his yarns as the occasion demanded"—or that he could get away with. The people of Brandon saw the strongest resemblances of the bass-voiced farmer in the grandson Stephen. His mother would remind Douglas of the contributions his grandfather Benajah had made to Brandon and would suggest that the boy reminded her of the family patriarch.[20]

Douglas's maternal grandfather Fisk had owned a farm about three miles north of Brandon. It was to this farm, operated by her older bachelor brother Edward Fisk, that Douglas's mother took daughter Sally and son Stephen after the doctor's death. The Fisk farm adjoined the three-hundred-acre Douglas farm, whose inheritor Sarah Douglas signed over to her brother.[21]

Farming was Brandon's major industry, and its hardships were heavy on the Douglases, who were forced to leave the less callused life of a physician's family in Brandon village. In the demanding tasks assigned to them, the Douglases earned their keep on the Fisk farm. Douglas described his uncle as "an industrious, economical, clever old bachelor, and [who] wanted some one to keep house for him."[22] That was his mother's chore. The boy willingly performed farm chores, tasks that were not easy, but assigned to him by his uncle, on a farm whose fields were rocky and undulating. Some of the land required trees to be cleared and rocks to be gathered and carried off. It was the boy's duty to split the hard woods and get them to the woodshed for the winter's fuel.[23] Douglas performed his duties industriously for nine months each year during his boyhood days and was enrolled in the Brandon District School for the three winter months between planting and harvest. The eighteen families of the district in 1804 built the one-room, hip-roofed schoolhouse from bricks that came from the nearby Leicester kiln.[24]

Douglas was particularly fond of his classmates, and as he grew nearer the day they would finish school he pined over the thought of leaving them. At fifteen years old, Douglas's affection for two of his closest classroom comrades was clear in a poem he composed, found in his 16-page school "Copy Book":

> When shall we three meet again
> When shall we three meet again
> Oft shall shimmering hope espire [sic]
> Oft shall weried [sic] love recline
> Oft shall death and [illegible] now reign
> Ere we three shall meet again.
>
> Though in distant lands we sigh
> Perch it beneath a hostile sky
> Though the deep [illegible] us rolls
> Friendship s[h]all unite our souls

> Still in fancy's rich domain
> Oft shall we three meet again.
>
> When round the youthful pine
> Moss shall creep and ivy twine
> When our burnished locks are gray
> Thined [sic] by many a toil spent day
> May this long loved bower remain
> There may we three meet again.
>
> When the dreams of life are fled
> When its wasted lamps are dead
> When in cold oblivions shade
> Beauty power and fame are laid
> Where immortal spirits reign
> There shall we three meet again.[25]

The Copy Book also showed the pubescent boy entertaining flights of fancy about girls. On the last page Douglas crowded in the name "Ellen Channing." Ellen Channing, Ellen Channing, Ellen Channing he wrote fifteen times down the length of the sheet. On the 16th line, the boy wrote "Ellen Channing Douglass."[26] Years later, Douglas would father two daughters, each of them dying in infancy. The first little girl died three weeks after her mother, Martha Martin Douglas, died giving birth to her. The second, born to Douglas and his second wife Adele Cutts Douglas, died in June 1860 at six months. Each child was named Ellen.

It had been Douglas's understanding that his uncle had promised to finance his education at the Brandon Academy when Douglas reached the proper age. It was this promise that had sustained Douglas in the devotion he rendered to the demanding tasks on his uncle's farm. Watching several of his friends preparing for entry into the Academy, Douglas at fifteen believed the time had come for his entry, as well. He approached his recently married uncle for permission and the expected sponsorship. The long-held dream dissipated in the uncle's description of the requirements of his own new family, which now included a baby boy. This new arrival, this new heir to the Fisk farm, including his father's farm his mother had given her brother, had eliminated Douglas's dream. In years to come Douglas would claim he was not "much dissatisfied with my good old uncle." The emerging politician would decide there was no benefit to criticism, and he burned no bridges. But it was evident that he was profoundly disappointed and hurt. In a later revelation, he would declare that Fisk was a "rather hard master ... unwilling to give me those opportunities of improvement and education which I thought I was entitled to. I had enjoyed the benefits of a common school education three months each year, and had been kept diligently at work the rest of the time. I thought it a hardship that my uncle would have the use of my mother's farm and also the benefit of my labour without any other equivalent than my boarding and clothes."[27]

No longer with any claim to the land his mother had signed over to his uncle—and against his mother's wishes, the teenaged Douglas decided to leave the farm. Sarah Douglas pleaded with him not to go. He never had been far from ill health. Unable to change her son's mind, however, Sarah released him. She warned him of the dangers and temptations of the world. And she advocated that he quickly take up a trade or some business that would provide steady employment.

"I promised to comply with her wishes," Douglas wrote in a biographical sketch years later, "that is, keep good company, or in other words keep out of bad company, avoid all immoral and vicious practices, attend church regularly, and obey the regulations of my employer; in short I promised everything she wanted, if she would consent to my leaving home."[28] Douglas left home determined, as he told his mother, to see what he could do for himself in a wide world of strangers. Douglas's first day was productive. He walked fourteen miles from the farm to Middlebury, Vermont, where he gained an apprenticeship in the shop of cabinet maker Nahum Parker. Parker's wife Sarah was a stepdaughter of Douglas's grandfather Benajah.[29] Fifteen-year-old Stephen Douglas was delighted with the job of hand-sawing pine planks and assembling table legs, bedsteads and washstands.[30]

"I have never been placed in any situation or been engaged in any business," he would write in 1838, "which I enjoyed to so great an extent as the cabinet shop. I then felt contented and happy, and never aspired to any other distinction than that connected with my trade and improvements in the arts."[31]

Middlebury offered other novel experiences, as well. Douglas joined a group in a weekly singing school. After one of the gatherings he walked home with a young lady, whose name is lost to history. When along the way a young man voiced what Douglas considered a slander toward the girl, Douglas defended her honor. The short but surprisingly pugnacious Douglas laid the offender on the ground with a single punch. A second lad was treated to the same righteousness.[32]

It was at Middlebury that Douglas developed an interest in politics. Although he had become comfortably "attached to the life of a mechanic," as he put it, he was spending more of his spare time reading. He and his friends were together most nights and Sundays reading and studying.[33] The subject was usually politics, and more particularly Andrew Jackson's politics. Douglas found in Jackson, who likewise had not known his father, his model for manhood. Young Douglas did not know it at the time, but the first decade of his working life was much like Jackson's. Both were teacher, lawyer, judge, politician, state legislator, congressman, and U.S. senator.

If he was impassioned when the sensitivities of his friends were bruised, Douglas became in youth just as pugnacious in his growing political interests. Adherents believed Jackson had been cheated out of the presidency three years earlier by a "corrupt bargain" between President John Quincy Adams and Henry Clay. And Clay in 1828 was challenging Adams once again.[34] With his employer Parker an advocate for Adams and with his recent experience of a gentrified uncle breaking what Douglas thought had been a commitment for the continuation of his study, Douglas was decidedly for Jackson. In Jackson was a hero who found virtue not in the aristocrat but in the commoner.

Douglas organized a "band of Jackson boys" who joined him in ripping down anti–Jackson "coffin handbills" that Adams supporters were posting around Middlebury.[35] In his physical assault on the accouterments of the more elitist party, Douglas was acquiring a visceral attachment to Jackson and the Jacksonian Democracy. He would say that it was the election of 1828 that led him to Jacksonian principles and his lasting "attachment to the cause of Democracy."[36]

Douglas ventured into "the wide world of strangers," which had concerned his mother. And he had never been happier. His first labors in politics exercised his mind as well as his body.[37] Parker was as instructive in politics as in the art of cabinet making. As an Adams man, he was a good mentor to his fifteen-year-old apprentice in carpentry and Jacksonian Democracy.

The Adams-Jackson contest grew muddier. Adams supporters claimed irregularities in Jackson's lineage and marriage. They charged that Jackson's mother had been a prostitute and his wife Rachel was an adulteress. Jacksonians responded in kind, claiming that Adams, while minister to Russia, had procured for Czar Alexander a young American woman for sexual pleasure.[38]

These were insensibilities enough for the young Jackson admirer. But Douglas felt his own sensibilities insulted when Parker insisted he perform some menial tasks in the Parker home. It was a presumption the young democrat would not accept.

"I was willing to do anything connected with the shop," Douglas said, "but could not consent to perform the duties of a servant in the house."[39]

He quit.

Douglas returned to Brandon and apprenticed himself to cabinet-maker Deacon Caleb Knowlton. Douglas was one of several apprentices who fashioned cured mahogany into raised-panel doors and fine furniture. The works of Douglas's craftsmanship found their way into the homes of Brandon and surrounding towns in the form of bureaus and cabinets and gate-leg tables.[40] Like Parker, Knowlton was an advocate of John Quincy Adams, more fodder for Douglas, whose fellow apprentices shared his affection for General Jackson.[41] The spirit of the presidential contest between these national figures had excited and firmly grounded him. But more, it became his life's political bedrock.

"From this moment my politics became fixed and all subsequent reading, reflection and observation have but confirmed by early attachment to the cause of Democracy," Douglas wrote.[42]

Having returned to his mother's home, Douglas began saving to fund his entry into Brandon Academy. The opportunity came more quickly than he might have expected or desired. During his apprenticeship with Knowlton, Douglas during the winter of 1829 fell seriously ill. His doctor told Douglas he would be unable to return to cabinet making and suggested he find another occupation. With what he had saved, Douglas took advantage of his condition. He achieved his earlier desire by enrolling in the Brandon Academy. There, he joined the school's debating society and found gratification in a growing talent for forensics and rhetoric.

The marriage of his sister Sarah to Julius N. Granger of Manchester Centre, Ontario County, New York, on February 14, 1830, was followed that fall by the marriage of their mother Sarah to young Granger's father, Gehazi. This alignment of families created an unexpected opportunity for Douglas, who moved with his mother to the elder Granger's residence at Clifton Springs in Ontario County, western New York. Granger was a man of means and could afford to satisfy Douglas's interest in furthering his education. Granger sponsored Douglas's entry into the Canandaigua Academy, about two miles northeast of the Granger home, to study Greek, Latin, mathematics, and rhetoric. Enrolling in 1830, Douglas boarded at the academy during the week and returned to the Granger home on weekends.

Douglas the Canandaigua student connected himself with the ideas of Jefferson for small government, state sovereignty, and strict construction of the Constitution. With a gift of vocabulary, a quick response to any challenge, and a capacious mind for historical and political information, Douglas was a frequent debater at Canandaigua. He championed Jackson, and when Jackson was re-elected president in 1832, Douglas's fellow Canandaiguans regarded him without peer. He was *the* politician.[43] His roommate, Marcus Willson, recalled Douglas's gallant and vigorous defenses of Jackson, which Willson later would say provided the foundation for some of Douglas's speeches as a freshman U.S. congressman defending the aged, retired president.

At Canandaigua three years, Douglas considered himself to have made "considerable improvement."[44] Having received credit for three years of classical studies, Douglas began the study of law. In January 1833, he left Canandaigua Academy and began a clerkship in the law offices of Walter & Levi Hubbell, both Democrats in a community made up largely of members of the National Republican, or anti–Jackson, Party. He pursued his law studies diligently five days a week and spent the sixth continuing classical studies. Often at dinner, his mentor Walter Hubbell would quiz Douglas on Chitty and Blackstone, commentaries on the laws of England and adopted common laws in the young United States, as well as Greek and Latin. Hubbell provided entrée for Douglas to Saturday discussions with other law students and prominent lawyers.[45] Hubbell invited Douglas occasionally to society parties at which Douglas, who was so comfortable among young ladies, was regarded as "literally a pet of the petticoats."[46]

This earliest known photograph of Stephen A. Douglas was believed taken at about the time of his entry into Canandaigua Academy in Canandaigua, New York. There Douglas began preparing for a career in law. And there he sharpened his oratorical skills, often defending President Andrew Jackson in debates (courtesy Abraham Lincoln Presidential Library and Museum).

The relationship with the Hubbell law firm ended in June 1833 when Douglas found himself in "straightened pecuniary circumstances." That wasn't the whole of it. His sister recalled that ambition and impatience were pushing Douglas to look westward. The idea of practicing law and the knowledge that practice in New York would be denied him for four years were stimulating his wanderlust. There were fewer standards for lawyers in the West.[47] Some states required little more than residency and the testimony of a lawyer or two.

Knowing that his mother was unable to support him through the remaining years of study that were required for admission to the New York bar, Douglas "determined upon removing to the western country and relying upon my own efforts for a support henceforth."[48] His mother worried that at twenty years of age her only son, always of delicate health, was too inexperienced to go west alone. As he had done when he left the farm five years earlier, Douglas brushed off his mother's plea that he remain in Clifton Springs. Finding his resolution "fixed and unchangeable," Sarah Douglas let her son go. She gave him $300, the last of his patrimony, which he carried along with letters of introduction from Francis Granger, Mark Sibley, and a few other lawyer friends.

"I bid farewell to my friends, and started alone for the 'great west,' without having any particular place of destination in view," he remembered years later.[49]

Douglas's mother asked him when she could expect to see him again.

"I will stop by and see you on my way to Congress within the next ten years," he answered.[50]

On the morning of June 24, 1833, Douglas, too short to do it himself, got help with heaving his single trunk aboard a stagecoach. He then hoisted himself aboard and began his journey west.

After brief stops in Buffalo and Niagara Falls, Douglas continued on to Cleveland, which he had set as his destination. His boat landed at Cleveland, slipping alongside the east government pier, built three years earlier, which made disembarking for passengers more pleasant than at other spots Douglas had seen. It was a sign of Cleveland's growing importance in processing and industry. A great advantage was the Erie Canal, finished in 1825, which connected Cleveland to New York, and the related shipping from there to the Great Lakes and commerce beyond.[51] The importance of such public improvements was filed away in the Douglas memory.

In Cleveland were acquaintances Douglas believed would welcome him. His cousin Daniel P. Rhodes, who had been born in Sudbury, Vermont, the year after Douglas's birth, had made his way earlier to Cleveland to seek his fortune in the West. Douglas had determined to reacquaint himself with Cousin Rhodes. He also decided to present the letters of introduction he had received from New York friends to Cleveland lawyer Sherlock J. Andrews.[52] Shortly after his arrival in Cleveland Douglas also looked up his Canandaigua Academy roommate Marcius Willson and three other Canandaigua classmates, whom he knew to be studying law with Andrews. He made it a point to see his Canandaigua friends nearly every day.[53]

The Andrews firm was among the most distinguished law firms in Cleveland. Graduating from Yale Law School in 1825, Andrews was admitted immediately to the bar and moved to Cleveland where he began his practice.[54] By the time Douglas arrived at the firm's offices in June 1833, Andrews was Cuyahoga County's prosecuting attorney, a position he owed to his affiliation with the county's Whig party. Whether Douglas or his friends had informed Andrews of Douglas's Jacksonian faith, Douglas so impressed Andrews that he immediately offered Douglas the use of his law library. Andrews promised Douglas a position in the firm once he passed the bar.[55] Such prospects at the beginning of his chosen career were for Douglas highly gratifying. He accepted Andrews's offer at once.[56]

Douglas's interests were similar to his cousin's: to take advantage of the opportunities the West offered and apply himself energetically in their pursuit. In his estimation, eminent men already had settled the East. They would not be competition for him in the west.[57] He believed a man of energy could build a reputation and livelihood in one of the new settlements that were springing up along the shores of the Great Lakes and the westward rivers like the Ohio and the Mississippi.[58]

Douglas promptly began his study of law. His future was promising. Andrews was a prominent lawyer who could assist the career of an ambitious young man. And he had encouraged Douglas. Learning that Ohio was a more expedient locale for the advancement of his career—Ohio required only a single year of study before admission to the bar, Douglas decided to make Cleveland home.[59] He threw himself into his new association with Andrews with characteristic energy. He reported to Andrews for work the next day.

On the fifth day, he was an absentee.

Douglas was stricken by what the doctor who examined him called "bilious fever." As it was understood at the time, it was a disease "generally suspected to be owing to, or connected with, derangement of the biliary system."[60] It was associated with the common symptoms of dysentery or malarial fever, which was said to lurk during the summer in the lowlands of the west. It was the kind of illness his mother had feared.

The fever confined Douglas to his bed for four months. Douglas was deathly ill. By the end of that time, he no longer had a position. Another apprentice had taken the position in the Andrews firm. Douglas was deeply disappointed, but his recovery was something more miraculous to him. He, even his doctors, had no idea that the cooler weather of fall, which nudged out the heat and humidity, also had nudged out the malady he had suffered during the summer months. Douglas recovered.

His illness and recovery had a profound impact on Douglas and his place in the world. The illness had taken full control of him and left him with no capacity to make choices.[61] No one while he was sick, he wrote his brother-in-law, could foresee what the next day would bring.[62] Yet the idea that fate was now in full control of his life, he became greatly intrigued by the nature of powerlessness and his own response to it. It was a great wonder to him:

> This sickness has often since been, and still continues to be, the subject of the most serious and profound reflection. My condition, the circumstances with which I was surrounded, the doubtful and sometimes hopeless issue, and especially my feelings, thoughts, and meditations, are all now fresh in my mind. I was among entire strangers. During the whole time I never saw a face I had ever seen before; I was so feeble as to be entirely helpless, unable even to turn myself in bed; I was advised by my physicians that there was no reasonable hope of my recovery, and that I ought to be prepared for my final dissolution which was then expected to take place from day to day.[63]

Douglas claimed that he had been fully conscious of his condition "and indifferent to the result." He had been ready to die: "I thought I was on the dividing line between this world and the next, must continue to exist in the one or the other, was willing to take either, and felt no choice which."[64]

His condition made him feel a "more perfect freedom from all care and trouble, except occasional body pain, and more negative happiness than during other similar period of my life."[65] His near-death experience would be a matter of great wonder and mystery to him for the rest of his life.[66]

Douglas's doctors still were uncertain that he was fully over the fever, believing it could easily return the following spring. Among other things, not the least of which was his loss of employment, that was reason enough for Douglas to leave Cleveland. Doctors, who had believed during the summer that his mortality draining from him, urged Douglas to return to Canandaigua. But Douglas was resolved to resume the journey west.[67] He did so in October 1833.

During his illness, Douglas had received $200 from home. After satisfying his medical and boarding expenses, he had $40 left. He bought passage on a boat operating on the Ohio & Erie Canal, built between 1825 and 1832. The infrastructure provided a successful transportation route from Cleveland, on Lake Erie, to Portsmouth on the Ohio River. It gave Douglas a reminder of how transportation improvements could link communities and commerce of a region to the rest of the settled eastern United States. From Portsmouth, Douglas proceeded by steamboat down the Ohio River. Unsuccessful in his search for a position, Douglas at Louisville was in something of an anxious mood. He was "ready to embark in any adventure adapted to my taste and feeling which should present itself."[68] Louisville offered nothing to keep Douglas and he boarded another steamboat bound for St. Louis. Fellow passengers included Dr. Lewis F. Linn, who would be elected to Congress from Missouri in the following year, and Colonel John Miller, who had been Missouri's governor from 1825 to 1832. Both were Jackson Democrats. Douglas found the conversations with them pleasant and easy.[69]

Arriving in St. Louis in November 1833, Douglas found it a busy port on the Mississippi River, about halfway between the river's origin at Lake Itasca, Minnesota, and its destination into the Gulf of Mexico about a hundred miles south of New Orleans. Boats arrived and embarked daily along the river highway, which separated Illinois, nominally a free state, and Missouri, whose founders, two years after Illinois had been denied it, welcomed slavery. His funds were nearly exhausted, and Douglas was anxious for a position. He set about the task almost as soon as the steamer was tied to the landing. He hoped to finance his living expenses while continuing his studies by working in a law office. He called on Edward Bates, one of the most prominent lawyers in the riverport city. A former Missouri Whig congressman and state legislator, Bates was impressed by the applicant and treated Douglas kindly. Bates offered Douglas the use of his firm's law library but he had no paying position available. It was disheartening. Douglas's attempts to find posts at other attorneys in St. Louis proved similarly unsuccessful.

Still intent on seeing Jacksonville, Douglas paid his tavern bill and took a boat to the new town of Alton, Illinois, opposite St. Louis on the eastern shore of the Mississippi River. Before dawn the next day, November 13, 1833, he boarded a stagecoach bound for Jacksonville. He still felt ill, which he attributed to the months of sickness and fever he had survived in Cleveland. The coach rocked along the bends and undulations of the Sangamon-Alton Trace Road, and Douglas felt nauseous. But the movements eventually lulled him into sleep, which refreshed him. His carriage traveling mostly north and northeast, he woke just as the sun began to rise over the prairie.[70] The brisk November had stripped the landscape of much of its vegetation, and Douglas could see broad vistas of pristine plains warmed by the sun coming up from the distant horizon. He was overwhelmed by its vastness.

"It was the first time my eyes ever beheld a Prairie and I shall never forget the impressions & emotions produced by the scene," he recalled.[71]

Douglas dropped particulars and decided he would take any kind of work when he arrived at Jacksonville in mid–November 1833. His pocket held $1.25, the last of his legacy, which experience told him would not pay board for more than a day or two at a tavern. It took little time for him to form a few acquaintants and begin looking for opportunities "to get into business of some kind, say teaching school, clerking, &c, but, again, without success."[72]

Putting first things first, Douglas sought lodging on the cheap. Asking around, he learned that Thomas Heslep, a cabinet maker of the Democratic persuasion, kept a tavern in his unusually large home two blocks west of the city square. Lodgers were boarded in a common apartment on the second floor. Heslep's son Joseph invited Douglas to lodge there, and Douglas did.[73]

From his temporary quarters overlooking a group of small white-chinked, grayish-logged cabins, Douglas could see the two-story brick courthouse on the public square's southwest side. Its weathervane and spire did nothing to beautify the building. Douglas was in no mood to criticize. More important was the need to acquire some way to pay for his housing. Douglas completed arrangements for his quarters at Heslep's tavern. He managed to sell some of his schoolbooks from his trunk to pay for them.

❖ ❖ ❖

Major Murray McConnel, Jacksonville's first Jacksonian lawyer, was working at his desk that Thursday, November 14, 1833, when the young man, whom nature appeared to have cheated in the length of his legs but had compensated by providing an unusually large head, entered the McConnel law office near the public square. The ruddy-cheeked, boyish Douglas presented to McConnel a letter of introduction. Looking into McConnel's sharp eyes, Douglas could see *the* exemplar of the worldly pioneer who had settled the town of Jacksonville nine years earlier. The two would find themselves much alike in their backgrounds—it was for similar reasons that they left their homes by the time they were fifteen—and took to each other at once in a friendship that would be unruffled for as long as the two lived.[74] To those who would tell McConnel that Douglas was only using him to advance his own career, McConnel said, "No matter, his ambition will probably prove of more worth to the Nation than all our modesty."[75]

Murray McConnel was the first lawyer in Morgan County and one of only two among the county's eleven lawyers to admit he was a Jacksonian. It was a reason he had to inform job-seeking Douglas that he did not have enough work to hire him. McConnel, however, saw great promise in the ambitious 20-year-old (courtesy Abraham Lincoln Presidential Library and Museum).

Douglas boldly asked for a clerkship in McConnel's firm. The growing threat in Douglas's financial condition was evident in the earnestness of his request. Yet McConnel's own situation was stretched. He and his partner Daniel Roberts were the only two Democratic lawyers among the 11 lawyers practicing in the town. And his situation was stretched further by the demands of a growing family. Douglas had arrived just a month before the McConnels expected the arrival of another child.[76] There was not enough business to support a clerk, McConnel told his visitor. Yet he was encouraging. He suggested to Douglas that he could learn and practice law before admission to the bar by traveling up the Illinois River to the new town of Pekin. There he could open an office and practice as a justice of the peace, for which he said a law license was not required in Illinois. Situated well north of Jacksonville along the east side of the river, Pekin boosters sought the advantage of its location on the Illinois between Chicago and St. Louis. Their vision was to make it a marketing and shipping port to serve agriculture in the region. Douglas could continue to read law, McConnel counseled, while working as a magistrate. Justices of the peace were permitted to administer summary justice in minor cases, commit cases for trial in circuit court, administer oaths, and perform marriages. For Douglas, it was a most welcome way to earn a living, study law, gain some experience, and ultimately seek admission to the bar. Told that Douglas had sold his law books, McConnel provided copies of some well used law books and copies of state statutes he said Douglas would need. McConnel valued the books at $30 and told Douglas he could pay him when he was able. Douglas subsequently satisfied the obligation.[77]

With the opportunity to fulfill his goal, Douglas did not hesitate to move toward the advantages McConnel described. Not doubting, now, that he would be able to apply for admittance to the bar, Douglas before he left the city filed his application for his law license with Associate Justice Samuel Drake Lockwood of the Supreme Court, who had lived in Jacksonville since 1828.[78]

Optimism in his gait and with his lightened, single trunk of belongings, Douglas departed for Meredosia, a village west of Jacksonville on the Illinois River, enroute to Pekin. He spent a week lodged at the Catfish Hotel, a white-framed tavern on the river's eastern bank, waiting for the boat, reading the books McConnel provided, and communing easily with the locals.[79] It was at this point that Douglas learned the last steamboat scheduled to travel upriver that year had blown up at Alton. There would not be another boat headed north until spring.

Good fortune put him in touch with a farmer from outside the town of Exeter, Morgan County's first settlement and located about 18 miles west of Jacksonville. The farmer told Douglas the town had been looking for a teacher to open a subscription school—public schools had not been established—for the area's children. He seemed confident enough that Douglas's education and demeanor could make him a teacher. The opportunity appealed to Douglas who, with only 50 cents remaining after paying his tavern bill, needed employment. Leaving his trunk of belongings at Meredosia, Douglas climbed behind the farmer on his horse and rode to Exeter.

The next day, Douglas and the farmer solicited Exeter's citizens without success. Not a single pupil was subscribed. Douglas was downcast, and even word that another small town in Morgan County named Winchester had been actively seeking a teacher did little to lift his spirits.

"I thought this was rather poor encouragement," Douglas thought, "but what was to be done? I was out of money, and still too feeble in health to perform any very arduous labor; and must do something to live."

He was, Douglas said of himself, "too proud to beg."[80]

Desperate for employment, Douglas walked the eight miles to Winchester. There he asked Winchester tavern keeper Ira Rowan to rent him a room on credit. In minutes, Rowan was able to detect enough promise in the young man who said he had come to Winchester to teach school that Rowan obliged. On the promise that he would take in Rowan's son Thomas Phillip, Douglas obtained lodging on the tavern's second floor.[81] He would lodge with the Rowans for the next few nights.

Douglas and Rowan spent their first evening together discussing travels and families. They talked about what seemed to be much in common. As had Douglas, Rowan had launched his journey from the East and had stopped in Ohio. There he had met Mary Kersey and the two were married October 26, 1826. In addition to son Thomas Phillip, the Rowans had a four-year-old daughter Sally—friends called Douglas's mother by that nickname—and a one-year-old boy, William Grainger. Douglas's attention was drawn to William, whose middle name was the married name of Douglas's mother and sister. The boy had been named for his great-grandfather Edward Grainger of Anne Arundel County, Maryland, but Rowan and Douglas were unable to make a connection beyond the last name of the families. Douglas also was able to acquire substantial information about the Winchester community from Rowan and felt a closer affinity to his host when he learned that President Jackson had appointed Rowan to serve as the community's postmaster.[82]

The next day, Douglas found more good fortune awaiting him.

Rowan introduced Douglas to Winchester's citizens as they made their way around town. Douglas was happy to find that the locals were eager to have a teacher for their subscription school. Within a few days, Douglas enrolled 40 students at $3 each for a term of three months.

Douglas also found a temporary job in Winchester. Local auctioneer John Pickering, who met and liked Douglas, told him he would pay him to help with the administrator's sale of the estate of the late Elihu Martin, a deceased Winchester retail merchant. Martin had left a sizable estate, which took three days to liquidate. Pickering offered Douglas two dollars per day.

"And board," Douglas bargained.[83]

The deal made, Douglas was employed for two and one-half days. It was time he used well. It afforded him the opportunity of acquaintance with many of the bidders while inducing them to up their bids for Martin's residuals. The excitement of the sale increased the auction's revenues. Douglas himself was excited enough to buy two pen knives, one lot of newspapers and three linen collars at a total cost of $1.36, a dollar more than the amount he had when he arrived in Winchester.[84] Pickering paid him $5.

"*I have become a Western man*," Douglas declared in a letter to his brother-in-law Julius toward the end of his first week in Winchester, "have imbibed Western feelings, principles and interests and have selected Illinois as the favorite place of my adoption, without any desire of returning to the land of my fathers except as a visitor to see my friends and the improvements that may be made from time to time in the country."[85]

This was an optimistic new Douglas, a brash, big-chested, slick-talking new Douglas who could respond easily to the first wink, the first smile, the first handshake that had made him a Western man. Winchester afforded Douglas his first wholly independent and self-directed occupation from which he derived real earnings. In just three months, he could earn nearly a fourth of the legacy he had received from the estate his father had built over a lifetime. Douglas's outlook reflected more than a newfound self-reliance. It was unbounded in Jacksonian principles, boundless in optimism born of a headlong confidence he would never lose. He felt part of the mission of Old Hickory to shape destiny, and not only his own.

"I emigrated when I was very young," Douglas recalled years later. "I came out here when I was a boy, and I found my mind liberalized, and my opinions enlarged when I got on these broad prairies, with only the Heavens to bound [*sic*] my vision, instead of having them circumscribed by the little narrow ridges that surrounded the valley where I was born."[86]

Distinctly different from urbane Jacksonville, Winchester was a place in which Douglas found himself at the center of Jacksonian egalitarianism. He could be bold without reservation and be forward without misstep. Whatever he chose to test, he had found a lively response from his new Winchester neighbors. As that auction proceeded, Douglas between lots found willing ears for political conversation and appreciation for Jacksonian Democracy. His abilities won him admiration not usually accorded to people of his age. It did not hurt that the politics Douglas spoke were Jacksonian politics. Although he was unaware of it at the time, most of the 60 families of Winchester were of the Democratic Republican persuasion. And Douglas was a Democrat, "a great Democrat, a natural man of the people."[87]

On December 2, 1833, Douglas opened his school in Winchester to 40 students, including Rowan's son Phillip, in a one-story wood building at Hill and Cherry streets with a three-posted porch on the front.

Douglas found more permanent lodging for his three-month stay in Winchester in the storeroom of village merchant Edward Griffith Miner. Miner also was from Vermont, a chance association that made the two ready friends. They "batched it," cooking for one another, spending time in "comfortable chats" with neighbors, and forming acquaintances.[88] Douglas served as Miner's best man at his wedding—but only after he talked Miner into furnishing him a new shirt. Miner's store provided a platform for Douglas to practice his oratory and politics. Although closed to business in the evening, the store was open to all comers as a caucus room and theatre. Boxes, bales, and barrels were seats for "the boys," who, with a plug of tobacco

His pockets empty and frustrated that he had been unable to find a position in law in Jacksonville, Douglas taught forty students at a three-month subscription school in Winchester, Illinois. He won many friends in the rural Morgan County community, whose residents were nearly all Jacksonians. So taken by his new friends, all of them successful on the frontier, and his own progress, Douglas within six weeks declared, "I have become a Western man" (courtesy Abraham Lincoln Presidential Library and Museum).

bulging from their cheeks or lower lips, fidgeted for an opening to get in a lick.[89] With the belly of the black cast-iron stove at their back, Douglas and his debating kin mixed the thick talk of liberty, fraternity, and Andrew Jackson with thick tobacco smoke and spit that stained the pine-planked floor.[90]

Having lived there for a time himself, McConnel retained the friendship of many residents of Winchester and visited the community once or twice a month. He recalled that one of the first things he heard about Douglas after Douglas's arrival in Winchester was that he offered himself as an independent candidate for the state legislature. McConnel noted that Douglas was not successful in his first attempt to win office,

> but that he so promptly made the attempt was characteristic of the man.
> He was filled with the commanding, irrepressible instinct of leadership, and the direction in which that leadership could be exercised was determined by another spontaneous quality, the civic interest.[91]

McConnel had clearly read in Douglas an unstoppable personality. His way was not dogmatic, McConnel said, and he was confident enough to listen to others: "He had no sort of disposition to go, like the Mohammedan, with a creed in one hand and a sword in the other, and a fanatic resolution that every man he met must swallow one or the other. The very first impulse of the man, when he found anyone dissenting from him in opinion, may be embodied in the familiar phrase, 'Come let us reason together.' It was as natural and spontaneous with him to reason, to argue, to seek to convince, as it is to all men to eat."[92]

Winchester gave the aspiring Douglas the chance to begin handling some legal work. With the used law books McConnel sold him, Douglas studied law after he dismissed his school students. He prepared and presented a considerable number of cases for his Winchester clients before the local justice of the peace on Saturday afternoons.[93]

Winchester also provided fertile ground for the young teacher, trained debater, and legal scholar to test his political skills. That winter, Winchester citizens organized a lyceum at which regionally renowned lawyer Josiah Lamborn of Jacksonville was to speak.[94] Although he was considered to have no intellectual superior in the practice of law, Lamborn had the reputation of a mudslinger. He was vindictive and utterly unscrupulous.[95] Lamborn quickly set the stage for his lyceum address, a brutal assault on President Jackson. A forceful speaker who was considered an unyielding advocate of causes he endorsed, Lamborn punctuated his charges against Jackson by pounding his heavy cane—he had been born with a clubfoot—on the platform.[96]

There was an inclination among some in the audience to agree with Lamborn. In the presidential contest of 1832, the county gave Jackson a ten-point edge over Henry Clay.[97] But public opinion was torn these days. Jackson's attack on the national bank had created a firestorm. The U.S. Bank was reducing its discounts and circulation after Jackson ordered the withdrawal of government deposits in September 1833. The contraction of credit was slowing growth and capital for internal improvements— public works like roads and canals, which the citizenry believed would stimulate the creation of new towns and businesses in Illinois. There was a decided new tone of hostility among the communities of Morgan County, which had begun permeating social and business affairs, so much so that "to be a political opponent was, to a great extent, to be a personal enemy, and an enemy to the country." In Jacksonville, the revulsion over Jackson's bank policy was so intense that it had catapulted the Whigs to power. Few openly defended Jackson or his administration.[98]

At Winchester that evening, hearing Lamborn vilify the measures of Jackson's administration, Douglas was unable to remain silent. He already had intensively prepared himself in the arguments, deeply learning as much as he could about both sides of the controversy:

> I was then familiar with all the principles, measures and facts involved in the controversy, having been an attentive reader of the debates in Congress and the principal newspapers of the day, and having read also with great interest, the principal works in this country; such as the debates in the convention that formed the Constitution of the United States, and the convention of the several States on the adoption of the Constitution, the Federalist, John Adams' work denominated a defense of the American Constitution, the opinions of Randolph, Hamilton and Jefferson on the Constitutionality of the Bank, and the History of the Bank as published by Gales & Seaton, Jefferson's Works, &c. I had read all of them and many other political works with great care and interest, and had my political opinions firmly established.[99]

When Lamborn finished his remarks, Douglas rushed to the stage and engaged him in a spirited rejoinder that Winchester friends found nothing short of courageous. Winchester had given Douglas his first political battleground and Douglas had not waited for an invitation to take advantage of it. His voice and command over his subject boomed. Douglas's attack was a fusillade of facts and arguments that poured forth with little eloquence but which mastered his opponent by the sheer weight of its volume. He was the master of his subjects. His listeners were astonished at the depth of his knowledge.[100]

"I engaged in the debate with a good deal of zeal and warmth," Douglas recalled, "and defended the administration of Gen. Jackson and the cause of the Democratic party in a manner which appeared highly gratifying to my political friends, and which certainly gave me some little reputation as a public speaker; much more than I deserved."[101]

Douglas was greatly encouraged that his neighbors declared him the victor in this first oratorical battle. His years of practice as the defender of Jackson at Canandaigua Academy had prepared Douglas for the very moment.

While at Winchester, Douglas stayed in touch with Jacksonville society—occasionally lodging on weekends in Jacksonville at McConnel's home—and its legal fraternity.[102] He fully expected to be a member soon. He ingratiated himself in ways that left his name on the minds and tongues of those he met. At a party in early 1834, Douglas gave one of the guests a picture of the Acropolis "as something rare amid our surroundings in that far land."[103]

During this time, Douglas made an important friendship in Jacksonville with Samuel S. Brooks, editor of the recently established *Jacksonville News*. Men were wise who were not misled by Brooks's deferential manner. The young editor was a determined Jacksonian Democrat, and from the first line of type set at the *News* it was clear that he was determined to be Morgan County's strongest advocate for President Jackson—and anyone who adhered to his principles. Through Brooks's stewardship the *News* became one of the most active Democratic voices in the Illinois.[104]

Brooks had the good fortune to work for Robert Goudy, a publisher who had recently moved to Jacksonville from Vandalia so that his children would be able to attend Illinois College. Goudy established the *News* in January 1834. As his career developed in Jacksonville (and later in Quincy, Springfield, and Cairo), Brooks would serve as one of Douglas's staunchest supporters throughout his political career, Goudy himself was just as spirited in his efforts to aid Douglas in his quest for political fame.[105]

It was a circular about his new newspaper in Jacksonville that brought Brooks and Douglas together. Brooks had distributed throughout the region an announcement of the newspaper's establishment and a copy landed on Douglas's school desk. The Winchester teacher was attracted to Brooks's first-page-editorial promise to espouse the democratic principles of Andrew Jackson and candidates of the Jacksonian persuasion.

"My prospectuses were circulated throughout Morgan and the adjoining counties," Brooks recalled, "and immediately after the publication of the first number of the paper [in February 1834], most of them were returned with lists of names of subscribers on them. Among the returned copies of the prospectus was one from Winchester, with a large number of names, accompanied by a very complimentary and encouraging letter, signed 'Steph. A. Douglas.'"[106]

When he met Douglas shortly after Douglas's return to Jacksonville in March 1834, Brooks was surprised by the appearance of the man responsible for the subscriptions to the *News* from Winchester, a beardless "youth apparently not exceeding seventeen or eighteen years of age." Brooks was even more surprised at the "strength of his mind, the development of his intellect, and his comprehensive knowledge of the political history of the country."[107] The admiration was mutual. Douglas would find in Brooks a most important partner in solidifying Morgan County's Democrats—and his own political prospects.

Douglas closed his one-room Winchester school on the last day of February 1834, and his students returned to their family farms to help during the new growing season. He believed his teaching was satisfactory to both students and parents.[108] Douglas had earned $120 for the term. With approximately $100 remaining he calculated that he had enough to carry him for the next several months, and he had completed what he believed enough reading of the law to gain admittance to the bar. Douglas's Winchester friend, Edward Miner, with as much moxie as his boarder, recommended Douglas for employment to Jacksonville lawyer Josiah Lamborn. Lamborn, whom Douglas had bested in the earlier test of oratory skills at a lyceum in Winchester, refused to consider even a clerkship for the teacher, saying the young man did not "know enough law to write out a declaration."[109]

The reproach did not bother Douglas. Douglas sensed "that the responsibilities of manhood were upon me, although I was under age ... and knew no one upon whom I had a right to call for assistance or friendship."[110] He was, he said, taking full account of his affairs: his "diminished health," his poverty, his place

Douglas had been thwarted in his first attempt at admission to the Morgan County bar. While teaching at Winchester, however, he studied law, wrote contracts, and helped settle some disputes. He was admitted to the bar on March 4, 1834, on his return to Jacksonville (courtesy Abraham Lincoln Presidential Library and Museum).

in the world. Douglas had reached an understanding that he believed would stay with him. His journey to the West had provided to him a great revelation. The circumstances he had faced—departure from the solace of his family, sickness that had taken him hopelessly to death's threshold, anxieties in his lengthy and untoward travels, and near poverty—Douglas believed had purpose.

"I am confident in the belief that all of these things will operate to my benefit and these very movements will prove the most fortunate in my life," he wrote.

Of all the lessons, Douglas believed the most important was in having discovered the true value of friends.

"I do not regret in the least the course I have taken," he wrote, "for wherever I have erred, I have a good lesson before me for the future— in being absent from friends in time of peril I realize their worth and importance— at all times and circumstances— and from every similar state of facts a corresponding lesson can be drawn and will be drawn which I shall make a living guide during my whole life."[111]

On March 11, 1834, Douglas wrote brother-in-law Julius Granger that he had decided where the Fates had directed him. He had fixed on Jacksonville. It was, he said, "probably the finest village in the State."[112] His opinion of the community would only grow. Within weeks he proclaimed Jacksonville to be "the Paradise of the world," his favorite place for his "future and permanent abode."[113] He recalled for Granger that his first letter had provided his early impressions of the town. Since he had left his family, his journey had taken him to "Chiliocotha [sic]," "Cincinatti [sic]," Louisville, St. Louis and Jacksonville. In Illinois, among all the places he had visited, he saw fertility in the soil, beauty in its location, and "the ease with which it can be reduced to cultivation." There were disadvantages, Douglas admitted, in the immature state, but they would yield to time.[114] Now, he said, he had been there long enough to judge that he would be pleased to call Jacksonville home.

"In my first letter I give [sic] you the first impression its appearance made upon my mind; I now add that those opinions have since been confirmed and stregthened [sic] by observation and mingling among the people," Douglas informed his brother-in-law.[115]

Mingling among the people.

Douglas had every right to feel giddy. He was, as he had told his brother-in-law, filled with Western feelings, principles, and interests. Douglas felt confident enough to write a self-congratulating letter to Henry Howe, principal of Canandaigua Academy when Douglas was a student there. Douglas acknowledged his debt to Howe for his "counsels and advice," which, he added, had "more than anything else [accounted] for what little success he may [have] had in his outset in life."

Douglas said that he had heard little of Canandaigua since he left, but reported he had seen school mate Henry L. Bryant, a recent graduate of Transylvania Law School, who was now looking for a permanent location.

"I cannot doubt Bryant will do well from the evidence he now exhibits," wrote Douglas, a sense of his own early success peeking through his words. "He often speaks of you and expresses his gratitude for the course of instruction and discipline that you established in the Academy."[116]

He said he hoped that each of his schoolmates would enjoy success like Bryant's and wrote with regret that he had not seen any of them.

"I would really be glad to hear what has become of Bull, Germaine, Griswold, Adams,

Ambrose Spencer, Codding, Bennett &c &c. I also feel a great interest in the class of young men or Boys, among who are John Bull, George Hubbell, Selden Marvin &c &c."[117]

The perfunctory indulgences being out of the way, Douglas got to the point of the letter: *himself*.

"You will indulge me in saying a few words about myself, although I may *smatter* of the *Egoist*."[118]

Reminding Howe that he left Canandaigua—"as you will recollect"—in June 1833, he detailed Cleveland, his bout with bilious fever, which confined him to bed into October, his boat trip from there to Cincinnati (he spelled it "Cincinatti"), Louisville and St. Louis, then to Jacksonville where he found himself "reduced in funds to less than five dollars, and was under the necessity of teaching a Common School for one Quarter."

If skepticism lurked in his principal's mind about the state of Illinois, Douglas recommended the works of Judge Hall[119] for accurate information. He also did his own part in describing the attractions of his adopted state and hometown.

> Illinois actually sustains a more elevated character in Morals and Religion that she is generally represented to do. In this Town we have a College with about one hundred and twenty-five students—one Female Academy with a large number of young Ladies in it a number of good Common Schools,—a Presbyterian, a Congregationalist, a Methodist, a Baptist and an Episcopal Church.... We also have many benevolent Societies, among which are the Temperance [*sic*], Education, missionary societies and a Lyceum &c &c.[120]

Douglas ended his letter with an apology for its length and a request that Howe from time to time send him reports of the activities of New York lyceums and societies.[121]

3. Party Democrat
Stephen A. Douglas

THE WEST! THE WEST! THE WEST! The West had begun to course through Douglas's veins. It was big country that could fulfill limitless dreams. Frontier life built men of sinew and self-reliance. The experience of common hardships was leveling. It was a frontier proud that it lacked institutions, a frontier in which settlers could create their own social conditions and political principles. Authorities that regulated life back east and sought to push such orthodoxies into the South and the West were as crushed here as the sod had been by the Wisconsin glaciers millennia ago, enriching the region's Jeffersonian independence. The farther west Douglas traveled, the more it appeared that bluntness and plain talk had smothered deference and authority. This was Jacksonian democracy, where men were direct, said what they meant without dressing windows, and had little use for abstractions. This was a democracy "intensely alive."[1]

Doctrines and institutions were falling to the will of the people, and will replaced money and property as the reckoning force in the west. The West had even changed the nature of religion. Men felt more and more comfortable ministering to their own souls. Questions about authority led to questions about the organized church. Primitive revivals had swept from Kentucky along the Appalachians from the beginning of the new century to challenge traditional religions. Educated clergy found their flocks making their way toward the appeals of hell-fire-and-damnation evangelists. These preachers, whose camp meetings could go on for weeks, cast out the unremitting claims of the hell of Calvinism, replacing it with promises of free will and personal salvation.[2]

"While a man remains a sinner he may come, as a free agent, to Christ, if he will, and if he does not come his damnation will be just, because he refused offered mercy," explained the Methodist circuit-riding preacher Peter Cartwright of Sangamon County. "But as soon as he gets converted his free agency is destroyed, the best boon of Heaven is then lost, and although he may backslide, wander away from Christ, yet he shall be brought in. He cannot finally be lost if he has ever been really converted to God."[3]

In 1833, the same year that Douglas reached Jacksonville, Dr. Barton W. Stone was winning converts to his evangelical church. His was the first independent congregation of the non-denominational church he founded in Kentucky. Stone had brought the "Second Great Awakening" to Bourbon County, Kentucky, in August 1801. Stone parlayed his newfound independent spirit to lead his two small Presbyterian Churches to host the most famous revival in the Upper South, the great "Cane Ridge Revival."[4] When Kentucky's Presbyterian Synod defrocked two ministers who participated, Stone renounced the church's standards and proclaimed that the Bible alone provided everything Christians needed to practice their faith. In Jacksonville, Stone won converts from among other Kentucky migrants to the Disciples of

Christ church he founded there. Unlike the stone-hard, doctrine of the Calvinists, independence was the foundation of each Disciples church. Calvinists held on to the doctrine of predestination—the elect of God were going to heaven and all others were going to hell, and neither sin nor good works could change that. Stone, however, reckoned a personal faith was the route to salvation. He had witnessed the joy and hope among multitudes of converts in the promise of it.[5]

In similar ways, Douglas shed his past in Jacksonville and became something of an evangelist himself. Reflecting on the time, he would say that he "discard[ed] all flings of the land where a man was born. I wish to be judged by my principles upon which the peace, the happiness and perpetuity of this republic now rest."[6]

There was a similar spirit in the transplants from the traditional South whom Douglas, the Easterner, joined in Jacksonville. Conventions here were not lordly given by the aristocratic among them. Hell, a man could do what he wanted. He could think for himself, no matter how much learning he had. He had to defer to no man.

On Tuesday, March 4, 1834, Douglas arrived in Vandalia, where the Supreme Court was meeting en bloc. He sought out Associate Justice Samuel D. Lockwood to be examined for licensing as an attorney.[7] Lockwood, tall and lean with hair that had turned white before he was fifty, was considered the personification of dignity and authority on the bench. The most cerebral of the state's four justices, he had been the chief compiler of the Illinois' first criminal code.[8] A New Yorker who piloted a flatboat on the Ohio River on his journey to Illinois in 1818,[9] Lockwood had made his way through several public offices, including Illinois state's attorney and, by appointment of Illinois' second governor Edward Coles in 1822, secretary of state. Lockwood resigned that office in 1824 to accept appointment by President Monroe as receiver of public monies in Edwardsville. The position paid considerably more, and Lockwood contributed the difference to Governor Coles's effort to prevent a legislative attempt to amend the constitution to permit slavery in Illinois.[10] The state's voters defeated the effort, and Illinois remained a free state. In early 1825, Lockwood was appointed a justice of the state Supreme Court, a lifetime position.[11]

It was Associate Supreme Court Justice Samuel Drake Lockwood of Jacksonville in late 1833 who denied Douglas admission to practice law in Illinois. Three months later, however, Lockwood certified Douglas an Illinois lawyer, though he remained ambivalent about Douglas's ability (courtesy Abraham Lincoln Presidential Library and Museum).

Guided by few standards required for admission to the Illinois bar, Justice Lockwood agreed to certify Douglas for the practice of law. Like Lamborn, Lockwood was not impressed with the young applicant before him. He admonished Douglas to "apply himself closer to the study of the law."[12] Lockwood issued Douglas a law license on the same day of Douglas's visit to Vandalia, March 4, 1834. Douglas became the twelfth lawyer in Morgan County, three now Democrats.

Douglas fastened his shingle to the front wall of the nine-year-old Morgan County courthouse in which he rented his first law office. He was six weeks from his twenty-first birthday.

Douglas was in his element at the Morgan County Courthouse, a forty-two foot square, two-story brick structure. The courtroom, situated on the second floor, provided space for meetings, "wrangles," and conventions of the political parties, as well as town meetings and, occasionally, church services.[13] Justice Lockwood, who would continue to consider Douglas unprepared for the law, presided from the second floor court room as circuit judge over the First Judicial Circuit, which included Morgan and seven other counties.[14]

A line of black locust trees grew around the courthouse, and hogs rooted around the mud streets of the square. The park area in the middle of the square was so overgrown by tall jimson weeds that even the hogs were unable to make their way through them. Unconcerned about the physical surroundings, Douglas more greatly appreciated the social occasions he found in and away from the courthouse and prided himself on learning the first name and some tidbit of information about everyone he met in his new professional quarters and beyond. No man, woman, or child ranked too low to pass unrecognized by Douglas. An admirer took notice of this habit of Douglas:

> I began to appreciate the truth that it was a wonderful power he had of recognizing at a glance each one of those unimportant units in our little corner of the world. "The power of calling 'Cap,' and Dick and John and Patrick each by his proper name on the instant, that he knew even the names of their boys and girls, never misplacing any of them, I could scarcely do that myself though I saw them every day, and saw few others. It is impossible for me to say how much effort this cost him, but I do know that it did not seem to cost him any at all. It seemed as spontaneous as breathing. There is no more subtle or more powerful flattery possible to man. He gave to every one of those humble and practically nameless followers the impression, the feeling, that he was the frank and personal friend of each one of them.[15]

Douglas's conversations could instruct and entertain. He could inquire about the well being of a woman hurt in a fall eight months earlier or wish a new settler all the luck. Hardly a man or woman who passed did not draw his attention, complimented that Douglas called him or her by a given name. Douglas was at ease with the politician, praising him in victory and commiserating in his defeat. He spoke to the tousle-haired girl whose head he patted—her parents looking on—and expected the father would remember the gesture at the next election.

"He knows everybody," an early historian recalled, "can tell the question that affects each locality, call the name of every farm owner on the way, tell all travelers something of the homes they left that they never knew themselves, and suggest what place they deserve in heaven."[16]

Douglas liked Jacksonville, which seemed as settled to him as "an old settled Country."[17] It seemed like a good town in which to build a career. He had bragged about the community's "advantages of good society," its morals, its literary and religious institutions, and its benevolent societies. It had a circulating library and a college of some 125 students, as well as the first female academy in Illinois. He reserved judgment toward Jacksonville's population of New Englanders, proud that they had founded the educational institutions, but overlooking their concern about slavery. About that Douglas said little. He considered the matter an abstraction. There were certain things for which any position was futile, and for which it was best to keep one's views closely held. It seemed more productive to let others place their bets and show their hands first.

Douglas was attached to the new country—the "Paradise of the world," he called it—and sought to convey its appeal to those he had left behind. How could any person content himself in New York "whilst there was a country like this at so short a distance abounding in all that can be made subservient to the wants, and that can conduce to the comfort and happiness of man," Douglas asked brother Granger. "If you have an opportunity of selling your farm immediately, be sure and embrace it, and all come on at once."[18]

Within only a few months after he chose to stay in Jacksonville, he wrote his brother-in-law again to report that Samuel B. Knapp, a banker well known to his family in Canandaigua, had arrived in Illinois and also had found it "highly pleasing." Douglas would say that the feeling was not "perculiar [sic] to Mr. Knapp or myself; but it is the common sentiment and spontaneous expression of every person who visits Illinois, and who possesses penetration enough to distinguish between what is and what is not calculated to promote his happiness. Under this view of the subject, if I can persuade you and father to come and see the country for yourselves the rest of my object will be very easily accomplished. For I do not pretend to deny that I am particularly anxious to have you all move to Illinois."[19]

In letters that followed over the next year, Douglas would continue to urge his family to join him in Illinois. The land, he said, was fertile—and lucrative.

"There are greater bargains to be had now and better locations than there will be at any future time."

Douglas did not plead, instead suggesting opportunity. He believed that values of land around Jacksonville, which he noted could be had for $1.25 per acre, would only go up. He predicted prices of from five to fifty dollars per acre within ten years. In 1835, Julius Granger acceded to Douglas's pleas, making a trip to Illinois and leaving behind money for Douglas to invest in land.

Of his own condition, Douglas wrote, "I am succeeding here far beyond my expectations, and the prospect before me is fair and flattering."[20]

The flourish was unmerited. There were more lawyers than legal business in Morgan County, and attorney Douglas's business was slow. He would later confess that his practice was not as rewarding as he had pictured.

"Law in the Sucker State will not make a man rich the first year or two," he admitted in a letter to Granger a year later.[21]

But if clients were fewer than he would have liked, there were townsmen who could appreciate the young man who had laid aside his eastern dress and manners for Kentucky jeans and frontier language whose Jacksonian volume had begun to increase.[22] Douglas was finding that the idea of constituents was more interesting and challenging than clients.

John J. Hardin was the leading lawyer at the Morgan County bar. His abilities by birth and breeding had assured his ascendency to prominence in the young Western Illinois town of Jacksonville. It was no disadvantage to him that he happened to be related to Kentucky congressman, former speaker of the U.S. House of Representatives and now U.S. senator Henry Clay.[23] Hardin's widowed mother Elizabeth had married Porter Clay, Henry Clay's youngest brother. The Hardins were esteemed residents of Jacksonville, Henry Clay and Daniel Webster visiting them at their home there from time to time. Their esteemed relations served the Jacksonville Clays in other ways. Porter Clay was able to ignore with impunity Illinois law and kept two Negroes to serve the family at their six-acre estate on the west side of Jacksonville.

The relationship with Uncle Henry also moved Hardin's Morgan County and neighboring Sangamon County to the forefront of Illinois's anti–Jackson politics. And Hardin, who bore the bearing of an aristocrat, was considered one of the most powerful politicians in the state.[24] He was the community's exemplar of wisdom and strength, looked to for guidance in matters of cultural, social, and political matters in the community.

Born in Frankfort, Kentucky, in 1810 and educated at Transylvania University, Hardin chose to move to Jacksonville in 1830, just two years after it was incorporated. Settlers were rushing onto the region. The 1830 census indicated the county's population was 12,714, a tenfold increase in just ten years,[25] much of it of Southern origin. Geography was mainly responsible for that. Before railroads, settlers followed trails and traces and the partially completed National Road, which had been designed eventually to reach Vandalia. Those from the Upper South followed the Ohio River, which joined the Wabash near Shawneetown, in deep Southern Illinois, and met the Mississippi River at Cairo, at the state's southern tip. Immigrants from the Deep South migrated upriver along the Mississippi.[26]

In 1831, Hardin began his law practice, interrupted for a period of service with the Illinois Militia during the Black Hawk War. Soon after his return to Jacksonville in 1832, Illinois governor John Reynolds, in accordance with the state's constitution, appointed Hardin state's attorney, the office he held at the time the 20-year-old Democrat Stephen A. Douglas arrived in Jacksonville, the Morgan County seat.

With men like Hardin to give the town a sense of urbanity, Jacksonville had taken on the mantle of a settled community. People knew their place—and were expected to remain in it—in accordance with the community's custom, a custom derived from the principles of virtuosity that came from the South. Douglas did not have a "place" and didn't want one. He was brash. He was confident. He was ambitious. He was full of bravado—and, as a newly certified attorney he was a little full of himself. Corresponding with his brother-in-law about his successes, Douglas boasted a little too much that he had claimed a "liberal share of law business, and took quite an active part in the political contests then pending."[27]

Saturday was the day of general rendezvous in Morgan County. A resident of Douglas's day described Saturdays on the Jacksonville Square as a "sort of Roman Nundinal, or general weekly holiday." It was the place "for various miscellaneous public purposes, political, social, commercial; for trading, horse racing, carousing, gambling, and fighting of all kinds; and especially for public discussion and electioneering addresses."[28] Douglas was known to participate, particularly in the spirited political conversation. He was a favorite among the tradesmen and farmers who gathered around the public square on Saturdays.

"I stood and listened to him, surrounded by a motley crowd of backwood farmers and hunters, dressed in homespun or deerskin," wrote William Millburn, recalling that as a boy he had attended a Douglas soiree in Jacksonville, "and he, only ten years my senior, battled so bravely for the doctrines of his party with the veteran and accomplished Hardin."[29]

McConnel's law partner, Daniel Roberts, admired Douglas's political instincts, exhibited in the exchange of his eastern dress for Kentucky jeans and his arm-in-arm intimacy on the street and in the saloon with men of Jackson stripe.[30] His brothers at the Morgan County bar were willing to recognize the efficacy of Douglas's demeanor but did not have to admire it.

With the threat of Douglas's popularity growing, the oppositional men of the Morgan County bar decided to "starve him out."[31]

The opposition party in Morgan County had President Jackson to thank for their ascendancy in local politics. Jackson's withdrawal of deposits from the Bank of the United States and the veto of its recharter, along with Jackson's veto of a bill to continue construction of a national road had advanced their political fortunes. Hardin men subscribed not only to the political standards of Henry Clay but, as well, believed in his "American System," a program of "internal improvements" financed by government. The county's Democrats generally opposed anything that portended bigger government or, closer to home, might enrich the likes of Hardin. But as credit had started drying up and the value of their land started to decline they were not that happy with their president, either. This was an opportunity not lost on Morgan County's Hardin men, who began recruiting dissatisfied members of the Democracy. Douglas commented on the losses.

"All the weak brethren among the friends of the Administration deserted and many others were scared, and the party were about to be used up," he explained to his brother-in-law.[32]

The breakdown of the Morgan Democracy was a gift to Hardin. Yet, Douglas, too, found in it a gift. He had made his first political speech for Jacksonian principles in Winchester; here was his first opportunity to test his own abilities, his personal political acumen—his first fight against an organized political opposition in Morgan County.

In the first week after Douglas returned to Jacksonville from Winchester, local anti–Jackson men held a county meeting at which their speeches and resolutions denounced Jackson's presidency and his bank and monetary policies. The attacks against Jackson and the Democracy were going unanswered. Mainstay Democrats like Murray McConnel saw nothing to be gained in answering. But young Democrats Douglas and Brooks believed otherwise and thought the response had to be made as soon as possible.[33]

Douglas and Brooks formulated a plan for a mass meeting of Democrats in Jacksonville on Saturday, March 29, 1834. While Jackson lost Morgan County but won Illinois in the 1832 election, Douglas calculated that he was willing to risk staking out a position for Democrats in Morgan County. The county's veteran Democrats believed the idea could only do more damage to the Democracy's cause. McConnel suggested the plan was "suicidal."[34] But buoyed by the success of his debate with Lamborn only weeks earlier, Douglas argued that if they understood the reasons for Jackson's actions, Morgan's Democrats would come out of the shadows to endorse the actions of their president. Douglas ignored all arguments against his and Brooks's idea.

Brooks printed handbills announcing the meeting that were distributed and posted throughout the county. The result was a public meeting at noon Saturday, March 29, at the Morgan County courthouse. It was recorded as the largest crowd ever assembled in Jacksonville.[35] It was a crowd much to Douglas's liking. It was, an enthusiastic Douglas would write, "one of the most numerous and spirited I have ever witnessed in that county."[36] Most of them were "farmers and mechanics, men who are honest in their political sentiments and feel a deep interest in the proper administration of the public affairs."[37]

Douglas had prepared a set of resolutions for the approval of these commoners and had arranged for McConnel, the county's elder Democrat, to present them. McConnel cowered at the last minute, however, reneged, and passed them back to Douglas, who did not hesitate. Introducing each resolution with an explanation, Douglas did not reject the idea of a national bank "consistent with the rights of the States, and the Constitution of the United States." But he raised the Jacksonian concern about any bank that would "interfere with the politics of the country" by political actions financed by public funds in the hands of the bank president. Douglas accused the bank of "interfering with the free exercise of the elective franchise, and attempting to control public opinion through the medium of the press." Accepting the importance of banks, Douglas wanted restrictions on them to prevent any chance of partisanship and power that could threaten the sovereignty of the people.[38]

He called on his fellow Democrats for approval. Before the crowd could respond, Lamborn, among the numerous anti–Jackson men who attended the meeting, interrupted. Poking his cane out, Lamborn lifted himself from his seat at the front. Excitement or earlier imbibing had flushed his face. From the front of the crowd he attacked the resolutions as well as the "inexperienced advocate" who had delivered them.[39] Lamborn accused Douglas of playing loosely with facts.

Douglas did not attempt to stop him. Only after Lamborn's lengthy retort did Douglas respond. He began an hour-long speech, beginning not with a defense of Jackson but with a public whipping of Josiah Lamborn. Douglas's darts pierced Lamborn mercilessly. Stung by the attack, Lamborn left. At that point, Douglas acknowledged his remarks were "rather severe." But they were highly exciting to his fellow Democrats, who at the end of the speech gave Douglas prolonged applause and then adopted his resolutions. The crowd was ecstatic with this new voice of Democracy. Still cheering, several denim-clad men approached Douglas. They lifted him to their shoulders and carried him away from the courthouse and twice around Jacksonville's square. There they knighted the squire Douglas, one month shy of 21 years old the "Little Giant." Whisking him past the court house, the appellation became a chant. "Little Giant, Little Giant, Little Giant." The sobriquet stayed with him the rest of his life. Douglas would say modestly that he was pleased that he had gained the "warm support of my own party."[40]

The speech drew the favorable attention of several newspapers in the region. Some reported that Douglas's success was returning the politics of Morgan County to the Democracy. The reviews from Jacksonville's anti–Jackson press were less complimentary. In three successive issues James G. Edwards, publisher of the *Jacksonville Patriot*, maligned Douglas. Douglas believed that John Hardin and associate justice Lockwood actually had written the attacks.[41] Ironically, the criticisms only served to make Douglas better known, so much so that he was able to pick up several new clients for his law practice. This amused Douglas. He mentioned to a friend that he wondered whether he was in some way obligated to pay Edwards for the free advertising that had boosted the success of his law practice.[42] There was a lesson here, Douglas said, for politicians:

> This incident illustrates a principle which it is important for men of the world and especially politicians to bear in mind. How foolish, how impolitic, the indiscriminate abuse of political opponents whose humble condition or insignificance prevents the possibility of injury, and who may be greatly benefited by the notoriety thus acquired. I firmly believe this is one of the frequent and great errors committed by the political editors of the present day. Indeed, I sincerely doubt whether I owe most to the kind and efficient support of my friends, or to the violent, reckless and imprudent opposition of my enemies.[43]

Despite the boost to his business, however, the boost to his political future that the speech had provided was of much greater value to Democrat Douglas. At this point, his sights were on political office. And his focus now was on its acquisition.

4. Sophisticates and Sophists

MORGAN COUNTY STATE REPRESENTATIVES Colonel James Evans, Colonel William Weatherford, and Captain John Wyatt, though by party affiliation Democrats, had become discontented with their party. Like Governor Joseph Duncan—indeed, like most Illinoisans, these leading politicians had been aggravated by President Jackson's anti-bank and anti-public works policies. They had become "milk and water Democrats." So soft was the loyalty to their party, these three Democratic legislators had been responsible for influencing their fellow Democrat, outgoing Illinois governor John Reynolds, in 1831 to appoint Jacksonville's John J. Hardin, a leader of the National Republican Party, to a four-year term as state's attorney.

Although he had been happy to accept their assistance, Hardin was arrogant and distant when the three Morgan Democrats, facing re-election, asked him the following year to reciprocate. Hardin refused to extend his help. What would make matters worse, Wyatt would be the only one of the three who would retain his seat in the next election. Hardin's recalcitrance upset Wyatt greatly. He squirmed and stewed, looking for some way to make Hardin pay for his ingratitude. Douglas suggested the opportunity.

Meeting in Douglas's courthouse office—door shut, Wyatt agreed with Douglas's offer to draft a bill that would change the way state's attorneys came to office. Douglas proposed filling the office of state's attorney by legislative election rather than by gubernatorial appointment. Wyatt liked the idea. The conspirators calculated that chances were far better than even since Democrats were the majority party in both houses of the General Assembly. After hearing Douglas's plan, Wyatt signed on.

"If I can only beat John Hardin, and beat him with little Douglas, it will be too good," Wyatt said.[1]

Getting the approval of Governor Duncan, former Democrat and now a close Hardin friend, would be quite another matter. Wyatt figured that the governor would be unlikely to concede to the legislature his power to appoint his own men to these powerful prosecutorial offices. There also were strong personal connections between Duncan and Hardin: they lived within a quarter-mile of each other in Jacksonville. Hardin's uncle, Henry Clay, had played a role in Duncan's conversion to the National Republican faith and, in fact, had introduced the governor to his wife.[2] Hardin had served on General Duncan's staff as brigade inspector during the Black Hawk War.[3]

The reaction of the Council on Revision, made up of the four members of the Supreme Court and the governor, to Wyatt's bill would be equally uncertain. These constitutional officers had the power to veto legislation, and while the measure did not directly impact the members of the Supreme Court, three of the justices were of the party Hardin led. One of them, Samuel Drake Lockwood, was a close associate and personal friend of Hardin. Theophilus Washington Smith was the only Democrat on the state's high court, and Wyatt was uncertain about Smith's loyalty.[4] Their roles as members of the Council on Revision reflected the nation's founders' idea that judges should be involved in legislation to trim the "excesses of democracy" by determining whether laws passed by the legislative branch were constitutional.[5] It was controversial at the federal level and even more so at the local level. Illinois Democrats saw the council injecting justices into political processes. Few believed the jurists were as impartial in their judgments about legislation as about interpretation of the law. Yet, as easily as he could dismiss the first objection, Douglas could dismiss the second. It took only a simple majority of the general assembly to override the council's veto. Douglas need only remind Wyatt that the Democrats controlled both legislative chambers. He was confident that a bill could be passed and, if vetoed, affirmed.

Like Wyatt, Douglas had reasons to work a setback for Hardin, but he was just as adamant about repaying Lockwood for perceived maliciousness. Douglas believed that Lockwood was working against him. Douglas told brother-in-law Julius Granger he had learned that it had been Hardin and Lockwood who "did the writing and worked the wires" to malign him in the county.[6]

Up to this time, Douglas—disingenuously, to be sure—said he "had never dreamed of being a candidate for any Office, but had acted the part I did because I conceived it to be right. But seeing the opposition were determined to put me down, and to starve me out as they expressed themselves, I thought it best to carry the war into 'Africa as of old.'"[7]

Douglas wrote Wyatt's bill to punish Hardin. And as payback to Lockwood, Douglas even more audaciously suggested a second bill that would hit the Supreme Court justices directly. Douglas's second bill, which Wyatt also sponsored, sought to reorganize Illinois' courts. The measure would remove the additional circuit court duties associate justices also carried. Douglas's idea was to dilute the political power of the justices, who while making their way around multi-county judicial circuits as circuit judges had plenty of opportunity for partisan politics.

Douglas's bill would curtail that.[8] It proposed that circuit duties of the Supreme Court justices be revoked and reassigned to judges of re-enacted lower courts. Circuit judges would be no less likely to politick, Douglas knew, but no matter. Controlled by Democrats, the legislature could be expected to appoint judges aligned with the Democrats. Wyatt introduced the bill and with Douglas promoting it from the platform of the capitol lobby state legislators passed the measure on January 17, 1835. Douglas had redesigned the state courts. Within five years, political expediency—which incidentally would also serve his own purposes—would motivate him to restore the structure he had just changed.

The law created six circuits, one more than Douglas had proposed, to which several rising stars were appointed. The appointees were Stephen Trigg Logan, future law partner of Abraham Lincoln; Thomas Ford, a future Illinois governor; Henry Eddy, an abolition-crusading newspaper man; Justin Harlan, a lifelong jurist; and Richard M. Young and Sidney Breese, each of them future U.S. senators. When Ford was temporarily detained from taking his seat on the Sixth Circuit bench, Logan filled in, earning the honor of hearing the first cases under the new circuit court system. The trial occurred in a rough-hewn log cabin, borrowed from its owner, on the south side of the Illinois River at a settlement known as "Bunkum."[9]

By 1834 the Illinois General Assembly was composed of eighty-four members, with only one a native of Illinois. Fifty-eight had come from slave states, mainly Kentucky and Virginia.

There were nineteen from New York and Pennsylvania, five from New England, and two from Ireland.[10] With fifty-eight representatives and twenty-six senators, it was a body small enough to encourage camaraderie. Whigs and Democrats communed easily together.

Vandalia had been the center of the state's government for more than a decade, yet in that time it had done little to cater to its regular guests of state government. There was not a sidewalk on any of the city's streets, which made getting from lodgings to the capitol a muddy business after a rainfall.[11] Douglas's Morgan County neighbor John Hardin summed Vandalia up by calling it "the dullest, dreariest place"—so dull and dreary, he said, that "it is not worthwhile to abuse it."[12] A mutual friend felt the same way. Abraham Lincoln wrote Mary Owens, an amorous interest, "I really can not endure the thought of staying here ten weeks."[13]

Finding so little to like, legislators and state officeholders who did not live in Vandalia left as soon as possible after the legislative session was over. Some did not wait that long. A joint session of the legislature had appointed Ninian Wirt Edwards, dandified son of former Governor Ninian Edwards, attorney general on January 1, 1835, to succeed James Semple, recently elected a state representative. Edwards had inherited his father's vanity and egotism, which cost him friends. Representative Usher Linder of Coles County in east central Illinois appraised Edwards the younger "naturally and constitutionally an aristocrat, and he hated democracy when I first knew him, as the devil is said to hate holy water."[14] Vandalia came no closer than associates like Linder to measure up to Edwards's tastes. He and his wife Elizabeth found the community so intolerable that he resigned the office of attorney general in little more than three weeks after Governor Duncan appointed him. On February 7 the Edwardses returned to their Italianate home on Aristocracy Hill in Springfield for good.[15]

There were a half-dozen boarding houses around the public square, and legislators, lawyers and litigants, office seekers, and those seeking favors kept their rooms filled during the sessions.

"The members were very much thrown together and learned to know each other very well. We had a very pleasant time," recalled Sangamon representative John Todd Stuart, soon to be the first law partner of his Sangamon colleague, Representative Abraham Lincoln.[16]

Milton Flack's Vandalia Inn, which the local newspaper said was in "every way calculated for a first rate tavern," was the liveliest spot in town when the General Assembly was in session.[17] Lawmakers and men who sought to influence them attended parties, cotillions, and banquets in the hotel's candlelit rooms. Although Abraham Lincoln wore a new sixty-dollar suit tailored for him in Springfield—the finest clothing he had ever owned, his deportment was considered a bit rough.[18] Reluctant to ask a dance of any of the young single ladies—who, in fact, seemed to be avoiding him—Lincoln found it less intimidating to ask Flack's wife Matilda to dance. Whether from kindness or fully agreeable, Mrs. Flack consented to Representative Lincoln's invitation. Lincoln's awkwardness—or nervousness—was apparent within the first measures of music. During their trip around the dance floor, one of Lincoln's size 14 boots trapped the hem of Mrs. Flack's dress against the floor. In the momentum of the dance, there was nothing an unbalanced Lincoln could do. He wobbled. The dress's hem tore and the party-goers' snickers resounded. Lincoln was mortified. The only thing to do was to plead genuine sorrow for the mishap. Mrs. Flack could not be mad at the highly embarrassed Lincoln.[19]

There were few houses in the capital city in 1836, even sixteen years after Vandalia had been chosen to replace Kaskaskia as the state capital.[20] Sangamon's representatives Stuart and Lincoln rented a room just opposite of Democrats Sidney Breese and Stephen Douglas on the second floor of one of Vandalia's frame rooming houses. It was the same house in which Senator Orville Hickman Browning of Quincy—joined occasionally by his wife Eliza Caldwell Browning—resided during his two terms between 1836 and 1840 in the state senate. Several Clay men, including Hardin and Edward D. Baker, boarded there, as well.[21] That they were of different parties made little difference in Vandalia's early days. Friends and deals could be made with a handshake. The Sangamon delegation's Stuart remembered that "at first there was very little of party spirit." A man's word was his bond in Illinois politics.

"Things were done and measures were carried very much by personal influence and personal arrangement." Stuart recalled.[22]

The limited lodging did not seem to bother the legislators as much as the fare they were served. Their foremost complaint was about the food they found on the tables. Most legislators were transplants from the South. Their palates were unaccustomed to the lean, stringy prairie chicken and venison, which were most often a meal's entrée. Quite unpampered, the men yearned for more familiar flavors and textures of fat-bellied pig's bacon that rarely came from Vandalia's kitchens.

"A piece of fat pork was a luxury in those days," recalled Stuart, a Kentucky-born legislator. "We had such longing for something civilized."[23]

A Springfield resident would say that "the most potent argument used against Vandalia" in the coming fight to relocate the state capital was that in Springfield legislators "would get hog meat."[24]

The capitol building at Vandalia was hardly any more commodious. Built only ten years earlier, already some of its brick walls bulged and plaster fell frequently from the ceiling, marking the pine floor with explosions of white powder. The capitol's appearance, said Governor William L. D. Ewing, was an embarrassment to the state.

"The State House at this place ... is manifestly inconvenient for the transaction of public business," Ewing declared. "The appearance of the building is not calculated to add either character or credit to the State. No member of the Confederacy, it is believed, has appropriated so small a portion of the public funds for the erection of public buildings as Illinois."[25]

As right as Ewing might have been and as much as fellow government officers might have agreed with him, no one in the Assembly had reason to listen to him. Ewing was a lame duck the moment he was sworn in.[26] But it was his moment. He delivered a highly detailed inaugural address, recommending new laws and amendments to numerous others. He did not mention the state's slave laws. With slavery a flashpoint among Illinoisans, Ewing ignored it.

Leaders of the largely Southern population had agitated for slavery in Illinois before it was admitted into the Union on August 26, 1818. Congressmen like James Tallmadge of New York, however, reminded Illinoisans that Article Six of the Northwest Ordinance of 1787 prohibited slavery in the Northwest Territory.

Slavery had been planted early in the western side of the Indiana Territory, the side that would become Illinois. At several points in their territorial history, Southern settlers in the Indiana Territory pleaded with Congress to repeal Article Six of the Northwest Ordinance, which prohibited slavery. When Congress refused, Indiana's territorial legislature in 1805 and 1807 passed laws to permit the use of indentures of unlimited duration to open entry to slaves.

Northerners poured into the east side of the territory and sought to separate themselves from the indenture systems, which were nothing more than slavery by euphemism. Illinoisans were just as alarmed that anti-slavery settlers could repeal the slavery-saving indenture laws and succeeded in winning the establishment of the Illinois Territory in 1809. Indiana lawmakers repealed the indenture laws soon after the separation.[27]

While slavery's proponents believed that rights to property included slaves, they decided to postpone further action on slavery until after statehood. Their reasoning was that the national government could require the state to have a republican form of government, the only requirement the U.S. constitution stipulated for a state seeking entry into the union, it could not dictate domestic institutions in a sovereign state after statehood had been achieved.

The Panic of 1819 was the first financial crisis Illinoisans felt. Land prices dropped. So did credit. Among Illinois leaders there was a belief that slavery would bring wealthy planters who would spend money freely for land owned by opponents of slavery, who could be expected to flee the state. The concept failed.[28] But the idea remained.

With the economy still in shambles and the rumblings for slavery shaking Illinois once again, Coles, elected the state's second governor in 1822, addressed the issues head-on in his inaugural speech to a joint session of the Second General Assembly. He discussed the state's economic condition, management of the new state bank, and the nascent canal project. He focused the second half of his address on his concern about the state's slavery policy. He called for the legislature to repeal the "black laws" passed by the first general assembly—the majority of whom still occupied legislative seats in the capital—and to erase the remnants of slavery. He faulted, for example, indentured servitude that could bind a person for up to 99 years. An indentured servant could be beaten legally, be uncompensated for work, and sold. Indenture was clearly a legal euphemism for slavery.

Legislators responded to the governor's call for action, but not for the purposes he had intended. They proposed, instead, a constitutional convention to legalize slavery in Illinois.[29] In opening the door to the question, Coles had hoped a discussion of slavery would enlighten citizens and move them against its curse. Instead, he had unwittingly thrown down a gauntlet. Coles had misunderstood his fellow Illinoisans. He had not considered the resentments he would raise among these pioneer democrats who heard and saw in him what they had sought to leave behind. He had not foreseen the indignation he would raise among Illinoisans who had not known—despised—the wealth and privilege he had enjoyed. He was from a family of Virginia plantation owners, had inherited his wealth, had been able to buy thousands of acres of Illinois land and hired laborers to farm it, freed slaves on his way to Illinois, and provided land and opportunity to them.[30] Coles was not one of them.

Riding a horse he had borrowed from Wyatt for the eighty-five-mile journey from Jacksonville, Douglas's first appearance in Vandalia was on December 1, 1834, the day before the Ninth General Assembly was to convene.[31] He was there to work his plan with Representative John Wyatt to oust State's Attorney John J. Hardin from office.

The General Assembly was convened in the first session of the Ninth General Assembly on the morning of December 3, 1834. The Democratic majority in the house honored their colleague from Morgan County, Representative Wyatt, by selecting him to call the House to order to elect a speaker and appoint a clerk and doorkeeper. From the gallery Douglas could construe the honor as a chit in his favor for the work he was there to do.

Along with others on the mezzanine above the chamber, Douglas watched the mechanics that on the first ballot put second-term Democratic Representative James Semple into the house speaker's chair. Following custom, Semple voted for his opponent, Representative Charles Dunn of Pope County, and Dunn voted for Semple. Also per custom, Dunn the vanquished escorted Semple the victor to the speaker's platform from which Semple took charge of the house.[32]

As the state constitution required, the speaker opened the returns cast in the recent fall election for Illinois governor and lieutenant governor. Semple declared that Joseph Duncan of Jacksonville had been duly elected governor and Alexander M. Jenkins lieutenant governor. A committee of the House and Senate was appointed to inform the executive officials of their election and arrange for them to take their oaths of office.[33]

Douglas was in the gallery to watch the proceedings. It took little time for him to descend the stairs and begin his personal effort to ingratiate himself with members of the General Assembly. Douglas was affable, had a way about him that was endearing and clearly without restraint. Another Jacksonville resident in Vandalia on business at the time saw Douglas working the lawmakers and marveled at how he had "become quite a pet with them, sitting on their knees even, and in every way making himself agreeable by assimilation."[34]

Douglas's co-conspirator Wyatt was not so sure that Douglas's way of attaching himself to all comers would work when it came to the serious task they had plotted. Certain that it would be controversial, even though the majority was made up of fellow Democrats, Wyatt quickly introduced Douglas's bill to change the way state's attorneys were appointed. Wyatt calculated the early introduction of the bill gave it its best opportunity of getting a serious hearing in the House. There already were whispers echoing through the statehouse that Wyatt had drafted a bill to exact revenge for Hardin's ingratitude and to get Douglas appointed to Hardin's government position.[35] It would not be a cake walk. Like many seated in the General Assembly, John Hardin was a Kentuckian, which gave him friends on both sides of the house. He was a lawyer, which itself gave him a virtue to vault him to leadership. As importantly, Hardin was related by blood or friendship to important people, particularly the men in the delegation from Sangamon County. They understood Wyatt's bill exactly for what it was.

Wyatt and his colleagues listened to the house clerk read a message from Governor Duncan. He called for schools, for a broad system of internal improvements, and opposition to a charter for a state bank.[36] That afternoon, in accordance with a House rule, Wyatt notified his colleagues of his intention to introduce his state's attorney bill. His was one of dozens of bill-filing announcements, which provided some cover for his measure.[37] The heat may have been on. The next day, acting in his role as a member of a select committee appointed to draft House rules, Wyatt reported a measure to strike the rule that required House members to announce their intention to file bills.[38]

On the following day, Friday, December 5, Speaker Semple referred Wyatt's plan to a three-member select committee. The committee ten days later reported the bill back to the House without amendment.[39] With Democrats providing the difference, both chambers of the General Assembly passed the bill. On January 30, 1835, the Council on Revision returned it with a lengthy veto message that was largely ignored.

Expecting the veto, Wyatt earlier had summoned Douglas back to Vandalia. Despite earlier misgivings, he believed Douglas was largely responsible for passing the bill and was needed once again to assure that the votes that had passed the measure would hold to override the veto.

Once the veto message had been read, the House took up the bill and Douglas actively

4. Sophisticates and Sophists

worked the hallway to preserve support for it. The governor worked the other side. Fortune smiled on Douglas in one of Duncan's tactics. The governor asked Democratic State Treasurer John Dement, a popular politician throughout Illinois, to help sustain the veto. A man shorter even than Douglas,[40] Dement, who with Duncan and Douglas was also from Morgan County, had been looking for just this opportunity. But it was not to help his Jacksonville neighbor. It was to embarrass him. Duncan had accorded Dement the same treatment Wyatt had experienced with Hardin. Duncan had refused to support Dement in his bid for re-election by the General Assembly to the state treasurer's office. Dement never forgave Duncan, who had misjudged Dement's popularity with legislators. Meeting in the house chamber on January 1, 1835, legislators retained Dement by a vote of 66 to 10 over five other candidates for treasurer.[41]

Wyatt was aware of Duncan's treatment of Dement—and Dement's aggravation—and saw in it the kind of leverage that could work in his and Douglas's behalf. He and Douglas visited Dement, who came up with his own nickname for the Little Giant. "Wyatt's tom-tit" is what Dement called him.[42] And Dement had been a Hardin man until Duncan's request to help kill Douglas's bill.

Dement had taken a liking to the gregarious Douglas. When Douglas was unable to find a room in Vandalia, the unmarried Dement shared his room. He counseled the boyish looking Douglas, advising him to smarten his appearance by getting a haircut and shave. Douglas did so the next day and was said to have worked the statehouse halls smartly.[43] Dement added his influence to Douglas's reasoning. They overrode the veto.

Some legislators looked upon the energetic young man from Jacksonville and judged him little more than an excited adolescent. His short stature made him seem a dwarf among men.

"He looked like a boy," said Representative Usher F. Linder, "with his smooth face and diminutive proportions." Linder represented Coles County.

But Linder quickly came to recognize an unusual ability in Douglas's maneuvering.

"But when he spoke in the House of Representatives," Linder would recall, "he spoke like a man, and loomed up in the proportions of an intellectual giant."[44]

On the afternoon of Tuesday, February 10, 1835, just three days before the Ninth General Assembly was to adjourn its first session, House and Senate members met in joint session to elect five state's

Illinois' second governor, Virginian Edward Coles, led the fight against an attempt by the southern-dominated General Assembly to make Illinois a slave state. Douglas in Jacksonville, where pro- and anti-slavery views simmered and boiled, would gain an education into the strong sentiments on both sides of the slavery issue (courtesy Abraham Lincoln Presidential Library and Museum).

attorneys under the new law. They would proceed in the order of judicial district, which meant the election of either Douglas or Hardin as the state's prosecutor in the First Judicial District would occur first. With the exception of Wyatt, Morgan County's senator and representatives voted for Hardin. So did Sangamon representatives Lincoln and Stuart.[45] When the vote was counted, however, 38 legislators voted for Douglas and 34 for Hardin. Speaker Semple declared Douglas the winner.

It was a stunning victory for Douglas in his first foray into the state's political machinery. As he would do as he made his way up the political ladder, Douglas would say disingenuously that he had not coveted the office and did not believe he was qualified for it. He immediately accepted, however, despite his virtuous performance of feigned reluctance. The new law elevated the twenty-one-year-old Democrat to a powerful office. Douglas was now the state's chief prosecutor in the largest judicial district in Illinois. Just as astonishing was that in doing so he had ejected from office one of the state's most powerful Whigs.[46] A tribute to his political maturity and unlike Wyatt's purposes for pushing the bill that unseated him, Hardin never held the defeat against Douglas. Although they would remain political foes, they also would remain personal friends throughout Hardin's life.[47]

Ironically, Douglas's maneuverings did not work out so well for the man who had provided the field for Douglas's strategy. John Wyatt had expected President Jackson to appoint him to the more lucrative position as register of the federal land office at Springfield. Instead, Jackson appointed the Whig-turned-Democrat, Illinois congressman George Forquer, to the post.[48] Wyatt became convinced that Douglas had turned on him to support Forquer. It was the reason Wyatt later would support John Todd Stuart when Douglas opposed Stuart for Congress in 1838.[49]

To Douglas, the prize for the games he had played seemed easily acquired. His own summation of his victories, indeed, sounded like a boy amazed but feeling entirely entitled to his plunder. Douglas wrote to his brother-in-law that the legislature had "done something for the 'Widows [sic] youngest and only Son.' I allude to my election by the legislature to the office of '*States Attorney*' for the First Judicial Circuit of this State, composed of the Counties of Morgan, Sangamon, Macon, McLean, Taz[e]well, Macoupin, Green, and Calhoun."[50]

Douglas's judicial reform bill also passed, and the legislature elected six new circuit judges. As a result, the high court's justices would be confined to Vandalia instead of presiding over the circuit courts. It meant, also, that Douglas as prosecutor would not have to try his cases before Judge Lockwood. Douglas certainly recognized the advantage. Speaking of the judge who had been appointed to Lockwood's former circuit as a result of the court reformation, Douglas said, "As a natural consequence we got an impartial and pretty clear fellow in the place of Lockwood my old enemy."[51] Stephen Trigg Logan, whose future would include a law partnership with Abraham Lincoln, was appointed judge in the first judicial circuit in which Douglas would serve as state's attorney.

These were important legislative and political successes, and Douglas's name reverberated throughout the state. Lockwood, recognized as one of the state's pre-eminent legal scholars and once a prosecutor himself, was not only critical of the new prosecutor. He was appalled.

"What business has such a stripeling [sic] with such an office?" Lockwood asked. "He is no lawyer, and has no law books."[52]

Only a year earlier Lockwood, when he certified Douglas for the bar, had suggested that Douglas needed to devote more effort to his study of the law. Lockwood, like Douglas, was a resident of Jacksonville. It was evident to Lockwood that Douglas was not seeing many clients at his law office, which was on the floor below Lockwood's courtroom in Morgan County's courthouse. One of Douglas's friends, Daniel Roberts, confirmed Lockwood's observation, noting that "clients were rare visitants at his office, nor was he a close keeper of his office for either business or study; but he was out among the 'boys,' assuming the part of politician from the start."[53] Douglas handled cases, but when he was in his first-floor courthouse office he was as likely to furnish it as a forum for Democratic politicians as for his own clients.

"A law practice with him was a secondary consideration," said one observer.[54]

In his own way, a freshman legislator who had watched Douglas working the House in behalf of his bills was of an opinion similar to Lockwood's.

"He was then extremely thin—being so short in stature, too—I think he was about *the least man I ever saw.*" That was how twenty-five-year-old Sangamon County legislator Abraham Lincoln summed up Douglas on his first sighting of him in late 1834.[55]

Lincoln's estimate of Douglas, who was just over five feet tall and weighed slightly more than one hundred pounds, was one of amusement.[56] He would not underestimate Douglas's political ability for long, however. With the exception of Lincoln's vote, Douglas's nomination for state's attorney won most of the opposition party's vote in exchange for Democratic votes to create an Illinois State Bank.[57] Lincoln could not go that far.[58] He voted against Douglas, voting on the losing side for his friend Hardin of Jacksonville. Lincoln's votes for other state's attorneys, however, were not strictly partisan. He voted, for example, for Democrat William Alexander Richardson of Schuyler County instead of his friend Orville Hickman Browning for state's attorney in the Quincy District. It was an interesting choice for the Sangamon legislator who would later see Richardson become Douglas's closest advisor and regard Browning as his.

In an autobiographical sketch, Douglas would suggest in a bit of false modesty that he was astonished to be a beneficiary of Wyatt's law:

> I will here remark, and most solemnly aver it to be true, that up to the time this charge was made against me, I never had conceived the idea of being a candidate for the office, nor had any friend suggested or hinted to me that I could or ought to receive it.... My short residence in the State, want of acquaintance, experience in my profession and age (being only twenty-one years old) I considered insuperable objections. My friends, however, thought differently, passed the bill, and elected me on the first ballot by four votes majority.[59]

It was a recollection substantially different from the self-praising Douglas did in the letter to his brother-in-law shortly after his election. Douglas reported the results of his court reorganization work at Vandalia "by which the Judiciary System was revised and the justices of the Supreme Court ... were relieved of the trouble of holding circuit courts and a new set of Judges were elected and as a natural consequence we got an impartial and pretty clear fellow in the place of Lockwood my old enemy and the opposition considered themselves pretty well *used up*. (I use this term because it precisely expresses my meaning.)"[60]

Douglas was reasonably proud of the extent of the victory and its impact on the "position I now occupy in regard to the present political situation of the State. Those who hitherto have been my most violent enemies have now laid down their weapons and sued for peace."[61]

For Douglas, who admitted the Hardin faction had caused him "tribulation" up to that point, there was a landmark lesson in these victories: he need not cower in the face of his enemies. In fact, Douglas's lesson was that attacks by the opposition strengthened him.

"So confident am I in this belief that I feel under great obligations to my opponents for 'past favors' and sincerely hope that they will continue the same hereafter. As long as they will do this I shall always know I am right, and shall have the confidence of the people, and carry a majority of them with me."

His victory affirmed his independence. He now criticized the opposition, "the self-stiled [*sic*] Whig Party," who make it an "article of their creed to put down every person who dares think for himself or has talents & the confidence of the People, so that he may [not] be in their way hereafter." It was a confident Douglas who would say, "At the present time I occupy precisely the position I have long wished for *Politically* and *Professionally*."[62] He would win accolades for his conduct in the office, though he continued to look to other offices that would serve other goals.

5. "The *Lord*, and the *Legislature*, and *Gen Jackson*"

THE BEGINNING OF STEPHEN DOUGLAS'S work as state's attorney was inauspicious. On a bright Sunday morning in March 1834, he left Jacksonville for his new job in Illinois' First Judicial Circuit riding a three-year-old mare he borrowed. Douglas had with him a single book on criminal law, which he stowed in a saddlebag borrowed from his mentor, Jacksonville lawyer Murray McConnel. Those who watched him leave Jacksonville for his first trip around the circuit snickered. His feet barely reached below the skirt of the saddle. The stirrups were cinched high enough up the saddle's fender for Douglas's boots to slide into them. Douglas, the state's chief prosecutor in its largest judicial district, was said to have made a most unimpressive figure.[1]

His duties, Douglas had told his brother-in-law, were "to prosecute all criminals in each county in the Circuit, and also all civil actions in which the People are concerned." To assure his family understood that petty criminals were not his only targets, Douglas pointedly noted that also included would-be pillars of the community like the "Pres & Directors of the State Bank, any county, or the Auditor of the Public &c."[2]

As state's attorney Douglas would earn an annual salary of $250, which he thought he could augment with as much as $350 in fees. He told his brother-in-law that he could tell Mother Douglas "that I am doing as well in my *'profession'* as could be expected of a Boy of twenty one." He underscored the importance of his victory: "In my Election I had to run against one of the strongest men in the State. My opponent John J. Hardin, having held the Office two years, and being a descendant of one of the greatest families in *Kentucky* (which in this country is the strongest recommendation a man can have for Office) and also having the influence of the governor in his favor. But as the *Lord*, and the *Legislature*, and *Gen Jackson* would have it, I beat him by four votes on the first ballot."[3]

To Douglas the victory was more than a defeat of a powerful Hardin. It was a blow for Jacksonian Democracy. Douglas said: "In Politics I can only say that the cause of the *Democracy* is triuphant [sic], and that the *People* are disposed to retain the advantage they have gained over the aristocracy."[4]

Douglas tried cases against some of the state's best defending attorneys, whose names would grow in state and national prominence: Edward D. Baker, Ninian W. Edwards, George Forquer, Hardin, Lamborn, Dan Stone, Stuart, Jesse B. Thomas, Jr., Samuel Treat, Cyrus Walker and Abraham Lincoln among them. These were towering men, in physique as well as in the profession of the law. But appearances seemed to make little difference in the case of anyone practicing at the bar at the time. A New York attorney visiting Sangamon County's courthouse was shocked by what he saw in the courtroom of the tousle-haired First Circuit Judge Stephen

T. Logan of Springfield. The visiting New Yorker was accustomed to the dignity that marked New York's courtrooms, not suspecting anything as different as he was to find in Judge Logan's court. As he entered the Sangamon County courtroom, he saw the short-statured Douglas prosecuting a case from the floor. Addressing Judge Logan, the bantam Douglas appeared to be speaking to the soles of the judge's unbuffed boots. Logan was tilted back in his chair, his feet crossed and resting on the desk in front of him higher than his head. A corncob pipe dangled from Logan's mouth, and garlands of white smoke leaked out of the bowl. Logan's hair was "standing nine ways for Sunday" and his clothing looking more like a woodchopper's than a judge's. On the other side of the railing that separated the judge from the lawyers and the day's spectators, the audience itself was getting a great deal of pleasure out of smoking, chewing, and expectorating tobacco on the yellow-pine planked courtroom floor.[5]

Douglas was more than comfortable with what was expected of him in the practice of law. Although the law was improving, there still was no love for anything English, including English common law. That was just fine with Douglas, who had no love for anything English.

For the novice lawyer-prosecutor, common sense was as important as knowledge of laws. Precedents were few. Case law was being written as these courtroom thespians argued their cases. Nubs and legal novelties lawyers raised in advancing their clients' positions often advanced the law in the circuits of the young state. The challenges of technicalities of law depended as much on an attorney's quickness on his feet and the strength of his common sense—or the strength of an argument, as incredible as it may seem to knowledgeable courtroom guests—as it did on his expertise in precedents or courtroom rules and procedure. A learned observer in Pike County, just southwest of Douglas's Morgan County, found Douglas's courtroom demeanor typical of the courtroom actors of the day:

Seeing him for the first time in the capitol building at Vandalia in late 1834, State Representative Abraham Lincoln (above) disparaged the 5'4" Douglas as "the least man I ever saw." Over the next quarter-century, Lincoln would see his own political career shadowed by Douglas's stunning rise (Library of Congress).

Of books there were few. Authorities and precedents slumbered not in the great handy libraries. The entire resources of the Bounty Tract could hardly fill out the shelves of one ordinary lawyer's library to-day.... He was a luckless lawyer who had to hunt his books to settle a suddenly controversial point, or answer a bewildered client's query; and he was a licensed champion, who, theorizing from his instored [sic] legal lore, or instinctive acumen, knew on the instant where best to point his thrust and was equally ready with every form of parry and defense. The off-hand action and advice of such men, nerved by necessity and skilled by contest, became of course to be regarded almost like leaves of law.[6]

On the circuit there was little time for much else. If there had been time to research a case for precedents or parallel cases, there were few communities on the circuit that had books in numbers approaching anything like a library. Douglas found few occasions in the courtroom for which he had to withdraw from his saddlebag the single borrowed law book that he carried with him on the circuit. Few cases required much beyond sound reasoning, an ability to organize words and sentences in ways petit and grand juries made up of callused men could understand, some shrewdness the grizzled could appreciate, and an ability to turn words in ways that could entertain. Moving from courthouse to courthouse in one county after another on the circuit, and mostly unprepared for trials that awaited him, Douglas had to rely on quick study and ingenuity to meet the tests erected by opposing attorneys. Fortunately for Douglas as well as his brother prosecutors in other circuits, most of the circuit's attorneys, representing clients they acquired on arrival, faced the same challenge.

Determined to master the requirements of his new position, Douglas had read a few of the latest works on criminal law available to him. As other lawyers did, he read Chitty and Blackstone commentaries on the law as he could. Armed with some law and an overwhelming self-confidence, Douglas proved himself apt. His cases were fairly innocuous: assaults and batteries, gambling, and complaints about saloons open on Sundays. One was more complicated and had the potential to stop his career it its beginning. Douglas weighed the issue and decided to challenge a decision by the judge in whose courts he had to practice, Stephen Trigg Logan. The logic in the case would be the foundation for one of the most important cases Douglas would pursue against an Illinois secretary of state, Alexander Pope Field. In that case, Douglas would take the exact opposite position.

State's Attorney Douglas challenged Logan's right to appoint his own circuit court clerk. Charles Matheny had been the First District's circuit clerk since his appointment by Judge John Reynolds in 1821. After he took the bench in 1834, however, Judge Logan named Mordecai Mobley to replace Matheny. On May 4, 1835, Mobley ousted Matheny and took control of the clerk's office. Matheny claimed that since the Illinois Constitution did not set a limit to the circuit clerk's term, he had a lawful right to continue in office. That was Douglas's position in a quo warranto proceeding—a hearing to determine by what authority someone holds an office—he filed in the circuit court. Losing there, Douglas appealed the matter to the state Supreme Court. In December, the Supreme Court ruled for Douglas's position, holding that Matheny rightfully held the office until the legislature specified tenure in the office. Douglas had proved that Logan did not have the authority to remove Matheny.[7] Logan did not hold what might have seemed impudence against Douglas.

In the courts of his circuit, Douglas found that he often was on trial as much as the men he prosecuted. The puncheon-floored courtrooms were theaters in which the actors declaimed sans script, thrusting and parrying for points drawn from recollection of legal principles or intuition—even on occasion a sophism—that produced oratory by which the actor sought to advance his position. The lawyer was an actor before an audience of farmers and mechanics who would serve as judges of his performance. Douglas's smaller stature often made volume and vehemence as important as well drawn reasoning in his courtroom performance.

"These lawyers were on exhibition," wrote an observer, "and they knew it. Every man in the county came to town Court week, if he could. There were but few people in the country then, and Court week was the natural periodical time for the farmers to meet, swap stories, make trades, learn the news, hear the speeches, and form their opinion as to which of the 'tonguey fellers it is safest to give business to or vote for the Legislater [*sic*]."[8]

There was among these lawyers, who prosecuted and defended, a genuine camaraderie and personal affection for one another outside the courtrooms of the circuit. Discussions could lead to debates, acts that honed skills for men like Douglas, Baker, Browning, Alfred V. Cavarly, Hardin, Hays, Lamborn, Lincoln, Lockwood, McConnel, Morris, Ralston, Richardson, Stuart, Trumbull, Whitney, Williams, Woodson, Yates, and numerous others who would rise from the circuit to state and national political offices.[9]

> They mingled in common, ate, drank, smoked, joked, disputed together. The Judge had at the tavern the spare room, if such a room there was, and the lawyers bunked cosily [*sic*], dozens together, in the "omnibus," as the big, many-bedded room was called, and there they had it. Whatever of law point past, pending, or probably could be raised, they "went for," discussed, dissected, worried, fought over it until, whether convinced or not, all knew more than when they commenced; and thus, struggling over these made-up issues of debate, became sharpened, by mutual attrition, the legal faculties that were panting for future and more serious contests.[10]

Among those points the young prosecutor found most educating was that at Bloomington, where seasoned lawyer John Todd Stuart of Springfield asked Judge Logan, to throw out some fifty indictments Douglas had drawn up. Stuart contended Douglas had misspelled McLean County as McClean. Since there was no such county as McClean, Stuart argued, there was no such place in which the offenses Douglas had charged could have occurred. Douglas considered Stuart's manner pompous and insulting, taking advantage of his youth and inexperience in front of a courtroom filled with people who knew Stuart but who were unacquainted with the young Jacksonville lawyer.

"I considered his [Stuart's] conduct extremely ungenerous," said Douglas. "Had it been done in a respectful and courteous manner, I should have made no objection to the indictments being quashed."[11]

It was an embarrassing moment for Douglas, whom his antagonists for days thereafter would call the schoolmaster who couldn't spell.[12] Douglas himself thought Stuart's motion was fatal to the indictments. But Douglas remained defiant. Stuart, had only a few clients among those named in the indictments, yet demanded they all be thrown out. This gentleman had to be rebuked.[13] Douglas might lose the indictments in the end, but if he could do nothing more than cause an irritating delay for his opponents, he would do it.

"When the Judge [Stephen T. Logan] asked me if I had anything to say in support of the indictments, I told him I did not consider it necessary as yet to say anything, Mr. Stuart having made the motion and having the affirmative of the question, the burden of proof of course rested upon him."

Judge Logan found logic in Douglas's argument that it was Stuart's responsibility to prove to the court the correct spelling of the county's name. The judge's ruling alone would have been enough to satisfy Douglas's objective. Having drawn up the indictments the night before, he knew that there was no copy of the statutes in the county, which meant Stuart would be put to the trouble, time, and expense of traveling to get one. Douglas's ploy imposed a two-day delay in the hearing and an irritating postponement for Stuart while the statutes were checked at the Tazewell Courthouse in the adjoining county.[14]

All were surprised when the statutes showed that the name of the county in Douglas's indictments was spelled correctly. Judge Logan sustained the indictments. Douglas was vindicated.

"It appeared that the name of the county in the indictment was right, and that the learned gentleman did not know how to spell the name of the county he had practiced in for years. It turned the joke upon him so completely, and excited so much mirth and humor at his expense, that he could not conceal his chagrin and mortification."[15]

On his next visit to Vandalia, Douglas checked the official records in the secretary of state's office and verified the spelling of the county's name. The correct spelling, as shown in the enrolled bill that passed the General Assembly, was McLean. He discovered, however, that the printer had spelled it incorrectly, which had been a lucky break for him in the dispute with Stuart.[16]

For Douglas the ruling taught him a lesson he would always remember: *"Admit nothing and require my adversary to prove everything."*[17]

Attorneys who opposed Douglas in the courtroom could have found that advice useful. Before a jury, Douglas was known to bluff, to turn facts, to distort evidence, or to have "made use of all his privileged makeshifts to win his case." Yet, while he might take every advantage to win a case, Douglas was known as a courteous and accommodating competitor toward young and obliging to older lawyers.[18] He was just as accommodating to those, including from the lowest of stations, who needed his services. A lawyer familiar with Douglas's come-one, come-all practice described him as a "hale fellow well met with the rudest and poorest man in the court room."[19]

Lawyers riding the huge First Circuit often had to be as enterprising on the road— if there was a road— as he found himself in the courtroom. On the prairies, lawyers might ride fifteen miles over thickly matted grasses that served as trails between communities. They might ride a day without passing a house or a farm. In the spring session they often faced muddy roads and streams swollen by downpours. There were few bridges, and that required the lawyers to innovate crossings. Lawyers continued to talk about a group of Eighth District lawyers that included Judge David Davis who stripped naked, threw their bundled clothing over their shoulders and rode their swimming horses across a swollen stream. Because of his long legs, Abraham Lincoln often was frequently the man appointed to test the depth of streambeds to find shallow spots at which he and his itinerant colleagues might cross.[20] Douglas was never asked to do that.

Lawyers like Douglas found that in the early days on a circuit, accommodations were few. Over in Christian County, for example, there were two primitive one-room buildings in rural Taylorville. One served as the court and the second as a saloon. Both were crowded. Christian County settlers served as jurors, witnesses, litigants, and spectators at the performances that went on during the day. And they crowded around the participants, the judges, lawyers, and defendants alike, patrons at the bar that night. Shelter was ten miles distant. It was not unusual for the lawyers to sleep on the floor or, when conditions were good, share a bed for sleep. Sometimes riding from daybreak to dark, the lawyers were fearless when it came to asking for—or simply taking—hospitality. Springfield lawyer James C. Conkling wrote of a trip on the circuit after a day of heavy rain: "At length I stopped at a cabin and knocked for admittance, but receiving no answer, I opened the door, and saw, by the bright moonlight, chairs and beds arranged in perfect order, but no inmates. Being very hungry I searched for something to eat, and fortunately found some meat and cornbread in nicely covered dishes. Of course I levied upon the provisions for supper; and took possession of one of the beds, where I slept comfortably and undisturbed until morning, when I went on my way rejoicing."[21]

Douglas considered his work on the eight-county First Circuit entirely satisfactory. He boasted after only his first six weeks of prosecuting cases that he had sent two men to the state prison and had not had a single indictment quashed. Nearing the end of his first season as state's attorney, he could declare to his brother-in-law that his effectiveness had exceeded that of his predecessor.

"Since my election I have devoted myself strictly to the duties of my office, and to my other business, not omitting however to spend a portion of my time to my Books, which is absolutely necessary of a young Lawyer. I have now been once around the circuit," he reported, "and have not lost an indictment, whereas my friend Hardin used to lose from one third to one half."[22]

Douglas called the courtroom his "theatre of action" in which he could find himself single handedly conducting a trial against "three or four of the best Lawyers in the State." He was not intimidated. He would neither ask favors nor grant them indiscriminately. With six weeks of what he considered nearly perfect service behind him and only two weeks in the Northern part of the circuit to go, Douglas was certain that his work had been capably performed.[23]

There were some on the circuit who did not share Douglas's critique of his own performance. Following a visit to Douglas in late 1835, brother-in-law Julius Granger wrote that during his return trip to New York he met a man on a steamboat who abused Douglas severely. Granger wrote to Douglas about it. Douglas's advice to Granger was to quit riding steamboats.

"I infer that my character does not stand very fair on the water," he said.[24]

Douglas knew his abuser and in his response to Granger let fly his own string of abuse against him: "He is a notorious desperado, devoid of character, was arrested for whipping his wife it became my duty to prosecute him, and had him fined $50 under [*sic*] the Corporation Law of the town and also divorced from his wife. The threats of such men do not frighten me. I come in contact with them too often to be intimidated by this blustering. I go prepared for such animals in real '*Kentuck style*.'"[25]

As Lincoln would do when riding his own judicial circuit, Douglas made a growing number of friends in the circuit's counties. He did not miss a chance to ingratiate himself with those he met out on the circuit. A comment here, a compliment there might pay off if a farmer or mechanic might someday find himself on a jury before which Douglas would perform. Neither did Douglas miss an opportunity to carry the Democracy Party's message in the large judicial territory. Within the first three weeks into his first travels around the circuit, Douglas was making himself popular with men of his age and bent.[26] It was clear that Douglas had found the people in this expansive western frontier more to his liking than others anywhere else he had known. They were, he would say, great commoners and great Democrats who would "ever give Gen Jackson and his administration a warm and enthusiastic support."[27]

"The people of this country are more thoroughly Democratic than any people I have ever known," Douglas wrote to his stepfather Gehazi Granger on November 9, 1835, from Jacksonville. He had just completed his first journey around the circuit. "They are democratic in principle and in Practice as well as in name. For every body is willing to assume that name, for the purpose of accomplishing his designs. But here equality and equal rights prevail. And no man acknowledges another his superior unless his talents, his principles and his good conduct entitle him to that distinction."

Douglas appreciated the leveling tendency of the Democrats of Jacksonville and found his attachment to them borne by their "Democratic character." It played a key role in his decision to stay there.

"I am firmly and decidedly of the opinion that those are matters not to be overlooked by a young man who feels an interest in the Politics and Political fate of his Country," Douglas told Granger. "I am free to confess that the character of the People of this Country, the Political principles that prevail here, and the bright and allureing [sic] prospects that greet and cheer on a young man and invite him to action, had a great influence on my mind in inducing me to remain here."

The people and politics in Central Illinois expressed the virtues and vision that Douglas had begun to dream for his nation. This was *the foundation* for which the 23-year-old lawyer and budding politician had been searching. Douglas laid out in his letter to Granger his head and heart in a personal manifesto:

> And I will also confess *to you* that these considerations weigh upon my mind and add an additional charm and a brighter luster to the beauty of the rolling Prairies and majestic woods with which our Country abounds. You may consider this vanity in me, and I confess it is. But it is a feeling that will obtain a place in every persons [sic] bosom who comes to this country and has a taste for those things, and who sees the advantage to be derived from them, and the benefits he can bestow upon others and upon his country.[28]

The problem as Douglas saw it was that "party" was an amorphous thing, vague and often shifting. It was an important observation, which recognized that the men and women who had arrived on the prairie sought self-sufficiency and not dependence. Governments had been everywhere. They had lived under them. Here, they sought and needed less of them. Thomas Ford, who arrived in Illinois in 1804 with his widowed mother and two siblings and became the first Illinois governor to grow up in Illinois, concluded that these Illinoisans "did not want government to touch them too closely or in too many places."[29]

One Jacksonville Democrat would put it this way: "It is difficult to catch the hang of parties here, for although there is considerable party feeling there is very little party organization."[30]

The young Jacksonian Democrat, Stephen Douglas, confident in his ability to lead the party, was about to change that.

Douglas's blossoming associations gave the young prosecutor a sense of the breadth and raw strength of the Democracy in Illinois. It provided confirmation that the power of the party of Jackson could be overwhelming if it was united. His friend Brooks had reached the same conclusion. What was needed was an organization that would end the absurdity of Jackson Democrats shooting themselves in the foot by practicing the kind of Jeffersonian idealism that encouraged anyone to enter political races. A future governor would note the lowbrow variety of politicians such politics produced: "From hence, also, comes the vulgar notion that any bellowing fellow with a profusion of flowery bombast is a 'smart man,' a man of talents, fit to make laws, govern the country, and originate its policy."[31]

As virtuous as they might have been, run-of-the-mill pioneers were little concerned about government or its minions. Wanting truly to live the Jeffersonian spirit, they considered the best government was the least. Such conditions, lethargic and indifferent, that were gold to the demagogues who cared not whether government was inefficient and irresponsible since "citizens were unable to assign credit for good measures or blame for bad, since responsibility could not be fixed clearly upon any group of public officials."[32]

Brooks told Douglas that he had seen as many as eighteen candidates for Morgan County sheriff on the ballot in a single election.[33] It might be good Jeffersonianism but it was not good politics. The Whig won that election. It was preposterous that a weak candidate should be elected over the strength of the people. The Democracy's failings in Morgan had been demonstrated in just a year since President Jackson's re-election. The county had become a Whig county, Brooks said. He had seen it time and again: good Democrats going for the same office would split the vote and assure the win to the minority party. To Brooks, the only chance for Democrats to succeed was to end the Whig-favoring split of the Democratic vote by uniting behind a single candidate.[34] The concept of a convention system would transform the nature of Illinois politics.

"It is a new era in our elections, and marks the origin, though not the completion, of a great revolution in men's motives for political action," Governor Thomas Ford said skeptically of the idea. "It is the point where the old system of electing public officers upon their merit and personal preference was about to terminate, and the new principle of 'measures, not men,' was to begin."[35]

The pattern of electoral wins by Democrats in Morgan County had proven to Douglas the merit of Brooks's suggestion to strengthen the party, the alternative of which condemned the Democratic candidates all to lose. Although these free-for-all contests might start in genteel fashion with candidates relying on popularity to appeal to voters, they often became vituperative, laced, as so many were, with personal attacks. And those attacks could be merciless, as democratic incumbent Congressman William May learned in the final weeks of his bid for re-election in 1834.

May had a lengthy record that had been rewarded by constituents and office holders from almost the day he arrived in Illinois from Kentucky early in the nineteenth century. He had been a justice of the peace in both Madison and Morgan counties, a captain in the Illinois militia, and a member of the Illinois House of Representatives. He had studied and practiced law until President Jackson appointed him receiver of public monies for the United States land office in Springfield. He won his first election to Congress on August 4, 1834, to take the seat of former Jacksonian Democrat Joseph Duncan of Jacksonville, who had resigned in protest over Jackson administration policies. In one of the stealthiest campaigns in Illinois history, Duncan ran as a Whig for governor. He did not convey to the state's hardcore Democratic electorate that he had switched sides, the key reason the Whig members of the legislature chose to run him over Lincoln, Ninian Wirt Edwards, William Fithian and Orville Hickman Browning.

"He was the only Governor of Illinois elected without electioneering or the making of speeches," said his daughter and biographer, who rationalized his absence by saying a family illness had been the cause.[36]

In office for fewer than four months, May was running for re-election in the Third Congressional District, which covered twenty-one counties and nearly half of the state's central and northern geography.[37]

Benjamin Mills of Peoria, a fellow Jacksonian Democrat, challenged May for the seat. It was toward the end of the campaign that a string of abuse against "Big Red May" started, and by an anonymous writer whose attacks were eagerly printed in the *Jacksonville Patriot*, a Whig newspaper. The Whigs did not bother fielding a candidate. The author of the attacks, calling himself "Illinois," told *Patriot* readers that May was unfit for office. May had been spared a conviction for burglary while he was a resident of Edwardsville, "Illinois" asserted, by inducing the witness to leave the state. There was more, May's attacker wrote. In 1825 May had seduced a woman living in Greene County with a promise of marriage, and she sued him for breach of promise when he failed to do so. In exchange for $200, she agreed to drop the lawsuit. Later contending he did not have the money, May was said to have given her a broken down horse and sidesaddle, which he said were his only possessions. And even after that, the paper's writer charged, May—by that time a married man—had returned to Greene County and resided with another woman for "some days, representing himself as a single and unmarried man, and courted a young woman who resided in the family."[38]

May was compelled to answer, but the editors of the *Patriot* and *Sangamo Journal* of Springfield refused him their columns to do so. Ignoring the *Patriot*, which gave space to his attacker, May paid for advertising space in the *Journal* to respond. Regarding the burglary, May denied any attempt to steal.

"I was there at that time by invitation from a female member of the family," he contended.

That was true as far as it went. Alfred V. Cavarly of Greene County, who was interested himself in entering politics, in a rather impolitic assertion said, "Your entry into the dwelling house was not to commit murder, but to have illicit intercourse with a female then residing there."[39]

May avoided prosecution. While some continued to believe he had suborned the witness, it did not hurt that the state's attorney happened to be the husband of the purported victim. May brazenly suggested that it was the prosecutor who was "anxious to hush it up, lest it should recoil with disgrace on himself."[40]

Just as brazenly, May admitted to the second charge, seducing the woman, whom he named in his paid response, under a promise of marriage.

"I have often freely acknowledged, that in youth, and in early manhood I have committed many follies and indiscretions," May's advertisement said, "and have been led by an ardent temperament to do what I have long and sincerely regretted, and for which I trusted I had long since made some atonement by an upright moral deportment before my fellow citizens."[41]

Lest it be said that Mills got a pass from abuse, similar personal attacks were aimed against him in the Whig press, as well. Among the charges was one that as a friend of Illinois College Mills had tried to steer some of the state's seminary funds, which the federal government had allocated to the state from federal land sales, to the Jacksonville school.[42] As Douglas knew, the college was the center of the anti-slavery controversy in Morgan County, the one issue that could taint beyond redemption any politician associated with it. The Illinois College matter became so hot that former Congressman Duncan, a College Board member, denied any connection with the college.[43] Duncan's denial was clear proof to men like Douglas that any mention of abolition or anti-slavery could escalate negatively the sensibilities of his neighbors, including the most aristocratic of them.

Despite the charges of theft and adultery—which the congressman quickly and freely admitted, May beat Mills in a landslide. That the voters were willing to forgive a man who could publicly admit such indiscretions recalled similar admissions by U.S. Treasury Secretary Alexander Hamilton, who also had admitted an extramarital affair.[44] In Morgan and Sangamon counties, where he was attacked most bitterly and publicly, May won almost 90 percent of the vote. Overall, he collected 73 percent of the ballots cast, 2,755 to Mills's 956. Ten write-ins collected a total of 59 votes.[45] And Duncan, who virtually hid during the campaign to avoid telling his former Jacksonian Democratic supporters that he was a Whig candidate, won by 53 percent of the vote over three other candidates, including the perennial candidate William Kinney of St. Clair County.[46] Douglas was pleased with the Democracy's triumphs.

"Illinois," he bragged, "still remains sound to the core, although she has got a *Traitor* for Governor."[47]

These renegade campaigns, even between faithful Jacksonians, and Duncan's furtive win of the governor's office piled up evidence for Douglas that organization was needed to impose party discipline and unity. Its focus would be a convention system, which would maintain Jeffersonian and Jacksonian principles of democracy by allowing public and then representative participation. A party platform and the men to carry it out would be the convention's key duties. The payment for party support was a candidate's adherence to its creed and principle.

Meanwhile, Douglas put up a good front: "In this State the Election resulted favourable to the cause of Democracy Liberty congressmen all being friendly to the Administration and opposed to *the* Bank, although one of them may be in favor of *a* Bank, unless Gen Jackson tells him better. In the legislature we have a decided majority, and therefore feel sure of electing a Jackson Senator."[48]

6. A New Party in Jackson's Image

Douglas was certain of his ability to attract voters, although he knew that others often had difficult times "in beating up" for them.¹ For Douglas, vote getting was not about brow beating but about building relationships. He made his acquaintances feel important. And he left them with an impression they had access to an important man. One of his friends noted this in Douglas's character: "I do not think he was ever with one of them for a minute without also leaving in his mind an ineffaceable impression of having been in contact with something immeasurably higher and deeper and broader than himself, of a great imposing personality, in a word."²

Douglas was unassuming and genuine around his constituents. He identified with their Southern beginnings, most often dressing in the same kind of Kentucky denim jeans they wore, symbols of their commonality—and Democracy.³ One summer afternoon while Douglas was campaigning in Greene County, a group of farmers were attracted to him at the court house. He excused himself for a few moments and bought a large watermelon. He sat down with them on the ground at the courthouse, cut the melon into wedges, and shared them with his correspondents.

A Massachusetts newspaper editor who witnessed Douglas campaigning observed that Douglas took notice of nearly everyone he passed.

"At one moment," the editor wrote, "he talks with the old, stern-visaged politician who had been soured by a thousand defeats and disappointments; in the next, to that well formed and genial Kentuckian, who has just sought a free State; now he sits down with the little girl approaching her teens, and asks of her school studies; and he pats the little boy on the head, and in presence of his mother and proud father ... says a word of his mild eyes and glossy locks."⁴

Douglas had learned how sweetly their own names sounded to his constituents and how grateful they were to the man who could remember them. He had learned how beholden they were to anyone who noticed their children—no matter how unwashed, how grateful they were for notice, any notice. Experience had taught Douglas that politics was about relationships and he knew why his constituents were attached to him: "I live with my constituents, eat with my constituents, drink with them, lodge with them, pray with them, laugh, hunt, dance and work with them," he wrote. "I eat their corn dodgers and fried bacon and sleep two in a bed with them."⁵

If he had learned how important intimacy was, it was demonstrated in an experience, likely more legendary than authentic, he had while campaigning. Douglas recalled staying one evening with a family at their cabin just under some water-cut bluffs along the Illinois River, approximately twenty miles west of Jacksonville. After an evening meal, Douglas said all of the family members except for a seventeen-year-old girl named Serena, whom he described as "plump as a pigeon and as smooth as a persimmon," went to bed. Douglas was tired and longed to be in bed, also, but would rather have taken his legs off with a wood saw, as he put it, than undress in front of the unstoppably talkative Serena. Concluding that she was determined "to outsit" him, Douglas "by repeated spasmodic efforts" took off his coat, waistcoat, cravat, and boots and socks.

Serena continued to talk with what Douglas said were unaverted eyes. He placed a chair between himself and the girl, whose voice and eyes were fully unfatigued. Douglas thought the chair would offer some security for propriety. He loosened his suspenders and lowered his trousers before realizing that a blanket between him and modesty still was 10 feet away. When Douglas arose from what he described as a stooping posture, and wholly disencumbered of clothes, he attempted to distract the girl by calling attention to something fantastic outside the window. The ploy failed. Douglas reported that as he dashed for the bed, Serena returned her gaze to him. As he dashed, she observed, "Mr. Douglas, you have got a mighty small chance of legs there."[6]

Up to this time, political campaigns allowed any man to announce himself a candidate for an office, then canvass the hustings for votes, make speeches, attract friends, attack opponents and suffer and, then, defend himself against similar attacks. As one political participant recalled: "In old times there was no such thing [as a nominating convention]—Every man became a candidate who wanted to—on his own hook—spoke for himself &c—All [the candidates] met and discussed questions together—[spent] days at it. People came 30–40 mi[les] to hear it &c—acted like People at church."[7]

These were men independent of party who could by sheer numbers of candidates split the vote. It meant that a minority candidate had as much a shot at election as those more attuned to the majority.

Jacksonians Douglas and Brooks recognized the weakness this loose political organization caused for the majority. In fact, this system of free entry split the majority. It was a political science that worked against the majority. Douglas's desire was for more democracy. With a belief that the majority supported Democracy party principles and candidates, Douglas could presume that the party should be the ultimate arbiter of political decisions. It was with this presumption that Douglas worked to impose a convention system for the Illinois Democracy in which the principles of the party would rise from the wellspring of the people, advancing principles, drafting agenda, and selecting candidates for state and local offices.

Douglas had some experience with effective political organizations. At Canandaigua, he had joined his political schoolmates to defend the Democracy against swelling voices of Anti-Masonry. Mixing frequently with local politicians, he studied the mechanics of party and political organizations. Although in the years ahead he would speak little of the Greek and Latin he learned at Canandaigua Academy, he would make the highest and best use of the lessons he learned there in the art of politics.[8] By focusing the vote of the party's faithful on selected men, candidates expressing the will of the majority acting in concert would be nominated for offices. The convention system, from district level to national, was the way to do it. The convention would seek and state the party's principles, nominate the candidate who best exemplified them, and then line up the party's loyal rank and file behind him to support them.[9]

This idea was outrageous to Jacksonville's Whigs. Even some local Democrats were suspicious.[10] The convention seemed a threat to patriotism and honor by denying the right of any man who wished to do so to declare his own candidacy to run for public office. It was a "Yankee

Trap," a reference to its effective use in New York, which political manipulators could use to game the system to thwart the electoral process.[11] But to Douglas the convention was a legitimate tool to assure a just defense of democracy in the face of an enemy with no regard for people. Douglas recalled the principle question of Thomas Jefferson about whether "the power of the people, or that of the aristoi should prevail."[12]

"There are two opposing parties," he would write in defense of the convention system. "The one advocates the rights of the People; the other, the advocates of the privileges of Property."[13]

The matter of local conventions reached the chambers of the Illinois General Assembly by December 1835. An Illinois Senate resolution declared that "every person eligible to ... office had a right to come forward as a candidate for it without the intervention of caucuses and conventions."

The conventions Douglas promoted, the resolution continued, were destructive of free elective franchise, dangerous to Republicanism and the right of a free people to vote for their own candidate of choice. It was a choice between being able to exercise free and independent suffrage or wearing shackles binding them to "a pack of demagogues, whose every move is self-aggrandizement!—office!—power!!!"[14]

Representative John Henry of Jacksonville introduced resolutions in the Illinois House that condemned as "anti-republican" a convention system for the selection of state and county offices.[15] Acting for the Democrats, Representative Uri Manley of Clark County immediately moved that Henry's resolutions be tabled until July 4. Since the legislature would have adjourned months earlier, Manley's amendment would have effectively killed them. Second-termer Abraham Lincoln, whose stature was growing among the Whigs, and Henry immediately called for a vote to keep the resolutions alive. Their motion failed thirty-three to nineteen, and Henry's hope to impair Douglas and the Democrats was laid on the table.[16]

The convention-approval bill came before the House again on January 5, 1836. Sangamon Whigs John Dawson and John Todd Stuart tried but failed to get their colleagues to table it. One more time, Henry moved his anti-convention amendments:

Resolved, That we regard the practice of holding conventions for the nomination of elective officers with the most anxious solicitude, and believe it to be destructive of the freedom of the elective franchise, and in its tendency calculated to take from the PEOPLE the privilege of making an unbiased choice for office from among their fellow citizens—opposed to Republican Institutions, and dangerous to the liberties of the People.

2d. *Resolved,* That every man who is eligible to an office within the gift of the people, has an undeniable right to become a candidate for the same, and that the people have a right to support him, without the sanction of a caucus or convention.

3d. *Resolved,* That the convention system ought not to receive encouragement or approbation from Legislative bodies.

4th. *Resolved,* That we believe with General Jackson, that public officers should not attempt to influence elections, because they hold the power and influence, and the People's money, by which they are enabled to establish Presses, support conventions and organize secret parties even against the interest of the people, and the democratic principles of this Government.[17]

After a motion to divide the amendments, the House voted separately on each of Henry's resolutions. Members passed the second and fourth.

Whig Representative Edwin "Bat" Webb sought to make Henry's offerings more palatable by recommending a series of resolutions taken from the Democrats' own playbook appealing to commoners. He moved that the price of public lands be reduced, that settlers on public lands be given pre-emption rights, and that all white male citizens 21 years of age and older have the right to vote whether they own real estate or not. There was one exception to Webb's resolution on suffrage. He moved that Illinois' elective franchise "be kept pure from contamination by the admission of colored votes." This last resolution stirred no controversy from Democrats. A third of the Democrats in the House joined Whigs to pass Webb's resolutions 35 to 16.[18]

Historian Richard Miller notes that the resolution was part of the Whig strategy to paint Martin Van Buren an abolitionist and amalgamator. It was designed to disrupt loyalty among the Democratic rank and file, where there were no known friends of blacks. The effort was gaining enough acceptance, Miller continues, that Sangamon County Democrat John Calhoun would be compelled to show that Van Buren did not support universal suffrage for blacks.[19] Calhoun, who was not related to the more famous John C. Calhoun of South Carolina, in the years ahead would become a central player in the Douglas—and the nation's—story on the plains in the Nebraska Territory.

Although some of the Henry and Webb amendments were passed, they were combined as a package for a final vote and were defeated. Without them, the main convention bill was taken up again and approved.

It was a victory for Douglas, who led the Democrats' efforts to mold the county organizations into a statewide power to coordinate the party's politics. His mission in Vandalia accomplished, Douglas returned north to Jacksonville.

Douglas saw the convention system as an assurance "to effect [sic] the popular will." It would level the playing field for the farmer, mechanic, and laborer with the advantaged aristocrat.[20] As an ambitious politician, Douglas also saw in the convention an instrument to create an advantage for himself. Instilling the need for party discipline to build the strength of party principles, the convention system could lessen the influence of the party's old guard and wealth. It would favor any man who was shrewd and clever at the art of political manipulation. Stephen A. Douglas exemplified such shrewdness.

The Democracy of Douglas's district had hosted its first convention in Morgan County in late April 1835. It was not just Democrats there. A substantial number of Whigs were there, too, expecting to see Douglas fall flat in his effort to organize the Democrats.[21] They were disappointed. The organization of the party lured a number of prominent Whigs into the Democratic fold— including attorney Alfred Cavarly of Carrollton; Peter Green of Clay County; Sangamon men William May, Peter Cartwright and George Forquer; Forquer's half brother Thomas Ford (a future Illinois governor) of Adams County; "and others who had been old Clay men."[22]

Brooks and Douglas succeeded in bringing together Democrats from every precinct in the county. The number of people seeking the numerous offices Douglas was to put before the conventioneers was large. They would nominate two candidates for the Illinois Senate, six representatives, a sheriff, three county commissioners and a coroner. The candidate nominated for sheriff, later believing voters would reject the new system, bolted the party and, running as an independent, was defeated.

Douglas did not seek nomination to an office. But when Democratic candidates failed out of fear to respond to the Whig legislative candidate John J. Hardin's severe attacks on a convention system and the men to whom it gave positions on the ballot, Douglas took to the stump. He met Hardin at every Hardin venue. With Douglas matching Hardin's attacks blow for blow, Whigs suggested that the Democratic ticket was weak if Douglas, who was not even a candidate, had to do all the speaking. The criticism was forceful enough that S.S. Brooks, one of the Democratic nominees, dropped out to make way for Douglas.[23] More and more typical of Douglas, in informing his relatives back east about his candidacy, Douglas indicated he had agreed only with the greatest reluctance. This was a way Douglas could avoid the appearance of managing politics, as his Whig friends charged were a perversion of the American Republican system.[24] It was, he told his brother-in-law, an "arrangement [that] is much against my will, for I did not desire to be a candidate this year, but rather make money—In this as in other things I yielded to the solicitations of my friends."

Douglas was artful in delivering the news. The fact was that Douglas had done little to develop his private law practice. A regular income from his work on the circuit made that unnecessary at this point. He believed that the reputation he was gaining as a lawyer on the circuit would pay dividends when and if he decided to devote himself full time to the practice of law.[25] Yielding to his friends or not, Douglas was not unhappy with the opportunity to contend for his first elective office. In fact, he approached it with the greatest of confidence.

"Judging from the prospects at present I ent[ert]ain no doubt of my success in the election," he wrote, adding with no lack of bravado, "I find no difficulty in adopting the Western mode of Electioneering by addressing the people from the Stump. John J. Hardin who was my opponent for States Attorney is now my principal opponent for representative. We have already had a number of pitched [sic] battles on the Stump in addressing the People, in which my friends & I believe this say I came out conqueror. We shall have a warm contest however—warmer the better for I like excitement."[26]

It was a vigorous campaign between Douglas and the man he earlier had removed from his state-appointed office. Douglas and Hardin debated in every precinct in the county. Although he later would find himself compelled to help organize a Whig convention, Hardin attacked Douglas's convention device. He and his fellow Whigs viewed the convention system as "a Yankee contrivance, intended to abridge the liberties of the people by depriving individuals, on their own mere motion, of the privilege of becoming candidates, and depriving each man of the right to vote for a candidate of his own selection and choice."[27] Abraham Lincoln joined the attack, saying it "ought not be tolerated in a republican government" because it was "dangerous to the liberties of the people."[28] Governor Joseph Duncan, like his Jacksonville neighbor and friend Hardin, predicted that the convention system would place a party's power into the hands of one man with a disastrous, undemocratic effect.

"You must perceive that all power will soon be centered in one man," pleaded Duncan with no little prescience, "and that our march to despotism is inevitable."[29]

Douglas bore the brunt of such attacks against the convention system—Hardin's main target— but the Morgan Democrat remained steadfast to the principles:

> That "the people have a right to assemble together in a peaceable manner; to consult for their common good," is a noble declaration of the constitution of our state; and contains the best gem of democracy, and is of so exhalted [sic] a character, and of such essential utility, as to place its propriety beyond all controversy. The depositories of liberty, and of power, the people, by frequent exercise of this constitutional privilege will be sure to maintain their just influence in the

management of the political affairs, and will always preserve that ascendancy over aspirants for power and dangerous distinction, which unholy ambition and love of glory too often instill into the hearts of men who, perhaps without being fully aware of it prefer personal aggrandizement to the happiness, and prosperity, and liberties of their country.[30]

Douglas and Hardin continued their debates to the day of the election on August 1, 1836. The results of the work in the Douglas convention system spoke convincingly. Morgan County Democrats swept nearly all of their elections, from the top of the ticket to the bottom and by pluralities larger than anywhere else in the state. Those who had been nominated in the convention won five of Morgan County's six House seats. Douglas won 1,926 votes, nine fewer than the leading vote-getter, the popular Democrat Newton Cloud. An influential farmer and preacher from Waverly in rural Morgan County, Cloud was re-elected to a fourth term. The pluralities of Douglas and Cloud were striking. Together, the two candidates won 3.72 percent of the 103,674 votes cast in the election statewide. Winning 1,732 votes, Hardin was the only Whig elected from Morgan County to the lower chamber. Democrats Richard S. Walker with 1,726 votes and William W. Happy with 1,694 finished close behind Hardin to win House seats. Morgan voters turned Whig incumbents John Henry and William Gordon out of office.[31] They also denied Democrat John Wyatt, who had helped launch Douglas's political career, his attempt at a promotion. After two terms in the House, Wyatt was trying to advance in 1836 to the State Senate in a four-man race. Democrat William Weatherford won one of the Senate seats with 1,875 votes and Whig William O'Rear won the other with 1,783 votes. Wyatt collected 1,668 votes. It was enough to shake Wyatt's faith in Douglas's loyalty to him. That faith was fully shattered in 1837 when Wyatt, still without an office, expected President Van Buren to appoint him register of the federal land office in Springfield. Van Buren appointed Douglas. John Todd Stuart remembered Wyatt's aggravation: "Somebody else received the appointment, however, which of course made Wyatt very angry—so much so that when I [Stuart] ran for Congress Wyatt went for me because Douglas had cheated him in reference to that appointment."[32]

The county's turnout in the August 1, 1836, election was most impressive. The 20,375 voters who went to the polls more than doubled the number of voters two years earlier and cast nearly twenty percent of all votes cast for House seats in Illinois. That was also two hundred votes more than the votes accumulated in Sangamon County, where the popular Abraham Lincoln of New Salem and members of his Sangamon County Long Nine in the House were elected. Lincoln's 1,716 votes led the Sangamon delegation.[33]

The Democratic Party's wins in Morgan County, orchestrated by the Douglas and Brooks organization, were enough to convince adherents of the Democracy throughout the state of the efficiency of the convention system. They also were enough to compel Illinois Whigs, who desired victory every bit as much as the Democrats, to form their own convention system.

Democrats from throughout the state revered what Morgan office-winners had done and venerated the men who had accomplished it. Pilgrimages from across Illinois ventured to the Central Illinois county to hear Douglas and Brooks teach how it could be done elsewhere. Conventions in other parts of the state soon followed.

Both Brooks and Douglas saw the exercises as important to the party. Douglas also was thinking about its importance to him. All-important public opinion had been consolidated. The power of the party—and the opportunity to favor the faithful and expect reciprocity through the power of patronage—had been concentrated. Leadership was able to exert complete control.

The newly recognized master of political mechanics, Douglas had organized Illinois' first Democratic machine.

As they approached a presidential election the following year—when they would have to elect someone to succeed Andrew Jackson—party coordination and discipline would be unusually important. On December 7 and 8, 1835, Douglas joined other Illinois Democrats in Vandalia to select five presidential electors. With the convention underway, an officer called on Douglas to address the delegates about their purpose. Douglas's baritone voice boomed through the hall, but delegates seated in rows distant from the platform complained they could not see him. Democrat John Dean Caton of Chicago lifted Douglas and put him on a table. Delegates applauded loudly, then listened attentively to Douglas.[34]

Responding to criticism of their convention system, delegates also passed a resolution urging Democrats throughout the state to engage in a "union and concert of action" but also to exchange ideas with their representatives.

"For without a frequent interchange of political sentiment, expressed by the people, and repeated by the delegates, properly authorized," the resolution continued, "the democracy cannot insure that success in their elections, which the purity and integrity of their principles, entitle them to claim."[35]

Douglas's idea for a convention system, operating statewide for the first time, could not be considered an outright success. Representatives from only five counties attended, and Southern Illinois delegates were relegated by their Central and Northern colleagues to doing more listening than being listened to. The convention system got a contested airing by old-line, as well as newer Democrats. In his young career of public service, Douglas for the first time would witness the bitterness in his own state of a sectional struggle over his convention architecture. Southern Illinois Democrats, stronger adherents to the Jeffersonian model of yeoman farmers, objected to a system of slating candidates that would deny anyone the opportunity to seek office. Northern Illinois Democrats, on the other hand, saw the convention system could work in the interest of the party's future successes, assuring party strength and unity, as Douglas had shown in Morgan County.[36]

An elector himself and soon to be the state chairman of the Democratic presidential nominee, Douglas had immediate reasons for wanting to assure the success of a statewide Democratic convention system. He had learned that the Whigs had devised a strategy that had the potential to elevate their candidate to the presidency in 1836. The twenty-three-year-old could see how the Whig ploy just might work. A sizable number of old-line Democrats, north and south, objected to the candidacy of Vice President Martin Van Buren, whom President Jackson had tabbed as his successor. Van Buren troubled western and southern Democrats, and Whigs saw advantage in the dissension. Whigs did not have a candidate considered strong enough to beat Van Buren outright. But in his announcement in 1834 that he would oppose Van Buren for the Presidency, Judge Hugh Lawson White of Tennessee gave Whigs an unexpected blessing.

White was an imposing figure. At six feet tall, he towered over his peers. His long face, made to seem even longer by flowing, straight white hair combed closely alongside his face and down over his shoulders, was a study in solemnity. His steel blue eyes were deeply set in hollows formed by high cheekbones and rugged zygomatic bones around them. He was thin, almost gaunt, a testimony to his routine for beginning and ending his workday in the dark. A prominent Knoxville lawyer, White had a distinguished record of public service. He became a judge in 1801, a Tennessee state senator in 1807, and was an associate justice on his state's Supreme Court from 1809 to 1815. He returned to the state Senate in 1817, after service as president of the state bank. The Tennessee legislature in 1825 elected him to take the U.S. Senate seat of General Jackson on Jackson's election as president.[37] He would serve eight terms. In 1840, the desires of his constituency did not accord with White's increasingly anti–Jackson principles and he resigned.

White entered the U.S. Senate in 1825 a whole-hog Jackson Democrat. But he found himself more often out of step with the president and agreeing with those in the camp of Jackson's first vice president, John C. Calhoun. White came to adopt Calhoun's view that the sovereign states had the authority to nullify federal laws with which they disagreed. With Van Buren President Jackson's heir apparent, White's State of Tennessee was drifting from Jackson also. White's presidential candidacy gained momentum in 1835 when the Tennessee and Alabama legislatures nominated him for president.[38] He was made to order for the Whig strategy, and Douglas was indeed concerned that White's candidacy could split Illinois' Democrats.

On December 19, 1835, the Illinois Senate backed White for the presidency by the closest of margins, 13 to 12, helped by a few Democratic senators who claimed they were Jackson men but who opposed Van Buren. Douglas believed that the Whigs had "bought out" at least two Democratic senators, who earlier had pledged themselves to Van Buren. The Whig strategy in the Senate, as Douglas viewed it, "is calculated to leave the impression that this State is favorable to the Judges [sic] pretentions [sic]."[39]

Although they did not believe White could win the presidency outright, Illinois Whigs thought he could win enough votes from dissatisfied Democrats to prevent any other candidate from winning the election at the polls. The goal of the Whig strategists at the national level was to have the election decided in the House of Representatives. Sangamon County Whig Representative Lincoln favored the strategy. When he announced that he would stand for re-election, Lincoln declared he would vote for White for president.[40] Douglas was all too aware of what could happen if the Democrats failed to elect their candidate outright at the polls. That had happened in the election of 1824, and Illinois politics were directly involved—and affected. None of the four candidates in the 1824 presidential election had won a majority of electoral votes. With 131 electoral votes needed to win, Andrew Jackson received 99 votes. John Quincy Adams won 84; William Crawford, President James Monroe's treasury secretary, won 41; and Kentucky Congressman Henry Clay won 37. In accordance with the Twelfth Amendment, the House of Representatives would decide the election and only the top three finishers were to be considered. That meant Henry Clay's candidacy was over.

Douglas knew that an election thrown into the House was fraught with danger. His own state's history provided a concrete lesson. In that 1824 election, Illinois congressman Daniel Pope Cook had publicly pledged to vote for the candidate with the highest popular vote should the House be called upon to decide the election. The pledge clearly required Cook to vote for Jackson, who won 41.3 percent of the popular vote. Adams had won 30.9 percent, Clay 13 percent and Crawford 11.2 percent. Although under pressure for his vote by his leader, Speaker Clay, and by death threats from home, Cook reneged on his promise to his Illinois constituents and voted for Adams. When his votes were aggregated with those of Clay's supporters, Adams won the election in the House.[41] Adams's subsequent appointment of Clay as secretary of state, angered Jacksonians, who called it a "corrupt bargain" and said it was the only reason for Adams's victory and Clay's ascension. Illinoisans repaid Cook for what they perceived was duplicity by replacing him in the next congressional election with Joseph Duncan of Jacksonville, who favored Andrew Jackson. Cook would say Illinoisans misunderstood his pledge. Yet his correspondence with Justice Lockwood, who strongly supported Adams, colors Cook's contention with doubt. As early as January 31, 1823, Congressman Cook had written Lockwood about the "subject of president making" in Washington where "Adams is the foremost horse at present, and I think gaining."[42]

Douglas saw clearly the purpose in this Whig-White scheme: "The Whigs are making a tremendous effort here to divide the Democratic Party by bringing out Judge White," he wrote back home in April. "But it won't do. We are determined to all go together and act in concert with our brethren in other parts of the Union."[43]

The Whigs saw just as clearly a scheme in the Democratic convention system.

"Is this Democracy?" a *Quincy Daily Whig* headline would ask. "Formerly it was held as a tenet of democracy, *that every office was open to every citizen;* that every man had a right to aspire to any office in the republic; and to solicit the suffrages of his fellow citizens.... But now the plan is changed. No man must dare to *nominate himself,* nor to accept the nomination of his friends! No man must *interfere* with the pleasure of a Convention, or a Caucus."[44]

White appealed to this kind of sentiment, which reckoned "management of men"[45] through parties and conventions similar to slavery: "I feel that I was not intended to be the *slave* of any man or set of men," White said of parties and conventions in 1835, "that I have some mind, and that the author of my existence intended that I should exercise it—that I should form opinions as to *politics and religion*, and freely and fearlessly act upon them without being intimidated by what either man or devils can do."[46]

The contest for the presidency between Van Buren and White in Illinois could be seen as a contest between convention and caucus. But Douglas could see also that the Whig strategy could produce a repeat of the kind of political ambiguity that had elevated a Jacksonian apostate, Joseph Duncan, to the governor's office with the help of Democratic-Republican voters in 1834.

Illinoisans had elected Duncan to Congress as a whole-hog Jacksonian in 1826, but over the course of his years in Congress Duncan's opinion of Jackson disintegrated. By 1834, Duncan was voting more often with Whigs than Democrats.[47] The Illinois congressman completed his break with Jackson and his party after the president vetoed the recharter of the Bank of the United States in June 1834. Within three months, Duncan resigned from Congress and announced for governor of Illinois. It was an unusual campaign—Duncan ran without once returning to or campaigning in the state. But he knew what he was doing.[48] Although the *Vandalia Whig* had predicted Duncan's gubernatorial candidacy as early as 1833, there were other influential Whig newspapers, like the *Sangamo Journal*, which charged that Duncan "sheltered" himself under the Jackson name while opposing Jackson principles.[49] By running in absentia, Duncan could avoid pesky questions about just what his principles were. With Whig newspapers keeping his name before their party's supporters, Duncan could presume the votes of Whigs. He also could presume the votes of the state's more moderate Democrats, known as "milk-and-cider" Jacksonians, like himself. The election on August 4, 1834, proved the effectiveness of Duncan's strategy. Running as a Whig, he won 17,330 votes to Jacksonian Democrat William Kinney's 10,224 votes.[50] His victory made Duncan the only Whig ever to win statewide office in Illinois.

Now, in 1835, Duncan's 1834 model of election lent greater urgency to Democratic Party unity. With William Henry Harrison and Daniel Webster also on the Whigs' presidential ticket, Douglas believed that Whigs did not care about electing White. They needed only to use him "to withdraw from the democratic ranks, a sufficient number to bring the presidential election before the H. of Representatives; and there by bargain & corruption ... change the unpolluted course of the free stream of democracy which now runs thro' every act and rule of the administration, and taint it with the rancor of bitter and illiberal federalism."[51]

Less than a month after Democrats at Baltimore in May 1835 nominated Van Buren, White supporters in Illinois gathered in Springfield, repudiated the Baltimore Democratic convention, and endorsed White's candidacy. Not long afterward, the Illinois Senate passed resolutions that did the same. Three votes came from the senate's 15 Jacksonian loyalists, demonstrating the threat of White's candidacy to Van Buren in Illinois.[52]

A Democratic convention in December 1835 created a committee of six Democrats to write a letter "To the Democratic Republicans of Illinois." Reputedly drafted by Douglas[53] and issued on December 31, 1835, it was credited with unifying Illinois Democrats, who supported Van Buren overwhelmingly at the November 1836 election.[54] Democrats nominated at convention in 1842 again won statewide offices.

In Springfield on March 1, 1843, Whigs met in a special meeting, whose object Abraham Lincoln described. He then introduced nine resolutions, half of them related to the creation of a Whig organization in Illinois. They were unaminously adopted.[55]

7. "The least man I ever saw"

STEPHEN DOUGLAS MADE his last rounds of the First Judicial District as state's attorney in September and October of 1836. He resigned the office on December 1, the day he was sworn in as one of six members of the Illinois House of Representatives from Morgan County. Elected at the age of twenty-three, he was the youngest member of the legislative body. Although elected for the first time, Douglas's work to engineer an upset of the Whigs in their own fortress made him the undisputed leader of the Morgan delegation. Thanks to the efforts of S.S. Brooks and himself, all but one member of the delegation, Douglas's earlier political foe, Whig John J. Hardin of Jacksonville, were Democrats. Douglas was returning to Vandalia, where his political opportunism under the tutelage of Democratic Representative John Wyatt had put him in his first public office. The man he and Wyatt had maneuvered out of office, John J. Hardin, would join him in the lower house.

It was virtually a new House of Representatives. Like Douglas, sixty-six representatives were newly elected, largely because of reapportionment. Only sixteen veterans of the Ninth General Assembly had returned. Nine of them had served in the Eighth. Of the twenty-eight senators, twelve were freshmen.[1] Not one of the members of the incoming Tenth General Assembly had been born in Illinois. The same was true of the governor, Joseph Duncan, and Supreme Court justices Thomas C. Browne, Samuel Drake Lockwood, Theophilus Smith, and William Wilson.[2]

The Tenth Illinois General Assembly was composed of a great number of able men who would earn honors in government service. Among them were Orville Hickman Browning, John Calhoun, Newton Cloud, Jesse Kilgore Dubois, William Lee Davidson Ewing, Orlando Bell Ficklin, Augustus C. French, Hardin, Lincoln, John A. Logan, Usher F. Linder, John A. McClernand, William A. Richardson, James Semple, James Shields, and John Todd Stuart. From this group would come a president, a cabinet officer, U.S. senators (one of them, Shields, the only man elected senator from three states), congressmen, governor and leading generals of the country's civil war.

When Douglas arrived at Vandalia in December 1836, he saw a city still pretending to the throne as the seat of government. The town had continued moving toward prosperity. Douglas could count fifteen wholesale and retail businesses. Around the square were a half dozen boarding houses and taverns, each claiming ample supplies of "choice liquors." Tradesmen and merchants were "all doing good business." There was water and steam power and a saw and gristmill. Vandalia editor James Hall's *Illinois Monthly Magazine* had heralded the nearby Kaskaskia River as a "potential great highway of commerce." (By 1833, however, Hall had been frustrated by too little growth in the commerce of Vandalia and moved to Cincinnati.[3])

The seed of a lyceum movement had been planted in Vandalia to inform, educate, and entertain its residents. There were three societies whose purposes reflected rising issues in the nation. One promoted Bible study. A second promoted temperance. The third promoted colonization of Negroes as a means to rid the nation of slavery—and, that accomplished, the black populations of Illinois and the United States.[4] One thing was noticeably missing, as even Governor Joseph Duncan reported: "There is no young ladies in Vandalia."[5]

The legislature that moved the capital from Kaskaskia to Vandalia in 1819 did not expect the state's second seat of government to be permanent—one reason the law required that decision to be reviewed before twenty years had elapsed. While the men appointed by the legislature to find the capital's new location believed activities associated with government would increase land values in a new capital city, Vandalia was doomed from the beginning in its hope to keep the state's headquarters. The promise of continuing improvements that might have been expected in a new capital city did not happen. There were no marked routes into the capital, which meant that first-term legislators had to find their way to Vandalia by landmarks and the kindnesses of settlers who directed them to the next navigation point. Many arrived with stories of hardship that did not favor Vandalia. Some had gotten lost. Evening accommodations for some enroute were found under the canopy of a tall oak or a ceiling of stars. Other towns were advancing more quickly.[6] There was a boom in sales of town lots in a village named Chicago, some two hundred, fifty miles from Vandalia in Fayette County.[7]

Once they had selected the site for the second capital, the legislature's committee hired surveyors and woodsmen to clear the heavily timbered land. The town was platted into sixty-four squares, the center two allotted for public use, and one selected as the site for a new state capitol building. An auction of 150 lots was held in September 1819 and raised $35,000, which was enough to assure the government's operations for the next two years. Expecting land values to appreciate quickly, state government officials or their agents at the sale bought several parcels. Surveyors, who were confident in the area's growth, invested, also. In the months and years ahead, however, many buyers failed to fulfill their contracts and the price of land declined.[8]

At 10 a.m. Monday, December 5, 1836, Douglas and his House colleagues were in their seats at a series of long tables arranged in rows in the House chamber on the first floor of the state capitol. Unpadded benches ran parallel to each of the tables on which the legislators were to sit three to a table. On each table were several cork inkstands, and interspersed on the floor were sand-filled wooden boxes that served as receptacles for the coarse brown spit of chewed tobacco. The same sand was used by legislators for blotting ink on papers they wrote, inelegant but utilitarian. Arranged along the tables were tall stands for candles that would illuminate the chamber during night work. The larger rooms provided the chambers for each house of the state legislature with fireplace and stoves heating the drafty spaces. Each chamber also had a single water pail and three tin cups from which legislators could draw refreshment.[9]

Sangamon delegation leader Abraham Lincoln had chosen a seat in a rear corner of the House. From there, he could keep track of who was talking to whom.[10] Because the new capitol building—the third one to be built in Vandalia in less than twenty years—remained unfinished at the beginning of the new term, Lincoln believed the legislature was likely to get little or nothing done.[11] Ironically, it would be Lincoln in only the next few months who would lead his colleagues in passing one of the most massive legislative programs—and spending sprees— in Illinois history.

Douglas's seat was just left of the platform from which Madison County's James Semple, whom Douglas helped elect House speaker a second time, managed the proceedings from the chamber's only armchair. Semple was something of a celebrity, a lowborn Kentuckian who had made his way into Illinois' political aristocracy. He had been a brigadier general during the Black Hawk war and afterward a tanner and lawyer. Tall and whiskered, he had entered the House in 1832 and quickly acquired his colleagues' respect as a knowledgeable gentleman.[12] While in Vandalia in 1834 for his own political purposes, Douglas had lobbied for Semple for speaker. In the days ahead, Semple would not forget Douglas's support, which elevated him to the speakership on the first ballot. It took seven ballots to elect the House doorkeeper.[13]

While members of the House and Senate spoke optimistically about the future of the state, rumors about relocating the state capital were stirring alarm among members of the Fayette County delegation and their constituents in Vandalia. Recognizing that the demographics of the young state were likely to continue to change, lawmakers in 1819 had mandated a review of the capital's location by 1839 to assure it was situated near the center of Illinois' population. Among the many who saw the rich gifts the law offered to those whose wit could win them were Douglas and Lincoln. This jewel, the capital, would foster the first legislative fight between them.

Joseph Duncan was in the middle of his first term as Illinois governor when the opening session of the Tenth General Assembly convened. Duncan was an imposing man. The six-feet-two-inch governor was a hero of the War of 1812. He moved to Illinois in 1808 and was elected to Congress in 1833. He was the only representative from the State of Illinois at the time. Although a relative newcomer to politics, having served just one term as a state senator between 1824 and 1826, Duncan had pulled off more than a victory. His win ended the political dynasty of Ninian Edwards in Illinois.

The eldest son of a Maryland farm family, Ninian Edwards moved to family-owned land in Kentucky before he was 20. Attracted to bluegrass law and politics, he was twice elected to the state legislature and won appointments to the Kentucky bench and the state supreme court. Henry Clay, who had been a U.S. senator, recommended to President James Madison that Edwards, although only 32 years old, be appointed governor of the Illinois territory when it was carved out of the Indiana Territory on March 1, 1809. Madison concurred, and for the next decade Edwards guided the territorial government until Illinois was granted statehood on December 3, 1818. On Illinois' admission as the 21st state in the Union, Edwards was elected to the U.S. Senate, served six years, and in 1826 was elected the third governor of Illinois.

Overall, Edwards could claim a good record of public service. He personally guided the territory through dark days during the War of 1812, to all accounts succeeded in his responsibilities as territorial governor to manage the salines of Illinois, and was credited with decisive leadership. His last actions were in public service, caring for his St. Clair County neighbors during the cholera epidemic in 1833.

As governor of the Illinois territory, Edwards had the power to configure new counties and appoint their leaders. He chose instead to allow the residents of new counties to elect their civic and militia leaders. He believed in the "good sense and justice of the people." He worried, however, that "violent parties" had developed in the territory by which "political controversies had degenerated into personal animosities of the most rancorous and vindictive nature."

He swore not to participate in them.

"I determined to risk the whole combined opposition of both parties rather than yield myself up to the control or enlist under the banners of either," Edwards resolved. Parties were evidence of demagogues operating in political society, operating out of self interest instead of the public good, he believed: "I will never admit that one, two, or three or more persons shall exercise the right and claim the privilege of giving life, shape, motion and effect to public opinion, where I am concerned. My appeal shall always be to the people; and at the same time that I most firmly declare that I never will yield to mere popular clamor, resulting from popular delusion artfully produced."[14]

Yet, Edwards himself and the so-called "Edwards Dynasty" defined politics in the first ten years of Illinois history. During Illinois' territorial stage, politics were categorized as either of the "Edwards" or "anti-Edwards" faction. Initiatives rarely involved matters of principle, nearly always related to personnel matters.

"Measures in their politics acquired importance only as they might favor the political fortunes of a friend or hinder those of an enemy," wrote historian Theodore Calvin Pease. "Usually active only when senatorships and other desirable offices were to be voted for, the rival groups in many, perhaps most, cases did not carry their feuds into elections for the legislature, letting the local influence of the candidates, and local maneuvers determine the issue."[15]

The Edwards party claimed men of strong influence and ability among its members. One was Edwards's cousin Nathaniel Pope, who had served as the Illinois territory's first secretary, its representative in Congress, and was now a federal judge. While in Congress, Pope on January 16, 1818, introduced the measure that sought statehood for the Illinois Territory, and the House referred it to the committee he chaired. It was Pope who won the approval of Congress to extend the state's northern boundary to forty-two degrees and thirty minutes latitude. That connected Illinois to the East by way of Lake Michigan and would make Chicago part of Illinois. The two houses of Congress passed Pope's statehood bill, which President James Monroe signed on April 18, 1818.

Another member of the Edwards Party was Pope's nephew, Daniel Pope Cook, who had married Edwards's daughter. Several others were Edwards's fellow investors in the Edwardsville Bank—in the community named for Edwards—and several real estate ventures. In an unwanted exchange of seats—and unfortuitously for Edwards and Cook—Edwards helped his son-in-law Daniel Cook defeat John McLean for Congress. McLean was then elected to fill the Senate seat that Edwards had vacated. McLean, because he was not pleased with the treatment Edwards accorded him, became a leader of the anti–Edwards Party. Democratic-Republicans Shadrach Bond, the state's first governor, and Jesse B. Thomas, who served with Edwards in the U.S. Senate from 1818 to 1829, joined McLean in the anti–Edwards group.

Although Joseph Duncan had not been associated with either group, the McLean anti–Edwards group recruited the war hero to run against Daniel Pope Cook for Congress. A former attorney general of the Illinois territory, Cook in his talents, sincerity, and kindliness won election to Congress in 1819 and re-election three times against McLean, who remained the powerful speaker of the Illinois House, Elias Kent Kane, Illinois first secretary of state, and Shadrach Bond. In the same charming manner by which he won the affections of the people of Illinois, Cook gained a high reputation in Congress and, with support of Southern men in the House, became chairman of the powerful Ways and Means Committee, in which revenue bills were passed or stifled. It was from that position that Cook persuaded Congress to donate 300,000 acres of federal land for the construction of the Illinois-Michigan Canal.

Yet, as esteemed as Daniel Pope Cook had been, his preference for John Quincy Adams over Andrew Jackson in the 1824 presidential election made him vulnerable in Illinois. In addition, Illinoisans had come to resent the sense of entitlement to public office exhibited by members of the "Edwards dynasty." At just this moment, Cook's father-in-law, Ninian Edwards, was seeking public office again. The aristocratic Edwards campaign did not connect with the rougher, white male Illinoisans who would vote. Edwards canvassed in fine-twilled fabrics, short pantaloons, high stockings, and freshly blackened boots. His arrival in a brougham driven by a black man drew more attention than his florid speeches.[16]

Duncan was an obscure state senator, but he would benefit from Cook's misjudgment in the 1824 presidential election.[17] Duncan had the credentials to appeal to the state's larger population of Jacksonians. He was a military hero, he was from the South, and he was a whole-hog Jackson man. That was enough for most Illinoisans. On Election Day on August 7, 1826, voters elevated Duncan over Cook by a margin of 12 percentage points, 6,322 votes to 5,619.[18] For the first time in sixteen years, Ninian Edwards found himself outside the doors of public office. It was just the beginning of tough times for Edwards, whose bank and land ventures sustained reversals.[19]

Just because Duncan had been elected a Jacksonian[20] did not mean he could not enjoy the perquisites of his new office offered by partisans on the other side. These included dining at the White House at the invitation of Andrew Jackson's political adversary, the National Republican (anti–Jackson) president John Quincy Adams. Duncan was a frequent dinner guest of President Adams. It was at the White House on one such occasion that he met Elizabeth Caldwell Smith of New York. Two feet shorter than Duncan, Smith was uncertain about the congressman. When Duncan asked her for her hand, it was Adams's secretary of state Henry Clay, often seated next to her at dinner, who interceded.[21] He encouraged Smith to accept. She did, and the couple was married in May 13, 1828. They left for Illinois two weeks later. Congressman and Mrs. Duncan relocated their residence from Southern Illinois to Jacksonville on August 1, 1830.[22]

Duncan's affection for the president waned as time progressed. He split with Jackson when he reneged on what Duncan believed had been a personal promise by the president for a civil service in government—to remove federal appointees only in cases of malfeasance or electioneering in office.[23] Duncan also opposed Jackson's suspension of the United States Bank as the government's fiscal agent as well as the president's rejection of improvements along the Illinois River and Illinois' Lake Michigan border. And Duncan strongly disagreed with Jackson's selection of New York Governor Martin Van Buren as his running mate in 1832. As did many Democrats, Duncan viewed Jackson's appointment of Van Buren as abandoning the West. With the disappointments having mounted up, Duncan left the Congress in the middle of his term to run for Illinois governor. He was elected in 1834.[24] Duncan said he never disliked Jackson. His votes against the president, he explained, were never because he had changed his position but because the president had changed his.[25] Duncan blamed Jackson's "Kitchen Cabinet" for the president's wayward decisions. He believed that the unofficial advisors with whom Jackson had surrounded himself were doing the president great disservice.[26]

Duncan in his inaugural message disclosed an interest in policies that took on the color of the Whig robe. He proposed state involvement in banks, even though the collapse of the state bank four years earlier had left the state holding $100,000 in debt.[27] Despite that experience and the Democracy's philosophical aversion to banks, Duncan was persuasive enough to get the legislature to consider a measure revitalizing state-controlled banks in Illinois.

Although several Democrats were determined not to vote for a system of soft currency, others, including Stephen Douglas, joined Whigs in favor of the idea. Douglas was not a member of the legislature at the time. He came to Vandalia for personal reasons: to meet with Supreme Court Justice Samuel Drake Lockwood to be licensed to practice law. While there, however, he recognized another opportunity. He imposed himself into the capital's "Third House," or "Lobby," which had been organized by J.W. Whitney of Quincy, who was called "Lord Coke." Unrestrained by House and Senate rules of decorum, speakers in the lobby could be as influential as legislators in discussing issues on the official agenda of the two chambers. Douglas's affable personality, grasp of all manner of facts, and reasoning won him favor in the lobby. There he supported the governor's plans for a state bank. It was not heresy for Douglas the Jacksonian to do so. In 1833, President Jackson had stopped the deposit of federal funds in the Bank of the United States and ordered them deposited in state banks. Douglas's logic fitted the president's. And Douglas agreed with views circulating in Vandalia that federal funds retained by Illinois banks, even if it meant the issuance of notes, would contribute to a healthier economy in the state.

When the proposal on the bank came to a vote, it won by a single vote. It took a great deal of "possum fat"[28] to get it done. It was not a party-line vote. A Southern Illinois senator who had been openly hostile to banks gave his support in exchange for help with his bill to tax land in the military tract to force non-resident owners to contribute to improvements.[29] A Central Illinois legislator, who told colleagues he would not support any state bank—unless his area of the state got some consideration— switched his vote when an amendment moved the bank's headquarters from Alton to Springfield.[30]

Democrats and Whigs alike were persuaded to lay partisanship aside "and all go, at least once, for the good of the country." That clause reflected the well-taken cynicism of Thomas Ford, who would become governor eight years later. Ford added to it, "Whenever I have heard this cry since, I have always suspected that some great mischief was to be done for which no party desired to be responsible to the people."[31]

Ford was astonished at the amount of self-interest in the bank issue. In his *History of Illinois*, he wondered whether the numerous favors that had been doled out to secure approval of the state bank would ever become known. Some did. For his vote, Senator Thomas Mather of Kaskaskia, who had previously opposed the bank, became president of the State Bank in Springfield. Senators Benjamin Bond of Clinton County, William Davidson, Cyrus Edwards of Madison County, Henry Mills of Carroll County, William Thomas of Morgan County and Archibald Williams of Adams County became bank presidents or branch directors, while continuing to serve in the Senate. Eight representatives who voted for the bank became directors.[32] Ford was aware that there was one more individual who had sought and received personal gain for his efforts in behalf of the state bank. The governor wrote, "That State Bank charter was passed in the House of Representatives by a majority of one vote; so that it may be said that making of a state's attorney made a State Bank."[33]

Ford never divulged the name of the man who "made a State Bank." John Todd Stuart, however, was not so reticent. Stuart revealed that the man was Stephen A. Douglas.

"Douglas was elected States Attorney over Hardin in order to get the vote to pass the Bank Bill," said Stuart who, as a state representative at the time the bank bill passed, would have known.[34]

Douglas was riding the first judicial circuit as a prosecuting attorney when the effects of the bank issue came to the forefront. He explained to his brother-in-law why he supported the bank bill.

"Capitalists are rushing in from all quarters to take our Bank stock which it is supposed will be very profittable [sic]. The stock [has] all been taken and the Bank will soon go into operation," Douglas predicted.[35]

Although he saw the subscriptions for the bank stock as signs of growth and prosperity in Illinois, Douglas made it clear that he remained a Jacksonian on banks. He explained:

> Here I must remark by way of explanation that I am no friend to the Banking System but on the contrary am in favor of the real Bentonian Shiners; But under existing circumstances a bank may be necessary in this State in self defense. We collect in the State about seven hundred thousand dollars of Public moneys at the Land Officers [sic] which together with a like sum from Missouri is deposited in the Bank of Kentucky at Louisville and from that place distributed again to the Indian Agents & the Officers of the Army. It was in view of the Public Deposits and Disbursement of Public moneys that our State Bank was established. It is not allowed to issue notes under five dollars, and after a certain period may be restricted to ten.[36]

The law capitalized a state-banking corporation at $1.5 million with an allowance for its increase to $2.5 million. Although the bank's charter gave preference to Illinoisans for the subscription for stock, schemes by four of the top five investors, including Senator Mather, who became the bank's president when it began operating in 1835, obtained controlling interest. The law had sought to prohibit large stockholders from controlling the bank by specifying a mechanism that lowered the number of proxies a stockholder could exercise as the number of shares he owned increased. The Mather combine got around this provision. They dispatched agents around the state who obtained grants of thousands of powers of attorney from people under whose name the combine's shares were then subscribed. The grantors never paid for the stock and never knew that their subscriptions made them bank owners.[37]

Among Mather's co-conspirators was John Tillson of Hillsboro, who had arrived in Edwardsville, Illinois, in 1819 as a land agent for Dr. Benjamin Shurtleff of Massachusetts. Tillson would buy thousands of acres in the Military Tract, land between the Illinois and Mississippi rivers in Western Illinois that Congress had set aside as bounty for veterans of the War of 1812. In addition to making Shurtleff wealthy, Tillson himself would become the second largest landholder in Illinois. By 1835 his land holdings totaled 2,651-quarter sections—424,160 acres, or 12 percent of the tract.[38]

Also involved in the bank scheme were Alton businessmen Benjamin Godfrey and Winthrop S. Gilman, who were heavily invested in the lead mines at Galena in northwestern Illinois. The Gilman firm's bank holdings were large enough that it alone could control the board.

Another was Samuel Wiggins, a Cincinnati financier and perennial player in Illinois finances. Wiggins in 1831 had personally bailed out the state, which faced an obligation to redeem the first state bank's heavily discounted notes at full face value in hard money. Legislators up to that time had ignored their duty, which required levying taxes to pay the notes to avoid the wrath of their constituents. There had been a source of funds—a common school fund into which federal dollars had been deposited—from which they might have borrowed to pay the notes. But with languid interest in education in Illinois at the time, the spendthrift General Assembly already had spent those dollars elsewhere and had evidenced no interest in repaying them. With no way to cover the call on the 1821 bank notes, the legislature authorized borrowing $100,000 from Wiggins, who had acquired a sizable number of the depreciated notes himself. The state's honor may have been saved, Governor Ford noted, but the public damned the legislature.[39]

"This loan was for a long time unpopular in many sections of the State," observers noted, "where it was currently believed, it is said, that the State was sold to Wiggins."[40]

The cost of Wiggins's loan was estimated at between $300,000 and $500,000, which went into the pockets of Wiggins and his associates—all at taxpayers' expense.[41] The cost was still a drag on state resources when Douglas in 1834 pushed in the statehouse lobby for Duncan's bank bill.

In direct violation of the bank law, the four private capitalists obtained most of the money to subscribe in the bank's stock from out-of-state investors. When Justice Theophilus Smith, the only Democrat and public office holder among the five largest holders, learned how his partners had obtained their positions, he moved that state subscription holders be preferred over those living outside Illinois and that proxy holders swear as to the residences of the share owners. The Mather combine, which would not be able to so swear to such an oath, got Justice Smith's proposal defeated, then united against him.[42]

Considered Alton's most enterprising merchants, Godfrey Gilman & Company's goal was to transfer control of lead from St. Louis on the west side of the Mississippi River to Alton directly east. St. Louis also served as the commercial port for shipments of commodities like pork, beef, wheat, and flour and as the center of trade for consumer goods from the east. Godfrey Gilman's interest was to make Alton a viable competitor for that business.[43]

Controlling the new bank, principals of Godfrey Gilman negotiated a loan of $800,000 to mount an attempt to corner the market in lead. Prices rose swiftly in the first few months. When the corner collapsed, Godfrey Gilman & Company collapsed with it. With Godfrey Gilman's demise, the loan failed. With carrying charges, the debt amounted to $1 million. It was the beginning of the end of the state bank, but Illinoisans would not find out about it for two years.[44]

Responding to threats that the state capital might be moved, Vandalia was in the midst of completing a new state house before the arrival of the Tenth General Assembly in December 1835. It would be Vandalia's third capitol building in fifteen years. The Second and Third General Assembly met in the first building, a frame structure destroyed by fire in 1823. Members of the next six general assemblies worked on sagging floors and rain-soaked plaster drooping from ceilings and bulging from walls in the second building, which Vandalians built from the shell of a burned-out brick bank building.[45] This third building turned out to be even more of a fiasco, which became evident more quickly. Examining the west end of the second floor, where the House was to meet, State Representative Douglas and his legislative colleagues, newly arrived for the start of the Tenth General Assembly's first session, found the building unfinished. The plaster still was damp and furnishings were largely holdovers from the older building. Worse, the House chamber was only slightly larger than the previous one. Planners failed to account for the growth in the House's membership, which came with the state's continuing growth in population. That growth was monumental. The number of the peoples' representatives had grown by nearly 70 percent—from fifty-three to ninety—in the two years between the Ninth and Tenth general assemblies alone.[46] It was just one more condition that

Douglas practiced his earliest political intrigue at the second state capitol in Vandalia. He found that political power resided in the legislative branch of Illinois government. With that knowledge, he cast from office one of the state's most powerful politicians and won his first political office (courtesy Abraham Lincoln Presidential Library and Museum).

would work against Vandalia's hope to keep the capital and work for those, including nine legislators from Sangamon County, looking for reasons to move it.[47]

At mid-afternoon on December 9, 1836, Secretary of State Alexander Pope Field delivered to the clerk of the Illinois House the governor's midterm message. It began exuberantly, glorifying the prospects of Illinois. With enterprising citizens reaping the rewards of their labors, the nation was enjoying "the full tide of prosperity." In the progress of their own state, the governor said, "her Representatives may look with becoming exultation." People were pouring in and settling Illinois' vast prairies, increasing its wealth, and promising a greater destiny. Abundant crops and high pay for labor were filling the coffers of mechanic and farmer, he said.[48]

The governor spent the balance of the first half of his speech discussing practical matters. He called for the state to have a stake in the capital stock of all canals and railroads to assure internal improvements, for which state residents were anxious, would get done. He called for

- amendments to the Revenue Law to have the state bank assume the costs of the Wiggins loan.
- funding for public education, without which "man becomes a savage."
- the state to subscribe to the stock reserved by charter of the state bank and an ambivalent support for paper currency to increase capital flowing in the state's economy.
- assuring a well organized and disciplined militia.[49]

It was the virulence of the second half of Duncan's message that caught House Democrats unaware. Duncan attacked President Jackson's administration, enraging Democrats, none more than Douglas. The freshman legislator concluded at that moment that Duncan, who was a good twelve inches taller than he, was a traitor to the Democracy. Douglas actually had an even greater, more personal reason for contempt. In a letter to brother-in-law Granger, Douglas revealed his belief that Duncan had worked against him and had worked instead for the Jacksonville Whig John Hardin in the recent legislative race.[50]

The acrimony between the two men should have come as no surprise to Douglas. After all, Douglas had upset the relationship between Duncan and Hardin. It was common knowledge that Douglas had written and spearheaded the bill that changed the appointment process that railroaded Hardin out of public office and railroaded Douglas in. It also was offensive to Duncan's belief that governmental

Formerly a whole-hog Jacksonian, Congressman Joseph Duncan did not reveal that he had switched to the party of Henry Clay before he ran in absentia and was elected Illinois governor in 1834. Jacksonians, including Douglas, who had helped him, got even (courtesy Abraham Lincoln Presidential Library and Museum).

appointees should not be removed from office except for malfeasance or electioneering in office. Hardin had not been accused of doing either. If Douglas was aggravated about Duncan's helping Hardin, turnabout was fair play. Douglas had worked for Duncan's opponent for governor, William Kinney.[51]

This rising animosity between these two prominent public figures from Jacksonville had little traction elsewhere. Members of this General Assembly were focused on more important game. They were hell-bent to emulate other states in developing internal improvements. Douglas himself favored the idea. He was "anxious to see one [a public works program] of reasonable extent and expense adopted." But he believed that what the legislature was asked to approve was too extravagant.[52] Extravagance was of no concern to the delegation from Sangamon County. Douglas's conservative spending perspective would match him against one of the legislature's most respected Whigs—and bring him trouble with his own constituents.

8. The First Douglas-Lincoln Contest

ALMOST FROM THE TIME HE ARRIVED in Illinois Douglas took part in the "rage for Speculation in Lands." He wrote father-in-law Gehazi Granger that "fortune after fortune is made as it were by magic, by entering Lands at $1.25 per acre and selling them again at advanced prices. Without performing a particle of labour you might make four fold the money you now do off your farm by all your labor and industry."[1] Douglas also sent a series of letters to his brother-in-law about the money to be made in land speculation. Douglas told Julius Granger that Illinois offered numerous inducements for the businessman, but land offered the quicker road to profits. "You can lay out your money here to a good advantage in almost any kind of business," Douglas wrote. "The most money is made here in speculating in Lands, for which this year presents the finest opportunities that have ever been afforded in this State."

He pointed out that a "great portion" of land in northern Illinois would be up for sale at $1.25 per acre in June and he predicted its value would increase eightfold "in a short time."

"Towns were being laid out every few days, and lots sold for a mere trifle which soon becomes valuable," he told his family. Lots bought in "flourishing towns" were rising in value—even without improvements—as the towns grew.[2] It was no exaggeration. Between 1835 and 1837, some 500 towns were laid out in Illinois. So many land titles changed hands that surveyors found themselves unable to keep up—the reason that over in Sangamon County surveyor John Calhoun, a Democrat, hired Whig Abraham Lincoln of New Salem as his deputy.[3]

Douglas believed he knew the reason and he bragged effusively about it: "Illinois is the best Agricultural State in the Union; that it contains a greater quantity of good Land; that the Land is of a superior quality; that it presents a more regular, rolling, and beautiful surface; that the Timber and prairie are interspersed in better proportions; that it affords greater facilities for internal improvements; and that in short, Illinois possesses more natural advantages, and is destined to possess greater artificial and acquired advantages, than any other State in the Union or on the Globe."[4]

Douglas's first foray into land speculation was in 1836 after he learned that some settlers in the interior of Adams County were agitating to move the county seat from Quincy. By law, the county seat was to be situated near the county's geographical center. That should have eliminated Quincy, Adams County's westernmost community, from contention. But Quincy founders Willard Keyes and John Wood hoodwinked two state-appointed commissioners whose duty was to locate the county seat in accordance with the law.[5] Keyes guided commissioners Seymour Kellogg of Morgan County and David Dutton of Pike through bogs, briars, snake pits, and quicksand up to their horses' saddle girths to what he claimed was the center of the county. The spot was near "Burton Cave," infested by millions of bats and a blind albino creature in south Adams. By their return that evening, the commissioners were exhausted—and disgusted. As one local, who saw design in Keyes's plot, put it, the commissioners were "ripened to a result."[6]

Wood the next day led Kellogg and Dutton over a much more pleasant route to a spot Wood easily convinced them was "sufficiently central." There, Kellogg was only too happy to drive a stake and proclaim it at the center of Adams County and site of Adams's central government. Disgusted that the seat of his own county, Morgan, was named for Andrew Jackson, Kellogg advocated that Adams County's seat by named for President John Quincy Adams, Jackson's political nemesis. The name held.

Wood had misled the officials, ending at what would become Washington Park in the center of Quincy, just a half mile east of the riverfront—and 17.5 miles west of the county's center.[7] No one contested the location until agitation for a new courthouse in Quincy in 1834 rekindled memories of the law that required a central location for the county seat. The stir became strong enough that proponents for relocation got the legislature to order another set of commissioners to determine the center of the county and allow voters to ratify the location for county government. This time the commissioners' stake was driven into soil near the middle of Columbus Village. In an election in August 1835 voters selected Columbus over Quincy 618 votes to 492.

Douglas smelled opportunity.

On May 27, 1836, Douglas and four other land speculators, lawyers James Berdan and Dennis Rockwell of Jacksonville, and J.H. Pettit and S.S. Brooks, publishers of the *Illinois State Gazette* and *Jacksonville News*,[8] ran an advertisement in the *Bounty Land Register*, Quincy's first newspaper, for the "Sale of lots in Adamsburg the Geographical Center of Adams County, June 21, 1836." These speculators were selling the idea that their Adamsburg site, "beautifully situated on a high, gently rolling prairie," was at the exact center of the county, "most central, eligible and convenient for the permanent seat of justice." Commissioners had planted the stake in Columbus, the ad said, only because they had been unable to find the owners of the property Douglas and friends now promoted. But by this time powerful county residents already had lined up for Columbus behind lawyers Archibald Williams and Abraham Jonas and merchants Clement Nance and Timothy Castle. Douglas's Adamsburg venture did not get off the ground.[9] The dispute over the Adams County seat would continue for several years. And Douglas had not heard the last of it.

Douglas was speculating on his own in the Illinois Military Tract. Before the end of 1836 he had acquired nearly 700 acres in Cass County, whose east side was bordered by the Illinois River. He bought the land for an average of twenty-five cents an acre.[10] In the years to come, he would acquire significant amounts of land in Illinois—thousands of acres in Cook County in northern Illinois alone—and elsewhere.

Like the nation's, Illinois' economy was flourishing, and it was believed that the development of the state's economy a massive public works program could bring—along with the proceeds from federal land sales—would pay internal improvements' costs. Although President Jackson had vetoed the Second National Bank charter, his treasury secretary Levi Woodbury encouraged the states to create banks to supply the expected deficiency in currency. This helped mollify ill will Whigs felt toward the national administration. For those in the Illinois statehouse, it was a way to assure the continuation of credit they considered so fundamental to growth. For the Democrats, however, there remained the memory of the failures in 1821 of the state's banks. But Woodbury's pronouncement "inferred it to be the wish of Gen. Jackson's administration that state banks should be created ... and with this view, the democrats were now in favor of the creation of state banks."[11] It would, they believed, provide the credit needed to fund a massive program of public works, which was about to dwarf all other issues that would come before the legislature. After a decade of division, northern Illinois counties had won the legislature's approval for the construction of the Illinois and Michigan Canal. Now, the rest of the state wanted a share. The swelling number of petitions for improvements that were flooding into Vandalia from throughout Illinois also motivated lawmakers. Stephen Douglas, named to represent Morgan County at an internal improvements convention in Vandalia in early December 1836—just before the start of the Tenth General Assembly, was not so sure that the race to build massive public works was a reasonable one.

Up to that time, waterways had been the key to locations and economies of most Illinois communities. They provided the most effective ways for produce to reach markets and destinations for goods that were not made locally. Steam had furnished motive power for railroad engines, but to that time they had proved dangerous and unreliable. The railroads that existed in the early 1830s were typically small feeder lines that connected a town to the river ports, which were the real muscle of transportation. State and federal governments tended to support projects for canals, rivers and harbors. In the second half of the decade of the 1830s, however, technological and safety improvements had elevated the stature of railroads as transportation systems. Mania for railroad construction followed.[12]

There was a raging fever for public works in Illinois, fueled by speculation in western land and the distribution of surplus federal revenue in state banks that came from its sale. President Jackson had blessed the nation with that surplus by paying off the national debt in 1834. That put an end to the program of President Washington's treasury secretary Alexander Hamilton, which began with the central government's assumption of the states' revolutionary war debts, and by which Hamilton said debt could be beneficial, even if never paid off. If the carrying costs were regularly paid, the nation's creditworthiness would increase, attracting more capital, which could finance additional business and generate additional public and private revenues. It was the first effort at a central bank, which Hamilton believed would strengthen the currency, commerce, and economy of the nation.[13] Hamilton's opposite, President Washington's secretary of state Thomas Jefferson, was fully opposed to the idea, protesting that fluctuating interest rates could devalue a man's labor and lead to uncontrollable speculation. Jackson sided with Jefferson in this debate.

Blessed with a swelling federal treasury, Jackson already had sent $640,000 to Illinois for public projects that the dreamers there believed could propel their state into prosperity.[14] There was every reason to think that as more land was sold there would be more federal money pouring into the state's treasury. Although sales in the military tract had been slow for more than a decade,[15] President Jackson, once in office, encouraged expansion. *To expand the nation was to extend the area of freedom,* Jackson had said.[16] Soaring land sales followed the pioneering spirits westward.

Revenues flowing into the federal treasury from sources like those land sales had enabled the Jackson administration to flow surplus dollars to the states. In Illinois the windfall pulled the state out of debt and created a surplus in the state treasury. One to notice opportunity was Abraham Lincoln, who was seeking a second term as a state representative. He picked up on his constituents' interest in massive public works.

What had begun in 1830 with simple pleas for macadamized or layered rock roads around the state by 1832 had become loud outcries for canals and railroads. The state's population was swelling and new and existing towns were growing with it. With agricultural areas developing rapidly, there were appeals for transportation systems that would take surpluses grown by more productive farmers to more distant markets. These pleas were being heard.

Elected from Vermilion County in 1832, Representative Gurdon S. Hubbard promoted state development of the Illinois and Michigan Canal along 300,000 acres of right of way Congress had granted five years earlier for that purpose.[17] When the Senate defeated his proposal, Hubbard proposed construction of a railroad on the canal right of way.

Hubbard's railroad was not built.

From then on Hubbard focused on the canal, which with Lincoln and Douglas's help was authorized by the Tenth General Assembly. Douglas and Lincoln were among the House members who agreed with Hubbard's recommendation that the canal's terminus be in northern Illinois instead of a point at the mouth of the Calumet River at Indiana. Hubbard convinced Illinois friends of the Calumet route that a great city would grow at the end of the canal. That city should be in Illinois, Hubbard reasoned, since "the entire expense of construction would devolve upon our state." The argument was convincing, and the canal terminus was settled at the mouth of the Chicago River. Illinoisans have Hubbard to thank for his vision, which assured the preeminence of the City of Chicago.[18] Hubbard himself would make the most of it.

State Representative John Todd Stuart in 1835 kept a promise to Circuit Judge Sidney Breese of Southern Illinois to introduce a bill to organize a central railroad from the Illinois-Michigan canal at Peru to the southern end of the state at Cairo from which Southern markets would continue to be accessible when the northern rivers and canal were frozen over.[19] The bill failed on the House floor, but Stuart, with Lincoln now working with him, promised another try if Breese would help them get Governor Duncan to appoint their choices for the first commissioners of the Illinois-Michigan Canal. Stuart and Lincoln had their reasons. Both were promoting a state bank and a state capital at Springfield, for which votes from the four corners of the state were sought.

Breese kept his part of the bargain, and Stuart passed Breese's resurrected railroad bill.[20] Governor Duncan in 1835 appointed to the canal commission William B. Archer, one of the wealthiest farmers of eastern Illinois; William F. Thornton, a wealthy mercantilist from the east central town of Shelbyville who also got into banking and brokerage; and Hubbard, who had left the legislature and had moved to Chicago. Hubbard was frequently in Vandalia, however, to lobby for commercial development and general prosperity—including his own. There were advantages to be gained. Hubbard's canal-related gains came with the businesses he created. He built a massive warehouse, which housed the first freight that arrived in Chicago, entered a partnership that built the Eagle Line of ships serving the upper Great Lakes to Buffalo, and established the Hubbard & Co. forwarding and commission business. In a corner of the warehouse was an Illinois State Bank branch, the first bank in Chicago, of which Hubbard was a director. He wrote the first insurance policy in Chicago for the Aetna Company, which he continued to represent for more than thirty years.[21]

Agitation for internal improvements was becoming the all-absorbing subject of public discussion. After all, New York by 1835 had had a canal for ten years. Pennsylvania was digging

914 miles of canal and was operating 218 miles of rail line. Even Indiana was pushing internal improvements projects forward. Why should Illinois fall behind, its citizens asked.[22] Railroads, canals, navigable rivers and accessible harbors were subjects of booming speeches, subjects on which elections could turn.

The Eighth General Assembly had passed charters for the construction of 344 miles of rail for the Vincennes and Chicago Railroad, the Alton and Springfield, and the Jacksonville and Meredosia.

None was built.

That did not stop the public's demands. And it did not stop legislators from passing more bills. At a special session on December 7, 1835, legislators passed charters for 2,524 more miles of rail and canals.

None was built.

The Ninth General Assembly added another 569 miles of tracks in the following months. All together, legislators authorized charters for a total of 3,437 miles for twenty-four railroads and a 150-mile-long canal.[23]

None was built.

Yet, there was no stopping Illinoisans' stubborn quest for internal improvements. Conventions in the summer and fall of 1836 demanded improvements. A mass convention in Sangamon County instructed its legislators "to vote for a general system of internal improvements."[24] Similar mandates came from conventions in Adams, Macon, Schuyler and Tazewell Counties—and dozens of other places, as well.

County after county instructed their representatives to support such schemes, giving even thinking representatives little choice.[25] The "right (or doctrine) of instruction" was serious business for the sovereign people of Illinois. It was an order by constituents that directed the actions of their representatives, no matter how unwilling they might be. Representative John Hardin called obedience to such instructions fundamental to representative democracy: "I avowed myself the advocate of the republican doctrine of the 'right of instruction,' and have often stated that it was the duty of the representative to obey the will of his constituents."

Representatives who did not obey instructions were expected to resign.[26]

Abraham Lincoln recognized opportunity. Launching his re-election campaign in a letter to the editor of the *Sangamo Journal* on June 13, 1836, Lincoln promised to be guided by the will of his constituents or their best interests. That would include their desire for internal improvements. Lincoln's pledge was not exactly outright pandering. At least he suggested a way to pay for the projects.

"Whether elected or not," he wrote, "I go for distributing the proceeds of the sales of the public lands to the several states, to enable our state, in common with others, to dig canals and construct rail roads, without borrowing money and paying interest on it."[27]

The Tenth Illinois General Assembly convened on December 5, 1836. By that time, the statewide internal improvements convention, chaired by State Bank President Thomas Mather in Vandalia, had completed its work. For three days delegates from every corner of Illinois piled on railroad projects, canal projects, and rivers and harbors improvement projects. Sangamon County alone sent sixteen delegates to Vandalia to promote their interests in the convention.[28] The matter of public works was so magnetic that delegates had to meet in the House chambers, the only hall in Vandalia large enough to contain their numbers.

The multitude of projects was "commensurate with the wants of the people."[29] While delegates to the internal improvements convention agreed on the need for public works, few had any concern about how to pay for them. They made it clear they wanted the legislature to figure that out.[30] David Davis, a twenty-one-year-old lawyer from the Illinois River community of Pekin, was one of five delegates sent to Vandalia to obtain a charter for a railroad to the Wabash River one hundred miles away. Davis stayed in Vandalia for all six weeks of the First Session of the Tenth General Assembly. He described the place, overrun by clamorous delegates, as a "madhouse."[31] While there, however, he made an important friendship with Lincoln. It would flower for them on the Eighth Judicial Circuit first as lawyers then as Lincoln the lawyer and Davis the judge. That friendship ultimately placed Davis as manager of Lincoln's 1860 presidential campaign committee.

Newly elected state representative Stephen A. Douglas was among the delegates to the convention. Before his election, Douglas had taken advantage of the excitement among his constituents for internal improvements. He announced that he favored them without qualifying his meaning. Later, however, he would say that he meant improvements of "reasonable extent and expense."[32]

In his House seat, Douglas sensed the potential for disaster in the euphoria, and on December 14, 1836, the ninth day of the Tenth General Assembly's First Session, he introduced a resolution to have the House instruct the Committee on Internal Improvements to limit the number of projects it would recommend. He called for completion of the Illinois and Michigan Canal, construction of a railroad from the southern end of the canal to the Ohio River in Southern Illinois, construction of a railroad from the far west side of the state to the Wabash and Erie Canal on its east side, and improvements for navigation on the Illinois and Wabash Rivers. Douglas's resolution also called on the House to require that projects be cost-justified, a proposal entirely ignored in the orgy for public works that was about to follow. History has largely reported that Douglas was a promoter of public works. What has been largely unreported was his work to bring sanity to the all-out mania for them.

"When I learned the nature and extent of the bill which the Committee on Internal Improvements were maturing," he later recalled, "I attempted to arrest it by introducing resolutions by way of instructions setting forth the kind and extent of a system I thought ought to be adopted…. I was willing and anxious to make these three works on the faith of the State; but was unwilling to go further [sic]."[33]

But reason was no antidote for the fever for public works that had blinded the boosters in Illinois.

"I found the people perfectly insane on the subject of improvements," said Congressman John Reynolds, the former governor, on his return from Washington. "No reason or argument would reach them."[34]

What the people wanted was almost unfathomable to Douglas. Though he considered himself a man of the people, Douglas also had the sense that their dreams of prosperity could end in the state's financial ruin. The people wanted more than 3,200 miles of iron rails to link the corners of the state. They wanted a canal to connect Beardstown to Springfield. They wanted bridges to cross rivers and turnpikes to cut through rough prairies. The people wanted to widen and clear Illinois' rivers and streams and to deepen its harbors. The people—nearly every person was now a visionary—saw cities springing up from the state's rich black soil as fruitfully as maize stalks. The growth would attract new capital, they predicted, and stimulate even more growth. And even more capital.

Freshmen legislators generally were expected to be seen and not heard. But Douglas's work to organize the Democracy in Illinois and his successes in Vandalia—even before he had been elected to a seat in the capital there—gave him standing that few other elected representatives enjoyed. Freshman Douglas played one of the most prominent roles in the Tenth General Assembly. Before the assembly adjourned, Douglas had been named to eighteen special committees and served as chairman for seven of them. His attendance record was among the highest where votes were recorded. His absences usually were recorded at the beginning of the day or right after lunch. Douglas was not a clock watcher.[35] A contemporary noted that "Douglas's towering intellect and impressive eloquence had ... already placed him in the front ranks of Illinois politicians, and presaged his future brilliant career. The power of his great mind influenced State legislation, as it afterwards swayed the councils of the nation."[36]

By the beginning of his second term in 1836 Lincoln had become the leader of the new Whig organization in the House. He had told the *Sangamo Journal* during his campaign for office that his objective was to assure suffrage for all whites—"by no means excluding females"—who paid taxes or bore arms and to follow the will of his constituents "on all subjects upon which I have the means of knowing what their will is; and upon all others, I shall do what my own judgment teaches me will best advance their interests." As Lincoln had construed their interests, they wanted public works. Confident that the distribution of excess federal receipts could fund public works, Lincoln told a friend that he wanted to become "the DeWitt Clinton of Illinois."[37]

As the Tenth General Assembly convened, Lincoln strengthened his position by winning an appointment to the House Internal Improvements Committee. It was a strategic appointment. From there, he could help manage decisions on the public works that would make it to the floor of the House. Lincoln had some "possum grease," as well. Friends of internal improvements had given him $200 "to sustain and Maintain the Internal improvement policy as well as himself as its defender &c." The mania was so pervasive he found no need for the donation. Lincoln would give back all but seventy-five cents, explaining later to friend Joshua Speed, "I didn't Know how to Spend it."[38]

Although Douglas considered himself a Jacksonian Democrat, he was not an ideologue. He believed internal improvements would stimulate investment, but he sought to return his colleagues to a more realistic, smaller program. In a strategy designed to slow the snowball his Sangamon colleagues had begun rolling, Douglas on December 14 filed his resolutions to preempt all but five state-sponsored projects. His plan called for the projects to be built and owned by the state. The state's related debt would be amortized in installments as the work progressed. Douglas also proposed that lands granted the state for construction of the Illinois-Michigan Canal be sold from time to time and proceeds used to pay amounts due on the loans until tolls for the public improvements were sufficient to pay them. He left blank the amount to be earmarked for the projects.[39]

When the measures emerged from the House Internal Improvements Committee on January 9, 1837, an amount of $7.45 million had been filled in and a board of commissioners was proposed to oversee its spending. In its preamble, the committee acknowledged the reluctance of some members to engage the state in a public works program but responded that the public expectation would be disappointed if some system were not adopted during the present session.⁴⁰ The plan was prudent, and the committee's report detailed revenue sources to indicate it could be paid for within a reasonable period of time.⁴¹ It was clear, however, that the scope of Douglas's plan was not good enough for Representatives of the people—and a herd of lobbyists—from other locations in Illinois. At nightly meetings in Vandalia, "large numbers of interested parties" demanded more. One orator at Lord Coke's Lobby proclaimed that "a hundred million would not be too much to borrow and spend."⁴²

This statewide lust for projects—and how it might serve the interests of a certain Central Illinois community—was not lost on the seven state representatives and two state senators, the Long Nine of Sangamon County.⁴³ Led by the six-foot, four-inch Lincoln, they saw a once-in-a-lifetime chance in the enthusiasm for internal improvements to achieve their own goal: the removal of the state capital from Vandalia to Springfield in Sangamon County. The Sangamon men were aware that others had sensed the inevitability of a move of the state capital. At the top of that list was Governor Joseph Duncan.

Throughout his four terms in Congress Duncan was acquiring real estate in Illinois. He saw the same opportunity the Long Nine saw, although his reasons were entirely personal. Duncan and two business associates, John Taylor and Eli Blankenship of Sangamon County, bought 1,600 acres east of Springfield at precisely the geographic center of the state. They laid out a town they called Illiopolis and in time would issue lithographic maps depicting the community's future glory and put hundreds of lots on the market. A good number was sold. The partnership employed Jesse Kent to manage a hotel. History doubts its potential for success. When it burned down it was not rebuilt.⁴⁴ The Duncan group's intention was to make Illiopolis the capital of Illinois and in doing so earn a return on their prescient investment. They initially worked behind the scenes to profit themselves from a move of the capital to the acreage they had bought in a speculation that the capital would be located there.⁴⁵

Sangamon County's legislators did not wait for the deadline that required a review of the state capital's location by 1839. The lust for the benefits and privileges that state government could bring a community had begun in 1832, a full seven years early. When Duncan announced his candidacy for the governor's office in 1833, some Springfield businessmen, who had been eyeballing the prize, feared Jacksonville had similar ideas. A handbill appeared in Springfield that warned of ulterior motives in Duncan's candidacy.

> If Gen. Duncan is elected ... Springfield will lose all possible chance of becoming the seat of government.... He is for Jacksonville and he dare not desert it. His own personal [real estate] interests, to the probable amount of fifty thousand dollars, would secure his support to that place.... If Duncan is elected the hopes of Springfield will be destroyed.... Let us then as citizens of Sangamon, give our votes in such a manner as to promote our interests. Let us think it more important to secure the seat of government than to elect any man; and let us give our votes to the man, most likely to advance our own interests, by the defeat of Duncan.⁴⁶

The irony was that Duncan had no interest in promoting Jacksonville for the relocated seat of the government. He and his partners were promoting their private interests.

It did not take long for the members of the Ninth General Assembly to realize that the site of the state capital was going to be in play. City after city was nominated. Democratic senator Adam Snyder of Belleville sought to bring order by striking everything after the enacting clause of a bill that dealt with the capital's move and suggested Illinois voters decide the issue by referendum in August 1834. Snyder suggested that Alton, Jacksonville, Springfield and, Vandalia be included in the referendum. Snyder's amendment was adopted 16 to 10 after it was modified to include Peoria. Governor Duncan also managed to get the "Geographical Centre of the State," Illiopolis, added to the list.[47]

Results of the referendum were disappointing to the promoters of Springfield. They organized a countywide public meeting in January 1834 at which they commissioned delegates pledged to Springfield at a capital relocation convention in April in Rushville. Central Illinois delegates provided broad support for a resolution recommending that voters choose Springfield for the state capital. Yet, when the ballots in the August 4, 1834, referendum were counted, Springfield with 7,075 votes finished behind Alton (8,175 votes) and Vandalia (7,730 votes).[48]

The referendum demonstrated that Illinoisans were not ready to decide where to relocate the capital. In fact, a fourth of those who went to the polls did not vote on the relocation question. While some 32,771 voters cast ballots in the four-way race for governor, the number of individuals who voted in the capital-relocation referendum totaled 24,449.[49] In most cases, voters who stood to gain from having the benefits of the capital near them voted for their own cause—with one notable exception. Vandalians and their Fayette County neighbors who hoped to retain the capital cast 658 ballots for Vandalia. Only ten people elected other choices.[50] All but 36 of the 2,297 voters in Sangamon County voted for Springfield. The same was true for Alton, whose Madison County voters provided 1,292 of the 1,316 votes cast for the river community. The exception was Jacksonville, county seat of Morgan County. Morgan had the state's highest voter turnout in the election with 2,717, but only 662 voters participated in the referendum. They gave 414 votes to Springfield and 185 votes to Jacksonville. All but nine of the remaining votes went to Alton.[51] Although he had gotten Illiopolis included on the ballot, Duncan apparently did nothing further to promote his site after he was nominated for governor. Statewide, his "Geographical Center" received 273 votes. Voters in Morgan County gave Illiopolis only seven votes. His own candidacy fared better. Duncan won election, taking 53 percent of the 32,771 votes distributed among four candidates for governor.

There were several lessons that Douglas and Lincoln—both experts at analyzing polling results—and other political strategists could learn from the referendum:

1. Population density determined the outcome of the referendum in the three geographic regions of the state. While the state's population overall was moving northward, in Southern Illinois it also was shifting easterly. The result was that voters in the southernmost counties gave Vandalia—the approximate center of Southern Illinois—6,737 votes. Alton, a commercial center on the Mississippi River just fifty miles to the west, got 5,802 votes. Population was also the reason the handful of northern counties made northernmost Peoria the leading vote getter. In Central Illinois, Vermilion County on the east side, Morgan and Sangamon in the center, and Pike and Adams on the west, made Springfield the clear winner.[52]
2. These metrics confirmed that as population continued to shift, so would preferences for the capital's location.
3. Such an amorphous condition suggested to strategists that it would be better to lead public opinion than to wait for it to solidify.
4. It also would suggest that the legislature pick a central location once and for all and make it permanent.

5. Abundantly clear from the referendum was that there was no preference for Jacksonville anywhere in the state, including Jacksonville. The community received a total of 274 votes, or about 1 percent of the total votes cast and only 2 percent of the vote from throughout Central Illinois. Morgan County voters themselves gave 414 votes to Springfield and only 185 to their own community.[53] Stephen Douglas would be a member of the legislature when the capital relocation issue returned. Although the referendum would convince Douglas that his hometown of Jacksonville stood little chance to win the capital, he would not forsake even his handful of constituents who expected him to work to win the capital for their community. He voted for Jacksonville in each vote on the state capital's relocation.

These lessons did not go unnoticed by state legislators. When none of the communities got the required majority, they ignored the capital relocation matter until 1836, when the dilapidating condition of the capital building at Vandalia—legislators arrived to find laborers putting in stoves to hurry along plaster repairs made to the walls and ceilings of the chambers—and the arrival of the Long Nine precipitated action.[54]

9. A Scheme to Capture the Capital

IN 1836 FEW ILLINOIS COUNTIES had more than one or two representatives in the state General Assembly.[1] The largest delegations by far were Sangamon County's with nine and Morgan County's with eight.[2] Every legislator wanted public works for his district. But if he were to win a share of such public prizes, he would need to ally himself with enough members from other areas to assure his interests were included in the final package. The Long Nine was willing to accommodate—as long as the beneficiaries repaid with votes to relocate the state capital to Springfield. Lincoln and his Sangamon colleagues understood the numbers and their power as the state's largest delegation. They worked their colleagues day and night trading their votes for railroads, turnpikes, canals and bridges in exchange for votes for Springfield.[3] It was the largest logroll in state history.

"This delegation from the beginning of the session threw itself as a unit in support of or opposition to every local measure of interest, but never without a bargain for votes in return on the seat of government question," recalled Governor Thomas Ford in his *History of Illinois*. "By such means 'the long nine' rolled along like a snow-ball, gathering accessions of strength at every turn until they swelled up a considerable party for Springfield, which party they managed to take almost as a unit in favor of the internal improvement system, in return for which the active supporters of that system were to vote for Springfield to be the seat of government."[4]

As governor several years later, Ford would have to face the challenge of the state's near bankruptcy the internal improvements program had caused. The Long Nine's design to move the capital, Ford claimed, cost the state $6 million. Half that amount, he estimated, would have bought all the real estate in Springfield at the time.[5]

"By giving the seat of government to Springfield was the whole State bought up and bribed to approve the most senseless and disastrous policy which ever crippled the energies of a growing country," Ford said.

The state's credit had been exhausted in the accumulation of debt for internal improvements.[6] Lincoln, who in his announcement for a second legislative term had called for public land sales proceeds to pay for internal improvements, was less concerned about how the bill would be paid as the logrolling progressed. Someone else would have to deal with the costs.[7]

In his resolutions, Douglas recognized the value of public works but in moderation. His limited projects he believed were of general utility to the state.[8] He proposed they be built at state expense on debt that would be repaid from sales of lands along the canal. But the enthusiasm at Vandalia provided little chance for moderation. Within days, the internal improvement mania resulted in committees in each house devising a system of projects throughout the state. The committees "cheerfully dispensed with inquiry into costs."[9]

Douglas was apprehensive about how effective his measures would be to limit the package the Long Nine was pushing. Lincoln, leader of the opposition party and chairman of the

House Internal Improvements Committee, was pushing hard. The younger strategist of the two, Douglas sought a way to neutralize the political power of Lincoln and the delegation he led. He discovered it in Lincoln's own history of public life in New Salem.[10]

A lover of history with a mind for research and retention, Douglas discovered that since 1830 the people of Lincoln's New Salem district had circulated petitions to instruct the legislature to carve a new county out of the northwest side of Sangamon County. Similar petitions circulated two years later when Lincoln made his first run for the legislature. Lincoln promised his New Salem friends that, if elected, he would work to put them in a new county. Lincoln scholar Michael Burlingame believes that is the key reason that although Lincoln lost his first race for the legislature, he won 277 of the New Salem region's 300 votes.[11] Others in Sangamon County had little use for severing a section of strength. Working to win broader support from other areas of Sangamon County in 1834, Lincoln did not mention the division of the county in his second campaign for the legislature.[12]

Thomas Ford (above) and Douglas were appointed associate justices of the Illinois Supreme Court under the law Douglas initiated to pack the court with Democrats. Later winning election as governor, Ford saved the state from bankruptcy created by the success of the Sangamon County delegation, which brokered votes for public works to legislators who supported their effort to relocate the state capital to Springfield (courtesy Abraham Lincoln Presidential Library and Museum).

Douglas knew that Lincoln, who had won election in his second attempt for a seat in the legislature, had presented a petition to organize a new county during the first session of the 1834 General Assembly. The Committee on Petitions denied consideration. With land speculators since then buying sites to develop, the division of counties would become a key issue for legislators in the Tenth General Assembly.

With the tenth assembly seated in 1836, petitions again called for the division of Sangamon County. A more serious effort was demonstrated in the measure, which proposed Petersburg as county seat. The level of interest alarmed the Lincoln team, which had just begun work to relocate the state capital to Springfield. Partitioning Sangamon County would reduce the strength of the Sangamon delegation, then the largest in the legislature. The delegation's size reflected the county's huge size. At the time it included what later became the counties of Logan, Menard, part of Mason, and most of Christian Counties.

In his research Douglas discovered the interest of Lincoln's New Salem friends in separating from their neighbors to the southeast. And although Lincoln had promised to take up the cause, he did little in its pursuit. Douglas persuaded Speaker Semple to appoint him to the

House's Committee on Petitions, to which requests for new counties were referred. Semple did so, and on December 20, 1836, Douglas introduced a bill to create a new county out of Sangamon. A legislator for less than three weeks, he had begun leveraging his position against the more powerful Sangamon delegation and their internal improvements logrolling. If his first internal improvement bills, designed to stop the orgy for public works—if those bills failed, Douglas's second bill would enable the Morgan Democrat to bargain with the Sangamon delegation from another position.

Douglas's proposal to divide Sangamon County was a great dilemma for Lincoln. A new county, splitting off a chunk of Sangamon's population, would reduce Sangamon's representation—its strength—in the General Assembly. Douglas's own eight-member Morgan County delegation might then become the largest in the General Assembly. Lincoln's fear would be that this Little Giant would then have the strength to serve his own goal, which, as Lincoln had come to find out, was *to make Jacksonville the state capital.*

The Little Giant, to whom nature had been extraordinarily stingy in the length of his legs but had blessed with an unusually large head filled with intelligence, cunning, and towering confidence, had succeeded as few had done before. The Little Giant had thrown Abraham Lincoln over a barrel. If Lincoln took too strong a position for or against the new county, his constituents on either side of the issue might be just resentful enough to fulfill his fear of reducing the size of the Long Nine—by not returning him to the legislature in the next election. On the other hand, if the division of Sangamon County were successful, the Long Nine might be transformed into the Long Six or the Long Five—and their chance of winning that great prize, the relocation of the state capital to Springfield, could be lost if it were not passed in this session.[13] Douglas the gamesman knew that even the threat of trimming the delegation's size threatened the Sangamon delegation's plan.

But Abraham Lincoln had not gained his position without political acumen of his own. Lincoln knew it would be impolitic for him to fight Douglas's measure publicly. Although Lincoln was not on Douglas's committee, he drafted a minority report and persuaded Robert Stuart, a Tazewell County Whig and committee member, to introduce it. Since he was not from Douglas's Morgan or Lincoln's Sangamon County, Stuart would appear to be independent of any controversy that might rise to public attention.

The Lincoln-authored minority report laid out several problems with Douglas's bill. First, it claimed the petitions did not have the legal number of signatures the law required. Second, it said there was no proof that timely public notice had been provided. Third, it said there were 1,200 signatures on another petition against the creation of a new county.[14] Finally, and here Lincoln designed to reverse the tables on Douglas, the report contended Douglas had ignobly ignored petitions from his own constituents that Morgan County be split. It was a good trump card for Lincoln to play. What Lincoln most importantly lacked, however, was a strong member on Douglas's committee. Stuart was not.

As the Democratic chairman of a committee reporting to a Democratic House, Douglas had the upper hand. Drafting the response to the (Lincoln)-Stuart report, Douglas on December 20, 1836, reported for the Committee on Petitions that it had found a majority (1,500 to 1,200) of Sangamon voters had signed the petitions that had been presented for a new county. Douglas, of course, denied that Morgan voters had ever done so.[15] In a fine example of his maturing sophistry, Douglas told his House colleagues: "Anxious to conform as near [*sic*] as possible to the wishes of a majority of the citizens of Sangamon County, a majority of the committee have directed me to report a bill for the establishment of a new county, out of that part of Sangamon described in the petition. And for the purpose of avoiding all difficulties that might possibly arise, they have inserted a provision referring it to the voters of Sangamon County for their approval or disapproval."[16]

Sophistry or not, this last sentence—"they have inserted a provision referring it to the voters of Sangamon County ... for approval or disapproval"—is intriguing. Douglas's measure would remove the controversy over a fight he just might lose—there had been rumblings to sever western Morgan County—from the halls of the legislature by requiring that the voters themselves decide. Douglas would submit the question to the voters in his first call for popular sovereignty. Letting the voters decide would avoid difficulties that might arise between Douglas and Lincoln factions in the statehouse. Two decades before the ruckus Lincoln would raise about popular sovereignty in Douglas's Kansas-Nebraska Act, Abraham Lincoln saw this fundamental Jacksonian principle—*the will of the people is the will of God*— thrown directly at him.

Lincoln was incensed when Representative Usher F. Linder, a Charleston Democrat, opposed as too costly Lincoln's motion to spread Stuart's report on the House journal. Lincoln wanted his constituents to see "his" arguments, which might moderate Douglas's upper hand.[17] Linder said if Lincoln's delegation wanted their constituents to see the minority report they could pay to print it themselves. Lincoln called Linder's opposition discourteous and meddlesome, hinting that Linder's actual purpose was to damage Sangamon County's position on the capital's relocation.[18] Lincoln could do little more than hint about Linder's motives. Lincoln could not risk alienating a large segment of his constituents by adamantly opposing the county's division.

The Morgan County delegation's lone Whig and Lincoln ally John J. Hardin successfully fought off what Lincoln considered another discourteous move by Linder to strike out an agreed amendment that required Sangamon voters to approve the creation of a new county. Lincoln believed the majority of Sangamon voters would reject the proposal to split the county. Douglas continued to side with Lincoln to have voters decide on a new county.

Concerned that Linder's continuing attacks on the bill were weakening Sangamon's position, Lincoln moved to send Douglas's bill to a select committee. The House agreed and named Lincoln chairman. Reporting the bill out of his select committee the next day, Lincoln proposed that a county named Marshall be organized and announced that he could accept it as amended. What he did not say was that he had drafted most of the amendments.[19] The measure retained the provision to require Sangamon voters to approve a new county, again reflecting Lincoln's belief that if the bill passed and was signed by the governor, it would be voted down in Sangamon County. Linder tried and failed again to remove the referendum provision. The Democratic majority in the House adopted a single amendment—to name the county Van Buren instead of Marshall, then passed Douglas's bill to carve up Sangamon County with the requirement that voters approve the idea. When the measure reached the Senate, where there was no Douglas, however, the Long Nine's Archer Herndon (father of Lincoln's future law partner, Billy Herndon) rose against it. He managed to kill the bill.[20] By that time, Lincoln had bettered Douglas in their tactical battle. With more to risk in Morgan County than to gain from this political confrontation, Douglas was content to be satisfied with a draw.

Douglas had proven himself a master at "wire-pulling." Lincoln had proved as clearly that he was no slouch at it. While Douglas continued to oppose outright what he called "the mammoth bill" for internal improvements, its friends, as Douglas called them, were working his own territory back home to pressure him to support it. The Long Nine sent minions to Jacksonville, where they informed Douglas's constituents that their representative was not acting in their interests.[21] They organized a meeting in Jacksonville at which they agitated Morgan County's citizens to direct their state representatives to vote for the internal improvements.[22]

Though he called himself young and inexperienced, the twenty-three-year-old Douglas was savvy enough to recognize when the public was unwilling to be led.

"So strong was the current of popular feeling in its (internal improvements) favor that it was hazardous for any politician to oppose it," he recalled.

Proponents of the measure knew that Douglas—this whole hog Jacksonian—favored the Democracy's principle of the "doctrine of instruction." It was for Douglas the principle at the heart of Republican Democracy. A legislator's obligation was to act in the interests of his constituents, who could direct his actions if it appeared he was not doing so. It was the means by which a legislator's constituents could direct him in the way they wanted him to vote on a matter.

"Accordingly," Douglas would say, "the friends of the bill got up instructions ... I did not feel myself at liberty to disobey." Ever afterward, Douglas would respond to critics of his vote for internal improvements that his support "was the vote of my constituents and not my own."[23] But the nature of the response was more than simple sophistry. Douglas's nature was one of practical politics, not ideology. It was a nature, Douglas wrote of himself, that was tempered by a "determination never to seek more than he thought politically possible."[24] Douglas believed in the sovereignty of the people. The people governed their representatives. The statesman had the right—more, the obligation—to make a case to the people. If the people were unwilling to accept the case, they were not at fault. Either the statesman had failed to make his case or the sum of the people's mind transcended the thinking of their representative.

"For Douglas, the statesman was he who would 'adapt his laws to the wants, conditions, and interests of the people to be governed by them,'" Douglas believed. He was no doctrinaire politician, who was willing to put principle above what was practical at the time. "A wise man," he said, "always conforms his actions to a policy which he cannot prevent."[25] The objective of the pragmatic politician was to get the best deal he could at the time. Douglas's ethic was the fair deal.

The internal improvements debacle was a good lesson for Douglas— and his House colleague Abraham Lincoln. Lincoln had gone into office saying he would be guided in all matters by the will of his constituents. He was as good as his word. It was Lincoln's exertions that brought forth the session's schemes: railroads from Galena to the Ohio, from Alton to Shawneetown and to Mt. Carmel, from Quincy to the Wabash, Bloomington to Pekin, and Peoria to Warsaw; rivers: improvements for the Kaskaskia, the Illinois, Great Wabash and Little Wabash, the Rock; the canal: completion from Chicago to Peru. All of this was accomplished without a single survey of any route, a single cost estimate, engineering, or other review.[26]

No project was too great for the Long Nine to accept so long as the prize remained in view. Even communities that did not share in the largesse of the Long Nine's pot of projects got a piece of pork. The internal improvements measure provided $200,000 for counties not part of the grander schemes.

The cost of the Long Nine's legislative package of January 1837 continued to mount.[27] At the end of that fiscal year, state Treasurer John D. Whiteside announced to the General

Assembly that the treasury contained $92.15. Levi Davis, the state's Auditor of Public Accounts, reported that total annual revenue of the State amounted to $67,500. In little more than three weeks the State would be obligated to pay out $123,571.52, or nearly double that amount. The outlook was not good.

"There is no probability," Davis warned, "that, under existing laws, the revenue of the State will increase."

Davis suggested that because of the state's fiscal condition "there cannot be a doubt that there is an imperative necessity for a new and improved revenue system."[28]

Legislators knew Davis's plea was for taxes. They ignored Davis. And if Davis inferred the need for fiscal restraint, that was ignored as well. The introduction of bills and resolutions for new internal improvement projects continued. Legislators introduced bills totaling $800,000 for waterway improvements and railroads.[29] Whig leader Lincoln continued to support them. He may have regretted the monster that he had helped create, but as he told his colleagues in the House, "We are now so far advanced in a general system of internal improvements that, if we would, we cannot retreat from it, without disgrace and great loss." Lincoln continued to pin his hope for solvency by relying on revenue from federal land sales. He reported a resolution from the Finance Committee to ask the federal government to sell to the state all unsold land in Illinois at twenty-five cents an acre. Lincoln projected that the sale of that land would net $5 million to the federal government. The only question, Lincoln said, was whether the federal government would be willing to participate in the scheme. He thought there were good reasons for it to do so. It would receive as much as one-third of what it had paid for the entire Louisiana Territory and stop "expensive and vexatious legislation," which he estimated was costing the federal government a tenth of what it received from land sales.[30]

"Should there be no *probability* of the General Government accepting our proposal, still, it is believed no evil can follow the making of it," he said.[31] To Lincoln, there was no harm in trying.

Despite the unquestionable precipice ahead, there seemed to be no stopping the drive for public works in Illinois. In much the same words as Lincoln's, Douglas noted that events had flown far beyond his control. He could not ignore the passion of the people for public works.

"It must be remembered that at that day the people were for the system—almost enmasse," Douglas wrote defensively.

He would note later that if the legislature had accepted his scaled down version of internal improvements, Illinois would have roads and prosperity instead of a scheme that had cast the fiscal health and reputation of the state into chaos. "If a limited and reasonable system, such as I proposed, had been adopted, instead of the one which did pass, I have no doubt it would have been entirely completed at this time, would be useful to the State and sustained by the people."[32]

Some of Lincoln's acquaintances got the feeling that Lincoln felt similarly, but that Lincoln thought any price for the state capital was worth the cost.

"I was in Vandalia that winter and had a talk with Lincoln," recalled Springfield attorney Stephen Trigg Logan, Lincoln's second law partner. "I remember that I took him to task for voting for the internal improvements scheme. He seemed to acquiesce in the correctness of my views as I presented them to him. But he said he couldn't help himself—he had to vote for it in order to secure the removal here of the seat of government."[33]

Although he continued to oppose the size of the public works program, Douglas was persuaded to help draft the House Committee's final compromise bill. He believed it was the best that could be done given the strength of public opinion. And both he and Lincoln put great stock in the power of the public mind. Lincoln believed that was the nature of republicanism. Douglas believed it was the nature of democracy. Both believed in doing the people's will.

In accordance with his constituents' instructions, Douglas voted for the internal improvements program. His constituents had instructed him. Douglas, whose only dogma was the Democracy and whose personal political purpose was paramount, felt compelled by honor and Jacksonian doctrine to obey.[34]

Years later, then-U.S. Senator Douglas still was ambivalent about his part in the public works failures, still trying to divorce himself from them. His vote was the vote of his constituents, he continued to say. The people had not held him responsible. In his *History of Illinois*, Governor Ford provides the explanation: "It was a maxim with many politicians just to keep along even with the humor of the people, right or wrong.... The politician felt assured that if he supported a bad measure when it was popular or opposed a good one when it was unpopular he would never be called to account for it by the people.... In fact it is true that a public man will scarcely ever be forgiven for being right when the people are wrong."[35]

Although he favored completion of the Illinois-Michigan Canal,[36] Governor Duncan, along with the Council of Revision, vetoed the internal improvements measure when it reached him. The legislation became law. Duncan would find himself the victim of Governor Ford's maxim. An unforgiving public, which Ford had described, refused to re-elect Duncan. Douglas and Lincoln would prove the other side of the maxim. The voters of Illinois never exacted vengeance on either of them—or on the several other legislators who would go on to the elected offices in the State of Illinois or in the halls of Congress, or upper echelons of the military.

Douglas had poured his energies into other issues during the 1836 legislative session. In one instance, he maneuvered his way onto a House Select Committee to which a resolution by Representative David Nowlin of Monroe County had been referred. The resolution called for the sense of the House about "President Jackson and his many violations of the Constitution of the United States." Angered by Nowlin's insolence, Douglas pleaded with Speaker Semple to appoint him to the committee. Semple concurred. The measure did not see daylight.[37]

Douglas had won Semple's patronage after Douglas in 1836 actively promoted Semple's name to fill the vacancy in the U.S. Senate caused by the death of Illinois Territory scion and father of the first Illinois State Constitution, Elias Kent Kane.[38] In an effort to bolster his own position on the local ticket, Douglas wrote Semple that the Semple name would strengthen the party in Morgan County. Semple took Douglas up on the recommendation but was unsuccessful. Semple reached the Senate in late 1843 when Governor Thomas Ford appointed him to succeed Senator Samuel McRoberts, who died in office. Douglas would succeed Semple as Illinois' junior U.S. senator on December 13, 1846.

With Semple's and Douglas's influence in the Senate and the Illinois House, Judge Richard M. Young of Quincy won election by the legislature to the U.S. Senate in 1837.[39] The Democracy's victory was a surprise to Abraham Lincoln, who had been encouraging the candidacy of another Quincyan, Whig Archibald Williams, considered one of the state's brightest lawyers.[40] Lincoln had been optimistic, believing the Democrats had been struggling to find a suitable candidate for U.S. senator.

"The opposition men have no candidate of their own, and consequently they smile as complacently at the angry snarls of the contending Van Buren candidates and their respective friends, as the christian does at Satan's rage," Lincoln had observed. He calculated it "probable we shall ease their pains in a few days."[41]

Douglas's work negated Lincoln's. On the third ballot, Douglas's candidate prevailed over Lincoln's, 62 votes to 17. Four other candidates shared 44 votes.[42] Following the custom of his party, Young sponsored a banquet that evening for Democrats to celebrate his victory. Douglas was among the attendees and drank his share of the free-flowing bourbon and champagne. Toward the end of the celebration, Douglas and Democrat James Shields jumped onto the table and danced together up and down its full length. To shouts of approval, Douglas and Shields's antics destroyed the tableware. According to custom, the winning senator paid the bill, which totaled $600.[43] Young soon would pay his debt, as well, to Douglas. Once in Washington as U.S. senator, the grateful Young figured into the appointment by President Martin Van Buren on March 4, 1837, of Douglas as register of the federal land office in Springfield.

As chairman of the Committee on Petitions, Douglas was perturbed that the legislature was adjudicating divorces, a role he believed the constitution had reserved to the courts. Four petitions had been directed to his committee within the first few days after the session began. Douglas led his committee to recommend that the legislature end the practice. It was just as easy, certainly constitutional, to file petitions for divorce with the courts, where they belonged. The only reason people chose to file in the legislature, he said, was that they knew they had no grounds for divorce and the courts would turn them down.[44] His legislative colleagues in both houses agreed and passed Douglas's proposition to remove divorces from the legislature.[45]

Douglas stepped to the forefront of debates on two resolutions Governor Duncan sent to the General Assembly in January 1837. The first was bound to draw the ire of Morgan's foremost Jacksonian Democrat, who, like others of his party, was angered by Duncan's apostasy and attacks on Jackson. To Douglas, Duncan's message was guileful. The governor again condemned the fiscal policies of President Jackson. Unless Jackson ended his hostility toward the Bank, Duncan warned, "We shall ... have established a despotism more absolute than that of any civilized government in the world."[46]

The House responded to the governor's message by creating a select committee, to which Douglas engineered his appointment, to consider the governor's accusations that President Jackson had violated the Constitution.[47] Douglas was largely responsible for the committee's response and assigned one of his closest allies, Gallatin County Democrat John A. McClernand, to deliver the committee's report. It defended Jackson and attacked Duncan. Answering one of the governor's allegations, committee members reminded their colleagues that Duncan had been a member of Congress when Jackson allegedly committed the violations. The tables were turned: "Governor Duncan as a representative of the people of the State of Illinois, and as a 'faithful sentinel on the watch tower of liberty, [should] have sounded the tocsin of alarm.' But this he did not; on the contrary, he sanctioned the wrong, if such it was, by his silence."[48]

Jackson had done no more in the exercise of his authority than previous presidents. There was no reason to condemn him, the committee concluded.[49]

Whigs had enjoyed Duncan's attack against the president. They were not as sanguine as McClernand dismantled the governor's charges point by point. When the committee recommended resolutions to state that it was the sense of the legislature to approve President Jackson's administration and disavowing Duncan's criticisms, Whigs like Douglas's fellow Morgan County representative John Hardin disparaged the committee's work as a waste of the legislature's time. Hardin argued there were too many other important subjects and moved a series of resolutions designed to divert attention from the Select Committee's report. His motion to strike the Democratic resolutions, however, failed by a margin of better than two to one, 57 to 24.[50]

Rising from his seat, Douglas won Speaker Semple's recognition. Presented with the opportunity to make his first speech in the legislature—he had done plenty of speaking in the Lobby, Douglas was not about to lose the gift Whigs had handed Democrats to embarrass the men whose purpose had been to embarrass his president.

"I am prepared for one to meet the message in the spirit in which it was sent," Douglas said.[51]

How amusing, Douglas said, that the same men who forced a political issue on the General Assembly should now find it so useless. It was their own governor who had demanded an expression by the House on the matter. Democrats were only acting respectfully in responding to the governor's request for action, "although the character of the message itself may be such as to forfeit the respect of any party or portion of the people."

The gloves were off. Douglas attacked Duncan for submitting the resolutions "as a firebrand to produce strife and distraction among those who were known to be opposed to its principles. It was intended as a rallying point around which the sinking fortunes of a desperate political faction might be collected and kept together ready for the presidential contest four years hence. I cannot repress the honest indignation which so extraordinary a document is calculated to create in my breast. I wish to unmask its deformities; to expose its insidious designs, and send it forth to the people, that it may recoil on the heads of those who propagated it."[52]

Hardin tried to finesse an exit for Whigs, once again by seeking to change the subject. He suggested substitute resolutions to turn the House's attention to internal improvements and education. Douglas would not let the other partisans off that easily. Hardin's was "an artful political maneuver" to distance himself from the governor, Douglas chided.

"Gentlemen [like Hardin] now discover for the first time that their servile submission to the will of the Governor had placed them in an attitude which they little expected or desired," continued Douglas. "And hence their extreme anxiety to avoid the question by adding matters which had nothing to do with the subject." The people would not be duped, Douglas declared.[53]

Whigs did all they could to end the debate, but Democrats had pinned them too well to the wall. An attempt by Sangamon Whig Abraham Lincoln to table the question was beaten back. Voting next on McClernand's resolutions, the House sustained President Jackson and rebuked Governor Duncan.

The governor's second set of resolutions placed before the General Assembly the issue of human slavery. Indignation over slavery, which had flowered in the east, was making its way west. Douglas knew the missionaries in Jacksonville, who had brought with them the cause of liberty for blacks. Alarmed by the rising tide of anti-slavery sentiment, legislatures of Alabama, Connecticut, Mississippi, New York, and Virginia in 1836 asked Northern states to officially disapprove of anti-slavery agitation. Slavery was a domestic matter, the resolutions contended, which put it solely within the states' jurisdiction to handle. Others had no right to interfere with the states' sole right.

The resolutions were assigned to a joint legislative committee of the House and Senate on December 29, 1836. The General Assembly sought to state Illinois' public position on an issue that would set the stage for argument between Douglas and his colleague Lincoln for the remainder of their lives. For each of them, it would be the first political confrontation with the issue of slavery.

The institution of slavery had been planted early in the western side of the Indiana Territory, the side that would become Illinois. At several points in their territorial history, Indianans pleaded with Congress to repeal Article Six of the Northwest Ordinance, which prohibited slavery in the territory. When Congress refused, the territorial legislature in 1805 and 1807 passed laws to permit the use of indentures of unlimited duration to open entry to slaves under another name. Northerners pouring into the east side of the territory sought to separate themselves from slavery-by-euphemism and carved off the Illinois Territory in 1809. Indiana legislators repealed their indenture laws after the separation.

The largely Southern population in the new Illinois Territory grew alarmed by the influx of Easterners who made known they were opposed to slavery. As the number of anti-slavery settlers grew, the number of Southern settlers declined, drawn instead to territories like Missouri, which were not limited by the Northwest Ordinance.[54]

Illinoisans had been split over the issue of slavery. Since 1820 the nation had dealt with it by the work of Lincoln's "beau ideal of a statesman," U.S. Representative Henry Clay of Kentucky, who with the help of Illinois Senator Jesse B. Thomas, had crafted the Missouri Compromise. That compromise held slavery to the area below the base latitude 36° 30,' or the southern border, of the prospective state of Missouri. The South had agreed to the limit on the basis of an unwritten agreement that the number of slave and free states in the Union would be equal. Thomas crafted that unwritten rule. At the instigation of Ninian Edwards, Illinois' territorial governor, Thomas as chairman of the Senate Committee on territories combined the bills so that Maine and Missouri would be brought into the union together.[55] Up to this time the measure had quieted southern agitation over the extension of slavery into the nation's territories, even if, as Southerners like John C. Calhoun contended, the provisions violated the principle of "equal footing" by which any entering states would be on an equal footing with the original states. By one of fate's great ironies, another U.S. senator from Illinois, Stephen Douglas, would disassemble Thomas's work. It would tear apart parties and union, which Thomas had pieced together.

Now, Governor Duncan had brought to the attention of the Illinois General Assembly complaints by the other states that were responding to renewed agitation over slavery.[56] On December 30, 1836, the seven-member joint committee responded with a report and resolutions that denounced abolition, denied that the national government had any right to control the institution in states in which it existed, and denied the ability to abolish it in Washington, D.C. Two Quincyans delivered the report, Whig senator Orville Hickman Browning, who drafted the resolutions, and Democrat James H. Ralston in the House.

In the report, Ralston and his colleagues contended abolition would be disastrous to slaves. They recommended the return of runaways to their own land where, with morals and intelligence improved, they could "scatter there the blessings of liberty, of learning and of religion." It was the committee's logic that Providence had worked through the agency of slavery to lift the black man from his wretched condition in Africa in contemplation of a nation of freemen enjoying peace and security on his return to his homeland.

"The intelligent slave himself, for such there are, instead of deploring his situation in

America as the most hopeless and degraded, rejoiced that his servitude was to be the precursor of freedom and happiness to his kindred beyond the Ocean," the committee reported.⁵⁷

Contrary to bringing the slave closer to freedom, the Select Committee contended, abolitionists were forging new fetters for the black man. Abolition excited and embittered citizens, aroused the passions of a monster mob, threatened rights of private property, would deluge the nation in blood, and rend the Union asunder. The South was no more to blame for slavery, the committee added, than the non-slaveholding states. It devolved to the present in the same spirit of amity by which the constitution had been created. "We would say in the language of the immortal Washington, 'let every violation of the Constitution be reprehended. If defective let it be amended, but not suffered to be trampled upon while it has an existence.' Whilst therefore we deeply deplore the condition of that unfortunate race of our fellow men whose lots are cast in thralldom, in a land of liberty and peace, we hold that the arm of Government has no power to strike their fetters from them. We are confident that an overwhelming majority of our fellow citizens [*sic*] would spurn indignantly, the man who would urge upon them an interference with the rights of property in other States."

The committee thought there was some importance in saying that its members were unaware that abolition had reached Illinois, nevertheless, the committee proposed three resolutions that

- disapproved of Abolition Societies.
- reaffirmed a state's rights to slavery under the federal constitution and denying any right to deprive a state of that right without its consent.
- denied the federal government had the power to abolish slavery within the District of Columbia without the approval of the district's white citizens.

These were matters on which Whigs and Democrats were unified. The House of Representatives passed the resolutions 77 to 6. In his first vote—and protest—against the agitation over slavery, Douglas voted with the majority.

In his first public action on slavery, Douglas's colleague Abraham Lincoln cast one of the six negative votes, which Lincoln left unexplained at the time. It was not until Lincoln had successfully orchestrated the move of the state capital from Vandalia to Springfield that he and Springfield Whig representative Dan Stone on Friday, March 3, 1837, three business days before the end of the legislative session, spread their protest upon the *Journal of the Illinois House of Representatives*. They could have felt slightly more at ease after February 23, when their colleagues resolved that it was imperative that the state's constitution be amended to prohibit domestic slavery within its boundaries.⁵⁸

Once Lincoln and Stone filed their protest on March 3, 1837, Douglas, if he gave it any consideration at all, might have wondered why all the fuss. The only apparent difference between the General Assembly's resolutions and the Lincoln-Stone protest was over whether Congress had the right to abolish slavery in the District of Columbia.⁵⁹

Although Lincoln and Stone rightfully have been praised for their belief that slavery was founded on both injustice and bad policy, it should not be interpreted to mean that they were mavericks on the issue in the General Assembly. While the Lincoln-Stone version might have been more precisely defined legalistically, the joint committee found deplorable the circumstances that had cast "our fellow men" into the "unfortunate condition" of slavery in a land founded on the basis of liberty and peace. The reference to peace signals that the committee's members considered slavery more than an aberration in a country built on freedom. In its juxtaposition with the term liberty, the committee drafters' use of the term peace implies they considered slavery a form of violence against humanity.

Concerned that the controversy could jeopardize the more important internal improvements legislation, the Illinois Senate on January 12, 1837, heard Browning out, and then tabled the resolutions ending any further action.[60]

10. Convening the Faithful

DOUGLAS HAD HIS OWN CONTROVERSY TO FACE—and in his own hometown—as the legislative session drew to a close. Jacksonville's *Illinois Patriot* newspaper on February 22, 1837, accused Douglas of making a deal with Lincoln and the Long Nine to trade his vote to move the capital for appointment to the lucrative office of register of the federal land office in Springfield. In a letter to the newspaper on March 8, just a day before the vote to move the capital, Douglas was clearly alarmed by the charge, challenging anyone who conveyed it, and strongly denying that he "had abandoned the interests of my own constituents and was acting in concert with the Sangamon delegation in supporting Springfield for the seat of government." If the capital was to be moved, Douglas had strongly promoted Jacksonville as the site and, in fact, had always voted in favor of Jacksonville. He would do so the following day.[1] Douglas pointed out that the recommendation for his appointment to register "was got up by my friends without my solicitation or knowledge." Not one member of the Sangamon delegation was among those friends, Douglas added. Douglas pointed out that his opposition to moving the capital to Springfield had hardly ingratiated him with the Sangamon delegation, who opposed him on most other legislative issues.[2]

Douglas wrote that there had been no arrangement or understanding about an exchange with the Sangamon delegation for the land office, the seat of government, or any measure. The record would show, he said, that in fact he had disagreed with the Sangamon men "on almost every important question that came before the Legislature, and more especially on the location of the seat of government, ... the all-absorbing topic with them.... To that bill I was opposed in every form and shape it assumed, from its first appearance in the House up to its final passage. My decided and uncompromising opposition to that bill, and the object intended to be accomplished by its passage, arrayed the Sangamon delegation *en masse* against me."[3]

The Long Nine and its friends were bringing the relocation of the Illinois state capital to a conclusion. Legislators dispensed with the results of the 1834 referendum in which Alton won a plurality in its bid to attract the state capitol. Legislators approved a bill by Lincoln's Quincy friend Orville Browning to make permanent the site chosen for relocation of the state capitol. Throughout the month of February, the Long Nine called in the favors they had amassed from the internal improvements package. On February 28, 1837, the Senate and House convened a joint session to vote on moving the state capital. On the first ballot, Springfield collected thirty-five votes, finishing first among nineteen communities seeking state government's seat. Although Jacksonville had finished last among the six communities offered as state capital locations in the 1834 referendum, Douglas had maneuvered his town into a position to be among the leading vote getters. On the first roll call, Jacksonville won fourteen votes, just behind Vandalia with sixteen and Alton with fourteen. Jacksonville tied with Vandalia with fifteen votes on the second ballot and dropped back to ten votes and fourth place on the third ballot when Springfield won fifty-three votes. By the fourth ballot, Springfield won seventy-three votes to gain the required votes. The speaker declared Springfield the duly elected seat of government of the State of Illinois.[4]

The House recessed until 2 p.m. That afternoon, the lid came off the internal improvements barrel. Legislators introduced a flood of new and amended projects, incorporating railroad, ferry, bridge, library, hotel, and numerous other companies. After dealing with dozens of House bills, the lower Chamber took up numerous Senate bills, which included more projects, a charter for a Machinists Union in Jacksonville, and relief for the infant heirs of the late James Woodside. Douglas voted for only one bill, an amendment the Senate attached to a bill on the Illinois-Michigan Canal. Late that afternoon, Representative Parvin Paullen of Pike County moved that the House recess until 7 p.m. John S. Turley of Shelby moved that the House adjourn. A quick vote dispatched Paullen's motion and the speaker adjourned the House until 9 a.m. the following day.[5]

Douglas worked state legislators to elect Judge Richard M. Young of Quincy to the U.S. Senate in 1837, which surprised Whig leader Lincoln, who had promoted the candidacy of Archibald Williams, another Quincyan (courtesy Historical Society of Quincy and Adams County).

Legislators might have been exhausted—but not enough to forego the celebration the victorious Sangamon delegation put on in Vandalia that night. Celebrants consumed eighty-one bottles of champagne, thirty-two pounds of almonds, eleven pounds of raisins, cigars, oysters, apples and other "eatables." Vandalia merchant Ebenezer Capps also billed the party two dollars for breakage. Ninian Wirt Edwards of Springfield paid the $223.50 bill for the party.[6]

It was at this time that U.S. Senator Richard M. Young paid his debt to Douglas by sponsoring his appointment to the federal land office in Springfield. Young had an additional motive. Aware of Douglas's growing reputation as the Illinois Democratic Party's leader, Young sought Douglas's help to thwart rumored senatorial ambitions of Democratic Congressman William May of Jacksonville.

The land office position promised multiple rewards to an ambitious appointee, as well. Federal registers were well compensated, receiving significantly better pay than a state legislator. Douglas could earn a salary of $500 per year and a commission of one percent of the value of land recorded. By law, the total commission was not to exceed $2,500 per year, and Douglas in his first year would earn the maximum allowed, $3,000.[7] Just as important to a man of political ambition was the ancillary opportunity for politicking the office provided. Douglas knew its importance. The state's second governor, Edward Coles, had launched his political career from his post as register of the land office at Kaskaskia. The year after Douglas's appointment as a federal land register, Thomas Carlin, register of the land office in Quincy, was elected Illinois governor.

From his position as register, Douglas could help Young in attacking May in the larger land office area of Central Illinois, most of which was within May's congressional district. Douglas's appointment was a fortuitous event that would incidentally lead to his new Democratic organization ousting the two-term congressman from office. Douglas's appointment as register came at an opportune time for him, as well. Taking office in April 1837, Douglas was able to avoid the wrath of the electorate against his former colleagues over the spectacular failures of the internal improvements measures passed a few months earlier. The public was blaming the policies and actions of Douglas's hero, Andrew Jackson, for the failures. Jackson on July 11, 1836, required that all federal land be paid for in gold or silver instead of bank notes. The effects of Jackson's "Specie Circular" in May 1836 reached Illinois in early 1837. Within months of passage of the internal improvements act, which would require massive infusions of credit, land sales sank, factories closed, and unemployment rose, values of stocks and commodities crashed, and economic depression was in full route.[8] Jackson's policies were initially praised by Illinoisans. After his veto of the recharter of the Second Bank of the United States, Jackson withdrew federal deposits and placed them in "pet banks," state-chartered banks favorable to Jackson. With no oversight or control by the U.S. bank, state banks opened the doors to borrowers on easy terms. Loans were largely going to speculative purchases of federal lands. What Jackson could give in easy credit, Jackson could take away in hard money. To slow down the speculation, his Species Circular required that federal land be paid for in specie instead of bank notes. This combination of forces has led most historians to lay the blame on Jackson for the Panic of 1837, which followed.

Economic historian Peter Temin's contra theory in *The Jacksonian Economy* holds that historians have been mistaken about the impact of President Jackson's fiscal policies. Temin argues that Jackson's veto of the Second U.S. Bank's charter, movement of government deposits to "pet banks," and the president's "Species Circular" did not launch the events that fostered the Panic of 1837. History has held that Jackson's veto eliminated the U.S. Bank's pseudo-role as a regulating central bank by deciding when to present for redemption in specie state bank liabilities, like state bank notes it held. Combined with Jackson's removal of government deposits from the U.S. Bank and placing them in "pet banks, bankers no longer had to be concerned about reserve ratios, specie, or currency ratio since there was no longer any oversight at the federal level to regulate or stabilize the currency. Uncontrolled, state banks expanded credit, which went not to real growth sectors of the economy like manufacturing, but to greatly increasing speculation in purchases of federal land, which soared. After it paid off the nation's debt with the resulting revenues, the Jackson administration chose to return excess federal revenue to the states. Illinois saw these funds as a foundation for financing its tidal wave of internal improvements. Historians also have held that Jackson reversed booming federal land sales and the wide-open credit policy of state banks that created them by issuing his "Specie Circular" in August 1836. It required buyers of federal land to pay in specie rather than bank notes. Temin demonstrates that arguments that one or a combination of these factors caused the Panic of 1837 are incorrect.[9]

Temin concludes that the actual causes of the panic are found in the Opium War involving Britain and China. In an exemplary use of hard data, he shows that the Opium War increased America's specie reserves more than enough to cover the nation's monetary expansion. Silver imports from Mexico and Latin America had provided silver specie for U.S. reserves. These imports had been balanced by outflows of silver to China until the mid–1830s, when the British introduced opium into the Chinese market. Since Americans had built up claims in Britain in the form of bills of exchange for the sale of cotton to the British, Americans could use the bills of exchange instead of exports of silver to pay for imports from China. This suited the Chinese, who, Temin writes, "abandoned their traditional desire for silver in favor of a demand for bills on London to buy opium from British India."[10] The net result was that silver imports subsequently swelled species in the United States and its monetary base.[11]

Although Jackson was no longer president in 1837, James Edwards, publisher of Jacksonville's *Illinois Patriot*, would write that he had predicted the failures in the economy and laid the blame at the door of Jackson's White House. While Brooks's *Jacksonville News* glorified every Jackson policy, Edwards had warned that Jackson's veto of the national bank had upset the stable engine that drove the country's economy.

"We have been led to look at the Utility of the *Bank* of the United States, especially in a community where no banking institution exists, and where no other notes are acceptable but those of this institution, and we have seen that it answered the purpose of a sound circulating medium," Edwards wrote. "The people have confidence in these notes, and appear the best satisfied when they have a great many of them."[12]

Although he had resigned from the legislature, Douglas returned to Vandalia on July 10, 1837, to attend the special session of the General Assembly Governor Duncan had called to deal with the results in Illinois of the nationwide economic Panic of 1837. Duncan, too, blamed President Jackson for them.

The chaos in the national economy had reached Illinois. As banks across the nation had done, Illinois banks in the spring of 1837 suspended specie payments since the Jackson pogrom had stopped redeeming state bank notes and required payments for federal land in gold or silver. Illinoisans had tried to get the Jackson administration to make the state bank a depository for United States specie. U.S. Treasury Secretary Levi Woodbury, a Democrat, however, was unwilling to help a state whose governor had turned coat against Andrew Jackson.[13]

This created a dilemma for Illinois' state bank. Under the law that created it, the state bank would be required to forfeit its charter if it refused specie payments for 60 days. Since large sums of money had been deposited in the state banks, which had been made the fiscal agent for the canal and railroads, the internal improvement program would fail with the revocation of the banks' charters. Addressing by message the returning legislators, Governor Duncan blamed Jackson for the mess and gave legislators a proposal for a way out. Duncan recommended repeal of the costly internal improvements program by turning over projects to private individuals and corporations who would build desired infrastructure with "suitable aid from the State."[14] Duncan also called for relief for the state bank. Legislators not only refused to repeal the internal improvements laws, they ignored the growing concern of many in the state and expanded public works projects by $800,000.[15] It was a major embarrassment for Duncan. But his plea for assistance for the bank did not go unheeded. Largely through the labors of second-term representative Abraham Lincoln, legislators suspended for a year the forfeiture of the state bank's charter by legalizing the suspension of species payments. The suspension was not revoked until 1841.[16]

Although Governor Duncan continued to blame President Jackson for the failure of the banks in Illinois, their failures were largely of the governor's own making. The state bank faced early trouble with the losses caused by the failure of Godfrey Gilman & Company, the largest subscriber in bank stock. The legislature had approved Duncan's proposal to increase the bank's capital stock by $2 million, all of it financed by the state. In addition, the state subscribed to $1 million of an additional $1.4 million capital infusion into the resuscitated Illinois Bank at Shawneetown.[17] That made the State of Illinois the majority holder of the capital in two insolvent banks. When added to the huge debt that was piling up for internal improvements in 1837, the condition of the state banks meant that Illinois was headed for financial disaster.

In Vandalia, Douglas found his old Democratic colleagues in desperation. They were feeling the antagonisms of their constituents not only as the local heirs of Jackson's fiscal policies but those of his successor, Martin Van Buren, as well. Van Buren had been inaugurated just four months earlier. His answer to the economic crisis was a sub-treasury plan by which the federal government would sever its relationship with the pet banks. The response was seen, even by Van Buren's friends, as desertion. The state's congressional delegation, whose members were all Democrats, opposed the idea.[18] Some of Illinois' Democratic legislators had gone so far as to bolt the party and align themselves with the Whigs.[19] Democrats had held the executive and legislative branches throughout the growing fiscal fiasco. The people were looking for answers—and retribution.

"If the Democrats did not bring about the present state of things, who did?" asked Springfield's *Sangamo Journal*.[20]

Douglas imposed himself into the fiasco. With the party of Jackson in deepening distress and major elections ahead in 1838, the twenty-four-year-old Douglas called together the Illinois legislature's Democratic members on July 27, 1837—his purpose to stop the disintegration of the party in Illinois. Douglas had a model that had proven its success. His Democratic organization in Morgan County had been effective—electing Democrats to five of six legislative seats just after he and S.S. Brooks had created it. He could point to that countywide victory and recommend the same type of organization to bolster the state's Democracy for the future. Douglas's fellow Democrats agreed and called the first statewide political convention to meet in Vandalia that December to nominate the party's candidates for state offices. They also created a statewide committee of 30 eminent Democrats, Douglas among them, to draft a broadside for publication throughout the state on political and financial affairs. Their work called on Democrats to reflect on which party advocated the "rights of the people" and which advocated "the privilege of Property."[21]

For the first time, also, the party appointed a state central committee, made up of five members from each congressional district who were to bring party policy and loyalty closer to the people.

At the same time, Douglas engineered his appointment to the chairmanship of the party convention. The convention was the center of the party's organizational apparatus at the time and used "committees of correspondence" to keep the party's view of issues alive in the counties. Douglas was soon to find himself engaged in such a task.

Illinois in 1837 was entitled to three congressmen. It was Representative William L. May's misfortune to represent the district in which Douglas resided. Like many of his Jacksonville neighbors, May had been born in Kentucky and took up politics soon after his arrival in Illinois. After a year as a Morgan County justice of the peace, May was elected a member of the Illinois House of Representatives and shortly afterward was appointed by President Jackson receiver of public moneys for the United States land office in Springfield. May succeeded Joseph Duncan in Congress when he left Washington in 1834. And just as Duncan had become disappointed with Jackson over fiscal policy, May parted with the Democratic administration for similar reasons. He believed that economic growth required the credit support of a national bank and regulation of state banks. Douglas, on the other hand, party man that he was, believed in Van Buren's sub-treasury proposal. It would separate the bank from government and require a hard money currency—gold and silver—only.

Before the creation of an Illinois Democratic organization, May could have expected to be returned to office by his party's electorate simply by announcing that he was running again. But his vote favoring the national bank had rendered him an apostate of the Democrats' Jacksonian principles. And now there was a party organization and Stephen Douglas was at its head. Douglas instructed May that to run as a Democrat he would have to be nominated by convention—like any other Democrat who wanted a position on the ballot—in accordance with the new rules of the party. Douglas's plan was to beat May in the convention.[22] May was flabbergasted, and he chose an unfortunate way to respond. He attacked Douglas personally. And brought Douglas's boss into it.

In a letter of September 15, 1837, to Treasury Secretary Levi Woodbury, May charged that Douglas, a federal employee, was "engaged in a political electioneering tour through his District in getting up [a] meeting of the voters to organize a Convention of delegates to nominate a Candidate for Congress who are to be pledged against [May]."[23]

Woodbury ordered Douglas to explain. Douglas acknowledged that he had travelled extensively in his land office district but explained it was related entirely to his official duties as the federal register. He was at a loss, he wrote Woodbury, to understand the grounds for May's charge, unless it was based on "a short paragraph in a late number of the Sangamo Journal an opposition paper in this Town which seizes every opportunity to impugn the notices, and misrepresent the acts of every member of the Democratic Party."[24]

Douglas gave Woodbury what he called the facts. Douglas wrote that May could have misunderstood that before his federal appointment Douglas had been devoting his energies to the unfinished business of his law practice, which took him throughout the fourteen-county Eighth Judicial Circuit.

"No political meetings were held and of course no delegates were appointed and pledged as stated by Mr. May, in any county that I was in during the time I was there," Douglas wrote, "nor have I attended or in any manner participated in the proceedings of any political meeting in Mr. May's District since I have held an Office under the General Government."

He suggested that May's charge was the "production of a suspicious jealous mind operated on by the slang of a petty newspaper managed and conducted for political and selfish purposes."[25]

In his response to Woodbury, of course, the register was stretching truth to its breaking point. Douglas was lying through his teeth. Nearly five months before the treasury secretary's inquiry about May's complaints, Douglas had been out lining up commitments for his own candidacy from delegates who would be attending the Democratic convention in Peoria that

November. He absolutely intended to take the nomination away from May.²⁶ Douglas had attended party conventions in Greene, Morgan, and Sangamon counties. At the Sangamon convention, Douglas not only won control of the delegation, but convinced its members to bind themselves to unitary voting at the convention. He convinced them that it was "the only safe and proper way of securing union and victory."²⁷

Then, there was this of August 12, 1837. Douglas wrote a letter that clearly implicated him in his attack on May. Responding to a letter from his friend Lewis Ross, a Fulton County, Illinois, lawyer, Douglas wrote: "In answer to your inquiry as to what I think of the difference between our Senator and representative in Congress, I will tell you frankly that I think there can be but one opinion upon the subject, and that is favorable to Judge Young and adverse to Col. May. The fact is our Party will never support Col. May again for Congress unless public sentiment takes a great change."²⁸

Douglas added, even more disingenuously, "*I am unable to say or even imagine who will be our Candidate for Congress.* I am decidedly in favor of a District Convention to nominate a Candidate, *and then let us all unite and elect him, be he who he may.*"²⁹

Douglas also worked to gently dissuade any notion that there might be other Democrats who would make attractive candidates. He modestly responded to an inquiry by Ross about whether Associate Justice Thomas Ford would answer a call to become a candidate. "As you suggest the name of Judge Ford, I will take occasion to say that there is no man in the District whom it would give me more pleasure to support than the Judge. *I am informed, however by his friends that he does not wish to run*, but is anxious to remain on the Bench."³⁰

Two exquisitely timed proposals arrived at this most opportune moment. The first indication that a sitting representative would be contested in his quest for re-election, the *Jacksonville News*, published by Douglas's friend S.S. Brooks, ran a list of Democrats Brooks believed qualified for the congressional seat. Brooks included Douglas's name on the list. Others were James Stephenson, the federal land register in Galena, and Sangamon County Surveyor John Calhoun of Springfield. This was the same John Calhoun who had hired Abraham Lincoln as his assistant. Considered a man of excellent mind and ranking second only to Douglas as a political debater, Calhoun keenly wanted the

Sangamon County Surveyor John Calhoun, a Jacksonian who once hired Abraham Lincoln as assistant county surveyor, met Douglas in Springfield and became one of Douglas's star protégés. In the years ahead, Calhoun as chairman of Kansas's Lecompton Constitutional Convention would play one of the most regrettable roles in Douglas's political career (courtesy Kansas State Historical Society).

party's nomination and had support from Democratic leaders unaware of Douglas's interest.[31] As bright as Calhoun was, however, he would remain only a stage player in Illinois Democratic politics. In Illinois, his party's leadership thought more of him than did the party's electorate—he served in more appointive offices than elective.[32] Within a decade, however, Calhoun would be at center stage in the great Kansas-Nebraska controversy that pitted his friend Douglas against James Buchanan, the 15th president of the United States, split sections, killed parties, and as Abraham Lincoln, as president-elect, said, was the proximate cause of the U.S. Civil War. Appointed Kansas Surveyor by President James Buchanan, Calhoun set himself up as Regent of the Kansas Territory and became chairman of the Lecompton Constitutional Convention. Douglas would learn in the decade of the 1850s that with friends like Calhoun, who was dubbed "Candlebox" Calhoun for hiding ballots in a wooden candle box, he had no need for enemies.

The *Illinois Republican*, a Democratic paper in Springfield, insisted that the party's congressional nominee be selected at a party convention. It was little known that Douglas himself was sharing in the editorial writing for the *Republican*.[33] Brooks took Douglas's lead and wrote in his *Jacksonville News* that if Congressman May decided to seek re-election, he should expect to submit himself for consideration as a candidate for any office to the convention, just as any other candidate was expected to do under the party's rules.[34] Some Democrats were alarmed at this new device by which the party, or more particularly, scoundrels within it, could dispense with volunteers for office in favor of a single candidate selected by convention.

Douglas and his friend Senator Young had been preparing for the anticipated clash with Congressman May. Young had turned on May on information from Douglas that the congressman had promised to help George W.P. Maxwell or Douglas if they would assist him in taking Young's seat in the Senate.[35] The *Illinois Republican*, with Douglas likely the author, was favorable to the Douglas-Young conspiracy. As early as April the newspaper began attacking May for his votes against President Jackson's distribution to the states the surplus proceeds from the sale of federal land. The newspaper also criticized May for supporting the repeal of Jackson's Specie Circular, which required payment for government land in gold or silver.[36]

May had done himself few favors among the adherents of either party in his attempts to appeal to both Whig and Democrat. While he backtracked to rationalize Jackson's war on the U.S. Bank, May complained that Jackson had failed to provide a currency as strong as the old bank's.[37]

The convention to nominate the party's candidate for Congress was held in November 1838 at Peoria. Delegates dealt summarily with May for voting with the "moneyed institutions that would be alike destructive to our happiness and prosperity, and subversive of the principles of our Republican system of Government." May had violated the trust of those who had elected him, delegates said. On the convention's first ballot, Douglas became the Third Congressional District's nominee.[38] May was appalled. Within months he withdrew from the Democratic Party. And there was not a little noise from lifelong Democrats who suspected the Little Giant of rigging the nomination. Only 40 delegates, representing only 14 of the district's 35 counties performed the service.

Whigs gloated that an ambitious upstart had ousted a veteran politician.

"No nomination could suit us better," crowed Springfield's Whig organ, the *Sangamo Journal*.[39]

❖ ❖ ❖

There was one more convention of Illinois Democrats to be held before Douglas could turn his full attention to his race for Congress. This would be the first statewide convocation of party regulars—to select the party's nominees for statewide office. Douglas would find there still was work to do, and the cause was the nominal head of his own ticket.

In Peoria, promoters of federal land receiver John W. Stephenson of northwestern Jo Daviess County for Congress had yielded to the better organized mechanics of Douglas's promoters. Stephenson became the Democrats' candidate for governor, not as payback, it was said, but because northern Democrats had earned a candidate from their section as reward for party loyalty.[40] The convention had done its work, and the party had a candidate. Unfortunately, the candidate did not hold up under scrutiny. With inside information on the nominee for governor, Secretary of State Alexander Pope Field whispered to a friend a plan to get May back on the ticket.

"Stephenson is a defaulter to the amount of 40,000 [dollars]," Field told Henry Eddy, a Southern Illinois lawyer and newspaper editor. "Say nothing about it to nobody. We will modestly set on foot an inquiry by our papers. They will of course deny it & then May has the Documents to prove the facts."[41]

May learned of the allegation of Stephenson's malfeasance and published details in his newspaper. Stephenson initially denied the charge, but party leaders were able to confirm it. Embarrassed Democrats caucused in Springfield and jettisoned Stephenson from the ticket. He was "too heavy a load for Douglas to carry in the congressional race."[42] Stephenson withdrew in May. The Democrats reconvened on June 5, 1838, and replaced him with Thomas Carlin, the federal land agent at Quincy. The nomination drew fire from Whigs, even some Democrats. Springfield's *Sangamo Journal* mocked the Democrats and their "LATE LAND OFFICE CONVENTION."[43] Stephenson had been a federal land office agent and was replaced by a land agent and friend of Stephen Douglas. And Samuel McRoberts, Democratic candidate for congress from the First District, was a receiver in a federal land office. Critics said it appeared that experience in a federal land office was the only qualification a Democrat needed to run for office. The critics raised a good point, but their concern may have been more about money. Federal land registers and receivers could earn as much as $3,000 a year, by which they were able to finance a large share of their campaigns themselves.

For Douglas it was time to turn attention to his own race. He could anticipate that winning a general election would not be easy. At twenty-four years old, he was not even old enough for a seat in Congress, although he would meet the age requirement by the time of the election in August 1838. Such pesky details were not all that important to the ambitious young politician, whose experience had proven that improvisation could be as useful as any thorough understanding or observance of rules. In the general election, Douglas would face a formidable adversary in Whig John Todd Stuart, the six-foot-tall Springfield law partner of Whig leader Abraham Lincoln.

Although May had beaten Stuart in the race for Congress two years earlier, Stuart remained popular throughout the district. Having jousted with Stuart in several First Judicial District courtrooms, Douglas was familiar with his opponent's forensic talents. Stuart was reserved and dignified. Douglas's experience told him Stuart was a good lawyer and smart opponent. He was a good judge of men. It was Stuart who encouraged Lincoln in the practice of law. It also meant that Douglas would not find sloughing and demagoguing easy—if he intended to do it in the campaign with Stuart.

Douglas also knew personally how effective Lincoln's support would be, even if he would not participate directly in Stuart's campaign. Leaving the full responsibility for the law office to his business partner, Stuart could be fully involved in the campaign against Douglas. Lincoln was not to leave Stuart unassisted in his Congressional campaign.

Lincoln had gained little more respect for Douglas than he had implied when he talked of his first sighting of Douglas at Vandalia in 1836. In notifying his friend William A. Minshall, a Schuyler County Whig representative, of Stuart's intention to seek the Congressional seat, Lincoln added a postscript—and another jab at the little man from Morgan County—to his letter: "We have adopted it as part of our policy here, to never speak of Douglas at all. Isn't [sic] that the best mode of treating so small a matter?"[44]

Stuart lost that 1836 contest to incumbent Democratic Congressman William May.

State representatives John Todd Stuart of Springfield and Douglas roomed in the same boarding house in Vandalia in 1836. Two years later, they would be opponents in the 1838 congressional race. Stuart won the election by 36 votes out of 36,472 cast and spent nearly a year refusing Douglas's pleas for a recount (courtesy Abraham Lincoln Presidential Library and Museum).

Both Lincoln and Stuart were well known lawyers who practiced across the state's large Eighth Judicial Circuit, which was approximately the same area included in the congressional district. Supporting Stuart's 1838 campaign, Lincoln cleverly attacked Douglas in letters submitted and published by the *Sangamo Journal* of Springfield under the pseudonym "A Conservative."[45]

With the pseudonymic attacks unceasing in the *Journal*, Douglas demanded that Simeon Francis, the newspaper's publisher and Lincoln friend, reveal the identity of the author. Douglas asked Francis twice to do him justice and publish Douglas's answer to "A Conservative's" charges that he had won his nomination by "corrupt bargain." It was a charge bound to incense Douglas, well aware that another "corrupt bargain" had kept his hero from the presidency. "A Conservative" claimed that Sangamon Democrat John Calhoun had agreed to help Douglas at the Peoria Democratic convention get the party's nomination for Congress. In return, Conservative continued, Calhoun was promised Douglas's place as register of the federal land office in Springfield. This was the charge that led to Douglas's demand for "A Conservative's" name. Francis rejected Douglas's request to reveal the name of the author. Nothing in the article justified it, said Francis, who simply recommended that Douglas consider him the author.[46]

"What! Are we to be told that a direct charge of *corrupt bargain and sale* 'does not contain *any thing* that requires an author's name to be furnished?'" an incensed Douglas wrote to Francis. "Is the charge of a 'regular transfer of a Land office *according to contract*' to purchase a nomination for Congress a mere trivial, unimportant circumstance, 'not containing anything that requires an author?' Is there nothing dishonest, disgraceful, and degrading in an act of this kind?"[47]

Four days later, Douglas asked George Weber, editor of the Democratic newspaper, the *Illinois Republican,* in which Douglas had an interest, to publish a response to the man who "*conceals* himself behind the mask of a fictitious signature" so that he could defend his "character against false accusations."

"My nomination as a candidate for Congress seems to have been the signal for a systematic and simultaneous attack on my character," Douglas wrote to his "FELLOW CITIZENS," "which has been followed up with a vindictive, fiendish spirit that shows that nothing but the sacrifice of its victim will appease its malice. My acts have been misrepresented, my opinions perverted, my motives impugned, and my character traduced in language as unkind and ungentlemanly as it was unjust and untrue. These outpourings of abuse and slander I have passed in silence, resting upon your intelligence and sense of justice for my vindication, against charges and insinuations, that bore the evidence of malice on their face, and I should not notice them on this occasion, had not my *private* and *moral*, as well as public and political character been assailed in a manner calculated to destroy my standing as a man and a citizen, if permitted to pass unnoticed, and my silence construed into an admission of guilt."

Douglas said he feared no investigation of the charges by this man who labeled himself "A Conservative."

"I invite, I challenge it," he taunted.

He said that when the curtain was raised to shed the light off truth on the attacks and the identity of the cowardly man who made them, it would clear the damage to his integrity by dragging his accusers from their hiding places.

"Let them cover themselves with infamy, which is the certain reward of the midnight assassin, and foul mouthed slanderer," he concluded.[48]

"A Conservative" was not alone in the accusations against Douglas. So, too, was David Davis, the 300-pound jurist from Bloomington who tramped the fourteen-county circuit with the two Sangamon lawyers, Stuart and Lincoln.

Davis, who called the campaign the hottest he had ever seen, would become intimately involved in the race as it approached completion. He charged that Douglas distorted facts, accusing "his adversary of favoring an [unpopular] measure ... whether he knew this to be true or not." Predictably, Douglas denied Davis's accusations. Davis replied that he was not mistaken. The proof that he was right would be exhibited at the polls in McLean County on Election Day, an assurance that was proven just as Davis had predicted. Stuart won McLean by 200 votes.[49]

In addition, Douglas would have to repair the disarray that had crept into the party, not only the challenge of the Jackson-Van Buren fiscal problems but the dissatisfaction members of his state party had with the party's new machinery—self-serving as it had proven to be, which Douglas and his cohort had introduced. There was also the question of Douglas's ability to run and finance a campaign for an office at the national level that was untried and, therefore, uncertain. It was a challenge, certainly, but one about which Douglas seemed unconcerned.

Stretching over thirty-four counties from Springfield and taking in all of northern Illinois, the Third Congressional District was the largest in the state. The Douglas-Stuart battle for the seat to represent the district in Congress started with the first good weather in March and would continue through the night before the election on August 6, 1838. Stuart, thirty years old, had as much energy and stamina as challenger Douglas, who was six years younger. Both would need them for the rigorous campaign they were about to undertake. For five months, the candidates rode from town to town in their canvass, breaking off their speech-making and debates only on Sundays.

An observer in McHenry County was amused by Douglas during his campaign appearance there. Riding in on a chestnut horse, Douglas surprised the onlookers. His legs reached only halfway down the horse's sides. If there was little of him— the onlooker carefully estimated Douglas's weight at 92 pounds, there was much that came from him. He might have "made the most ludicrous appearance of any person I ever saw," said one of the observers at McHenry, "yet was a full match in a political argument with any man in the state." Standing on a whiskey barrel where the Rev. Joel Wheeler of McHenry, who chaired the meeting, placed him so his audience could see him, Douglas spoke for nearly two hours on bank and tariff issues. His observer said listeners thought it "one of the most convincing speeches that was ever delivered in the country."

Douglas stayed in the town for several days, fishing and playing euchre with his partisans and some who were not.[50]

Douglas flabbergasted even members of his own party, who had given him little chance against the better-known Stuart.[51] With just as much stamina and the willingness to expend it in the cause, Douglas kept up with Stuart throughout the campaign, willing to speak anywhere in the state at any time to any group of any size that offered listeners. Northern Illinois Democrat John Wentworth reported that Douglas spoke for more than four hours at Dixon's Ferry, an outpost in far northern Illinois, where only 40 or 50 people showed up.

"He performed his part with such,—we shall say adroitness, that that part of the State was carried against predicted defeat," Wentworth said.[52]

The campaign of the combatants was, as campaigns were in those days, routinely intimate. Douglas and Stuart often rode together, ate meals at the same table, and, at the end of the day occasionally shared a bed.[53] A young man named John Reynolds, whom Douglas would help become a lawyer, remembered meeting Douglas and Stuart at the end of one of their days of campaigning in Hancock County. Reynolds and fellow clock salesman Sands N. Breed had rented and been assigned separate beds by a Mr. Swope, a tavern landlord. That evening, with no spare beds available, Swope brought the two congressional contestants to the bedroom and introduced "Mr. Stuart and Mr. Douglas, opposing candidates for Congress." Swope informed Reynolds and Sands they would have to share their beds. Douglas asked the men their politics. Breed informed Douglas he was a Whig and that Reynolds was a Democrat.

"I will sleep with the Democrat and Stuart may sleep with the Whig," Douglas instructed.[54]

As they moved northward, Douglas departed Stuart for the canal territory at Joliet in northeastern Illinois, where he sought to appeal to the Irish immigrants who were laboring there. Stuart had visited the canal workers earlier and, claiming a familial relationship—Stuart told the Irish canal builders that he had descended from a neighboring Scot clan, sought their votes. Douglas's ancestry was Scottish, too, but he became carried away by the enthusiastic reception the hundreds of Irish laborers gave him. He admitted later that he had stretched the truth about his ancestry.

"I had an appreciative audience," said Douglas. "They cheered me; in fact, they were too friendly. I was extolling the patriotism of Ireland, the virtues of her people, the bravery of her sons, and beauty of her daughters. I even referred to myself as being descended from a long line of patriotic sires of Irish descent."[55]

Douglas told the story about his personal appeal to the Irish workers to the family of Jeriah Bonham, later publisher of the *Illinois Gazette*, with whom Douglas stayed overnight while enroute north from Peoria. He told Bonham about his claim of Irish ancestry, making fun of his own short stature.

"When I had said that," Douglas recounted, "a great, big, burly Irishman, over six foot high, rose and said, 'Do you say Mr. Dooglas, that you discinded from the great McDooglases of Ireland?' Coming forward where I was talking the big man patronizingly leaned over me, spreading out his brawny arms (and said), 'What a devil of a discint.'"

Douglas reckoned the story perfectly excusable because it served an honorable purpose. As Douglas biographer Frank Stevens observed, "...If Stuart could get no nearer Ireland than through a Scotch ancestry he was entitled to no consideration, because he (Douglas) himself was a real Irishman whose ancestors were the McDouglases and as such he expected to receive the vote of every Irishman in the district."[56] Douglas, in fact, had every confidence that would be the result. That was the honorable result.

"I expect to get all their votes," he boasted to Bonham.[57]

The small Douglas's big swagger was a winning attribute. His victory in the "canal ring," as the center of Irish laborers was called, was overwhelming.[58] Douglas won only twelve of the Third Congressional District's thirty-four counties.[59] The huge margins of Douglas's victory in the canal counties were compelling enough to generate a Whig lawsuit that ended up in the Illinois Supreme Court to stop the so-called "alien vote" in Illinois.

The distortion of facts when they seemed harmless but useful for his own purposes was becoming more and more characteristic of Douglas. There were some in his adopted hometown of Jacksonville who believed his success as a lawyer "lay largely in his utter indifference to the line that separates truth from falsehood. If he could but win he did not hesitate about the means."[60]

After the "McDooglas" episode, Stuart decided he would be better served if he were present when Douglas spoke. He agreed to Douglas's request for joint debates.

The Stuart-Douglas debates were spirited. The contestants would speak to audiences from any venue at which Douglas was able to get his head above the crowd. As at McHenry, that occasionally meant a friendly partisan lifting Douglas onto a whiskey barrel or wagon buckboard. Stuart and Douglas each would speak for as long as two to three hours. Douglas would sweep the platform with gesticulation. Arms flying, Douglas rose, almost flew. He would use all of his height, extend it, stretch it into an illusion of towering genius. His exertions, generated by an inner steam that at moments reddened his face and choked his voice, were nearly limitless.

The stress of the campaign wore on both men. The rigors removed Stuart for the week of May 10, 1838. Lincoln filled in for him at Bloomington that Thursday.[61] Douglas, who sought to meet every demand and expectation of those who were kind enough to listen to him, was nearly exhausted himself. On his arrival to Chicago during that period in the campaign, a resident who saw him observed that "when Douglas came in from that canvass he was the most forlorn object [he] ever saw. His horse, his clothes, his boots, and his hat—all were worn out. He had to use ropes for his bridle, and his saddle-bags looked as if they had seen a century's service." Douglas, nevertheless, said the spectator, still appeared to be "light and agile, a sparkling boy, vital, keen, impulsive, and confident." His fellow Democrats outfitted Douglas with new clothes and riding gear and "sent him on his way rejoicing."[62]

The heat that summer was extraordinarily oppressive. The Illinois prairie, even in the shorter summer days of July and early August, drenched the partisans in heavy humidity that, daily, drained them. Conditions added to the unyielding demands of the drawn-out campaign. Neither Douglas nor Stuart, however, ceded anything to the other. The demanding schedule and heated attacks continued. On at least two occasions the forensics became physical. A witness to a heated Douglas-Stuart argument in Archer Herndon's "Indian Queen" grocery—a euphemism of the period for tavern—in Springfield saw Douglas and Stuart spar to exhaustion. The tavern floor, "slippery with slop," prevented either from doing much damage to the other, though at nearly a foot shorter than Stuart Douglas could not have done much damage to his opponent. An observer said Douglas's heart "was so valiant that he made nothing of assaulting men of ... great height and strength like Stuart." Another bystander, however, recalled that "Stuart jes mopped the floor with him [Douglas]." The contest apparently ended in good humor. Stuart ordered a barrel each of whiskey and wine for his foe and his friends.[63] Douglas did not turn Stuart's kindness down.

The other occasion came toward the end of the campaign when Douglas decided to canvass in Morgan and Sangamon Counties, the district's most populous areas. Three days before the election Douglas met Stuart for a debate in front of the Market House in Springfield. Their colloquy grew more contentious in their appeal for voter sympathy. Stuart was a seasoned politician and as a lawyer used to attacks on his character. But apparently offended by one of Douglas's verbal assaults, Stuart locked Douglas's head under his right arm and carried him squirming around the public square. Douglas disengaged himself from his opponent's grip by biting Stuart's right thumb so hard that Stuart was said to carry the scar for the rest of his life.[64]

It would be months before the results of the August 6, 1838, election were known, although some two thousand Stuart supporters were confident enough to celebrate at a barbecue in Springfield in October. Democrats were less surprised by the amount of time it was taking to count the vote. It turned out to be a heavy vote. Few had given Douglas any chance of beating the popular Springfield Whig. But when the vote was counted, it showed Stuart had won 18,254 votes. Douglas won 18,218 votes. It was a difference of only thirty-six votes, slightly more than one vote per county in the thirty-four-county Third Congressional District.[65] Increasingly confident throughout his campaign, Douglas was pleased by the battle few said he would win. But he also was deeply distressed to have lost by such a small number. He had been confident of victory, albeit a narrow victory. He told a friend he believed he had won by about 100 votes.

Douglas began to hear reports of vote tampering by Whigs and he thought that Gov. Joseph Duncan had refused to count some Douglas votes. He did not explain how the governor would have been involved in vote-counting.[66] Friends believed some disgruntled Democrats also had hurt Douglas in the election. Usher Linder charged that "old Jim Turney," a former

Sangamon County state's attorney,[67] had gotten the Irish canal workers to vote for a John A. Douglas and a James A. Douglas and many other Douglases. Those votes were discarded. Linder claimed Turney thought he should have been slated to run for the office and, aggravated when he was not, worked to undercut Douglas.[68]

The editor of the *Vandalia Free Press* refuted all such claims, reporting that he was present when the secretary of state, the state auditor, and state treasurer examined the returns. There were indeed votes, the *Free Press* reported, for "Wm. A. Douglass" and "John A. Douglass." And they were awarded to Stephen A. Douglass, the newspaper said, adding that every vote Douglass could claim had been awarded to him. The editor noted that the Treasurer John D. Whiteside, a Democrat (who later would take a place in history as General James Shields's second in the Shields-Lincoln duel of 1842), was one of the examiners.[69] It was another one of the other examiners in whom Douglas would take a greater interest, Secretary of State Alexander Pope Field. Ironically, Douglas's successful effort to end *viva voce* voting when he was a state representative played a role in his defeat. Judges found numerous mistakes on ballots that had been cast for Douglas. In one case, the ballot had listed him as a candidate for the state legislature instead of Congress. Had the voters entered the polling places and publicly declared their vote, one election observer thought, Douglas would have won.[70]

For months Douglas vigorously pursued a recount. On March 4, 1839, Douglas wrote to ask Stuart to join him in asking for recount of all votes, looking for misspelling of names, and mentioning particularly the spelling of his last name as Douglas instead of Douglass. If state officers declined to recount, he asked that a recount be made by their friends. A third suggestion was for the appointment of a three-member committee who would examine the poll books in each county. And short of accepting any of those options, Stuart should join Douglas in running the race again.

Stuart declined each proposal. Douglas remained unsatisfied.

"I feel it my duty to my country, to those kind friends who have sustained me, and to myself, to contest the election in vindication of the right of a majority of the people to rule," he told a friend in later that month.[71]

Lincoln certainly had expected Douglas to contest the election vigorously and proposed a stealth investigation of the alien vote. He suggested that Whig operatives audit every poll book to assure that Stuart got credit for every vote that had been cast for him. Lincoln also advised Whigs to make a "collection of proofs" of the votes that went to Douglas by determining "whether any persons voted for Mr. Douglas in your County who were *minors*, or who had not been *Residents* of the state *six months* preceding the Election [and].... Whether any *unnaturalized foreigners* voted for Mr. Douglas in your County?"

Encouraging his detectives to proceed without delay, Lincoln said he wanted the "*names of the illegal* voters refered [*sic*] to in the last two questions ... [and] the names of the individuals by whom the fact of their illegality can be proved and the name and the residence of a justice of the peace before whom Depositions can be taken and a proper place to take them. When informed by you of the fact we will immediately take steps to procure the proofs."

This was clearly an important matter to Lincoln. He suggested that political friends be solicited to help with the investigation and, to expand it, appoint precinct committeemen to help where they thought it advisable. Lincoln asked that the investigation and any discoveries be kept as confidential as possible.[72]

In November Douglas wrote Francis Preston Blair, once one of President Jackson's closest advisors, and now editor of Washington's *Daily Globe*, the Democratic organ, for advice on how he might contest the election. Douglas suggested to Blair that his election was important to the principles of the national Democracy, between Democratic and federal principles, particularly on the issues of a subtreasury and a national bank. Douglas noted that if the next presidential election, only two years away, were to be decided in the House of Representatives, his presence there would be important.[73]

Douglas sought similar advice from Missouri's Democratic senator Thomas Hart Benton, who heartened Douglas by opining that Stuart's certificate of election would not be conclusive if the poll books showed Douglas had won a majority of the votes.[74] Unsuccessful because financing the contest was beyond his means, Douglas was said to be vacillating. Knowing Douglas, however, Lincoln warned Stuart not to trust the rumor.

"A report is in circulation here now, that he [Douglas] has abandoned the idea of going to Washington; though the report does not come in a verry [sic] authentic form, so far as I can learn," Lincoln wrote to Stuart on November 14. "Though, by the way, speaking of authenticity, you know that if we had heard Douglas say that he had abandoned the contest," Lincoln said, "it would not be verry [sic] authentic."[75]

Lincoln was right. Douglas continued his campaign.

In early March of 1839 Douglas appealed to Stuart directly. Saying he believed he had received the majority of votes, he wrote to Stuart that he would not desire the House seat on less than honorable grounds. His appeal to Stuart, though, was anything but the appeal of a supplicant.

"I cannot believe that you will claim a seat in Congress upon the mere ground that you have been so lucky as to receive a certificate of election, made in violation of law[76] and in opposition to the votes of a majority of the people," Douglas wrote in his lengthy letter to Stuart on March 4. Douglas suggested four options for determining the accuracy of the vote count or, if Stuart found none of those acceptable, running the race again.

Whig newspapers had long since tired of what they considered Douglas's distasteful persistence. The *Quincy Whig* called for an end to it. Readers would note the *Whig's* dig at Douglas's capture of the massive Irish vote, which brought him so close to Stuart's heels.

"We would suggest to McDouglas and his *Spirit*ual friend,[77] that as the people of all parts of the district have not *properly* appreciated their merits, they pull up stakes and locate in such parts of it, as have shown, by the recent election, so strong a devotion to their *peculiar* principles. 'Go where glory waits ye,' gentlemen— you are not sufficiently appreciated in Morgan and Sangamon."[78]

Stuart quickly and directly responded to Douglas's proposals for recount or re-running the election.

"No," he answered.

Stuart followed up on that answer with a letter on March 13, 1839, in which he told Douglas that to accept his proposal would be to acknowledge that he (Stuart) doubted the outcome of the election.

"I do not consider your various propositions worthy of a more particular reply as they are all evidently intended for the Public and not for me," Stuart wrote.[79]

The contested election lost urgency over the ensuing months. By mid–November Lincoln would tell Stuart that no new returns were coming into the secretary of state's office, and he would note that Douglas had stopped coming in, as well. In a subsequent letter, Lincoln told

Stuart the legislature had killed the State bank "without *Benefit* of *Clergy*" but confined notice of Douglas to a brief postscript: "The Democratic giant is here; but he is not now worth talking about."[80]

His personal finances were the key reason Douglas finally decided to discontinue his challenge of the results of the election. Initially enduring some criticism for continuing to draw his federal salary while campaigning, Douglas had quit his post as federal register and had thereafter largely financed his campaign himself. His resources had dwindled. When he finally resigned himself to the results of the election's outcome, Douglas decided to turn his attention exclusively to the practice of law. From early 1839 to November 1840, he began beating the eighth judicial circuit for law business. His recent campaign against the Stuart had made a name for Douglas and he was sought considerably more often for legal advice. He entered into a partnership with attorney George F. Markley of Bloomington. He and William Archer of Pittsfield in October 1839 announced a partnership to handle cases in Calhoun and Pike Counties. Although such arrangements by Springfield lawyers with lawyers elsewhere on the circuit were typical—the Springfield lawyer assisted in handling cases appealed to state and federal courts in Springfield—the theatre for Douglas's partnerships was in the counties.[81] Democratic attorney John D. Urquhart of Springfield, Governor Thomas Ford's stepbrother, formed a partnership with Douglas at about the same time. Within weeks, the two were on the opposite sides of the courtroom from Stuart and Lincoln. The case, in which Douglas and Urquhart represented a widow who sought to obtain her interest in her deceased husband's real estate against the wishes of her sons, was quickly settled, as the attorneys for both sides had advised, out of court.[82]

The regular practice of law was improving Douglas as counselor. His peers considered him a strong lawyer and as advocate for his clients one of the ablest. One of his colleagues of the bar said a client on the wrong side of the law would find Douglas his best defender. Douglas's record before the Illinois Supreme Court was admirable. He won ten of thirteen cases he presented there in 1839.[83] Colleagues marveled at his ability to extract and absorb information from experts and associates.

"He so perfectly assimilated the ideas and knowledge of others that all seemed to be his own, and all that went into his mind came out improved," wrote John McAuley Palmer, an Illinois governor who had practiced at the bar with Douglas.[84]

Palmer had reason to appreciate Douglas. After studying law in Edwardsville, Palmer arrived in Springfield in December 1839 to obtain his license to practice. He met Douglas shortly after arranging for a room at the Globe Hotel, and Douglas took an immediate interest in him. Douglas made out the paperwork required for Palmer's application, then persuaded Jonathan Young Scammon, an able lawyer who had just become the reporter of cases and decisions of the Illinois Supreme Court,[85] into serving with him as the committee to examine Palmer. Scammon and Douglas received the court's appointment for that purpose. After interviewing and concurring in the legal skills of the young candidate, Douglas personally drew up Palmer's license and had it signed by Supreme Court Justices Theophilus W. Smith and Thomas C. Browne. Palmer would remember Douglas's "cheerful kindness which always characterized him and made him so popular." Douglas was, said Palmer, one of the most considerate lawyers he knew.[86]

Although it appeared Douglas was settling into the practice of law, he continued to dabble in politics as well. He could not keep himself from involvement. He took a close and clandestine role in a special legislative election in 1839 to fill a vacancy in the Sangamon County delegation. Douglas was known to be encouraging Democrat Thomas J. Nance of Petersburg to seek the office against Whig candidate John Bennett, who owned a hotel in nearby Petersburg.[87] What was not known publicly was that Douglas also was quietly encouraging a few Whigs to compete as well. That tactic was a page taken from the book written in Morgan County five years earlier. As an election there taught Douglas, a larger number of Whig candidates would split the party's vote. An organization of the other party's voters virtually assured their man's election. Lincoln suspected something wily going on. He wrote to Stuart on November 14, 1839, of his suspicion: "I am afraid of our race for Representative. Dr. [Moses L.] Knapp has become a candidate; and I fear the few votes he will get will be taken from us. Also, some one has been tampering with old Esqr. [Samuel] Wycoff, and induced him to send in his name to be announced as a candidate. [Simeon] Francis[88] refused to announce him without seeing him, and now I suppose there is to be a fuss about it."[89]

Douglas never revealed that he was the operative behind the fuss. His candidate, Nance, won the election.[90]

11. The Contest for Miss Mary Ann Todd

DOUGLAS MET MARY ANN TODD during her three-month visit to Springfield at the invitation of relatives in the summer of 1837.[1] This was Todd's second visit to Springfield. In May 1835 she had accompanied her father on one of his semi-annual trips to Springfield to visit daughters and nephew John Todd Stuart. On each of her visits to Springfield, Mary Ann stayed at the home of her sister Elizabeth, wife of attorney Ninian Wirt Edwards.[2] He was the aristocratic son of Illinois' third governor, Ninian Edwards.

Twenty-four years old—and five years older than Mary Todd, Douglas had arrived in Springfield in March 1837 as the newly appointed register of the federal land office. Named to the position by President Van Buren and already having been a judicial circuit's prosecutor and state legislator, Douglas's stature was growing because of his uncanny proficiency at the art of politics. And Mary Ann Todd had a lively interest in politics. Her father was a Lexington lawyer, banker, slave owner, and Whig politician whose home was regularly frequented by Whig politicians of Kentucky.[3] The Todd family lived near one of the nation's best known politicians, Henry Clay, in Lexington, Kentucky. Mary Ann was known to have boasted, even as a child, to Mr. Clay that she would one day be the wife of a president of the United States.

Todd was seventeen when she first visited Springfield in 1835. And for the first time in eleven years, she was free of her controlling stepmother Betsy Humphreys Todd. Mary Todd's own mother, Eliza Parker Todd,[4] a cousin of Mary's father Robert Smith Todd,[5] died when Mary Ann was six.

The Edwards home was situated on "Aristocracy Hill" just a few blocks west of the site at which the new state capitol, recently won for Springfield, would be built. A Todd relative, Dr. John Todd, built the first house on "The Hill" in 1827 in a grove of trees on the north side of Washington Street between First and Second streets. Bordered by hazel and brier bushes and a few tall oaks, as John Todd Stuart recalled, Second Street, then called Edwards Trace, was the main entrance into town from the south. The Hill was more of a ridge than a hill, but with its number of affluent residents in homes of grand size and style, it drew comparisons to Boston's Beacon Hill. Aristocracy Hill was separated from the commercial area of town to the east by a small stream called Town Branch. It was a boundary not only physically but socio-politically as well. Within a few years, other homes were built for more of Springfield's elite, families of men like George Forquer, Lawrason Levering, Thomas Mather, and John Huntington. It was a neighborhood of lawyers, merchants, bankers, builders, and other well-to-dos.[6]

Its southern settlers initially named the town Calhoun to honor Vice President John C. Calhoun of South Carolina. They changed the name to Springfield when Calhoun created a national crisis in heralding his state's right to nullify federal law.

Todd's residence with the Edwards family accorded her a good deal of social standing in the capital city, and she enjoyed the attention she received as a member of the state's "Edwards Dynasty," even if it had languished a decade earlier. Her physical appearance made Todd a proper match for Stephen Douglas. At five feet four inches, she stood eye to eye with him. With her brown hair pulled back and secured by a barrette, Todd's broad forehead was exposed above wide-set blue eyes. A frequent girlish excitement would show itself in the quick-to-blush cheeks of her pixie-like face. Her figure was considered beautiful and one observer said that "no old master ever modeled a more perfect arm and hand."[7] Todd was an animated young woman, her hands moving in quick gestures as she spoke. Her new friends considered her willful and emotional. She had spirit and a quick temper, they said.[8] There was no one in Springfield who could hold Miss Todd's spirits in check. She had found a sense of freedom not present to her at Lexington. Yet, although she felt unfettered, she had not come of age, and any interest she had in the beaus who were interested in her would have to wait. After a few months with the Edwardses, Todd was summoned by her father to return to her Lexington home.

Todd left Lexington once again for Springfield in October 1839. This time she would complete the break from her stepmother. Once again, she lived in the capital city with the Edwardses, once again at their invitation. What she remembered of Springfield from her earlier visit was now even more exciting. The relocation of the state capital had brought innumerably more beaus to the city. It seemed a worldlier place for the finished Todd, who spoke French fluently, was widely read, had a grasp of politics, and possessed a manner at once refined and audacious. She was considered a "good talker ... capable of making herself quite attractive to young gentlemen."[9] Those who became acquainted with Todd on her return to Springfield described her as "'gifted with rare talents' ... 'high-bred, proud, brilliant, witty,' as 'aristocratic' and 'accomplished,' and as coming from a 'long and distinguished ancestral line.'"[10] Her brother-in-law would worry that she was dangerously attractive.

"Mary could make a bishop forget his prayers," Ninian Wirt Edwards once said about her.[11]

Todd had another side, which she was readily willing to display. She quickly gained a reputation in Springfield for a disposition that tended toward domination rather than adaptation, and for being

Mary Ann Todd arrived in Springfield just months after Douglas and Lincoln in 1837. As politically astute as either man, Todd played each against the other (Library of Congress).

tempestuous and resentful.[12] Her sister Elizabeth said Mary "loved glitter, show and pomp and power" and sought "place and public distinction." Todd's ambitions arose again in Springfield. She was ambitious, Sister Elizabeth said. She was as confident as the child in Lexington had been, whispering into friendly Springfield ears that she was destined to be the wife of a President."[13]

Todd came with a pedigree that included her family's close relationship with the national Whig statesman Henry Clay. Her father, like Clay, had served in both houses of the Kentucky General Assembly. The Todd and Clay families were neighbors in Lexington, and Mary had attended Madam Mentelle's fashionable boarding school with the Clay children across the road from Ashland, the Clay family estate.[14] As a girl Todd had been bold enough to summon Clay from meetings at his home, once to show off a horse. She had a child's fancy for the elder Clay, sometimes would sit on his lap, considered him handsome, and told him she would marry him if ever he became president.[15]

While Todd had standing in Springfield because of her relationship to the Edwardses, she had other important relatives in the area, as well. Cousins John Todd Stuart and Stephen Trigg Logan of Springfield and John J. Hardin of Jacksonville were each making his mark as a lawyer in his community and as a politician in the state.[16] It was Cousin Stephen Logan who introduced Todd to Abraham Lincoln, his junior partner.[17] And it was Cousin John Todd Stuart who had encouraged Lincoln to practice law, then brought Lincoln into his firm in Springfield in April 1837. In social soirees at the Edwards home, politics were uninvited but usually found their way in with the arrival of young men like Todd's relatives and Lincoln and Douglas, who were frequent and welcome guests there.

Politics and the law having dominated his life since his arrival in Illinois, Douglas in Springfield had begun to polish his social skills with the city's young women. He was at ease with any in the Springfield set and very much enjoyed moving among them. The pleasurable development of his skills made him a welcome beau. Douglas's attentions were returned. He was particularly partial to Miss Sarah Dunlap, daughter of the wealthy businessman and cattle breeder Colonel James Dunlap of Jacksonville, and Miss Julia Jayne, daughter of Dr. Gershom Jayne of Springfield.[18] Each young woman was known to the eligible bachelors who came to Springfield for the beginning of the Eleventh General Assembly. And each would marry political men who would become important in the stories of Lincoln and Douglas. Dunlap married John Alexander McClernand, then a rising young attorney from Jacksonville and a Douglas political colleague from their earliest days together in Vandalia. McClernand would become an even more important political friend when the two reached Washington in 1843 as freshmen Illinois congressmen.

One of Mary Todd's closest friends, Julia Jayne would become the wife of Lyman Trumbull. It was these two young ladies who conspired to write anonymously the "Rebecca Letters" critical of Democratic State Treasurer James Shields. When Shields demanded to know the authors, Lincoln took on the responsibility for which Shields challenged him to a duel. It was the only duel Lincoln accepted and for which he was forever embarrassed. Todd would end her friendship with Jayne—completely and permanently, without ever a hint of regret—for an unforgivable slight of one husband by the other. It happened this way:

In 1855 Trumbull, an anti–Nebraska Democrat and an Illinois Supreme Court associate justice, would defeat Todd's husband Lincoln in Lincoln's first bid for a U.S. Senate seat from Illinois. In that day the two houses of the General Assembly meeting in joint session elected the state's U.S. senators. By her count of the legislators expected to vote for her husband, Todd-Lincoln had convinced herself that Lincoln had the votes to replace Democrat James Shields as U.S. senator from Illinois. The states' senior U.S. Senator Stephen A. Douglas had created the opportunity with his Kansas-Nebraska Act in 1854. It replaced the Missouri Compromise, the federal law that had held slavery below the southern border of Missouri since 1820, with "popular sovereignty." Although Douglas pointed out no federal law had ever stopped slavery, slavery had not existed where the people did not want it, that Congress had rejected each of his attempts to extend the Missouri Compromise line west so he could limit slavery while organizing western territories, and that history proved pioneers had always prohibited slavery when allowed to decide, his rationalizations avoided the question of slavery's morality.[19] Douglas's measure sectionalized and killed the national Whig Party and caused the departure of many Democrats from their party. Trumbull, who still called himself a Democrat, was one of them. The Lincolns believed that as a moderate on the issue of slavery Lincoln would appeal to old Whig friends, many of whom at this point were referred to as the "Opposition Party," and disaffected Democrats like Congressman William Bissell and his friends in the state legislature who now called themselves "Independent Democrats."[20]

On the first ballot, legislators cast forty-four votes for Lincoln, only six fewer than the number needed to win. Trumbull received five. As she and her friend Julia Jayne-Trumbull watched the proceedings—state legislators casting one ballot after another—from the gallery above the House floor, Todd-Lincoln watched her husband's lead shrink. By the ninth ballot, the number of Lincoln's electors had diminished to fifteen, twenty-nine fewer than the number the first ballot gave him and thirty-five short of the number needed to win. Legislators on the ninth ballot gave Douglas's candidate, Governor Joel Matteson, who had been waiting in the wings for just this moment, forty-seven votes. The risk that Matteson might get three more votes to win the Senate seat "forced me and my friends the necessity of surrendering to Trumbull," as Lincoln explained later to a friend.[21] He knew that Douglas had hatched a plan that under such circumstances was designed to send the Democracy's Matteson to the U.S. Senate. Lincoln saw it working as those legislators he called the "Nebraska men" (supporters of Douglas's Kansas-Nebraska Act) on the seventh ballot began switching their votes from him to Matteson. Unless Lincoln released his supporters, the Douglas plan would be achieved.

Lyman Trumbull had thirty-five votes in the ninth ballot. Lincoln released his friends to vote for Trumbull. Lincoln's concession assured Trumbull's election.[22]

Whether or not Lincoln explained to his wife the reasons for his actions, Mary Todd-Lincoln was devastated by the result—the loss of the prestige of being the wife of a U.S. senator to someone so dull as the Connecticut Congregationalist Lyman Trumbull. Julia Jayne-Trumbull, an innocent observer no more or no less than Todd-Lincoln herself, had nothing to do with the outcome. That was of no consequence to Todd-Lincoln, who never again spoke to Jayne-Trumbull.

Douglas was among sixteen men who joined Ninian Wirt Edwards and Abraham Lincoln in sponsoring a Cotillion Ball at Springfield's elaborately decorated new American House Hotel in Springfield on December 16, 1839.[23] The purpose of the event was to celebrate the move of the state capital from Vandalia to Springfield and to welcome the wives and members of the first legislature that would meet in the state's new capital city.[24] It provided a setting for attentions between Todd and numerous young men, including James Shields, Lyman Trumbull, Joshua Speed, Edwin "Bat" Webb, James Matheny—and, particularly, Abraham Lincoln and Stephen A. Douglas.[25] These last two were known to Todd from her stay in the Edwards home in 1837. Each of them had moved to Springfield in the spring of that year, and the political star of each seemed on the ascendancy. Douglas had arrived in Springfield to become the federal land register, appointed by no less than the president of the United States himself. Lincoln's abilities had just been demonstrated by his leadership of the team that won for Springfield the Illinois state capital and the gifts that would go with it. Todd heard firsthand some of the praise for Lincoln that followed in the months afterward.

It was Speed, a frequent guest at the Edwards Home, who introduced Lincoln to Todd, and Lincoln began spending more time there.[26] Todd's brother-in-law Ninian Wirt Edwards did nothing to discourage her interest in the taller gentleman. His own law practice would benefit from the new government offices in Springfield. Todd had heard the erudite Edwards predict that Lincoln "would be a great man."

The Edwardses, however, came to believe that Lincoln and Todd were unsuited for each other.[27]

Todd attended the Cotillion Ball. Douglas, by now considered one of the most polished young gentlemen in Springfield,[28] was said to be as graceful as Lincoln was ungraceful on the dance floor, and Todd was more complimentary toward him than toward Lincoln. Douglas and Todd had what appeared to be a flirtatious relationship and saw each other occasionally. Yet, Todd had an interest in Lincoln, and, as perfectly intended by Miss Todd, Lincoln saw Douglas and her together.[29]

Harriett Chapman, a daughter of Lincoln's stepsister Sarah Bush Chapman, claimed that Todd had told her she and Douglas had been betrothed until Todd contracted a serious illness—conveniently. Her own machinations were the cause.[30] Friends noticed that she had grown nervous and could easily become irritated at the slightest provocation. She confided her worries about her conflicting infatuations to her brother-in-law, Dr. William Wallace of Springfield. Were they for Douglas? For Lincoln?[31] Todd decided to break the engagement with Douglas.[32] According to Chapman, Douglas wanted to continue the engagement, but Wallace, Todd's physician and the husband of Todd's sister, Frances, personally pleaded with Douglas to end it.[33] Douglas did so "with great reluctance," according to Chapman. Todd had told Chapman that she "loved Douglas, and but for her promise to marry Lincoln would have accepted him."[34] Years later, on hearing Chapman's claim, Todd disputed the recollections. She said it was she who broke the engagement.

"I can't consent to be your wife," were the words, Todd later told a confidante, she used to recede from Douglas's proposal of marriage. "I shall become Mrs. President, or I am the victim of false prophets, but it will not be as Mrs. Douglas."[35]

Chapman's memory is suspect. She was sixty years old when she told Lincoln biographer William Herndon the story of the Todd-Douglas engagement and break up. Yet she had had such an unusually close relationship with the Lincolns that she had access to their most intimate conversations and confidences. She had lived with the Lincolns for approximately two years as a housekeeper while she attended the Springfield Female Academy.[36] Given President Lincoln's rightful elevation to civil sainthood after his assassination and the place Douglas took as the foil to the saint, Todd had nothing to gain and much to lose if she were to confirm Chapman's story. Whether Chapman's story is accurate, Douglas and Todd did have a relationship so flirtatious that it convinced other friends that it influenced Lincoln's decision to leave her at the altar on what Lincoln would later call the "fatal first" of January 1841.[37]

Herndon was close enough to Lincoln, Todd, and the young society of Springfield to conclude that Douglas, indeed, wanted to marry Todd. But as little as he liked Todd, Herndon credited Todd's insight into human behavior for leading her to transfer her affections from Douglas to Lincoln. As Herndon recalled, "Douglas wanted to marry Mrs. Lincoln when a girl. Mrs. Lincoln, when a girl, was courted by Douglas and Lincoln at the same time. Mrs. Lincoln was a keen observer of human nature, an excellent judge of it, none better.... Mrs. Lincoln saw in Mr. Lincoln honesty, sincerity, integrity, manliness, and a great man in the future. Mrs. Lincoln saw in Douglas a rake and a roué by nature, a demagogue and a shallow man. This I *know*."[38] The emphasis was Herndon's.

For her part in the relationship, Todd was said to have refused Douglas because of his "bad morals."[39] Douglas was not unlike other young men of his day—he smoked, drank, cursed, chewed tobacco and occasionally "expectorated"—spit tobacco juice—and on the carpet, no less. Lincoln was the notable exception with regard to such disgusting practices.

"I liked him [Douglas] well enough but that was all," Mary Todd told her sister Elizabeth Edwards.[40]

Todd's observation came at a moment in which she needed to soothe some distress about the deteriorating relationship with Douglas. The fact was that Douglas seemed to be losing interest in her. Todd had gotten the feeling that the popular Douglas had no lasting fancy for her. She said as much to her friend Mercy Levering. Todd had developed a close relationship with Levering, a young woman from Baltimore who in the fall of 1839 came to Springfield for a stay with her brother Lawrason in the house next door to the Edwardses. In a letter of July 23, 1840, regarding Douglas, Todd revealed to Levering an unusual sentiment for one who seemed so disinterested in another: "*There* [with regard to Douglas] I had deemed myself forgotten."[41]

There was, in fact, another woman, and Todd seemed jealous. Douglas had become interested in Ninian Wirt Edwards's cousin, Matilda Edwards, a tall, eighteen-year-old blonde, who recently had finished studies at the swank Monticello Female Academy at Alton. That November in 1840, Matilda Edwards accompanied her father Cyrus, who had been elected August 3 to the House of Representatives, to Springfield. Cyrus had been a member of the old "Edwards Dynasty," which had grown up around his brother, Governor Ninian Edwards. For Cyrus it was a return to the state capital as an elected official. A former state representative and state senator, he had lost his bid for governor in 1838 to Democrat Thomas Carlin of Quincy. Now, however, Cyrus was back in public service and his daughter Matilda would find her way into the public spotlight. And she attracted the spotlight.

Her beauty made Matilda Edwards an immediate sensation in Springfield. Even Lincoln's friend and roommate Joshua Speed, who had just sold his store to return permanently to his native Kentucky in a few weeks to manage his family estate, was smitten unmistakably by her. Speed's attraction to Matilda could hardly be misinterpreted. In language that would inspire a poet, Speed described her "two clear blue eyes, a brow as fair as Palmyra marble touched by the chisel of Praxalites" and "lips so fresh, fair, and lovely that I am jealous even of the minds that kiss them." Speed could not hide his interest in Matilda even from Mary Todd. She acknowledged Matilda's loveliness, adding: "*Mr. Speed's* ever changing heart I suspect is offering *its young* affections on her shrine, with some others."[42]

One who was aware of the Douglas and Lincoln attractions to Matilda was Orville Hickman Browning of Quincy, who knew both men well. Browning and Douglas had been "youngsters together," as Browning characterized their relationship, when they met in December 1836 at the Vandalia state capital as freshman legislators. They had lodged and boarded at the same house.[43] Likewise, Browning and Lincoln, both natives of Kentucky, had begun a lifelong friendship during that same time in Vandalia. Considered one of Western Illinois' best lawyers, Browning occasionally referred to Lincoln legal matters from Adams County that advanced to state or federal courts in Springfield. The partnership was efficient and economical for Browning and remunerative for Lincoln. Lincoln had a particular fondness for Browning's wife Eliza, who joined her husband in Vandalia. That is where Lincoln met her. Mrs. Browning, who enjoyed an occasional pipe bowl of tobacco and who had an unusually perceptive political acumen, recognized Lincoln's awkwardness around women. She appreciated Lincoln and always was able to make him feel comfortable around her. Eliza Caldwell Browning descended from Joseph Caldwell and Jane McGrew, which made her a distant relative of U.S. Senator John Caldwell Calhoun of South Carolina.[44] In 1836 when she accompanied Orville from Quincy to Vandalia, the couple had only recently married. Both would establish a close relationship with Lincoln that would continue into his presidency. The 29-year friendship between Lincoln and Eliza was the longest female acquaintance in Lincoln's life.

By the time Matilda Edwards arrived in Springfield, Mary Todd had jilted Douglas, who, therefore, felt free to pursue the wavy-blond-haired eighteen-year-old. Browning's recollection was that Douglas quickly fell in love with Edwards and proposed to her. She refused him.[45] Like Todd, Edwards considered Douglas a character of "bad morals."[46] Although the sequence of these events indicates Douglas and Todd were beyond a close relationship, residents of Springfield continued to see the two arm-in-arm on the streets of Springfield. At least one observer believed Todd had an ulterior motive for continuing such exhibitions with Douglas. Billy Herndon was convinced that Todd used Douglas to regain the affections of Lincoln, who had broken his engagement with her.[47] Friend Browning believed Lincoln's decision to call off the engagement was the result of a troubled conscience. Although engaged to Mary, Lincoln, too, Browning believed, had fallen in love with Matilda Edwards.[48]

"It seems to me—infer it that Mary Todd flirted with Douglas in order to spur up Lincoln to a greater love," Herndon recalled.[49]

Like Herndon, Browning recalled that Todd's efforts to attract Lincoln were frequent. He believed she was most anxious for their marriage. It always seemed to Browning that in the Lincoln-Todd relationship "Mary Todd did most of the courting."

"I always doubted whether, had circumstances left him [Lincoln] entirely free to act upon his own impulses, he would have voluntarily made proposals of marriage to Miss Todd," remembered Browning. "There is no doubt of her exceeding anxiety to marry him."[50]

Douglas was not the only man with whom Todd was seen. She also took the role of coquette with Edwin "Bat" Webb, a widower with two children,[51] and acted amorously with Joseph Gillespie. Each had arrived in Springfield for the convening of the Eleventh General Assembly. These flirtations were less effective than Todd might have wished. She discovered that she had overplayed her hand with Lincoln.

"Lincoln soon regarded himself as being treated dishonorably in public and made to feel unendurably inferior in her eyes to his arch rival, Douglas, by the woman he would marry," an observer concluded. "Naturally needing to receive confirmation of his personal superiority through getting spontaneous signs of whole hearted devotion from his fiancée, he grew increasingly self-doubtful and despondant [sic] as he realized her impulses to continue flirting with Douglas were irrepressible."[52]

At least they seemed that way. What else was Lincoln seeing them together to conclude?

Matters grew complicated as soon as Lincoln returned to Springfield on September 16, 1840, from a four-month journey around the Eighth Judicial Circuit. It had been an especially demanding summer. He was chairman of the presidential campaign of Whig William Henry Harrison in Illinois and campaigning for election to become a Harrison elector. He also had some four dozen cases pending in the Sangamon County circuit court and Illinois Supreme Court. With enough on his shoulders to bear, he did not need to see Todd again with Douglas. But he did. He was not interested in antics of a fiancé playing games with his psyche.[53]

The day after his return to the city, Lincoln left Springfield on September 17 to go to "Egypt," Southern Illinois, to campaign for Harrison. He did not turn to Springfield until November 2.[54]

His first glimpse of Todd when he got back to Springfield surprised him. She had put on weight. And it was noticeable, evidence of an inner turmoil of her own. Todd had spent that summer in Columbia, Missouri, with the family of her uncle, Judge David Todd. In a lengthy letter on July 23, 1840, to Levering, Todd described her stay and odd occurrences. Her new acquaintances were kind and hospitable, she wrote, but she was not interested in forming any close relationships, which she knew would soon have to be severed. Todd reported to Levering with evident surprise that she had received newspapers from Springfield, notably *Old Soldiers, Journals* "& even the *Hickory Club* [the newspaper was actually named *Old Hickory*].... This latter, rather astonished your friend, *there* I deemed myself forgotten.—When I mention *some letters* I have received since leaving S[pringield] you will be somewhat surprised, as I *must confess* they were entirely *unlooked for*. This is *between ourselves*, my dearest, but of this more anon. Every day I am convinced this is a stranger world we live in, the *past* as the future is to me a mystery."[55]

The emphases were Todd's. They made it clear that she was astonished to have received "*some letters*" from someone whom she "deemed [had] forgotten" her. That someone was Douglas. Her reference to "even the *Hickory Club*," so named for Old Hickory, Andrew Jackson, was telling. Douglas, who was leading the Illinois campaign for the Democratic presidential candidate Martin Van Buren—against Lincoln for Harrison, had helped establish the *Old Hickory* newspaper as the Van Buren campaign mouthpiece. Its first edition appeared February 17, 1840. It was published to compete with the Harrison campaign publication *Old Soldier*, which Lincoln and four other Whigs edited. Clearly, Todd, who asked Levering to keep such musings confidential, was still thinking about Douglas, still speaking about him with continuing affection.

What Todd did not say in her letter was as enlightening as what she did say. While clearly interested in the renewed attentions of Douglas, she gave no notice to her other Springfield suitor and purported fiancé, Lincoln. She had good reason to have been just as enchanted with Lincoln as Douglas and to have reported it to Levering.

Lincoln that same summer had attended a Whig convention in Rocheport, Missouri, approximately 15 miles due east of Columbia. After the convention, Lincoln went out of his way—15 miles in the opposite direction and 15 miles back—to call on Todd at her uncle's home.[56] Todd did not even mention Lincoln's call in the Levering letter. In another confidence,

Todd spoke in a tone that ridiculed Lincoln's impoverished state. Lincoln's once-black suit had become so worn it had "faded to *Lincoln green*," she wrote.[57]

Todd's routine of nighttime parties and daytime naps in Columbia had rendered her appearance corpulent by the time she returned to Springfield on September 21.[58] As Lincoln had noticed her fuller figure, other friends were just as observant.

"Verily, I believe the further [*sic*] West a young lady goes the better her health becomes," Lincoln's friend James C. Conkling of Springfield wrote about Todd near the end of September. Conkling had become the fiancé of Todd's friend Levering. In dripping sarcasm he added, "If she comes here she is sure to grow. If she visits Missouri she will soon grow out of your recollection, and if she should visit the Rocky Mountains I know not what would become of her."[59]

Todd was as much concerned about her figure's new fullness as her friends were. In an admission to Levering, she quibbled that she was not quite as heavy as she once had been, but she admitted her weight was still of "quite a sufficiency."[60] Lincoln once before had weaseled out of a relationship with a woman whose weight gain during a three-year absence disturbed him when once again he saw her. He managed to break that earlier engagement to Mary Owens of Kentucky whose size, as he wrote to Eliza Browning, made her a "fair match for Falstaff."[61] Whether for a similar reason or not, Lincoln's affections toward Todd had cooled. His eyes turned elsewhere.

On the evening of January 1, 1841, the Edwards's classic Italianate home on Aristocracy Hill in Springfield was filled to overflowing with neighbors and other guests there to witness the wedding of Miss Mary Ann Todd of Lexington, Kentucky, and Mr. Abraham Lincoln, Esq., a Kentucky native, Whig Party leader, and now a Springfield attorney.

The rooms of the Edwards home had been festooned in finery. It had taken the day to prepare a dinner that awaited the guests and wedding party after the ceremony. Three bridesmaids, three groomsmen, and the houseful of guests awaited the betrothed couple.

Two of the city's best known young men did not show up for the wedding. One was Stephen Douglas, who had not been invited. The other was Abraham Lincoln, who was responsible for the festivities.

Lincoln later explained to Speed he was suffering a bout of the "the hypos" and could not bring himself to be married.

Speed's description of his friend was more direct.

"Lincoln went Crazy," was Speed's belief.

Lincoln's friends found him early the next morning. Their concern could not penetrate his gloom and desperation.

"—had to remove razors from his room—take away all Knives and other such dangerous things—&c—it was terrible," Speed recalled.[62]

Within the week, Martinette Hardin McKee wrote her brother John Hardin, "We have been very much distressed, on Mr. Lincoln's account; hearing that he had two Cat fits and a Duck fit since we left."[63]

Three weeks after deserting Todd at the altar, Lincoln wrote Stuart that he felt as if he was "now the most miserable man living. If what I feel were equally distributed to the whole human family, there would not be one cheerful face on earth."[64]

During his four-year stay above Speed's store, Lincoln took most of his meals—without having to pay for them—at the home of William Butler, a Springfield hotelier and Lincoln benefactor.⁶⁵ It was there that he met sixteen-year-old Sarah Rickard, the sister of Butler's wife. Rickard was staying with the Butlers.⁶⁶ Lincoln was smitten with the brown-eyed, brown haired girl, who was half his age. He proposed marriage. She acted with a maturity well beyond her juvenile years.

She told Lincoln, "No."

"Mr. Lincoln did make a proposal of marriage to me in the summer, or perhaps later, in the year 1840," Rickard told Lincoln biographer Herndon nearly three decades afterward. "He brought to my attention the accounts in the Bible of the patriarch Abraham's marriage to Sarah, and used that historical union as an argument in his own behalf. My reason for declining his proposal was the wide difference in our ages. I was then only sixteen, and had given the subject of matrimony but very little, if any, thought."⁶⁷

If Herndon's informants are correct, Lincoln's attentions continued to be directed toward very young women. Denied by Rickard, he turned them next toward Matilda Edwards, who was only two years older than Rickard. Todd had become aware of Lincoln's interest in Edwards. In conversations with Orville Hickman Browning—some of them lasting until midnight—in the Edwards home she angrily referred to the relationship. She was bitter about Matilda, she told Browning. Her confidant Browning had access to both sides of the Todd-Lincoln relationship. He roomed at the Butler home, where Lincoln took his meals.⁶⁸ Browning surmised that Todd's resentment was because Lincoln told her he loved Edwards.

"Mr. Lincoln became very much attached to her [Miss Matilda Edwards] and finally fell desperately in love with her, and proposed to her, but she rejected him," Browning recalled.⁶⁹

In reflections provided to Herndon, several correspondents cited other reasons for the failed engagement of Lincoln and Todd. Even two of the people closest to Lincoln and Todd disagreed about their breakup. Her brother-in-law Ninian Wirt Edwards believed that it was Lincoln's love for Matilda had caused the split. Edwards told biographer Herndon directly "that he, Lincoln, fell in Love with a Miss Edwards." In the Herndon interview, Edwards reported that Lincoln did not directly or indirectly make Matilda aware of his feelings. Edwards said somewhat inanely, "She became aware of this—Lincoln's affections—The Lincoln & Todd Engagement was broken off in Consequence of it."⁷⁰

Yet Edwards's testimony pointed out that Matilda was casting off all comers, including Speed and Douglas. In a telling revelation, Edwards said that Matilda married none of her Springfield suitors. Instead, she married Newton Deming Strong of Alton on September 24, 1844. As Rickard had done, Matilda Edwards told Lincoln that the difference in their ages was the reason she could not be serious about him. Her explanation was seemingly disingenuous. Age had made no difference in regard to the man she chose to marry. Strong had been born in 1809, which made him the same age as Lincoln. Edwards finally admitted to Elizabeth Todd Edwards, cousin Ninian's wife, that age had nothing to do with it: "Miss Edwards one dy [sic] was asked why she married such an old dried up husband—such a withered up old Buck. [She was twenty-two. Strong was thirty-four.] She replied: 'He had lots of houses & gold.'"⁷¹

While her husband believed Matilda Edwards was the direct cause of the Lincoln-Todd breakup, Elizabeth Edwards at the same time told inquisitor Herndon that she doubted Matilda had anything to do with it. "Mr. Lincoln loved Mary—he went Crazy in my own opinion—not because he loved Miss Edwards as was Said, but because he wanted to marry and doubted his ability & Capacity to please and support a wife. Lincoln & Mary were engaged—Everything was ready & prepared for the marriage— Even to the Supper &c—. Mr. L failed to meet his Engagement— Cause insanity. In his lunacy he declared he hated Mary and loved Miss Edwds. This is true, yet it was not his real feelings."

If Lincoln had been so love struck over Matilda Edwards, any affections he may have had for her escaped *her* notice. Elizabeth Edwards asked Matilda if Lincoln had ever mentioned the subject of love for her. "Miss Edwards Said—'On my word he never mentioned Such a Subject to me: he never even Stooped to pay me a Compliment.'"[72]

While history generally has looked to other women as the wedge that came between Lincoln and Todd, Todd herself did not believe another woman to be the cause. She blurted that out the moment Lincoln confessed to her that he did not love her. Todd believed the cause to be her relationship with Douglas. Herndon describes a telling scene in his biography of Lincoln. It is in his report of a conversation between Lincoln and Speed, who had been waiting for Lincoln to return from an interview in which he was to tell Todd they were finished.

"Well, old fellow, did you do as I told you and as you promised?" Speed asked Lincoln when he returned.

"Yes, I did," responded Lincoln, "and when I told Mary I did not love her, she burst into tears and almost springing from her chair and wringing her hands as if in agony, said something about the deceiver being himself deceived."[73]

Mary knew immediately that the root cause of Lincoln's loss of affection for her were her ill-advised dalliances with Douglas. She told Lincoln, "The deciever [*sic*] shall be decieved[;] wo[e] is me." Lincoln said she was "alluding to a young man She fooled."

Todd now regretted her attempt to use Douglas—who was, indeed, the "young man She fooled"—as a tool to win Lincoln's affections.[74] Lincoln's longtime law partner William Herndon, who had been present when Lincoln asked Speed's advice, believed Lincoln had grown so jealous over Todd's flirtations with Douglas that he could not marry her.[75] Whatever the cause, Lincoln in the interview with Todd once more committed himself to her. It happened after that tear burst when Lincoln told her he did not love her. The passion of Todd's reaction was too much for him, Lincoln later told Speed.

"I found the tears trickling down my own cheeks," Lincoln said. "I caught her in my arms and kissed her."[76]

Speed, the mentor who had sent Lincoln to personally break the engagement off, was irritated. That was foolish, he said, "a bad lick." Speed reminded Lincoln that in the custom of the time, Lincoln's pathetic reaction had been "tantamount to renewal of the engagement, and in decency you cannot back down now."

"'Well,' drawled Lincoln, 'if I am in again, so be it. It's done, and I shall abide by it.'"[77]

Lincoln realized he had been hooked again by Mary Ann Todd. The engagement was on.

12. The First Douglas-Lincoln Debates

DOUGLAS HAD PROMISED HIS FAMILY several times that he soon would return home to Canandaigua, New York, for a visit. He did not keep the promises. His sister Sarah reprimanded him for paying more attention to politics than family. Douglas acknowledged "the justice of her chidings" and promised to do better.[1] He did not.

Douglas's assurances to his family of a reunion continued to be broken. Business and the string of offices into which "friends placed him" were denying him the time even for personal relationships in Illinois. Each opportunity, he explained in letters home, required his "personal attention, and blast all my anticipations of enjoying the society of a Mother & Sister, a Father and a Brother, the only persons on earth to whom I feel any peculiar attachment."[2]

Douglas sounded resigned to and exhausted by the demands of his friends, demands, which he very often had arranged himself, that again and again denied him the pleasure of family and friends. As he complained: "I assure you that I have been so completely engrossed with the excitements and strifes of partizan conflicts and official stations," he wrote his brother-in-law in New York, "that office and honors have lost their charms, and I desire and seek repose and the society of friends."[3]

Although Douglas was artful in these sorry pleadings to his family, it was true that the young politician's party recognized his personal magnetism with others and continued to call on him for leadership. He was by no means unwilling to accommodate.

Douglas biographer Martin Quitt argues convincingly that Douglas, in fact, had conscientiously estranged himself from his family. Quitt points out that all of his correspondence home went either to brother-in-law Julius N. Granger or stepfather Gehazi Granger. While Douglas sent 15 letters, several of them quite lengthy, to his brother-in-law, he did not write a single letter to his mother from Illinois.[4] Quitt's analysis of Douglas's family relationships would explain that by considering the family's cross-marriages in relationship with the cultural conventions of the day. Douglas's Uncle Edward Fisk married Emily Granger, who was the daughter of Gehazi Granger, whom Douglas's widowed mother Sarah Fisk Douglas married. Douglas's sister Sarah married brother-in-law Julius. This would have made Emily Douglas's aunt and step-sister and Julius his stepbrother as well as brother-in-law. Quitt speculates that Douglas may have worried "about ridicule sparked by the complicated relationships that the three marriages produced.... The early nineteenth century labeled as incest marriages that broke traditional barriers, for which there was a good deal of confusion. The crisscross of affinal relationships that the Fisks and Grangers created was better left out of Douglas's story, even though they did not transgress a particular taboo."[5]

❖ ❖ ❖

Stephen Douglas was astute enough to recognize that party politics were best relegated to proper forums, that they were tolerated only so far—particularly when the discussion involved more erudite opponents. Even the devoted Jacksonian Democrat realized that an opinion stated too strongly was better saved for a forum in which there was something to gain.

That was the unspoken rule, as well, for a loose association of young Springfield lawyers, politicians, and political aspirants who frequently gathered around the wood-burning stove at the rear of Joshua Speed's store for what Speed called "a sort of social club without organization."[6] Speed was the resident partner in the Bell & Company general store, housed in a two-story wood-frame building at Fifth and Adams Streets on the southeast corner of Springfield's public square. It was a large country store, as Speed called it, selling dry goods, groceries, hardware, books, medicine, bed clothes, mattresses, and other sundry items.[7] Just northwest, at the center of the square, huge brown blocks of stone, hewn in quarries at Cotton Hill, ten miles southeast of Springfield, had begun forming the large Greek Revival building in which the new state capital would be housed.

The gatherings at Speed's store, said Herndon, were a "society for the encouragement of debate and literary efforts."[8] Weather notwithstanding, eight to ten young men—Herndon regretted that women were not allowed—gathered at Speed's every winter evening.[9] The regulars among them were Douglas, Herndon, Lincoln, James Matheny, Noah Rickard, Evan Butler, Edward Baker, Joseph Gillespie, James Shields, Nathaniel Pope, Milton Hay, and Newton Francis. Others attended irregularly. At Speed's the young men shared confidences and stories of the day and learned what made the other guys tick. According to Herndon, it was poverty. Poverty was, he said, "staring us all in the face."[10] It was at these gatherings that Speed became intimately associated with Lincoln and Douglas and their friends, he revealed in a later reminiscence.[11] These were occasions at which the young men would present original literary productions, read poetry, and hone their ability at public speaking and debating. Chief among the performers in partisan discussions were Douglas, who led the Democratic side, and Lincoln, who led the Whigs. Lincoln called on his additional talent—a talent Douglas admired and regretted he did not have—to deliver homespun stories that would take the sharpness off conversations when they turned too serious.

Since 1837, when he moved to Springfield to practice law with John Todd Stuart, Lincoln had resided above the Bell & Company store with Speed, the spirited Billy Herndon, who was clerking at attorney Stephen Logan's law firm at the time, and Charles R. Hurst, who clerked in Speed's store.[12] The brash and boisterous Douglas, though squat, cast the longest Democratic shadow at these affairs. He had been one of Lincoln's chief opponents during the Tenth General Assembly. But any rancor one might have expected the two men to have toward each other did not extend beyond the doors of the state capitol in Vandalia at the end of the session. Douglas was just as fond of Lincoln's homespun yarns as any of the members of the "social club." Lincoln enjoyed the give and take of similarly unattached Whigs and Democrats. Like many of his counterparts, Douglas did not have his friend's gift for folksy stories and greatly enjoyed Lincoln's.[13] To a point.

The conversations of Lincoln and his Whig friends could border on the provocative, sometimes intentionally. Douglas would wheedle and hedge when he could not answer Whig points authoritatively. When driven to the point he could no longer ignore the attacks on Jackson, Van Buren, or the politics of the Democracy, however, an enraged Douglas would dodge by lashing out blindly against any Whig excess that his mind could, on impulse, send to his tongue. With the usual crew of young Democrats and Whigs, and with a presidential election approaching, the conversation one evening in November turned to politics. Billy Herndon, seated on a wooden keg, listened eagerly to the escalating debate, and saw Douglas's ire escalating with it. "Douglas, I recollect, was leading on the Democratic side. He had already learned the art of dodging in debate, but still he was subtle, fiery, and impetuous. He charged the Whigs with every blunder and political crime he could imagine. No vulnerable spot seemed to have escaped him."[14]

The argument between Douglas and Lincoln grew more and more heated. Pestered by his party foe-friends, an exasperated Douglas sprang up and challenged anyone who disputed him to debate the matter publicly.

"Gentlemen, this is no place to talk politics," he said. "We will discuss the questions publicly with you."[15]

In leading the statewide campaign to promote the candidacies of Ohio Whig William Henry Harrison for president and John Tyler of Virginia for vice president, Lincoln had cast aside the candidacy of Henry Clay, the politician he had most admired throughout his life. In earlier days, Lincoln frequently called Clay his "beau ideal of a statesman." In 1840 Lincoln believed—and convinced his Whig friends—that Clay could not win. The old General Harrison, the Hero the Battle of Tippecanoe, was electable, Lincoln explained in a letter to the *Sangamo Journal*.[16]

Speed noted that this was the latest in the forensic rivalry between Douglas, who led the Van Buren campaign in Illinois, and Lincoln that had begun with their first acquaintance. It was clear to Speed, who was close to both men, that the differences between the two—in personality and character—were as distinctive as the state's north and south.

> "They seemed to have been pitted against each other from 1836 till Lincoln reached the Presidency," Speed recalled. They were the respective leaders of their parties in the State. They were as opposite in character as they were unlike in their persons. Lincoln was long and ungainly, Douglas short and compact. Douglas, in all elections, was the moving spirit in the conduct and management of an election; he was not content without a blind submission to himself. He could not tolerate opposition to his will within his party organization. He held the reins and controlled the movement of the Democratic chariot. With a large State majority with many able and ambitious men in it, he stepped to the front in his youth and held it until his death.
>
> Mr. Lincoln, on the other hand, shrank from any controversy with his friends. Being in a minority in the State he was forced to the front, because his friends thought he was the only man with whom they could win. In a canvass his friends had to do all the management. He knew nothing of how to reach the people except by addressing their reason. If the situation had been reversed, Lincoln representing the majority, and Douglas the minority, I think it most likely Lincoln would never had place. He had no heart for a fight with friends.[17]

Douglas's departure from Speed's store that night was acknowledgment that the work of lifting up their candidates was becoming more acrimonious. This night at Speed's store would mark the beginning of what would be two decades of public debates between Lincoln and Douglas. At the fireplace in the backroom of the store on this evening in November 1839, Lincoln responded to Douglas's flare up and challenged the Democrats to a series of public debates of Whig and Democracy principles and policies. It would be no momentary flash of a contest. The two agreed that their adherents would join them for eight evening debates to be held in the Second Presbyterian Church in Springfield.

When the first series of debates was considered a draw, the debates were extended with a second round in December.[18] The resumption of the contest would be mounted in a series of orations that continued for another eight evenings in the House of Representatives at the state capitol. Douglas would organize the orations, which would bring to the platform John Calhoun, Josiah Lamborn, and Jesse B. Thomas, Jr., for the Democracy and Lincoln, Edward D. Baker, Orville H. Browning, and Stephen T. Logan for the Whigs.[19] The topic of the debates was to be a discussion of President Van Buren's proposal for a sub-treasury to replace the defunct National Bank.

Douglas scheduled himself for the first speech on the evening of November 19 with Lincoln getting in a final word. Douglas and Lincoln were the combatants on the issue of the national bank. Lincoln's supporters admitted Douglas won that debate. As might have been expected from the voice of the Springfield Democracy, the *Illinois State Register* thought Lincoln's performance was "clownish" and said his parries with Douglas were ineffective.

"He could only meet the arguments of Mr. Douglas by relating stale anecdotes and old stories," the newspaper critiqued, "and left the stump literally whipped off of it, even in the estimation of his own friends."[20]

"Lincoln did not come up to the requirements of the occasion," according to one of Lincoln's closest friends, Joseph Gillespie. "He was conscious of his failure and I never saw any man so distressed."[21]

In his inimitable way of using any available tool to his advantage, Douglas fixed the schedule to the advantage of the Democrats. Douglas assigned Lincoln to speak on the last night, December 26, 1839, the evening after Christmas, when only the most dedicated partisans might be expected to attend. As Douglas had intended, by the time came for Lincoln to speak, attendance had dwindled considerably. Lincoln's disappointment tested the limits of despondency:

> Fellow Citizens:—It is peculiarly embarrassing to me to attempt a continuance of the discussion, on this evening, which has been conducted in this Hall on several proceeding ones. It is so, because on each of those evenings, there was a much fuller attendance than now, without any reason for its being so, except the greater *interest* the community feel in the *Speakers* tho addressed them *then*, than they do in *him* who is to do so *now*. I am, indeed, apprehensive, that the few who have attended, have done so, more to spare me of mortification, than in the hope of being interested in any thing I may be able to say. This circumstance casts a damp upon my spirits, which I am sure I shall be unable to overcome during the evening. But enough of preface.[22]

Despite his disappointment in the turnout, Lincoln spoke masterfully for more than two hours against Van Buren's sub-treasury. He responded point by point to Douglas's explanation that while Democrats sometimes erred in practice, they were always right in principle. That explanation actually scored the point for the Whigs, Lincoln said. He remembered a germane anecdote:

> A witty Irish soldier, who was always boasting of his bravery, when no danger was near, but who invariably retreated without orders at the first charge of an engagement, being asked by his Captain why he did so, replied, "Captain, I have as brave a heart as Julius Caesar ever had; but some how or other, whenever danger approaches, my cowardly legs will run away with it." So with (Douglas's) party. They take the public money into their hand for the most laudable purpose, that wise heads and honest hearts can dictate, but before they can possibly get it out again their rascally "vulnerable heels" will run away with them.[23]

Lincoln had been in Douglas's audience and in his own speech Lincoln would hold the Little Giant accountable for his loose use of facts. Douglas had defended Jackson's veto of the national bank and Van Buren's sub-treasury system. In addition, Douglas had argued that unusual one-time expenditures required during Van Buren's Presidency explained the higher cost of government during the Van Buren administration. One by one, Lincoln debunked every one of Douglas's claims. Lincoln's attack then turned personal.

> Those who heard Mr. Douglas, recollect that he indulged himself in a contemptuous expression of pity for me. "Now he's got me," thought I. But when he went on to say that five millions of the expenditure of 1838, were payments of the French indemnities, *which I knew to be untrue;* that five millions had been for the Post Office, *which I knew to be untrue;* that ten millions had been for the Maine boundary war, *which I not only knew to be untrue, but supremely ridiculous also;* and when I saw that he was stupid enough to hope, that I would permit such groundless and audacious assertions to go unexposed, I readily consented, that on the score of both veracity and sagacity, the audience should judge whether he or I were the more deserving of the world's contempt.[24]

Although he believed Lincoln had lost the first debate with Douglas, Gillespie said Lincoln's second effort, even if poorly attended, "transcended our highest expectations. I never heard & never expect to hear such a triumphant vindication as he then gave of Whig measures or policy." It was for Lincoln a turning point in the art of debate, according to Gillespie: "He never after to my knowledge fell below himself."[25] Lincoln was pleased to be able to tell Stuart in a letter on January 20, 1840, that his speech had been so well received that the Whig Party was publishing it in pamphlet form.[26]

Lincoln's speech was delivered "without manuscript or notes," as Speed recalled, and took up seven columns in the *Sangamo Journal*, which transcribed and printed it in pamphlet form as faithfully as it was given. The party would distribute the pamphlet in the upcoming presidential campaign Harrison and Van Buren.[27]

Illinois Whigs liked their chances for electing Harrison electors on November 2, 1840. For the first time they had organized, adopted the convention system, held a state convention to select delegates to the first national convention, and sent four delegates in December to the convention in Harrisburg. It was largely the doing of Lincoln, who encouraged the organization of Illinois' Whigs.

At the Harrisburg, Pennsylvania, convention the Whigs' national platform was simple: oppose Democrats.[28] Whigs were holding "Harrison Festivals" throughout Central Illinois, at which campaign planners like Jesse Fell, Asahel Gridley, and David Davis were organizing parade units of veterans who had served under Harrison in the War of 1812.[29]

Illinoisans, including many Democrats, were susceptible to the patriotism these promotions conjured up. They were more positive than the continuing effects of the Panic of 1837—still felt in Illinois, for which people blamed Van Buren. All this while as President Van Buren was living lavishly and had been just as profligate in government spending. State Senator Orville H. Browning of Quincy told the ungentrified of Illinois that Van Buren spent $85 on a pair of shears to trim hedges at the White House.[30] In addition, the president was thought to favor abolition and Negro suffrage.

Democrat Adam Snyder, a state senator from Belleville, had never seen anything like these attacks on Van Buren.

"We are in the midst of one of the hottest contests for the Presidency that has ever taken place in this country," he wrote. "The opposition have united all their forces on Gen'l Harrison. All the disaffected and disappointed of all differences of opinion and incongruities—Abolitionists and Southern states rights men, bank and anti-bank, tariff and anti-tariff men ... have joined forces for Harrison. The opposition has never before taken the field with such zeal and unanimity as in this campaign. Money, labor, and unremitting exertion are employed to effect their purpose."[31]

The Whigs blamed Democrats for every state and national ill, "for all the disasters and calamities (they had experienced), including droughts and overflows, crop failures, bank suspensions, and hard times; but were discreetly silent on internal improvement failures."[32]

By March 1840, Lincoln, the Harrison campaign's leader and principal speech maker in Illinois, was growing ever more optimistic. In January he had written his law partner Stuart, who was serving in Congress, "You know I am never sanguine, but I believe we will carry the state. The chance for doing so, appears to me 25 percent better than it did for you to beat Douglas."[33]

Within a month of that letter, Lincoln had a measure to validate his opinion. Since its first issue on February 1, 1840, subscriptions to the Harrison-booster *Old Soldier* newspaper were skyrocketing. Subscribers numbered 8,000 in the first month of publication, and Thomas C. Browne, an associate justice on the Illinois Supreme Court, told friends he expected subscriptions would reach 20,000.[34] Lincoln was one of five editors of the tabloid, published in the *Sangamo Journal* office in Springfield. He was ecstatic about the paper's success and his next letter to Stuart was even more glowing.[35]

"I have never seen the prospects of our party so bright in these parts as they are now," Lincoln wrote.

Lincoln was delighted that his counterpart, Douglas of the Van Buren campaign in Illinois, appeared to be on edge. Lincoln told Stuart of an incident in which Douglas had been insulted by something he had seen in the *Springfield Journal* the day before. Walking with party operative John Calhoun, Douglas met the *Journal* Editor Simeon Francis on a Springfield street. Douglas grabbed John Calhoun's cane and tried to beat Francis with it. Francis, at six feet tall and rotund, manhandled Douglas, grabbing him by his hair and pinning him against a market cart, as Lincoln described it, holding him there until he was pulled off.[36]

"The whole affair was so ludicrous that Francis and everybody else (Douglas excluded) have been laughing about it ever since," said Lincoln.[37]

Time and Stephen Douglas proved Lincoln a bit too buoyant. Big men frightened Douglas not at all and he was not one whit less confident about his own man's chances than Lincoln was for his. Douglas also was confident about his ability to lead his team to victory. Others were just as confident about Douglas. Sangamon County Democrats elected him a delegate to the state convention. Party officials elected him chairman of the state central committee and in February 1840 elected him manager of the Democratic campaign in Illinois. Early that year Douglas helped start *Old Hickory*, a campaign newspaper to boost Van Buren and Democratic principles. He denied that he was editing the newspaper—John Calhoun was doing that—but Douglas was directing *Old Hickory's* editorial policy.[38] He was fully engaged in the Van Buren campaign and admonished friends around the state to do the same.

"Energy and activity are all that is necessary to gain the victory," he wrote to Lewis Ross, a Democratic leader in Fulton County along the Illinois River. "Let us not relax our exertions because we feel confident of success."[39]

As if to assure his campaign's workers that he was not asking them to do more than he was doing himself, Douglas told Ross he was in this campaign wholeheartedly: "We keep up the fire wherever we go."[40]

Douglas himself was, indeed, on fire in this campaign. If any man was doing the hard fighting for his man, it was Douglas. Between March 1 and the election November 2, he delivered 207 speeches—nearly one a day—in his statewide canvass.[41] It frequently put him on the platform with Stuart, his old foe for Congress a few years earlier, with Edward D. Baker, with his old nemesis John J. Hardin of Jacksonville, and with Lincoln several times. At Springfield in October, Douglas debated two experienced campaigners in one day and was so engaged in the second contest that he ordered supper brought to him on the platform. Douglas's defense of Van Buren was fearless. The Whigs had mocked the president as "Van, Van the used up man." With the ex-governor present, Douglas skinned Joseph Duncan as "the worst used up man" he had ever seen.[42]

Lincoln—and Douglas—may not have fallen below the esteem of their friends, but they did reach a low point in their attempts to outdo each other on the matter of race. In preparing for a debate in Jacksonville in March 1840, Lincoln had worked up a charge that as a delegate to a New York constitutional convention nearly twenty years earlier Van Buren had championed universal black suffrage. When Lincoln asserted the charge, Douglas bounded forward to interrupt him. Not true, Douglas screamed. Lincoln calmly awaited Douglas's return to his seat, then read a passage from William M. Holland's biography of Van Buren. When Douglas called the text false, Lincoln produced a letter Van Buren had written to Dr. William Fithian of Danville confirming the information.

"Damn such a book," Douglas yelled as he snatched it from Lincoln's hand and slung it, pages flying, into the crowd.[43]

Fithian actually had twisted Van Buren's actions in the 1821 New York convention at which suffrage was a major issue. Holland's biography of Van Buren reported that Van Buren was silent during the convention's debate over suffrage for free black residents. He voted with the majority, however, in rejecting a proposal to restrict the votes to whites. And he voted to require a property qualification for free black candidates for presidential electors.[44]

Whether Lincoln ever learned the truth of Van Buren's actions, Lincoln found it continued to work for him across Illinois. He repeated it, finding that he could win "spontaneous bursts of applause from the People, [which] gave evidence that their hearts were with him."[45]

Illinois' legislative elections in August 1840 were the first important harbinger of the effectiveness of the presidential champions Douglas and Lincoln, and they foreshadowed a Van Buren victory in Illinois in November. Democrats took twenty of twenty-seven seats in the state Senate and forty-five of the eighty-five seats in the house. Seeing the results of the fall election, both parties and their leaders redoubled their efforts to elect their man in November.

The presence of Irish canal and railroad workers among voters in congressional elections in 1836, 1838, and 1840 and the presidential election in 1840 stirred Illinois Whigs to white heat. It was time to do something about it. Ironically, many of the emigrants had come to Illinois to work on projects in the massive public works program Lincoln's legislative delegation from Sangamon County had passed in 1837. By that summer, for example, a small army of Irishman arrived in Quincy to work on the Northern Cross Railroad, which was to be built from Quincy to Springfield.[46]

The *Quincy Whig* was displeased with the Democrats' invention of party organization and its appeal to the foreign vote. The *Whig* warned that all this Democratic architecture was going to leave the Whig ship "sailing under bare poles." The newspaper was particularly disturbed by the so-called alien vote: "When we saw Captain (Timothy) Kelly with his sixty odd Irish volunteers march up in a solid body to the polls and deposit their votes as one man we were strongly impressed with the idea that the elective right in the state was a mere mockery."[47]

There had been a barrage of criticism of these foreign or so-called alien voters following the 1836 congressional election in the Third District. Democrat William May whipped Whig John Todd Stuart 11,764 to 10,001. Although Democrats took the three other congressional seats in that election, May's lopsided victory was largely because of the heavy vote in and around the counties in which construction of the Illinois-Michigan Canal had just gotten underway. Irishmen who furnished the labor for the canal furnished the vote for May's win.[48] The *Chicago American* led the attack on ethnocentric grounds and demanded an end to the alien vote.

"No man of foreign birth should be admitted to the political rights of an American citizen," said the *American*.[49]

Then, in 1838, the upstart Democrat Stephen Douglas, not even old enough during the campaign to meet the age requirement for a seat in Congress, came within a hair's breadth of beating Springfield's popular Whig John Todd Stuart. Once again, it was the foreign vote that tightened the race. The *Quincy Whig* alleged that "EIGHT HUNDRED of those that voted for Douglas and Carlin, on the Canal, have dispersed to parts unknown.... The people of the State can now see, to whom they are indebted for '*Democratic majorities*'—to an itinerant rabble, who vote here to-day, and perhaps would be found in arms fighting the battles of their Queen against us, to-morrow."[50]

The *Whig* demanded a constitutional amendment so that "the growing interests of this large state ... be under the control of her own citizens.... We are confident if this question should go to the people, a large majority of them would say—*Let emigrant foreigners, first become citizens of the UNITED States, before we grant them ALL the privileges which belong to the citizens of our own.*"[51]

Lincoln reached an ironic conclusion that business conditions would ultimately do away with the foreign vote. He wrote Stuart in early January 1840 about rumors that the state's financial woes would bring an end to internal improvements, which would alleviate a need for alien workers and voters.

"The Whigs say that the canal and other public works will stop," he wrote, "and, consequently, *we shall then be clear of the foreign votes*, whereas by another year they may be brought in again."[52]

Whigs continued to look for a way to overcome the voting block made up of the thousands of Irish laborers who resided in the northern part of the state to work on the Illinois-Michigan Canal. Nine tenths of them were reckoned to be Democratic voters.[53] The Democratic vote in the canal counties was clear evidence that the alien vote had the power to decide elections.

Whigs knew their party would continue to be relegated to the minority unless they found a way to overcome it.[54]

Two Whigs in a far northwestern Illinois county found the opportunity.

Horace H. Houghton, who grew up on a Vermont farm, took up the printing trade at the age of eighteen. He advanced himself in his work, made his way to New York for a stint with Harper Brothers Publishers, to Boston for a season, then returned to Vermont to take charge of *The Statesman* newspaper in Castleton.

Houghton was drawn west in 1834, within a year after Stephen Douglas started his journey. Like Douglas, Houghton traveled to Ohio where he found work in Marietta, then moved on to Cincinnati and Louisville. He continued west, stopping in St. Louis, where he worked for a brief time in the office of the *St. Louis Republican*. Hearing about the prosperity being generated by lead mines in northwestern Illinois, Houghton migrated to the region. He joined in managing *The Northwestern Gazette and Galena Advertiser* in Galena, the county seat of Jo Daviess County at the northwest corner of the state.[55] Eventually Houghton bought the newspaper.

Houghton was Whig and he made his newspaper editorially Whig. He also was an innovator. He invented a device to remove single sheets of paper from the printing press. It became standard equipment on Adams and Hoe presses, preferred by publishers because it eliminated the need to pay a man to remove the printed sheets. In 1839 Houghton came up with another novel device, this one having the power to pitch Illinois Democrats like sheets of paper out of political office.

On Election Day, August 6, 1838, Whig election judge Thomas Spraggins allowed Jeremiah Kyle, an Irish canal worker, to vote in Jo Daviess County for county officers and for representative in Congress. Kyle had lived in Jo Daviess County for more than six months but, never naturalized, he was not a U.S. citizen. Houghton saw in an elegant convolution of law the opportunity his party had been seeking.[56] It was in a little-used provision. Houghton became a "whistle blower."

He filed a *qui tam* writ in the Jo Daviess County circuit court of Judge Dan Stone, whom Douglas had known as a Whig in their days together in the state legislature. It was the same Dan Stone who had joined Representative Lincoln on March 3, 1837, in protesting anti-abolition resolutions the General Assembly had passed two months earlier. Lincoln had solicited other representatives to join him in the protest. Stone was among the five who signed on.

Under *qui tam* a private individual was incentivized to bring suit against a person alleged to have committed fraud against the state. The law did not require the plaintiff to be damaged by the defendant's conduct. It recognized, instead, that whistle blowing could discourage such fraud. And it encouraged whistle blowers to do so by permitting judges to award to the whistle blower part or all of any fines they imposed.[57] A voting rights law in 1829 provided a fine of $100 against an election judge who permitted an unqualified voter to cast a vote. With defendant Spraggins agreeing to be sued, Houghton alleged that Spraggins as an election judge, a government official under the election law, had improperly allowed an unnaturalized Irish resident of Illinois vote in the congressional election.

There had been little notice of the case. There was little to notice. Neither Houghton nor Spraggins submitted arguments, leaving Judge Stone, strangely, to privately infer the circumstances of the case.[58] The judge ruled in favor of plaintiff Houghton in October. The state did not have the authority, went Judge Stone's ruling, to authorize unnaturalized citizens to vote. Spraggins, therefore, had violated the law.[59] The judge fined Spraggins $100, the full amount allowed by the voting rights law.[60]

The ruling shocked the state's Democrats, none more than Douglas.[61] They saw in it a Whig conspiracy to disenfranchise lawful voters. Both parties to the suit, Houghton and Spraggins, had been Whigs. A Whig judge had heard the case. Three of the four justices of the Supreme Court were Whigs. The track had been laid, Democrats complained, for a "railroading" that would exceed all the rail that had been laid by the failed internal improvements program.

Stone's decision had far-reaching implications that challenged for the first time in Illinois history a provision of the state constitution that had worked to the advantage of the state's Democrats. In a twenty-year-old state whose stock was composed of immigrants, Illinois always had allowed any free white male "inhabitant" over twenty-one years of age and who had resided in the state for at least six months to vote in state elections. Up to this time, that included suffrage for Illinois' unnaturalized residents so long as they met those tests. It was clear why the Whigs celebrated Stone's ruling and the Democrats detested it. There were as many as ten thousand foreign residents in the state at the time, and ninety percent of them voted Democratic.[62] A look at the electoral maps would have been enough to convince Democrats that the "Galena Alien Case" would be fatal to the future of the Democratic Party in Illinois. And it could happen as early as August 3, 1840, when voters would elect nineteen members of the Illinois Senate and all ninety-four members of the House of Representatives. The presidential election was scheduled for November 3, just three months later.

Douglas's own experience in his contest against Whig John Todd Stuart the year before had demonstrated the importance of these blocks of unnaturalized voters to the Democratic Party. The Third District's Irish residents had been the difference in bringing Douglas to within 36 votes of a seat in Congress. Added to that was the possible loss of the unnaturalized German population in Southwestern Illinois. Judge Stone's decision had the power to cast Douglas's Democrats into a political abyss in which they would no longer be the majority party in Illinois.[63]

"If allowed to stand as law, that decision would have the effect of delivering the state and all the branches of government to the Whig party," observed one of Douglas's Democratic friends. "Mr. Douglas saw the importance of the decision not only to the thousands who were disenfranchised by it, but also the importance in a political or party view."[64]

With congressional elections occurring every two years, Douglas understood the urgency to act. He quickly appealed to the Illinois Supreme Court, which granted certiorari for the court's December 1839 term. With his Jacksonville friend, Democratic attorney Murray McConnel his co-counsel, Douglas appeared in December before the four justices of the Supreme Court in Springfield to argue the case. Opposing attorneys were Virginia-born Cyrus Walker of Macomb, part of the erstwhile "Edwards Dynasty"; Schuyler Strong, who had arrived in Springfield "advanced in years" from New York; and Justin Butterfield of Chicago. These lawyers were recognized by their peers as strong advocates for the Whig position.[65] They argued that in exercising its constitutional power over naturalization itself Congress required immigrants to reside in the country for five years before they could attain rights of citizenship, including the right to vote. As the Whig lawyers argued, this confirmed that the authors of the U.S. constitution had never envisioned an unnaturalized resident having a right to vote after only six months of residence.[66]

Douglas argued that the Illinois constitution drew a distinction between naturalized citizens and inhabitants and that the U.S. constitution enabled it. He conceded that the U.S. constitution provided for the country's naturalization laws in the manner the Whigs had described. But he pointed out that the second section of the constitution's first article left entirely to the states the control over the privilege of voting. Illinois had never surrendered that control of suffrage to the federal government, argued Douglas, and the state's constitution gave "inhabitants" the right to vote. Douglas pointed out that in Illinois inhabitants were defined as any white male over twenty-one years of age who had lived in the state for at least six months. He referred to numerous acts of Congress, federal court decisions, and state laws to show that the word inhabitant included aliens.[67] The arguments of both sides were compelling. Yet Douglas knew that the logic of neither argument got at the real issues.

"The point," wrote one of Douglas's closest friends, "was not whether the state *ought* to admit aliens to vote, but whether the state, having already conferred the privilege, had the power and authority to do so or not. The case was the first involving the point ever tried in the United States."[68]

That was the legal concern. Douglas's more practical concern was the politics of the case. Three of the four justices were "a formidable auxiliary of the Whig party. Its members, as the Council of Revision [with veto power over legislation], could hold governor and legislature in check, and accomplish indirectly all the ends sought by the minority."[69]

Douglas believed the Whig-dominated Court would likely decide the *Spraggins v. Houghton* case to the advantage of the Whig Party.[70] The only Democrat on the high court was Justice Theophilus W. Smith, a man so notorious for his personal ambitions—party be damned—that assistance from him was uncertain. Justice Smith's dream had been to be elected to the U.S. Senate, and he was known to have schemed, even from the bench, to achieve it.

A New Yorker, Smith had studied law in the law offices of Aaron Burr. Trained in the art of political intrigue in Tammany Hall, Smith was known to his fellow Illinoisans as a self-serving trickster.[71] He "never lacked a plot to advance himself. He was a laborious and ingenious schemer in politics, but his plans were always too complex and ramified for his power to execute them. Being always unsuccessful himself, he was delighted with the mishaps alike of friends and enemies; and was ever chuckling over the defeat or the blasted hopes of some one," his colleague from the bench, Thomas Ford, said about him.[72]

The arguments before the Supreme Court in the alien case completed, the justices announced they would take the case under advisement until their June 1840 term.[73] At least, this meant that Douglas and his Democratic colleagues had six months to find a way to resolve the dilemma in their favor, or risk the loss of control of the government.

13. Creating a Constitutional Crisis

As grave and demanding as these matters were, Douglas and Lincoln, leaders of the two parties at war over the right of the state's foreign inhabitants to vote, still had to earn a living. That summer and fall they were engaged in their law practices, traveling across the judicial circuit and at stops along the way debating presidential election campaign issues.

A murder trial in DeWitt County in May 1840 brought Douglas and Lincoln together on the same side of the courtroom, the only time in their twenty-six year acquaintance that they would be on the same side of a case. Along with attorney Kirby Benedict of nearby Macon County, they served as co-counsel for Spencer Turner of Clinton, who was accused of mortally bludgeoning Martin K. Martin of Clinton on April 15. The facts were arrayed strongly against Douglas and Lincoln's client. There was a witness to the crime. William Dishon on April 19, the day after Martin died of his wounds, swore to Justice of the Peace J.C. McPherson he had seen Turner attack Martin "with a piece of timber of considerable size." It was enough evidence for McPherson to order Turner arrested. A grand jury handed up an indictment "that Spencer Turner not having the fear of God befor [sic] his eyes but being moved and seduced by the intigation [sic] of the Devil ... feloniously willfully and of his malice afore thought did strike giving to the said Martin then and there with the wooden stick ... one mortal wound of the length of two inches and of the depth of one inch."

Reporting the grand jury's indictment, State's Attorney H.B. Campbell concluded that Turner "did kill and murder [Martin] contrary to the ... Statute in such cause made and provided and against the peace and dignity of the same people of the State of Illinois." The indictment that Campbell drafted to report the grand jury's findings filled the better part of two pages. The verbiage totaled 388 words in a single sentence with 22 misspellings and malapropisms. Illinois did not require unblemished literacy of lawyers who practiced in the state, as both Douglas and Lincoln themselves exemplified from time to time.

At the same time Campbell was presenting evidence in the case to the grand jury, McPherson empanelled a coroner's jury. The county had just been organized in 1839, so there was as yet no county coroner to conduct an inquest. For the same reason, there was no resident attorney in DeWitt to defend Turner, which is why Douglas and Lincoln were working in his behalf.[1]

The inquest framed the main facts of the case. Martin had been found "helpless and speechless" near Miles Gray's garden in Clinton and taken to Gray's house. He remained in a coma and died at about 5 a.m. on April 18, 1840. That evening, the coroner's jury conducted an inquiry, gathered evidence, and carefully examined the body of the deceased. The jurors concluded Martin "came to his death by a severe blow upon his head with a club struck by Spencer Turner ... which blow was struck on the 15th day of April 1840 near two o'clock p.m."

Damning evidence, indeed. But Douglas and Lincoln noted one additional comment by the coroner's jury: "Together with his [Martin's] own imprudence in keeping himself in a state of intoxication and exposure in rain and inclemency of the weather on the night previous to his death."² It was enough for Douglas and Lincoln to plant doubt in the minds of the jury members about the cause of Martin's death. Was it the blow? Was it the liquor? Or was it exposure to the elements?

"Admit nothing and require my adversary to prove everything."

Henry Wilbray, who had been elected foreman from among the twelve jurors who heard the case that morning, submitted the jury's decision later in the day: "We the jury find the Devendnt [sic] not gilty. Clinton, May 23—1840."³ For their work in the case Douglas and Lincoln earned $200 each. Lincoln was willing to accept a ninety-day note. Douglas demanded that he be paid immediately. After waiting eighteen months, Lincoln had to sue Turner for payment.⁴

The year 1840 had opened with alarm growing among the Democrats about the looming possibility of an unfavorable ruling by the Illinois Supreme Court in the Alien Case. Such a ruling could disenfranchise large blocks of German and Irish voters who favored Democratic candidates. Democrats could sense something unseemly at the moment the decision was expected. Whigs seemed uncommonly celebratory. In unusual pageantry and pomposity, the state's Whig party had organized a Central Committee and was raising the flag of William Henry Harrison to oppose the re-election of President Van Buren in November. This was the same group of Whigs who earlier had reckoned the convention system a fraud on the people and a fungus on the constitution.⁵ Stuart, Lincoln, Baker, Logan and Henry were the key organizers of a two-day "Young Men's" Whig convention in Springfield, which they called for June 2, 1840.⁶ It seemed more than a coincidence that the affair had been arranged for the same time the Supreme Court was to reconvene for their summer session. Democrats feared the large gathering of Whigs from across the state would influence the justices, if in fact they had not already telescoped their decision to the Whigs.⁷

Thousands came from all over Illinois to participate in the Springfield Whigs' celebration of the Harrison "log cabin and hard cider" campaign. They camped on the prairie, drank cider, and sang campaign songs. A delegation from Chicago had spent a week traveling to the rally, bringing along their own band, a six-pound cannon to fire salutes, and a thirty-foot miniature brig drawn by a team of six white horses. Even though it had been a group of Springfield Whigs, the "Long Nine," which had won the state capital from them a few years earlier, Fayette County Whigs pulled an entire log cabin some eighty-five miles from Vandalia to be part of the convention.⁸

Veterans of the American Revolution and the War of 1812 led a huge Whig parade that began at 10 a.m. June 3, followed by the Chicago Whigs' band and miniature brig. Delegations from the states of Indiana, Iowa and Missouri, and from fifty-nine of the Illinois' eighty-four counties followed.⁹

Democrats reckoned the Whig shindig cost a hundred thousand dollars. They had it from good Whig authority that at a free public "Barbacue" [sic] party-goers had consumed "six thousand pounds of fresh beef, eighty head of sheep, and hogs, bacon hams by hundreds, with numerous other articles of refreshment ... furnished at an immense cost."¹⁰

With Douglas a co-author, the Illinois Democrats' Central Committee issued an extensive condemnation of the Whig Springfield party. In a series of resolutions about the convention,

Douglas and colleagues considered it their duty "to warn the honest and unsuspecting to beware of hypocrisy, treachery, and deceit." The Democrats were "mortified" by the ends to which the Whigs went. The inventory of offenses included "stockjobbers and bankers" in silks and satins, images of log cabins stamped on gilt buttons worn by the gentry, "and above all, the full-length portrait of Gen. Harrison borne among a deluded crowd, commanding their shouts and huzzas." These were gimmicks, the Democracy's defenders wrote, drawn from British pageantry by which politicians deigned to "mislead the people by shows and exhibitions instead of argument and reason."

The Whig pageant was designed to appeal to the basest of human emotion, Douglas and colleagues wrote. "The degradation of the intellect of man is, and always has been, one of the most efficient means of destroying free and representative Governments: and if ever the liberties of the people of this Republic are to be lost, and forever destroyed, it can, alone, be accomplished by such means as those now in progress, where reason and intellect are utterly disregarded, and nothing but the baser passions of our nature appealed to."[11]

It took less verbiage for the *Register,* Springfield's Democratic newspaper to sum up its opinion of the Whig gathering.

"Humbug," said the *Register* unceremoniously about the Whig affair.[12]

The Democrats earlier that spring had called off their own convention by an excuse that it had been scheduled unwittingly during the busy time of year for Democratic farmer-delegates. Now, however, they asked that the party faithful gather at their county seats at noon on July 4, "the great and glorious anniversary of our national birth." And just as they sought to attach themselves to the glories of the Revolution, the Democrats sought to cast the Whigs as just the kinds of aristocrats the rebellion had overthrown. Douglas made no little point of the fact that the Whigs had chosen to start their convention on the birth date of George III, the British king "from whom our ancestors wrested our liberties from sacrilegious destruction."[13]

Douglas's anxiety about Justice Theophilus W. Smith's position on the Alien Case was dispelled by highly unusual—if not unethical—actions. Justice Smith was now communicating regularly with Douglas about the case—and not only about his own views but about those of his fellow justices, which he had learned in confidence in conferences of the justices, as well.[14] Smith secretly warned Douglas that the three other justices—Samuel Drake Lockwood, William Wilson and Thomas C. Brown, all Whigs—had made up their minds. Smith revealed that even before the arguments that were expected to be heard when they resumed hearing the case, the Whig justices already had written their decision. Justice Smith told Douglas the majority was going to dismiss Douglas's appeal.[15] The revelations outraged Douglas. But he saw in the court's premature action a misstep that he later would be able to use to advantage. For now, he had ammunition enough. Smith had revealed some important clerical errors in the record. Douglas sent for a copy of the record. In it he found what he believed was a fatal—even if it was only technical error.[16]

The Supreme Court reconvened in June and began handing down decisions in cases heard and taken in December. *Spraggins v. Houghton,* the vehicle for the Alien Case, was called. Douglas sprang from his seat and moved for dismissal of the case based on "defects" in the record.[17] Douglas pleaded that the case was fictitious and no violation could possibly have occurred. One of the justices noted that the parties had agreed that only the constitutional issue was to be decided and that the Court was ready to make its ruling.

"That was and still is the agreement," Douglas answered, "but ... the defect in the record was of such a nature that no decision could be made upon it, even on the constitutional question, unless the record was corrected."[18]

In his review of the record and Justice Smith's notations, Douglas had discovered an error so mundane that it had been overlooked. But given the seriousness of this matter the mundane could be of gargantuan importance to Douglas. To paraphrase one of Douglas's first lessons in practicing before the court, *require my adversary to prove everything.*"[19] The detail Douglas found was that in logging in the case the Supreme Court clerk had recorded a file date of May 1839. That was three months before the August 6, 1839, election during which the violation was alleged to have occurred. Douglas pounced. There had been no election in May. The violation Houghton had alleged could not possibly have occurred, Douglas argued. The entire case had been a fiction, he said, and must be dismissed.[20] The opposing lawyers, flabbergasted, now asked the court for time to allow them to review and correct the record. The court acceded to the request and refused Douglas's motion. Douglas was not ready to yield. There was more to show that the case, in fact, had been a hollow political trick. Houghton and Spraggins had concocted a ploy that did not involve a controversy at law. Both litigants were Whigs, Douglas argued, and neither of them put on a case before the judge. Therefore, there had been no contest. Douglas pointed out that the judge was a Whig who decided a case that did not exist. The motive was purely political and on its face demanded dismissal. Here was a dilemma for the court. While Douglas's argument did not persuade the court to dismiss the case, the justices agreed there was the matter of a faulty record and a need to correct it. That would take time. If it were to avoid being cast as conspirators in a weak and political case, the court had little choice other than to continue it.[21] The court did so.

Douglas did not get all he wanted. But there was no need to further argue principle when what he got was, for now, enough. The second continuance meant that a ruling in the case would have to wait the court's winter term, which was to begin in December 1840. By that time, the August gubernatorial and legislative elections and the November presidential election would have been conducted. Douglas's discovery of a single detail would preserve the alien vote for the Democrats in the two upcoming elections.[22] The continuance also would give Douglas the time to air the case in the most important court of all, public opinion.

Although the vote in the subsequent presidential contest was close—Van Buren won 47,443 votes and Harrison won 45,576,[23] Illinois was one of only two states the president won in the northern, non-border states. New Hampshire was the other. Douglas's effort surpassed Lincoln's. Although he was a Yankee, Van Buren won 61 percent of the vote in Southern Illinois. He also finished strongly in the counties along the Illinois River, where Irish laborers were working to build the Illinois-Michigan canal. It was that Irish vote, which on average increased voter rolls some 30 percent in the river counties, which gave Van Buren Illinois' electoral votes. It also served up the main factor in a battle over the right of immigrants to vote. Douglas once again would put himself in the middle of that controversy, a renewal of the same controversy that followed his 1838 race for Congress.[24]

Although Van Buren had lost the Jacksonian affections of many Illinois Democrats, the heavy returns for his electors along the Illinois-Michigan Canal—the "alien" vote as Whigs referred to it, where Douglas had focused much of his effort, helped make up for the defections. Disappointed Whigs like Lincoln's McLean County friend and fellow lawyer David Davis blamed Harrison's loss of Illinois on the foreign vote.

"If the Irish did not vote more than 3 times we could easily carry the State," Davis complained.[25]

There was no failure in the strategy of either Douglas or Lincoln. Except for the vote along the canal counties, the Whig vote was up significantly. Democrats got the canal-side vote, but Mormons on the west side of the state contributed Illinois' strongest showing for Harrison. Sixty-eight percent of the vote from Hancock County, where the Latter Day Saints had established their New Zion, went to the Whigs. Mormons scratched out the name of Whig Elector Abraham Lincoln, however, and replaced it with James H. Ralston, a Quincy lawyer and Democrat—as Douglas, in his effort to capture the Mormon electorate, had instigated.[26]

"The continuance [of the Alien Case] saved the day to the Democrats," a Douglas biographer would sum up. "During the months following, until the elections had been passed, no Supreme Court has ever received the denunciations that Douglas poured out upon the heads of its members."[27]

By the time the Supreme Court reconvened in December, Douglas and his Illinois Democrats had conducted a campaign for the public mind that blanketed the justices in criticism. The strength of Douglas's effort to get the court to change what Douglas had understood would be the way the court would rule backfired, however. He had not anticipated that the court, assailed as it was at Douglas's beckoning, might alter its opinion, which was written by his old nemesis Samuel Drake Lockwood. Attacked by those who predicted the court would issue a political decision, Lockwood and his colleagues watered down their decision. Lockwood wrote for the Whig members of the court:

> The question, then, whether Kyle was an inhabitant, and entitled to the right of suffrage, within the meaning of that word in the Constitution, is not a subject of enquiry by the judges of the election. I am, therefore, of opinion, that Spragins [sic], in admitting Kyle to vote, has not violated the statute, and is consequently not liable to the penalty. On the constitutional question, whether unnaturalized foreigners, who are permanent residents of the State, have a right to vote, I forbear to express an opinion, as I believe, while our election laws remain as they are, the judges of elections are bound to receive the votes of such persons.

Based on the record, the court determined that by agreement of both parties the alien voter in question met the qualifications required by the law of 1829. Stone's court had erred in imposing the penalty. Justice Smith, the court's only Democrat, agreed with Lockwood's ruling.[28]

Foul, cried Douglas. The threat to the Democracy had centered on the crucial constitutional question of suffrage for "unnaturalized foreigners," as Lockwood termed them in his opinion. Avoiding that question now, Douglas knew, meant that Lockwood had left the door open for a renewed attack in the future. Douglas took his complaint to the "Third House" of the state capitol. In a speech in the lobby Douglas got to the nub of his complaint that the Supreme Court had issued an opinion steeped in politics. He charged that the court had purposely evaded the main issue in the Alien Case to quiet the Democrats in order to defeat Douglas's bill for judicial reorganization.[29] The opinion in the Alien Case gave Douglas evidence that he would have to redouble his effort to reorganize the court. In the statehouse lobby and around Illinois he decried the court's apparent partisanship and worked even harder for his party's, and with no less vigor, his own interests.

"It [Douglas's argument] gave strength to the advocates of a reorganization of the judiciary," wrote Douglas's biographer and longtime friend James Sheahan. "The political characters of the court, and the partisan nature of their official acts as judges and as members of the Council on Revision, were held up in the strongest light, not only in the legislature, but in the more animated debates in the lobby."[30]

Douglas's arguments would excite the electorate of both parties in the days ahead.

Douglas's name had been among the 195 signatories to an announcement published in the *Illinois State Register* on March 27, 1840, calling on precinct delegates to attend a Sangamon County convention to nominate candidates for the state legislature and county offices in Illinois. Focused on a greater political prize—although he spoke of considerations of a private nature, Douglas declined his party's nomination to run for the legislature from Sangamon County. Douglas already had served in the Illinois General Assembly as the representative from Morgan County. With loftier goals in mind, Douglas viewed a return to the legislature as a step backward. In a letter about the nomination to Col. Robert Allen, a Springfield merchant on whose stagecoach Douglas ridden into Central Illinois six years earlier,[31] Douglas reported he had too little time to devote to the canvass.[32] It was a ruse. He already had begun pulling wires for another office, one more step up that could help assure he would win his coveted seat in Congress. This plan was Douglas's most outlandish. It was a strategy that ultimately would result in a self-serving alteration of the state's highest court. It would be Douglas's greatest ploy—could put him on the state's highest judicial bench—and this after having been told just five years earlier that he was not competent enough to practice law. If he was successful, he would become at age twenty-seven the youngest Illinois Supreme Court justice ever.

Alexander Pope Field was particularly proud of his middle name. It connected him to one of the founding giants of the State of Illinois, Nathaniel Pope. Field had been Illinois secretary of state since 1828, appointed to the post by Illinois' third governor, Ninian Edwards, another Field relative. It was his connection to his famous uncle Nathaniel, who in 1809 had been appointed the first secretary of the Illinois Territory and in 1816, was elected the Territory's delegate to Congress. Nathaniel Pope had been a tenacious congressman, introducing the legislation to make Illinois a state and persuading his colleagues into fixing its upper boundary far enough north to assure the new state would have broad access to Lake Michigan. Pope recognized the importance of that access. It would connect Illinois to the commercial centers and seaports of the East.[33]

Upon admission of Illinois to the Union, Pope, a lawyer, was appointed United States district judge for the state. At about the same time, his nephew Alexander Pope Field arrived in Illinois and was elected from 1822 to 1828 to the General Assembly from far-south Union County. Field looked as if he had been stretched to a straight-standing six feet, three inches tall. He was so thin that he looked even taller. His proportionally small head, with thin lips, squinty eyes and protruding nose, seemed ill fitted for the length of his body. Trousers belted well above his midsection gave his legs the appearance of stilts on which a small torso rested. The appearance of his boots indicated narrow feet.

Pope became secretary of state in 1829 and held the office without the re-nomination by any of the three governors during that time, John Reynolds, William L.D. Ewing, and Joseph Duncan. Field had in his twelve years grown comfortable and complacent. Running a successful law practice that frequently took him away from Vandalia for lengthy periods of time, he had no intention of vacating his executive post. There was no reason for him to feel compelled to do so. The state's constitution provided for appointment by a governor to the office of secretary of state but said not a word about a term of office—when the holder was to leave, or under what conditions.[34] Without that direction in the constitution, Field believed he was entitled to remain in office unless the constitution was amended, the legislature created a law to remove him, or a court convicted him of some official malfeasance, all reasons Reynolds, Ewing, and Duncan did not attempt to remove him from office.

Although he had entered office a Jacksonian Democrat, Field's interest in party or loyalty had declined over time and he had strayed into the Whig party. Governor Thomas Carlin of Quincy, however, was a Jackson man in principle, who believed that to the victor belongs the spoils. Yet Carlin waited. The word in the Democratic Party's inner council was that Douglas was working with Field on a deal that would enable Field to keep his office in exchange for certifying Douglas the winner of the Stuart-Douglas congressional contest. Field already had issued a certificate of election to Stuart, but a certificate to Douglas would allow him to follow Stuart to Washington where, if Illinois had not done so, the House of Representatives would decide who was entitled to the Third Congressional District seat from Illinois. The *Vandalia Free Press*, a Whig newspaper, caught wind of a Democratic conspiracy and aired it. The public announcement of the theory outraged Douglas. He told the *Illinois State Register* that the allegation was "false in every particular."[35] The *Springfield Republican*, however, carried the story without a Douglas retort. The lack of denial from Douglas led Springfield citizens to believe the report was credible and that Field would issue Douglas a certificate. In the end, however, Field did not.[36]

Rumors behind him, Carlin in January 1839 fired Field and appointed John A. McClernand to the post. Field refused to vacate the office, and on a vote of 22 to 17, the Whig-controlled Senate sided with Field and refused to consent to McClernand's appointment.[37] McClernand filed suit to take the office, and Judge Sidney Breese, who had been a Democratic partisan before taking the bench, ruled in McClernand's behalf. Field had been prepared for Breese's ruling with two quick actions. He moved his office's files and the state seal for safekeeping to the Springfield store of Robert and John Irwin. The Irwin store often served as that city's unofficial Whig headquarters. Next, Field appealed to the state Supreme Court, which docketed the case for its 1839 summer term.[38]

McClernand, who had been elected to the House of Representatives from Jacksonville after Douglas's departure, enlisted Douglas's help to get the files that Field had secreted away. Douglas sought an order from the Sangamon County circuit court for the files. The court, however, sided with the arguments of Abraham Lincoln, who represented the Irwins against Douglas, and quashed Douglas's request to compel Field to do anything.[39]

The main case continued in the Illinois Supreme Court. For four days, solicitors on both sides argued the case before the four justices. Douglas's oration was a powerful precursor to the idea that had become his Jacksonian philosophy—to *let the people rule*. Douglas admonished the court to believe in the "intelligence and virtue of the people, and their capacity for self-government." The accountability of public officers to the people, he said, was "essential to the very essence of republican institutions…. All power is inherent in, and derivable from the people; that our government was instituted by them, for their mutual benefit and protection; and that government possesses no powers, except those granted, by the people, in the constitution."[40]

They were impassioned, powerful words. Douglas's argument was so highly regarded that it was published widely throughout the state. Published in full by the *State Register* of Springfield, it filled eight columns in the August 17, 1839, issue. The speech may have been exciting to Jacksonian partisans, but they had no effect on the court. While Justice Smith, Douglas's earlier confidant, took the side of McClernand, Justices Lockwood and Wilson made up the majority of the court in the case. Justice Brown, claiming he was related to McClernand, recused himself.

In a 106-page ruling in December 1839, the Court decided the governor had no authority to remove a secretary of state and held for Field. Once the secretary was appointed, wrote Lockwood, he could not be removed except for bad behavior or until the legislature limited the term of office or authorized his removal for cause.

The decision set off a firestorm of controversy throughout the state among Democrats, who were convinced that the decision had proven that the court itself was not impartial.[41] The case's final hearing came in the court of public opinion. Douglas helped see to that. Voices of outrage attacked an aristocracy of the Whig majorities in the state Senate and the judiciary, which prevented the Democrats their right to occupy a key governmental office.[42] Lockwood was the chief target. Douglas's newspaper charged that Lockwood himself, believing Cyrus Field would be elected governor over Carlin, had an obligation to remove Field.

"Does he [Lockwood] recollect that he told a certain member of the legislature last winter that it was an outrage for Field to hold on to the office?" the Democratic *Springfield Republican* reflected. The newspaper contended Lockwood's decision was designed to protect Stuart's certificate of election to Congress.[43] Likewise, the Democratic *Illinois State Register* charged that Lockwood had a personal interest in protecting Field. As secretary of state Field was the official who certified elections. The Whig Lockwood could be certain, said the newspaper, that a Democrat appointed secretary of state would certify that Douglas had been elected.[44]

The state Democratic convention in the fall of 1839 had attacked the "Federalist" judges and senators who favored lifetime appointments to insulate themselves from the will of the people. This was, as Douglas saw it, a party question, which he promised would be decided by the people at the ballot box in August 1840.[45] Douglas's prediction was correct. The fall election made Democrats the majority party in both branches of the legislature.

The Supreme Court's ruling gave Democrats time to challenge the matter over what appeared to be lifelong appointments for Whigs. With Democrats now controlling both the House and Senate, Carlin now appeared to have the opportunity to appoint a man of his own choosing. For Carlin, however, it still did not work out that way. And this time, it was a Democrat, his man Stephen Douglas, who got in the way. Carlin wanted to appoint—even already had invited him to Springfield for that purpose—Quincy Democrat and friend Isaac Newton Morris, to whom he had promised the office. Carlin made the mistake of leaving Springfield—with Douglas in it. On his return to the capital, Carlin found a petition signed by so many members of the legislature's Democrats that he had to appoint Douglas.[46] With the wires apparently already pulled and in the interest of preserving the peace with his party, Carlin was left with little choice.[47] Rebuffed by the Whigs in his nominations of McClernand and now finding members of his own party for someone other than Morris, the governor on March 1840 submitted to the Senate another name for the statewide executive office. Carlin's submission of his nominee to the Senate on January 31, 1840, was terse: "I nominate Stephen A. Douglas to be Secretary of State."

Whigs pounced on the nomination. The Supreme Court had just ruled, said Whig senator William H. Davidson of White County, that no vacancy existed, and the governor had no power to appoint a secretary of state. Davidson moved that "the Senate do not advise and consent to the nomination of Stephen A. Douglas as Secretary of State." The Senate did not.[48]

With the August 1840 elections putting Democrats firmly in charge of both houses of the General Assembly, Carlin on November 30, 1840, once again nominated Douglas. Douglas's friend, Senator William A. Richardson of Quincy—the same Richardson who became Schuyler County state's attorney in 1835 under the law Douglas authored to change the way prosecutors were appointed—quickly

William A. Richardson of Schuyler County, Illinois, was among local lawyers the state legislature appointed state's attorneys under Douglas's earliest measure. In the years ahead, Richardson would become one of Douglas's closest political friends and a powerful politician in his own right (Library of Congress).

moved Douglas's appointment. Just as quickly Senator Davidson again argued the secretary's office was legally occupied, making Douglas's appointment superfluous. Davidson's motion to end the nomination this time was defeated 23–15. Richardson called for the original question—to appoint Douglas—and by the same vote, Douglas was confirmed secretary of state.[49]

The twenty-six-year-old lawyer, who had argued before the Supreme Court the governor's right to appoint the secretary of state, now accepted Carlin's appointment to the position. Douglas had advanced to one of the state's highest offices and, even then, saw the opportunity for—and coveted—something greater. That something was achieved in less than three months.

To Alexander Pope Field the judgment of the people—and members of the Illinois Senate—was clear. Field, who had been so free with invectives during the attacks on him, chose not to fight and surrendered the secretary of state's office to Stephen Douglas.[50] President William Henry Harrison in early 1841 appointed Field secretary of the Wisconsin Territory.[51]

14. The Move to Pack the Court

Governor Carlin had called a special session of the newly elected members of the General Assembly on November 23, 1840, to deal with the continuing disastrous effects of the internal improvements program of 1837. With a 51 to 40 majority, House Democrats elected party leader William L.D. Ewing speaker over the Whig candidate Abraham Lincoln on a strict party-line vote. In customary fashion, Ewing had voted for Lincoln and Lincoln for Ewing. Democrats also organized the Senate.

The Democratically controlled legislature turned its attention to the two state banks, which had suspended the requirement that they redeem the notes they had issued by paying for them in specie. The quick and fully expected result was the depreciation in value of the banks' currency. The Democrats were not deadset against state banks. A Democratic legislature had created them. But Democrats from the beginning claimed that Whigs, whose adherents largely had administered the banks, had managed them poorly.[1] Still facing debt payments well beyond the state's means, the General Assembly of 1837–38 had authorized the suspension of specie payment by the banks until the end of the next General Assembly. If the current special session ended without extending the suspension, which is what the state banks desired, specie payments on the overwhelming internal improvements debt would have to resume at once. To prevent that, Whigs devised a plan to merge the special session into the regular session so that no break would occur. In this way they could extend the suspension to the end of the 1841 legislative session[2] and relieve the state—and an empty state treasury.

Lincoln believed the Democrats planned to end the special session on December 5, two days before the regular session was to begin. If that happened, the state with no other choice would be compelled to resume payments in specie. Whig Representative Joseph Gillespie framed the danger. Banks of other states, which also had suspended specie payments, would have the opportunity to remit Illinois notes they held for payment in specie and drain it from Illinois banks. With no other option left, Whigs planned to prevent the legislature's adjournment by having enough members—including a handful of concerned Democrats—absent so there would not be a quorum when the Democrats moved to adjourn the special session *sine die*. Although the Senate already had voted to adjourn, the House without a quorum could not vote to adjourn. A *sine die* motion would require a counting of the ayes and nays. Lincoln and only a handful of Whig colleagues attended the House session just to make sure there were too few votes for a quorum, thus preventing a vote to end the session.[3]

When the Democrats discovered the Republican strategy, Speaker Ewing ordered the sergeant at arms to round up absent members, including Democrats who had claimed to be ill. Counting heads, Lincoln and Whig colleague Joseph Gillespie suspected the number of members had reached a quorum. They had failed in their efforts to get the Whigs, who the sergeant at arms had rounded up, to withdraw. But they did get them to agree to call for the ayes and nays. Thinking they might still be able to create too few members to make a quorum, a few Whigs attempted to leave through the House chamber door. When they found the door locked, three of them—Lincoln, Gillespie, and McLean County Whig Asahel Gridley, recorded their "nay" votes against adjournment, then jumped from the second-floor window of the Second Presbyterian Church, in which the legislature had been meeting while awaiting the completion of the new capitol building.[4]

The Democrats achieved their quorum, however, and the General Assembly adjourned. Lincoln's only prize was some heavily partisan ridicule. For Lincoln, the event became the severest kind of embarrassment.[5] His action continued to come up in jest from Whigs and Democrats alike. Even his friend John Hardin of Jacksonville considered Lincoln's action childish.[6] At the end of the session, while the House was considering a resolution to adjourn for a half-day to commemorate the Battle of New Orleans, Democrat William Bissell of Monroe County mentioned the incident in a mocking tone. Lincoln was perturbed.

"As that jumping scrape has become so celebrated it appears necessary that I should say something," Lincoln said in a speech forever memorialized in the *Illinois House Journal*. Speaker Ewing gaveled Lincoln out of order. The speech was not germane to the resolution the House was considering. It was important for Lincoln to get in his lick.

"As to jumping, I should jump when I please and no one should hinder me," an irritated Lincoln muttered.[7]

By the end of 1840 Douglas was at the next step of his climb. Lincoln, on the other hand, was at one of his lowest. Political and personal pressures were weighing on him. He was on the verge of his greatest bout of melancholia in his life. He told Stuart he was suffering from the "hypos," or hypochondria.[8] Emotional distress kept him absent from the legislature more and more frequently. Humiliations seemed to pile up on him. The internal improvements program, for which he had played a leading role, had created a massive state debt, which was discouraging settlers from moving to Illinois and causing some Illinoisans to move out. As a result of falling demand, land values were plummeting and the fear of growing taxation was rising. More worrisome for Lincoln was the fear the legislature would repudiate the debt and fail to pay interest on it. To Lincoln that would bring long-lasting shame, not to mention credit unworthiness, to the state.

"The State will be bankrupt," he warned.[9]

Lincoln, like his Whig party, for which he was the undisputed leader, had become disheartened by mounting problems and losses. In the August 1840 election, he was re-elected to the legislature but this time by the narrowest margin of any member of the Sangamon delegation. In the following November presidential election, his candidate William Henry Harrison, for whom he had campaigned tirelessly across the state and at the expense of his own law practice, lost to Douglas's candidate Martin Van Buren. At a special session of the General Assembly, called in November to deal with the state's mounting debt, it was left to Lincoln to recommend increased taxes.[10]

Lincoln suffered personally. He had always "stood true to his ideas of Whiggery," a party general confirmed.[11] He might have rightfully expected to be accorded the honor of heading his ticket. Yet Lincoln himself in 1840 rejected a proposal from several Whig leaders that he run for governor in 1842.[12] The astute student of the state's practical politics knew no Whig could win statewide office in Illinois, as he told his suitors. The Democracy's strength in the precincts of Illinois had seen to that. Lincoln's Whig friends were likewise despondent. David Davis of Bloomington sadly concurred with Lincoln in saying there was "hardly the faintest hope of this State ever being Whig.... There is precious little use for any Whig in Illinois to be wasting his time and efforts. The state cannot be redeemed. I should as leave think of seeing one rise from the dead."[13]

All of this was caused in great part by the methodical and effective mechanical engineering of Stephen Douglas.

To have been denied the opportunity to fill the state's highest office was difficult for Lincoln, whose ambitions were well known by his friends and associates.

"He was always calculating, and always planning ahead," said partner Herndon. "His ambition was a little engine that knew no rest."[14] And yet, to what purpose?

Added to this "strain of politics" were tests of a more personal nature to Lincoln. By January 1, 1841, Lincoln's best friend, Joshua Speed, had announced he was leaving. It was Speed, the Springfield Samaritan, who had offered Lincoln shelter when he arrived in Springfield in April 1837. Speed said he had never seen so gloomy a face.[15] It was with Speed that Lincoln had communed for nearly four years. Speed allowed that he planned to sell his part in the store to Hurst, who had clerked there and lived above it with Speed, Herndon, and Lincoln. Speed planned to return to Kentucky permanently. It was a severe blow to Lincoln. No friendship or association had been more important to Lincoln than Speed's.

It was at this low point for Lincoln that on the evening of that January 1, 1841, which Lincoln called "the fatal first," he failed to keep his engagement to wed Mary Todd in her sister and brother-in-law's fine, two-story brick home on "Aristocracy Hill."

Lincoln's absence in early 1841 played large in one of the most brazen political moves in Illinois history—orchestrated by Stephen Douglas. Douglas and Illinois Democrats had reason to fear that the Supreme Court's Whig majority would rule against voting rights for unnaturalized citizens after six months of residency in the state. An ethically questionable warning to Douglas by the court's only Democratic member, Justice Theophilus Smith, that the court was going to rule against the "alien vote" gave Douglas information he used to win a delay in the court's ruling—time enough to work a plan that would end the Whig majority on the court.

In a purely partisan move, Douglas sought to reduce the power of the Whig majority on the Illinois Supreme Court. For Douglas, the effort was a 180-degree reversal from the position he had taken six years earlier. In 1835, he had drafted the measure approved by the legislature that removed the responsibilities of the four justices to serve as circuit judges, as well.[16] That kept the court's majority Whigs off the circuit where they could politick in their off-duty hours. Douglas had a penchant for changing his mind once he had achieved his goals, which marked his character throughout his life. Although it was he who had engineered a change in law to get himself appointed state's attorney, he changed his mind about that practice within three years. "Although I wrote this bill and reaped first fruits under it, and was inclined at that time to think it correct in principle and ought to become law; yet subsequent experience, observation and reflection have convinced me of my error; and I now believe that all Legislative elections ought to be abolished, and the officers either appointed by the Governor and Senate, or elected by the people."[17]

Now Douglas in 1841 proposed to repeal his earlier action, as astounding and purely political as the earlier bill, for which he was responsible, had been. He now proposed to abolish the circuit courts entirely and expand the state Supreme Court to nine members with each justice once again presiding over the circuit in his judicial district. It was a move for which the public mind was prepared. The high court had come under intense fire in Illinois for the two political controversies involving the secretary of state and the "alien" case.[18] In the public forum, Douglas and other Democrats primed for the battle had turned the public mind against the court. The justices had ruled against the Democrats in saying that Alexander Pope Field could remain Illinois secretary of state indefinitely, a decision tantamount to despotism in Democratic eyes. In a republican government, power comes from the people and, through elections, reverts to them, wrote George Washington at the time of his first inauguration.[19] Without such a check on government and those who serve the people in it, the risk was despotism.

Although the Democrats ultimately acquired the office with Field's resignation, the "alien" case remained unresolved. And because it was a key to winning future elections, it was much more important to the Democrats.

That secret information from Justice Smith during the Supreme Court's consideration in 1839 that the Whig justices were going to rule against suffrage by unnaturalized immigrants—nearly half of the Democrats' electorate, Douglas and McConnel had won a stay of the Court order on a technicality. Now, in 1840, Democrats knew the case again would be before the court, and they had no reason to suspect the decision would come out differently.

Democrat Adam W. Snyder of St. Clair County, situated across the Mississippi River from St. Louis in southwestern Illinois, had been elected to the Illinois House of Representatives in 1836 and established a close political friendship with another freshman Democratic legislator that year, Douglas of Morgan. By 1840, Democrats controlled the legislative and executive branches. Snyder's constituents had moved him up to the Illinois Senate. Friend Douglas was now Illinois secretary of state and like Snyder recognized the importance to the Democratic party of the growing number of immigrants. Under Illinois' constitution, although they might be unnaturalized, they still could meet the state's voting requirements if they had lived in the state for at least six months before an election and were white men over twenty-one years of age. Douglas was well known to the large block of alien voters in the North, the Irish workers on the Illinois-Michigan canal. He reminded some of them of Louis Napoleon, appearing of medium height but with unusually short legs. He struck them as pleasant in conversation, full of blandishment, one said, and with a magnetism that was nearly irresistible.[20]

Snyder's senatorial district contained the state's largest bloc of foreign voters, including young German men recently arrived.[21] So it was understandable that, to the dismay of Whigs—and even some Democrats, Snyder would introduce the bill to reorganize the Supreme Court in an attempt to stop the decision anticipated to end alien suffrage. Few were not aware who really was behind the legislation. The bill was in short order dubbed the "Douglas Bill," a recognition of its promoter.[22] The measure would abolish the six circuit courts, remove their circuit judges from office, increase to nine the number of Supreme Court justices, and assign circuit duties to each of them. With Democrats holding the executive branch and reclaiming the majority in the General Assembly in the August elections, no one doubted that all five additional justices would be Democrats. That would give them control of six of the high courts' nine seats and secure their power of state government for the life of the majority of men who would serve lifetime appointments.

The current Whig court, alarmed by the partisanship the alien issue was generating, handed down the decision later in the month of December 1840. While Justice Smith, in a lengthy dissent, wrote that unnaturalized inhabitants had the right to vote, Justices Lockwood and Wilson, seeking to mitigate the attacks on the Supreme Court that the anticipated decision was generating, ignored the constitutional issue. Instead, they issued a narrow ruling dealing with the facts of the case only. Lockwood's decision simply reversed the circuit court's ruling on a technicality that the law did not give an election clerk the power to inquire whether a voter was an alien. The ruling ignored the explosive constitutional issue of the status of the alien vote, which greatly aggravated Douglas and Democrats. It was a clear effort by the Whig-dominated court to calm the Democratic furor over their electorate, in Douglas's view. With the proper orchestration, the court's ploy could be used to Douglas's advantage.

On December 10, 1840, Senator Snyder introduced "an act re-organizing the judiciary of the State of Illinois." Whigs made the debate over the judicial reform measure as arduous as they could. They saw the outlandish partisanship it represented and called it revolutionary and anti–Republican. Douglas would not have disagreed. But the Democrats had seen a reactionary propensity in the Whiggish high court's decision in the secretary of state case and the "Alien Case."

Lincoln's stalwart friend Baker and five more Whig senators filed a protest that was published in the *Senate Journal*. Douglas's bill, it said, was a cynical measure "to obtain a democratic majority on the Supreme Court, that they might decide questions of law according to the principles of democracy, or in other words, according to the will of the party in power." The judiciary, "the surest shield of public welfare and public right," was being politicized, being brought down in an outrageous scheme to make the legislature the pre-eminent authority in the state. Not above a bit of scheming themselves, and without reminding their readers that they had been the chief promoters of many of the state's ills, Whigs said all the other misfortunes of the state had taken a back seat to Douglas's party bill. They itemized the misfortunes: "an empty treasury—our internal improvement system a wretched skeleton—railroads half finished, or half decayed—iron without roads, and roads without iron—the canal so surrounded with

Governor Thomas Carlin, who had been a federal land officer in Quincy, appointed Douglas secretary of state and later associate justice of the state's state's supreme court, posts that would serve Douglas's interests in political advancement. Although he had selected other candidates, Carlin found himself outflanked by Douglas (courtesy Historical Society of Quincy and Adams County).

difficulties, that even its truest friends were almost found 'to stop, too fearful and to faint to go'—our scrip, issued on the faith of the State, spreading like leaves every where and, like leaves almost valueless: these were some of the difficulties of our condition; and these it was supposed required our utmost wisdom and patriotism."

The authors added that while faced with all these matters, the single part of the state's government against which there was no complaint and for which no change was required, was under attack. "How strange it must appear, that, while all the rest of these great interests remained unprotected, almost untouched, this system of circuit courts has been attacked and destroyed."[23]

Democrat Lyman Trumbull responded with a closely reasoned argument for reformation of the judiciary, which filled ten columns in the April 9 issue of the *Illinois State Register*. Trumbull was not a disinterested party. When Douglas captured one of the five new spots on the expanded Illinois Supreme Court, Trumbull succeeded him as Illinois secretary of state. John J. Hardin, Cyrus Edwards, and William Gatewood answered for the Whigs in arguments published verbatim in the Whig organ, the *Sangamo Journal*.[24] This attack on the court harkened back to the chaos and barbarism of Jacobin France, they charged.

"A more perfect despotism never existed in the Legislature of a free people," the *Journal* asserted, "except for bloodshed, it would have resembled the General Assembly of France in the time of Robespierre and Marat."[25]

Democrat Thomas Ford, who would be appointed to one of the five seats created on the Supreme Court, found himself agreeing with such claims. It was, he said, "confessedly a violent and somewhat revolutionary measure."[26] In a separate attempt to unmask the reasons for the bill, Lincoln and his five-member Whig committee against the Judiciary bill argued that the measure was designed to destroy the independence of the Judiciary.

"The declarations of the party leaders, the selection of party men for Judges, and the total disregard for the public will, in the adoption of the measure, prove conclusively that the object has been, not reform, but destruction, not the advancement of the highest interests of the State, but the predominance of party," Lincoln wrote.

After the court's narrow ruling, Douglas in the "Lobby" charged that the justices had disposed of the case in a manner that was simply designed to entice Democrats to abandon their plan to reform the court. Douglas's arguments were effective, although the vote in the legislature was close. Snyder passed the bill in the Senate by a vote of twenty-two to seventeen. The margin in the House was smaller, forty-five to forty, with all Whigs and three Democrats voting against it.[27] With one additional opportunity to stop the reform, the Supreme Court justices vetoed the measure three-to-one in their roles as members of the Council of Revision. As a member of the council, Democratic Governor Carlin favored the bill and refused to sign the objection. By February 10, 1841, both houses of the legislature, each controlled by Democrats, overrode the veto. In his public comments, Douglas took no credit for the victory. But he had worked hard behind the scenes to get the bill passed and its veto overridden.[28]

The new law outraged Whigs. On February 26, thirty-five House members entered in the *House Journal* another lengthy protest against Douglas's reorganization of the judiciary.[29] Lincoln registered the protest. In his seven-point criticism, Lincoln called the measure a fatal blow to an independent judiciary and the constitutional term of its officers since the legislature had imposed itself in the fundamental formation of the Judiciary. It was a revolutionary measure to Lincoln's way of thinking, an anti–Republican, purely partisan measure, unwanted by the people, from which "no practical good" but the possibility of "immeasurable evils," could come. Lincoln recognized that it had increased the court's political and partisan character. Nine members would increase the court's expense without improving the public's confidence.

Lincoln must have known how useless his appeal would be. There was little outcry against it. But for the record, Lincoln would say, "The blow has already fallen; and we are compelled to stand by, the mournful spectators of the ruin it will cause."[30] As he would demonstrate in years ahead, Lincoln was no revolutionary bent on ignoring law by the legislature or interpretation of law by the judiciary.

Lincoln's friend Hardin could easily predict the appointment of Democrats to all five new seats.

"A beautiful set of scoundrels they will elect to those offices," he said.

The *Chicago American* seconded Hardin's remark, saying, "Men with whom you would not trust your dinner are now seeking situation on the bench of the Supreme Court."[31]

Even some Democrats were dumbfounded about the tilt the court would take once five more Democrats were appointed to the bench. Fearing that politicians could extract vengeance on those who has opposed them, there was concern among Douglas's own party members that those who had resisted his bill would find themselves subject to "party abuse & personal crimination." Likewise, there were lawyers who had opposed the measure who pondered with some alarm their future appearances before the high court. They voiced concern about recriminations over their response to the Douglas bill. One observer wrote that if the measure failed judges could be "expected to display the malignity of their hearts against lawyers who advocated the bill. I have heard many gentlemen of the bar of the first respectability declare that they could not again appear before the Supreme Court unless that court should be reorganized."[32]

Such fears were not hollow. The organization Douglas had created was steeled in a demand for loyalty. Many of those who strayed from the party line—even those who subsequently returned to it—would never regain its confidence. Governor Ford, one of the five beneficiaries of Douglas's bill, would write, "These democrats, many of them, are still under the ban; so true it is that in all party matters a breach of discipline, a rebellion

This painting of Douglas by 19th century portraitist Charles Loring Elliott was completed just months before the state legislature on February 15, 1841, appointed Douglas an associate justice of the Illinois Supreme Court (courtesy Mr. George Buss of Freeport, Illinois).

against the leaders, is regarded as infinitely more offensive than the mere support of wicked or unwise measures or opposition to good ones."[33]

Five days after the court's reorganization was enacted, the Democratically controlled House and Senate met in joint session on February 15, 1841, and elected the new judges the law provided. All were Democrats. Those selected were Circuit Judge Sidney Breese, Thomas Ford, Samuel H. Treat, Walter B. Scates, and Douglas. With Democratic associate Justice Theophilus Smith, this would give Democrats a six-three edge on the court. Though it would make no difference in the outcome of that ratio, one appointment raised eyebrows. It was that of Douglas. This was exactly the kind of partyism, the kind of spoils about which the Whigs had harped. It was seen a payback for the Democratic and political operative, his appointment to the judicial branch, whose independence was considered most important. The Whig press and several conservative and older lawyers of the state opposed Douglas's appointment, contending his legal qualifications were too sparse to merit consideration for such an important judicial post.[34] Even Douglas's friend and the bill's sponsor, Senator Adam Snyder questioned the appointment. Douglas was twenty-seven years of age, too young to be a justice, Snyder believed. Still, Snyder would say, "we could not do much better than to have elected him."[35] Douglas's old friend and mentor Murray McConnel, who had hoped that his own name might have been among the five considered for the court, was flabbergasted by the appointment of Douglas.

"Dug a great *Supreme Squire*. I tell you we are a great people," McConnel wrote in an unusually sarcastic comment.[36]

Abraham Lincoln found the occasion of Douglas's appointment remarkable for another reason. He was amazed that Douglas, who had opposed "life offices," had accepted such an office as a Supreme Court justice.[37]

15. Judge Douglas

THE NEW JUDGE AND JUSTICE, the Hon. Stephen A. Douglas, with characteristic feigned surprise ignored criticism that he had schemed for his appointment to the bench. In fact, he answered that he had to surrender himself to a judicial career at great personal sacrifice.

"But friends asked the sacrifice, pressured it, urged it, and he consented," said his newspaper friend and apologist James Sheahan.[1] Indeed, Douglas's associates considered "his removal from the social, political and legal atmosphere of Springfield a matter of supreme regret. [But] Douglas knew his business. He desired the appointment."[2]

As usual, Douglas kept his counsel close and did not elaborate on the nature of his personal sacrifice. It would not have been a pecuniary one, since the job paid $1,500 a year, an increase over the salary he had received as secretary of state (although only half of what he had earned annually as a federal land register). The comment indicated the sacrifice was political in nature. But was it? Douglas had been appointed to preside in the Fifth Judicial Circuit, headquartered in Quincy, on the west side of Illinois. It was a region growing fast. From the time in 1821 John Wood of New York and Willard Keyes of Vermont had landed in the region called "The Bluffs," now Quincy, the community's population had been doubling every five years: from 20 in 1825, to 350 in 1830, 753 in 1835 and 1,850 in 1840.[3] The congressional district's population between 1830 and 1840 had exploded from 8,000 to 68,000[4] as immigrants from New England, Germany, and Ireland arrived. Douglas's judicial district included the 3.5 million-acre Illinois Military Tract wedged between the Mississippi and Illinois Rivers. Congress in 1811 had provided the land as bounties to volunteers, an inducement for enlistments when a second war with Great Britain appeared imminent. In 1836, Samuel Alexander, register and receiver of the federal land office in Quincy, recorded sales of 569,367 acres of land, a massive jump of 1,576 percent in sales in only the second year of its existence. By 1841, when Douglas arrived in Quincy, the land office there had posted the highest sales of all ten offices in Illinois in two of the most recent five years.[5] That record reflected the strongest growth in commerce, population and votes along the Mississippi River.[6]

The strength of the Whigs in Western Illinois, evident in the ratio of Whig to Democratic office holders, was not as great as in the Sangamon region. The judicial reorganization would be even tougher on Whigs. Douglas's circuit duties, which would take him at least twice a year around the large judicial circuit, would afford Douglas the chance to meet with the increasing numbers of voters in his district. In Illinois, judicial districts largely coincided with the state's congressional districts.

Governor Lilburn W. Boggs's order to move Mormons from Missouri blessed the west side of Illinois with another large block of voters. The state's westernmost town, Quincy, had provided refuge to the fleeing Mormons. With a desire to be independent of government, the Saints found a permanent site for their theologically oriented community in Hancock County, just north of the Fifth Judicial District seat at Quincy. Stephen Douglas on first hearing of the embattled Saints knew it offered a significant opportunity for the politician who could win the friendship of such a huge, new political constituency. Douglas next worked to ingratiate himself with the church's leadership and members.

Taking advantage of opportunities as they became available to him. Douglas's successes since his arrival in Illinois satisfied to his ambitions. He had managed to maneuver out of office the apparent lifetime secretary of state, Alexander Pope Field, then persuaded Governor Thomas Carlin to appoint him Field's successor. The new role put Douglas in a position to gain the favor of Mormon founder, leader, and Prophet Joseph Smith. As secretary of state, Douglas found himself in a spot to be the foremost proponent of the charter to make Nauvoo the Mormons' new Illinois home.

Senator Sidney H. Little, a Hancock Whig, introduced the bill to change Commerce City in Hancock County to Nauvoo—and give free rein to Joseph Smith for the new city's governance. Douglas, though secretary of state and not a legislator, managed the bill in the House.

Smith and John Cook Bennett, the Illinois quartermaster general who had been converted and baptized a Mormon, drafted the Nauvoo charter. The document maximized local self-rule, not so unusual in that day. To that point, the Illinois legislature had approved only four city charters, and those for Chicago and Alton contained provisions similarly liberal.[7] With an allowance to establish its own militia, independent judiciary, legislative council and a government with almost unlimited power, Nauvoo's charter for all practical purposes exempted the religious community from the U.S. and Illinois constitutions.[8] The doctrine of separation of powers was wholly disregarded, as were fundamental constitutional provisions that governments be republican. There was nothing republican about the Nauvoo charter. Nevertheless, Whigs and Democrats alike coveted this new constituency, and the charter moved with unusual speed through the both the Senate and the House. The bill was approved by the Council of Revision and on December 18,1840, Governor Carlin signed it into law.

Little and Douglas each believed Smith and the church would favor his party enough to influence the huge electorate in his direction.[9] It was Douglas, however, who was singly favored by the Mormons, whose Prophet granted him the "Freedom of the City of Nauvoo."[10] It would not be luck that placed Douglas in Quincy. He certainly was aware of the importance of the large block of voters that had moved into far Western Illinois and had found a new home just north of Quincy. Douglas believed the new residents could be moved to favor him.[11]

Douglas had been Illinois secretary of state less than three months when he resigned the post on February 16, 1841, the day after he had been selected an associate justice of the Illinois Supreme Court. His term as secretary of state was shortest in history. But it was long enough for the ambitious 27-year-old to win the friendship of Mormon leader Joseph Smith and the affections of Smith's vast phalanx of voters on the far west side of Illinois. By managing the movement of the legislation, Douglas had helped secure passage of the charter for the Mormon City of Nauvoo. He needed the secretary's office no longer. To assure he had burned no bridges with Carlin, Douglas in his letter of resignation wrote that "justice to my own feelingswill not permit me to say less, than to express to you my grateful acknowledgements for that kindness, frankness and generous confidence which have characterized your intercourse with me, whilst I have had the honor of an official connection with you."[12]

On March 1, 1841, James W. Keyes, former Springfield postmaster and now a justice of the peace, administered the oath of office to Douglas, who had personally written it on a half sheet of paper for his swearing in ceremony. Douglas solemnly swore to administer justice "without respect to persons and do equal right to the poor and rich without sale or denial promptly without delay conformably to the laws, favor, affection or partiality." He swore to uphold the constitutions of the United States and the State of Illinois.[13]

The state's Whig press attacked Douglas's appointment to a position that required the highest standards of impartiality. It did not take long for him to demonstrate that such concerns were not without foundation. In one of their first acts Douglas and his colleagues of the new Democratic majority on the Supreme Court appointed Democratic state representative Ebenezer Peck of Chicago the court's clerk. To an outsider, the advancement of Peck as the court's highest civil servant was considered nothing less than astonishing. Peck had joined Whigs in voting against the judiciary bill. But his position changed after the Council of Revision vetoed it. It was Peck's vote to override the veto of the bill he earlier had opposed that now made it law. The reason became evident when the court organized. Without consulting their Whig associates on the bench and not saying anything about it in their first meetings in open court, the new Democrats on the bench summarily removed incumbent court clerk J.M. Duncan to move Peck into the post. The court's Democratic members said nothing of the appointment. It was Peck himself who announced shortly after the court adjourned that a majority had voted to elect him clerk of the court.[14] It was clearly Peck's reward for his vote to override the veto of Douglas's bill to pack the court. And Douglas's handwriting was all over the appointment.[15]

On March 3, 1841, Douglas, the new associate justice and circuit judge, moved to Quincy, the largest city in the Fifth Judicial Circuit. He lodged for several weeks in the Quincy House, regarded as the finest hotel in the West. It had been built at a cost of $106,000 in 1838 by John Tillson, a New Englander whose land speculations made him one of the wealthiest men in Illinois.[16] Douglas eventually rented rooms in a small brick boarding house, known as the "Brigham House," within a half-mile south of the Adams County courthouse on the east side of the public square and within a ten-minute walk.

Douglas's circuit court office was on the upper floor of the two-story Greek Revival court building, its large pediment resting on four huge fluted columns. From his vantage points at work and home, Douglas had an unobstructed view of the Mississippi River to the west and the slave state of Missouri on the river's opposite bank. Douglas's evening walk from the courthouse to his home took him past the two-story brick home of Dr. Richard Eells, a physician. The Eells house at Fourth and Jersey Street was a half block east of the community's first church building, an unpretentious wood frame building Quincyans called the "Lord's Barn." Both structures were Quincy wellsprings of sympathy for the treatment of the Negro. Yet, Quincy's toleration of blacks, slave or free, was an uneasy one. Lives and property of those who agitated in behalf of the black were never considered far from danger.[17]

Douglas's first duty was to unseat Peter Lott, a fellow Democrat who for two years had been the residing circuit judge. Douglas could rely on the fact that the action was simply in accordance with the court reorganization law.[18]

Douglas could claim several friendly acquaintances in Illinois' westernmost community. He had been long acquainted with J.W. Whitney of Quincy, who as "Lord Coke" ruled over the so-called "Third House" at the state capitals in both Vandalia and Springfield. Coke had

Shortly after his arrival in Quincy as a supreme court justice, Douglas rented rooms in the Brigham House. The residence was within walking distance of both his Adams County Courthouse and the home of Dr. Richard Eells, whom he found guilty of aiding a fugitive slave. The Eells case was appealed all the way to the U.S. Supreme Court, which upheld Douglas's decision (courtesy Historical Society of Quincy and Adams County).

been an important personage in politician Douglas's schemes. Coke's court was "The Lobby," the place in the capitol buildings where legislators, lawyers, and others could orate and persuade freely. In Coke's lobby, remarks were unfettered by rules of the House or Senate. It was Coke who made the rules, under which he would stop a speaker only if, in his opinion, the speaker failed to inform—or amuse. Douglas often had found the platform Whitney's Lobby offered useful for arguing causes with less restraint than the rules of decorum required in the chambers of the legislature. He had been an active member of Lord Coke's retinue. It was this "Third House" platform Douglas had lobbied for his self-serving legislation to change the way state's attorneys were appointed, for a charter that granted Mormon leader Joseph Smith almost unlimited power in Illinois, and for the bill he had crafted to pack the Illinois Supreme Court with Democrats. The passage of each measure for which he lobbied had gained momentum from Whitney's platform.

Another important Quincy friend was Governor Carlin, who had resigned himself to Douglas's effort to remove Alexander Field from the office of secretary of state. It was Governor Carlin whom Douglas snookered into appointing him. Carlin was more favorable to Douglas's plan to reform the Supreme Court. And he acceded to Douglas's request that he be appointed one of the five new associate justices. Douglas wanted the Fifth Judicial District bench in Quincy, from which he could implement the final phase of his scheme for election to Congress. Carlin complied with the request, facilitating the last stage of Douglas's career plan.

Likewise, the new judge was well acquainted with Quincy Whigs like Orville Hickman Browning, who was elected a state senator from Quincy when Douglas was elected a state representative from Jacksonville in 1836. The two had boarded in the same house together in Vandalia, and both had opposed the size of the Sangamon delegation's internal improvements program.

Douglas struck those who watched the diligence with which he applied himself to his courtroom responsibilities as a "steam engine in breeches."[19] He had maneuvered himself to the Fifth District, however, not just to decide cases. Knowing that the state's growing population would merit as many as four additional congressional districts and understanding the significant block of voters the Mormons might bring him, Douglas once again worked to solidify the affections of a political block for a future higher office. He renewed his association with the Mormons. He had worked with John C. Bennett, the Mormon emissary whom he had helped obtain the charter that made Commerce City the Mormon City of Nauvoo. And such continuing interest in the Mormons raised suspicion about the reasons for his championing the causes of the religious community. Douglas's attentions to the Mormons struck some more like political opportunism, which it was. When he appointed Bennett, now the first mayor of Nauvoo, the Fifth Circuit Court's master in chancery, a paid administrative post, non–Mormons of Hancock County pitched a deafening protest. Douglas ignored it. Likewise, he felt no reason to be concerned about a similar reaction from the circuit's largest community, Quincy, to the move. During the Winter of 1838–39, 1,500 Quincy residents provided shelter to 5,700 Mormons after Missouri Governor Boggs's Executive Order 44 on October 27, 1838, forced them out of the state or face extermination.[20] The "Quincy Democratic Association" labored in behalf of the Mormons, raising funds and helping to supply food and shelter. The *Quincy Whig* complained that the "Ass-ociation" had ulterior motives. Putting words into the mouth of J.W. Whitney (Lord Coke) the *Whig* charged that Democrats would help the "latter day saints [sic] *provided*, this people will claim kindred with us of the 'association,' and agree to sustain such men for office next August, as we may set up for their support."[21]

Misunderstanding and maltreatment seemed destined to follow the Mormons. Such conflict began in New York with threats of mob violence after Smith's publication of the *Book of Mormon* in January 1830. It followed them to Kirtland, then to Far West, Missouri, and now in 1841 into Western Illinois.

In Missouri it had not been enough that the Mormons were being driven out by threat of death. Governor Boggs declared church leaders enemies of the state and ordered them held for treason. Smith, his brother Hiram, and three others were arrested on November 1, 1838, and a two-week preliminary hearing, at which dozens of others were released, found cause to hold them.[22] They were taken to Liberty Jail in Clay County, Missouri. In April 1839, the Mormons escaped during a transfer of venue to Boone County and fled to Quincy, where Smith's wife and four children had been sheltered.

Still sought by Missouri, Smith eluded capture until June 4, 1841, when once again in Quincy to visit church members he called on Governor Carlin at his home. Smith said that although the governor treated him kindly, there was no mention of an arrest warrant from Governor Boggs that Carlin had forwarded to local law enforcement officers for execution. That night Adams County Sheriff Thomas King, Quincy Constable Thomas Jasper, a posse, and a Missouri officer arrested Smith at Heberlin's Hotel at Bear Creek, about twelve miles north of Quincy. Smith was returned to Quincy the next day and appearing before Charles A. Warren, master in chancery of the Circuit Court, obtained a writ of habeas corpus, which enabled him to appeal to Judge Douglas. Douglas returned to Quincy later that day and ordered a hearing on the matter for Tuesday, June 8, in circuit court at the Warren County courthouse at Monmouth.[23]

By agreement of Smith's defense, led by Orville Browning and Archibald Williams of Quincy, and State's Attorney Morrison, the hearing was delayed a day, which gave an excited crowd more time to fester against Smith. A rumor circulated that the evidence would not justify a conviction, and by the next day a gallows had been erected in the court yard and a mob pushed their way into the courthouse. Douglas ordered the sheriff, a short and gentlemanly sort, to clear the courtroom. When he failed to perform his duty, Douglas stood and loudly appointed a tall Kentuckian whom he knew capable of handling the job.

"I appoint you sheriff of this court," Douglas bellowed. "Select your own deputies, and as many of them as you require. Clear this courtroom."[24]

The Kentuckian, said by observers to have thrown some men out the courthouse window, the courtroom was cleared in twenty minutes. Telling the story, Douglas biographer James Sheahan noted that Douglas had no authority to appoint another sheriff since the county's elected sheriff was present. But this was an emergency, Sheahan continues, and there was no time to debate the fine points about the constitutional limits of Douglas's power. By Douglas's quick action Smith had been saved from the makeshift gallows. Smith was exceedingly grateful.[25]

Smith's lawyers argued that the purported facts of the case were fraudulent, which could have discharged process.[26] In his ruling, however, Douglas ruled on a narrow procedural matter. The state had not objected to testimony that the warrant under which Smith had been arrested was the same one Carlin had issued earlier and had been returned unserved. Douglas declared that the warrant had expired with the failure of execution the first time. "The writ once being returned to the executive, by the Sheriff of Hancock County was dead and stood in the same relationship as any other writ which might issue from the Circuit Court and consequently the defendant could not be held in custody on that writ."[27]

Douglas freed the church prophet. Smith was inclined not only to praise the judge but to urge favor to the judge's Democratic Party.

"Douglas is a Master Spirit, and his friends are our friends— we are willing to cast our banners on the air, and fight by his side in the cause of humanity, and equal rights— the cause of liberty and the law," the prophet wrote. "We will never be charged with the sin of ingratitude— they have served us, and we will serve them."[28]

Douglas's ruling fostered numerous complaints. Joseph Duncan, running as a Whig in 1842 for governor, charged that Judge Douglas was unethically courting the Mormon vote for the Democratic candidate, Adam Snyder. Smith was not exempt from criticism, either. The *Alton Telegraph* was amused that Smith, saved by Douglas from the Missouri Penitentiary, was willing to march against the Missouri Penitentiary to free three imprisoned students from Quincy's abolitionist Mission Institute. The *Telegraph* was astonished that Smith would avow abolitionist principles and at the same time support Snyder, "WHO IS HIMSELF ONE OF THE LARGEST SLAVEHOLDERS IN THE STATE."[29]

Missouri sought Smith's extradition from Illinois once again in July 1842 after an assassin shot and wounded Governor Boggs on May 6. Former Nauvoo Mayor John Bennett, whom Smith had excommunicated that spring for seducing women under the guise of "spiritual wifery," insinuated Smith was involved.[30] Assured he would not be removed to Missouri, Smith in December traveled to Springfield and surrendered. There he consulted with Douglas, who advised him to ask Governor Ford, elected Carlin's successor in November, to rescind the arrest warrant. It would be the last official visit between the Mormon prophet and Douglas while he was a judge.[31] Ford was unsure he could withdraw the previous governor's order and, after consulting with other associate justices, decided against Smith's petition to vacate the warrant. Douglas then suggested to Mormon friends that the Missouri order alleged no crime against Smith and that Smith could not possibly have been culpable in the assassination attempt. Douglas had seen Smith in Nauvoo the day after the alleged attack, a distance too great to have enabled Smith to participate. Since he had not been in Missouri at the time of the assault on Boggs, he could not have been a participant and, therefore, would not have been at the scene from which he was charged to have fled.

At trial in Springfield in the federal court of Judge Nathaniel Pope on January 4, 1843, Smith was represented by Justin Butterfield of Chicago and Benjamin Edwards of Springfield, brother of Ninian Wirt Edwards. Josiah Lamborn prosecuted the case. Lamborn argued that since the case involved a warrant between Illinois and Missouri, the case was before the wrong court. Pope would decide his court had jurisdiction since the warrant was issued under the constitution and laws of the United States.[32]

Rising to deal with the matter of the exculpatory evidence, an observant Butterfield took note of his special surroundings, which several ladies, including Judge Pope's daughter and Mary Todd Lincoln, were beside Pope on the bench.[33] Butterfield uttered these classic remarks: "I appear before you today under circumstances most novel and peculiar. I am to address the 'Pope' (bowing to the judge) surrounded by angels (bowing still lower to the ladies), in the presence of the holy Apostles, in behalf of the Prophet of the Lord."[34] Butterfield won the prophet's acquittal.

Douglas had plunged into his work as judge of the Fifth Circuit. Within a month after assuming the bench, he summarily cleared between 300 and 400 cases, some of them seven years old, from the docket in Fulton County alone. He told James Shields he believed the members of the Bar were "entirely satified [sic] with the Judicial Change."[35] As state auditor, Shields issued Douglas his first paycheck for $112 on July 1, 1841, for his first three months service as associate justice of the Illinois Supreme Court.[36]

Douglas was an unusual judge in both appearance and demeanor. He could be as informal as the courtrooms of the circuit, a few still operating in rough-hewn log houses. The bar often was primitive: occasionally little more than a pine plank or plain table perched on a platform high enough to assure justice was positioned above the attorneys and their clients as a reminder of the supremacy of law. Like Judge Stephen Logan, in whose Sangamon County Court Douglas had practiced, the young judge would lean back in his chair and prop his feet up so that the soles of his boots were nearly all the attorneys in his court could see of the man. One was aggravated enough to tell Judge Douglas that he preferred addressing his arguments to the intelligent part of the judge's body.[37] The attorneys often rode with the judge from county to county where they would find clients—and audiences—awaiting them. "To go to court and listen to the witnesses and lawyers was among the chief amusements of the frontier settlements ... and Judge Douglas was thoroughly at home in this primitive environment."[38]

He could be informal enough in warm weather to conduct his hearings in shirtsleeves. He was known to come off the bench and mingle with the crowds at recess or "take a seat on the knee of a friend, and with one arm thrown familiarly around a friend's neck, have a friendly talk, or a legal or political discussion."[39]

Occasionally, Judge Douglas would not wait for recess.

> When presiding as a judge on the bench he would frequently, while the lawyers were addressing the jury, go down among the spectators and seat himself beside an old friend and visit with him, all the time keeping cognizance of what was going on, ready to respond when his attention to the case at bar was required, maintaining all the time the most perfect order. He has been seen at Knoxville, when the court room was crowded, to seat himself upon the knee of old Governor

Douglas's first paycheck as associate justice for three months' service was $112. It was signed by Treasurer Milton Carpenter and Auditor James Shields, a man unique in several respects in politics. He was the same Shields who challenged Abraham Lincoln to a duel, which Lincoln accepted and ever afterward regretted. He is the only man in U.S. history to have served as U.S. senator from three states: Illinois, Minnesota, and Missouri (courtesy Mr. George Buss of Freeport, Illinois).

McMurtry and, with his arm upon his shoulder, talk with him for a considerable time, which, diminutive as was his stature, and great as was that of the Governor, did not seem incongruous.[40]

Douglas liked a good cigar and after the court's adjournment for the day a good drink with the locals, sometimes to excess. But he was resilient and always ready for court the next morning.

Douglas's qualifications and ability to serve as one of the state's nine justices was still questioned by some, including editors of Quincy's *Whig* newspaper. Those who practiced in his courts, however, were gaining a respect for the now twenty-eight-year-old judge. Few of the cases Douglas decided required new principles of law—seemingly borne out by the fact that the new judge was provided only one law book for his duties. What the job required was a good well of common sense, worldly skill, and tact to maintain his position as a Supreme Court judge "before a bar which included many able and alert minds, making up in shrewdness what they lacked in legal training."[41]

Douglas's eyes might have rolled to the back of his head over some of the cases brought to him. Wealthy Quincy merchant John Bartlett, who had emigrated from Barbados, was walking home from his Quincy store through a deep snow one winter day. As he made his way, he approached a man walking a bulldog in the sidewalk's narrowly cleared path. Bartlett demanded the man and dog step aside. Neither did, and Bartlett punched the dog in the snout with an umbrella. Thinking better of pounding Bartlett, the dog's owner swore out a warrant for the merchant's arrest. Bartlett was taken into custody, appeared before Justice of the Peace J. Quinn Thornton, and fined. Dissatisfied with decision, Bartlett appealed to Judge Douglas, arguing he was the one in the altercation who had been assaulted. Douglas ruled that there had been no assault under the statutes.

"What sort of a country is this?" Bartlett demanded. "An old man is made to get out of the way of a dog, and is threatened and bullied and then made to pay costs." Douglas summarily dismissed him from his courtroom.[42]

During the July 1841 term of the Supreme Court, Douglas issued the opinion of the court that overturned a lower court's decision by which a circus was fined under "'An Act to prohibit wax-figures, tricks of jugglers,' &c." Orville Browning represented the circus owner.[43] More serious were cases like the one Judge Douglas heard in Morgan County in May 1841 against George Gardner of Scott County. Gardner was accused of firing a shotgun into the chest of Philip W. Nash. Only the second murder trial in Morgan County history, the case was referred to Judge Douglas from Scott County on a change of venue, where he expeditiously meted out justice, both at the lower court and at the Supreme Court levels. Tried in June, Gardner was found guilty and Douglas ordered him to be "hung by the neck until dead" on July 23. Before the date of execution, Murray McConnel appealed the conviction to the Illinois Supreme Court, alleging several errors and defects in the case. Douglas, now acting in his role as an associate justice and writing the opinion for his brethren, dismissed each of the errors McConnel had alleged and upheld the conviction. Douglas's brother justices agreed unanimously with his opinion.[44]

The Gardner case gave Douglas the distinction of issuing the only order in Morgan County in which a man was to be hanged. It was a distinction whose execution Douglas escaped. The promise of a hanging brought many people to town on a sultry Friday morning. They were disappointed to learn that the execution of Douglas's order had been put off until November.⁴⁵ Gardner avoided hanging then, too. He broke out of the county jail a few days before the date of execution and was never heard from again.⁴⁶

In an unusual action by a Supreme Court justice during the July 1841 term, Douglas reversed himself in a Hancock County case involving a breach of contract. Calvin A. Warren, a Hancock County lawyer and merchant, had backed out of a verbal land contract with one Edward Nexsen and other partners. Warren was known in Quincy, where he had resided before moving to Hancock County in 1839 and to which he would return a few years later. He was a well known real estate speculator. One of his grand speculations was in the future town of Oquawka, north of Hancock County and just inland from the Mississippi River. He had expected to sell properties there to the Mormons as they fled from Missouri into Illinois. He had convinced former Governor Joseph Duncan, also a real estate speculator, to invest $50,000 for a quarter-interest in the project.⁴⁷ It failed only because of Warren's own avarice, an attempt to take advantage of the Mormon refugees by price gouging and selling rancid commodities. The Mormons abandoned Oquawka as their new home and settled on Commerce City, then Nauvoo, instead.

In the circuit court case, Douglas found that Warren had not sufficiently answered the two charges and ruled against him. When Warren sought to fill in the blanks of his earlier responses, Douglas denied him the opportunity. Warren appealed to the Supreme Court and Douglas was assigned to write and deliver the court's opinion. Douglas believed that in his actions as circuit judge that he was on firm ground. He cited numerous precedents that held incomplete answers to declarations would cost the loss of all. On the second point, however, while Douglas acknowledged that "some of the old cases seem to sustain the position" that a defendant was not entitled to correct the record, more recent authorities favored a more liberal rule "one better calculated to promote the rules of justices, by permitting the party to correct his mistake, at any time during the same term, upon the payment of costs." In his written ruling, Douglas admitted he should have allowed Warren's motion to correct the record and reversed himself.⁴⁸ For Douglas, rule of law was more important than the fact that his ruling favored a scoundrel.

When the Board of Statehouse Commissioners notified Governor Carlin that suitable rooms were ready in the new capital, the governor issued a proclamation on June 20, 1839, that directed state offices to complete the move to Springfield by July 4. A large turnout celebrated the occasion that day.⁴⁹ There was no indication that controversy surrounding state government's relocation had subsided. The matter came before the state's Supreme Court, and Douglas once again was involved. His brethren on the state's high court looked to Associate Justice Douglas to draft the opinion after State Treasurer Milton Carpenter sued former senator and now Illinois State Bank President Thomas Mather for money he and forty-nine other sureties had pledged on Springfield's behalf in the bargain to move the seat of government from Vandalia. A lower court had ruled that Mather, the only bond holder the State sued, was not liable as a private citizen for a state project. The nub of the case stemmed from an amendment that Representative Abraham Lincoln had rushed through the legislature as a tactic to limit the number of communities competing for the capital. Lincoln's bill required that the winning community contribute $50,000 and two acres for the construction of the new statehouse.⁵⁰ After Springfield won the capital, Douglas proposed a bill to release Springfield from the requirement. Although he was said to have "fully appreciated the kindly feelings that prompted the proposal," Lincoln asked Douglas not to introduce it. Arrangements were made to have the amount paid in three installments.[51] Fifty of Springfield's most prominent residents signed on as sureties for a bond for $50,000 after the adjournment of the Tenth General Assembly. Unfortunately, the financial Panic of 1837 made it difficult for the guarantors to meet their obligation. The first two of three installments were paid—both late. (Lincoln was among 101 Springfield citizens who had signed a note by which they pledged to back a city bond issue to pay the second installment of $16,666.67.)[52] Mather and his colleagues who had acted to secure the final payment apparently believed that the first two payments were enough.[53] Douglas refused to let Mather off the hook and reversed the lower court's decision to free him of his responsibility. The state had authorized bonds for Springfield citizens to pay its share of construction in exchange for the benefits the city would realize from the relocation of the seat of Illinois' government. Justice Douglas believed Springfield would get its money back and more.

"The increased value of the property in the vicinity of public buildings, would seem to require that those who are benefitted, should contribute some part of the increase, for the purpose of erecting them, rather than that the whole advantage should accrue to them, and the expense be borne by the citizens generally," Justice Douglas opined. "We can see no foundation for the objection made to this subscription, on the ground of public policy, or propriety."[54]

Douglas's stature grew because of his administration of his court. Throughout his district, the judge cleaned up hundreds of languishing cases. He gave attorneys who were lax in pursuing matters of various kinds as little as a day's notice to be prepared to present their cases or see them summarily dismissed. His stature also was growing because of the quality of his acumen in the law, as well. Whig attorney Justin Butterfield, who had argued against Douglas in the "Alien" voting case, thought he could handle the "little squatty Democrat" in his courtroom. Butterfield ended up being an admirer.

"He listens patiently, comprehends the law and grasps the facts by intuition; then decides calmly, clearly and quietly and then makes the lawyers sit down. Douglas is the ablest man on the bench today in Illinois," said Butterfield.[55]

To this point, Douglas was not known to have been driven one way or the other on the issue of slavery. His first official action with regard to treatment of blacks came in the state Supreme Court's ruling in *Bailey v. Cromwell* on July 24, 1841. The court affirmed the argument of appellant attorney Abraham Lincoln "that the presumption of law was, in this State, that every person was free, without regard to color." The court added pointedly, "The sale of a free person is illegal." Douglas concurred in the opinion, written by Justice Sidney Breese.[56]

His assignment to Quincy put Douglas in the center of the anti-slavery movement in Illinois. The city's founders, John Wood and Willard Keyes, along with dozens of others were anti-slavery proponents. Both signed on to the creation in Quincy of the first Anti-Slavery Society in Illinois on August 25, 1835, and Keyes became its first secretary.[57] Signing as Vice President was Dr. Richard Eells, whose home at Fourth and Jersey was one-half block from the abolitionist church, the Rev. Asa Turner's "Lord's Barn" and within a block of Judge Douglas's residence at Third and York. Eells and Douglas's paths would intersect in 1842 when Douglas would try the doctor for assisting a fugitive Missouri slave.

It was Quincy's opponents of slavery who suggested that the Rev. Elijah P. Lovejoy organize a convention in either Quincy or Alton to establish a statewide anti-slavery society. Lovejoy approved the idea, and the Quincy society's organization became the model for the Illinois Anti-Slavery Society Lovejoy proposed in 1837.[58] The strength of Quincy's enthusiasm for the abolitionist movement was recognized in the convention that created the state anti-slavery organization. Judge Henry H. Snow, a member of the Rev. Turner's church in Quincy, was elected a vice president. Other Quincy men were elected to seats of the Illinois Anti-Slavery Society's board of managers.[59]

After learning that some of the city's leading citizens blamed the Rev. Elijah P. Lovejoy, publisher of the abolitionist newspaper *Alton Observer*, for the continuing mob action in Alton, fearful Quincy anti-slavery men repeatedly urged Lovejoy to bring his press to Quincy. They assured Lovejoy that he and his press would be protected. Lovejoy's friend David Nelson was one Quincyan who did not promote the idea. While he found Quincy's New Englanders and Congregationalists "intelligent and lovely," he likened others of the river town to "boiled ... scum."[60]

Judge Douglas presided at one of the most important antislavery cases in U.S. history, the only Underground Railroad case to reach the U.S. Supreme Court. In its ruling several years later, the Supreme Court upheld Circuit Judge Douglas's decision.

The matter involved Douglas's own neighbor, Dr. Richard Eells, who had been whispered to be aiding slavery's victims in their attempts to escape their bonds on the Underground Railroad.[61] When he arrived in Quincy in 1835, Dr. Eells brought with him from his Connecticut home a strong spirit of abolitionism. By 1836 Eells had found kindred spirits in Quincy who formed the first of Illinois' three loosely organized starting points on the Underground Railroad, which helped carry fugitive slaves to freedom.[62] Over the next few years, he would be credited with helping to freedom dozens of blacks who had been referred to him.

Eells established his practices—medical and humanitarian—in one of three single-story frame buildings in the middle of the south side of John's Square, at the time mostly a patch of unkempt rough hazel trees. A popular spot for those looking for entertainment was at the square's southeast corner in front of the courthouse. A large stump had been left by the removal of an aged tree that often served as the platform for political speeches, sales, and sermons.

Although German immigrants who traded at the town's few dry goods and grocery stores paid in money, merchants sent it on in payment for the goods they sold. Little currency circulated. Like most of the town's other purveyors of goods and services, Eells often received produce and farm goods for his work. That was eased in 1841 when Eells was named Quincy's first city physician and was paid regularly by the city for his ministrations.[63]

In 1835, Eells and his wife Jane built a small brick Italianate home on Jersey Street within a minute's walk east of the "Lord's Barn." The primitive wood-frame structure was the first church building—and the first sanctuary of the anti-slavery movement in Quincy. The pastor was the Rev. Asa Turner, a member of the Yale Band, the seven divinity school graduates who founded Illinois College in Jacksonville in 1829.[64] Turner moved the following year to Quincy, where he built his church and a reputation for anti-slavery. He preached this message within ear shot of the slave state of Missouri.

"I told them what anti-slavery was," Turner recalled. "Every man has a right to the avails of his own labor. Abolitionists want free speech, a free press, and all the freedom God has given every man. Our Declaration of Independence and Constitution have guaranteed it."[65]

Dr. Eells had fully committed himself to Turner's message.

Late one summer evening in 1842, Berryman Barnet, a black Quincyan and an agent for the local underground railroad, arrived at Eells's home to report that a man named Charlie was running for freedom and being pursued by a Missouri search party. With directions to the fugitive's hiding place, Eells reached Charlie about two miles east of Quincy. He gave the man a dry shirt and pair of pantaloons.

The two set off for Quincy's Mission Institute, a college for Presbyterian missionaries and safe haven for contraband blacks. Dr. David Nelson founded the institute approximately one mile farther east after being chased out of Missouri in 1836 for teaching abolitionism at Marion College. He had founded the college near Palmyra, Missouri, in 1831.

Nelson was considered one of Presbyterianism's great preachers. Among his converts was Elijah P. Lovejoy, the young minister who filled the columns of his St. Louis newspaper with stories of slavery's horrors.[66]

From a distance, a group of the pursuers, sent by Charlie's Monticello, Missouri, owner, Chauncey Durkee, approached Eells's buggy and ordered him to stop. Eells steered the buggy to the edge of a cemetery near a cornfield south of the Institute and instructed Charlie to jump and to stay hidden. Before morning, however, Charlie was discovered, captured, and taken back to Monticello. The angered Missouri vigilantes chased Eells to his home. Confronted by the agitated group at his door, Eells denied that he had helped a fugitive slave, claiming he had been home all evening. One of the pursuers, however, had found the black man's wet clothing in the doctor's buggy, confirming his complicity in the slave's attempted escape. The next morning, Quincy Justice of the Peace Henry Asbury bound over Eells for trial. The jury trial would take two days in Judge Stephen A. Douglas's court room.[67]

The issue was a knotty one. In Article Six of the Ordinance of 1787 the U.S. Congress prohibited slavery in the Northwest Territory. Despite that decree, the territory's settlers, Southerners and Northerners, remained divided over the question of slavery. There were those who believed it meant an absolute prohibition of slavery, others who considered the ordinance beyond the authority of Congress and, therefore, unconstitutional, and some who suggested that it applied only to black children born after 1787. When Illinois was admitted as a state, the drafters of its constitution ignored the prohibition of slavery, drafting a document that permitted limited slavery, though it required that anyone held to involuntary servitude be removed from the state within one year. It was a construction of law that Douglas would reflect in his decision in Eells and consistently throughout his government service, including his response in 1857 to the U.S. Supreme Court's ruling in Dred Scott: no federal law had ever freed a slave. American history had shown that the people in determining their own domestic institutions would end slavery.[68] They could effectively ignore federal mandates by not adopting regulations needed to enforce them. Although he had come from the east, Douglas brought with him no sympathy for abolition—or Anti-Slavery Societies like the one liberal Quincyans had created in August 1835. As a representative in the Illinois legislature, Douglas had voted with the majority of his colleagues for resolutions that sought to end the agitation in the state over slavery. And the legislature had indicated its intentions regarding flights to freedom by passing its own Fugitive Slave Act.

Although his position on the bench precluded any participation, Douglas witnessed in his adopted city of Quincy the acrimony of the debate caused by this matter of abolition. In Quincy there were abolition and anti-abolition meetings, and the attentions of either side seemed only to elevate the agitation. Concerned that such activity could damage the city's reputation, there were calls for moderation. Quincy attorney Orville Hickman Browning reflected the views of conservatives who saw slavery as a domestic institution legally free to operate in the states in which it existed. He castigated abolitionists who continued to agitate about it. It was Browning who as a state senator in 1837 drafted the Illinois legislature's resolutions agreeing with requests by Southern states to condemn abolitionists. In Quincy six years later, Browning again took the lead against abolitionists as the featured speaker at a meeting whose purpose was to denounce the agitators.[69] While Browning personally believed slavery was immoral and an unjust, he ultimately decided the best course was to discourage his neighbors from arguing about it.[70]

The Eells case reached Douglas's courtroom in April 1843. The trial of the prominent doctor highly affected the community's citizens—creating estrangements in business and social relationships.[71] Leading citizens were on both sides of the issue. It also strained relations between Illinois and Missouri's governors. Missouri governor Thomas Reynolds, himself a former Illinois Supreme Court justice, demanded that Illinois extradite Eells to Missouri for aiding the Missouri fugitive. Illinois Governor Ford refused. Ford defended Eells by saying the information he had convinced him Eells had not been in Missouri for two years, meaning the allegation brought by Missouri could not have occurred. But Governor Ford, in his lengthy letter, bemoaned a larger controversy:

> And permit me to assure you, that no one feels more deeply than myself, the obligation of promoting and maintaining amongst the States of this Union, the utmost harmony and reciprocal regard for each other's rights. The people of this State recognize in the fullest manner, the perfect right of the people of Missouri, to make and execute such laws, in relation to persons and property, within their own jurisdiction, as may seem good to themselves, without any interference on our part, either in making or executing those laws.
>
> This is the disposition and feeling of ninety nine out of every one hundred of our citizens; who look with indignation and abhorrence upon the conduct of an incendiary and misguided few amongst us, who have interfered, and are disposed to continue that interference, with the right of the people of Missouri, to a class of persons there made private property by the constitution and laws of your State. In that disposition and feeling, I myself, fully participate with the great mass of the people here.[72]

Eells's attorneys contended that the U.S. Supreme Court in a recent ruling, *Prigg v. Pennsylvania*, made the federal government responsible for apprehending fugitive slaves and that Congress could not require a state to execute a law of the federal government. As a result, they argued, Eells was answerable not under the state law but under the federal Fugitive Slave Act, so should be released. Douglas decided against those arguments on the basis that Eells's arrest had been made with the objective to preserve the peace in accordance with the Illinois' "Black Code." The law made it a crime to harbor a person legally held to service in Illinois or any other state.[73] The jury held, therefore, that the state had the right to arrest Eells.[74] Although he didn't imprison Eells, Douglas fined him $400, half the market value of the slave Charlie, and $100 less than the maximum fine the law allowed.[75]

The *Quincy Whig*, which more often was critical of Douglas, approved of his ruling in the Eells case.

"We hope this will prove a warning to the abolitionists in the future," wrote the editor. "If prudence, and a due regard for the rights of a neighboring State, will not hold them in check, the laws should."[76]

Douglas's Jacksonville friend John J. Hardin summed up the feelings of Central Illinoisans about conductors like Eells along the Underground Railroad. In an editorial in the Jacksonville

Illinoisan—Hardin frequently wrote editorials for the Whig-oriented newspaper—he wrote, "One Dr. Richard Eells, notorious for having attempted last summer to steal and run off a negro, the property of Mr. Durkee of Missouri, was recently tried for his rascality and found guilty."[77]

Eells appealed Douglas's decision to the Illinois Supreme Court, whose members two years later upheld Douglas's decision. In the meantime Eells gained enough notoriety to gain the presidency of the Illinois Antislavery Society in 1843 and the nomination as the Liberty Party's candidate for governor in 1846. Ultimately, the Eells case reached the U.S. Supreme Court, where William Seward of New York and Salmon Portland Chase of Ohio, who would become members of President Lincoln's cabinet, were Eells's defending attorneys. The nation's highest court in 1853 also affirmed Douglas. By that time, impoverished by the cost of his trials, Eells had been dead seven years. And Douglas by that time had been a member of the U.S. Senate for six years.

Mormon Prophet Joseph Smith regarded Stephen Douglas as a "master spirit" of Smith's Mormon Church. As secretary of state and circuit judge, Douglas had pursued and protected the interests of Smith's church. For that, Douglas believed he would earn the votes of the thousands of Smith's followers (Library of Congress).

16. Quest for Congress

THE STRENGTH OF QUINCYAN THOMAS FORD'S VICTORY in 1842 at the head of the state ticket carried Democrats into offices throughout the state. Ford's party maintained control of the Illinois legislature, a circumstance whose possibilities were not lost on the twenty-nine-year-old Douglas. Illinois' U.S. Senator Richard Young hoped to be re-elected, but malfeasance as one of the state's commissioners charged with negotiating a loan in the foreign money markets to pay the debt left by the internal improvements debacle doomed his re-election.[1] Democrats in the legislature, with whom Douglas was closely tied, had turned against Young. As a legislator in 1836, Douglas had promoted and voted for Young's election to the United States Senate, a favor repaid when Young helped Douglas win appointment by President Martin Van Buren in 1837 as register of the federal land office in Springfield. From Douglas's perspective, the score was even.

It was rumored that Judge Douglas was not only willing to be a candidate for public office. He was discretely campaigning while making his way around his Fifth Judicial Circuit and communicating regularly with party associates in Springfield to keep abreast of offices, candidates, and implications.

Douglas had quietly decided to seek the seat of Senator Young, whose term was expiring. In a confidential letter to Harry Wilton on March 27, 1842, Douglas began by gratuitously praising Wilton as the best candidate for the State Senate: "I don't know whether you are a candidate for the Senate or not but hope you are. I believe all the aspirants would give away to you cheerfully; and am afraid they will not unite cordially on any other man."

Douglas then got to the point. Wilton, he wrote, was "first to solicit me to become a Candidate for the U.S. Senate" but reporting that "our friend [Sidney] Breese is in the field actively electioneering for himself. "He has written to the senator in this county soliciting his support, and I presume has written to each senator & candidate in all other Democratic Counties to the same effect. This is a pretty strong game & may do mischief if no[t] counteracted."

Douglas's direction by indirection was apparent in his request to know "whether there is any danger of divisions which will result in defeating any members of the Legislature."[2] That intelligence was important to Douglas, since it was the legislature that elected the state's U.S. senators. Douglas campaigned guardedly, but it was hardly sub rosa. Too often he had been at the meetings of what the *Springfield Journal* derogatorily called the Loco Focos. Acquainted with Douglas's caginess, the *Journal* figured Douglas to enter the race and was willing to "bet a ginger cake against an 'apple' on Douglas."[3]

The maneuverings of Douglas and friends was so pervasive that the Springfield newspaper, the *Illinois State Register*, itself a Democratic journal, grumbled that an insurgent clique was dominating the Democratic Party.[4] Certain that his friends were promoting his candidacy in the legislature, Douglas confidentially confirmed himself a candidate to take Young's place in the U.S. Senate. What Douglas had not calculated—and his intimate colleagues in Springfield had not detected—was that his older associate Sidney Breese, who had risen to the Supreme Court along with Douglas, indeed was campaigning for Young's job.[5] So, too, was Democratic state Representative John A. McClernand. Little concerned about McClernand's entry into the race, Breese expected his young colleague Douglas to consent to his Democratic elder's request that Douglas drop his candidacy. When Douglas refused, Breese suggested strongly that he postpone his ambition. Once again, Douglas refused and continued to campaign tirelessly for the nomination. Although Douglas's intractability rankled Breese at the time, he would be helpful when Douglas again sought Illinois' second Senate seat in 1846.[6]

House and Senate Democrats caucused on December 16, 1842,[7] to select the next U.S. senator from Illinois. Both Breese and Douglas had closely worked their associates throughout the state, expecting that local grass-roots support would buoy the confidence of the men who would vote that day. The contest brought hundreds of the state's leading men, most of them not members of the legislature, to Springfield. Their presence that evening was designed to demonstrate not only their own support for their candidates but enthusiasm by their regions, as well. The enthusiasm grew rowdier as the results of each of the nineteen ballots were announced. Commotion and agitation rent the caucus, which began shortly after 7 p.m. The incumbent Young, who still chased after the office, led the voting with 38 votes when the first ballot was counted. Douglas was second with 29 votes, Breese third with 28, and McClernand fourth with 18. The politicking and voting went on for six hours and eighteen more ballots. Young's chances diminished as the voting continued, and he withdrew from the contest after a promise that he would be appointed to take the vacant position on the state Supreme Court of Thomas Ford, who recently had been elected governor.[8] When legislators cast their nineteenth ballot, they gave Breese fifty-six votes to Douglas's fifty-one. McClernand received three and Young one. The full legislature the following day elected Breese to the Senate. True to their word, the legislature's Democratic majority appointed Young an associate justice.

The scuttlebutt-analyses about the closeness of the election focused on Douglas's age. The Constitution required senators to be at least thirty years old. At the time of the election of Illinois' next senator, Douglas was twenty-nine. The new Congress would convene—and Illinois' new senator would assume office—on March 4, 1843. Although he had been an Illinois Supreme Court justice, the highest position in the state's judicial branch, for two years, Douglas still would have been too young to be seated in the United States Senate. Continuing to fight for Douglas's election, his friends argued he could wait until his thirtieth birthday, April 23, 1843, little more than a month hence, before taking his seat. The argument was not persuasive, the reason the full legislature elected Breese to the Senate.[9] Douglas maintained no hard feelings about his loss. He attended the traditional celebration at Springfield's American House for Judge Breese's election. Douglas was said to have taken "an active part in the dancing."[10]

Judge Douglas returned to his bench in the vast military tract in western Illinois. But having just missed the most prized office in government service, the taste for elective office was in his mouth. With Douglas's fellow Quincyan and Democrat Thomas Ford elected to the state's chief executive office and Democrats in control of both houses of the General Assembly, attention now shifted to state reapportionment. The migration into Illinois of New Englanders, Germans and Irish—and in his own Western Illinois, some 15,000 Mormons just north of Adams County in his judicial district—had boosted the state's population significantly, Douglas anticipated the 1840 census. It demonstrated that Illinois merited four additional congressional districts. The legislature completed the job of redistricting by March 1, 1843, which opened a new congressional district, which the legislature's Democratic majority generally superimposed over Douglas's judicial district. A special election to select congressmen in the new districts was set for August 7, 1843.

Douglas's friends in the new Fifth Congressional District encouraged him to seek the party's nomination for Congress. Douglas's health was of concern at the time, and he was unsure he would have the strength to campaign and declined. At one point he considered resigning his seat on the bench to spend time recuperating.[11]

While Douglas hesitated, others were quickly announcing for the western region's new congressional seat. Already, the Whigs announced that Orville Hickman Browning of Quincy, considered one of the state's ablest lawyers and a familiar face in Western Illinois politics, would be their candidate.

Several Democrats indicated interest in the seat, among them former Governor Carlin, state Representative A.W. Cavarly of Carrollton; William A. Richardson of Rushville, who did not seek re-election at the end of his recently completed Illinois Senate term; even U.S. Senator Young. Apprehensive about their strength in the newly redistricted congressional district, Democratic Party leaders were concerned about the number of their party's candidates announcing for the race. With Douglas offering some helpful nudges, they called for a party convention at which they wanted delegates to select and support a single candidate. Although he had denied he was a candidate for Congress, by the time the thirty-seven delegates met convened in Griggsville, Illinois, on June 5, Douglas had miraculously recovered his health and let it be known he was available. There were signs that Douglas and his supporters had done more than provide mere notification. Their advance work for the nomination was solid. When Governor Carlin led in the first vote, delegates were called into an unexpected—and unexplained—recess. Returning in a half-hour for the second vote, delegates immediately and unanimously nominated Douglas.[12]

Douglas was presiding at court in Knoxville when he got the news about his nomination as his party's candidate for Congress. Courtroom spectators heard it and erupted in excitement, enough so that Judge Douglas had to adjourn the court. Everyone—the judge, jury, lawyers, and spectators—spilled out onto the public square.[13]

Douglas was not alone in seeing an opportunity to be sent to Congress. His friend Abraham Lincoln of Springfield in the Seventh Congressional District had taken note of the reapportionment and began contacting friends for support after the new districts were drawn. Lincoln began hinting that he was interested in a Whig nomination for Congress.

"Your county and ours are almost sure to be placed in the same congressional district," he wrote to his Whig friend and state representative Alden Hull of Tazewell County. "I would very much like to be it's [sic] Representative."[14]

And to Richard S. Thomas, a lawyer and active Whig in Virginia, Illinois, Lincoln wrote, "Now if you should hear any one say that Lincoln don't want to go to Congress, I wish you as a personal friend of mine, would tell him you have reason to believe he is mistaken. The truth is, I would like to go very much."[15]

Whigs met in Springfield to create a series of party resolutions on the same day the Democrats in the legislature were completing the reapportionment. Lincoln's draftsmanship created two sets of guides: the first reflecting Whig founder Henry Clay's American System, calling for a tariff on imported goods to protect American industry, opposition to direct taxation, a national bank for maintenance of a sound currency, and distribution to the states of the proceeds of public land sales. The second set of guides reflected the practical politics like those of young Douglas. Lincoln called on his Whig colleagues to build a convention system for the nomination of the party's candidates and a detailed party organization of county delegates to fill all vacancies.[16] After trying like Douglas to maneuver himself into a position to run for Congress, Lincoln had to admit failure. In a letter of March 24, 1843, to his friend Joshua Speed, now living in Kentucky, a greatly disappointed Lincoln reported that the convention's Whig delegates had nominated Edward D. Baker as their district's candidate for Congress. Lincoln was disheartened more that he had been appointed a delegate to the district convention for Baker, "so that in getting Baker the nomination, I shall be 'fixed' a good deal like a fellow who is made groomsman to the man what has cut him out, and is marrying his own dear 'gal.'"[17]

Lincoln continued to hold out some hope for a nomination and quietly let friends know it. Disappointed that his Sangamon friends preferred Baker to him, Lincoln told Martin S. Morris of Petersburg how he and friend Mason with only three votes had the power to give the victory to either Baker or John J. Hardin of Jacksonville. If something unexpected happened, Lincoln authorized Morris of the Menard district to support him for the nomination.[18] On the following Saturday, delegates to the Menard Whig convention at Petersburg instructed Morris and the County's other delegate, George U. Miles, to vote for Lincoln on the first ballot and Hardin on the second.[19] The plot was unsuccessful and Hardin won the nomination.

Douglas, as usual, feigned surprise when his fellow Democrats at Griggsville nominated him. Publicly he had implied he would decline such an honor. But when the Democrats nominated him unanimously for the seat that a growing population and redistricting created in the Fifth District, he bowed to the public's wishes and offered himself as a candidate.[20]

Douglas was all too cunning, his community's newspaper blared. For some time Douglas had been itching to move up, the *Quincy Daily Whig* editor charged. The paper had had it with him. It called him one of that "clique of selfish politicians, that have governed the State with a rod of iron" and, moreover, even while on the bench "one that has assisted in pulling the wires, and giving direction to the movements of his party."

"Crafty, and ambitious as crafty, among all the party movements he has participated in, he has never forgotten number one," the *Whig*'s attack continued, "and we find him during the last ten years, either in one office or another, or always on the look out for one a higher grade, and that would pay better."[21]

Since his arrival in Jacksonville nearly ten years earlier, Douglas had craftily reacted to events and opportunities to make moves designed to advance his own interests. Pay made no difference. He had earned $3,000 as federal land register in 1837 and earned half that amount as a state Supreme Court justice four years later. Douglas's chess playing focused not on tactical loss but on strategic gain. The depth of intrigue made no difference. Whether it was ejecting the powerful from office or ignoring friends who had helped him in his project, Douglas's game was to make the moves that moved him forward.

The *Whig* had erected its opposition to Douglas from the time he arrived in Quincy. Considering his moves from one office to another, the newspaper opened up on him, asking how long it would be before the judge would be seeking another higher office. In 1843, voters of the large Fifth Congressional District would elect a new congressman. Suspicious of Douglas's intentions, the *Whig* attacked him in May for a ruling in his circuit court that appeared to have more political than legal implications.

On the second day of the court's spring term, the Adams County grand jury asked Judge Douglas whether they were authorized to indict offenders in the recently legislated but as yet unorganized Marquette County. The state legislature had created the new county by carving it from the eastern half of Adams County. Douglas took what the *Whig* considered several unusual steps in answering the question. He reduced to writing his decision. That was such an extraordinary step for the judge, even he admitted it.[22] Douglas went well beyond the grand jury's single question by broadening his decision to the entire issue of Marquette County's organization. From the newspaper's perspective, Douglas was using the bench to pad his and his party's political future. The judge had no reason to decide anything more than whether the grand jury had the power to indict in the unorganized county. To step beyond that question, as Douglas did in upholding the validity of the legislature's creation of a new county and in counseling the proposed county's voters on the election of its officers, was too much for the *Whig's* editor.

> I object to his forcing opinions on the grand jury and the people of Adams County, when such were not called for. He was merely asked to say whether the grand jury had jurisdiction over offenses committed in what was intended by the legislature for Marquette County; and in answering this question he adds, that for election purposes the counties are not united. This was gratuitous, uncalled for, and although probably given in all honesty, yet many will say, that Judge Douglas, in volunteering his opinion on this point, intended to benefit his *political* friends in what he believes to be Adams County.[23]

The *Whig* said little about the motives of the political men who, following the editor's logic, would have had similar reasons for the opposite view. In addition, the *Whig* did not attack that side's argument that the legislature's creation of Marquette County should have been nullified. Whig lawyer Orville Hickman Browning made that argument.

What Browning and Douglas each knew was that the decision would play heavily in the upcoming congressional election. They knew that Whigs were stronger than Democrats in Quincy and the rest of the western half of Adams County. Their numerical superiority was favorable to the Whigs, who controlled Quincy and county political appointments and could be expected to work for a Whig victory. Splitting Adams County would not change the Whig strength in Adams County, but it would provide patronage workers and political strength in a new county for the Democrats. It would have given the Democrats a separate block of voters, whose inferior numbers would no longer be mooted by the Whigs of Adams County.

What was unusual about Douglas's ruling, however, was that it reversed his ruling in February 1842 when he prohibited county commissioners from moving the county seat—and the county's power—to Columbus in the eastern half of Adams County. What had changed was that a nomination now loomed for the office he had been seeking since he left New York.

Douglas ignored the *Whig*—and the practical advice of his friends to retain his seat on the bench until his election was certain. With his perfunctory expressions of regret and personal sacrifice, Douglas on June 28 resigned his position on the Illinois Supreme Court. The *Whig* would question just how much Douglas would be sacrificing, charging that it had proof that although Douglas had sent his letter of resignation to Governor Ford, he had continued to draw his salary throughout the canvas and up to the day of the election.[24] The *Whig* was quick to attack Douglas as an interloper, asking in a headline in June, "Where does Judge Douglas reside?" The newspaper accused Douglas of not living in Quincy and of not paying his share of taxes. It charged that other residents bore the burden of the municipality's costs, including Douglas's share.²⁵ Some circles thought Douglas a bit big for his breeches, always had aspired for offices beyond the one he held, which should have been enough to suit any man of ordinary ambition.²⁶

Douglas knew he faced a formidable opponent in Browning who had been nominated by his fellow Whigs meeting on May 1 at the Pike County courthouse in Pittsfield. Browning and Douglas had been acquainted since their elections in 1836, Browning to the Senate and Douglas to the House, at Vandalia. Having resided in the same boarding house at Vandalia, they enjoyed each other's friendship. After Lincoln and his Sangamon Long Nine had secured the state capital for Springfield, Browning and Douglas had been among the 150 men at the party in Athens, Illinois, some fifteen miles north of Springfield, to celebrate the achievement.²⁷ It had been Browning who introduced in the Senate the bill to permanently relocate the capital, once a site had been chosen. Douglas, who had left the legislature for Springfield and his new post as register of the federal land office there, saluted the victors.

"The last winter's legislation [moving the capital to Springfield]," Douglas said in a toast at a celebration in the Sangamon County town of Athens, "may its results prove no less beneficial to the whole state than they have to our town."²⁸

At the same time, Browning and Douglas were accused of trading their votes for a share of the Long Nine's internal improvements largesse. Neither had done so. The vote-trading related to the capital's relocation had been in exchange of public works projects. Although of different political parties, Browning and Douglas both had opposed the massive program orchestrated by Browning's Whig friends from Sangamon County. Neither had a reason for trading votes. A fiscal conservative, Browning stubbornly refused to vote for the program, one of only eight senators who opposed internal improvements but who voted for the capital's move to Springfield.²⁹

A Kentuckian educated at Transylvania Law School, Browning had the reputation of a "dandy." A light handkerchief usually dangled from the single breast pocket of his Prince Albert-style dress coat. Large cuffs emerged from its sleeves and ruffles were behind its buttons. Browning's thinning hair, combed with great care over the top of his head, was stroked forward at the sides conveying the appearance of a Roman senator's olive crown. He had a fine forehead, a skin fold over his eyebrows, large "darkish" and piercing eyes, and an aquiline nose. Despite this air of aristocracy, Browning's smile was genuine and had earned him the friendship and respect of his community. Eloquent in speech, personally or in the courtroom, Browning enjoyed a reputation that frequently attracted business for his law practice from across the state. That did not make Browning a favorite among his peers. He was aloof and arrogant, conceited, always carrying himself with an air of pomposity and superiority. It was for this reason, said the German emigrant-turned politician Gustave Koerner, who had served with him the state legislature, Browning was not loved.³⁰

The Fifth Congressional District, including the vast Military District between the Illinois and Mississippi Rivers, was the largest in Illinois Because he and his partner and fellow Whig Nehemiah Bushnell had practiced in land transactions, Browning was well known and respected throughout the eleven-county congressional district.³¹ Although fellow Democrats were concerned about how well he might do, Douglas was certain that he could count on the Adams County and Mormon vote. And he was confident that the party was organized by the time delegates left the Griggsville convention. They marched out as precinct and county committees, district correspondence committee, and district central committee. They had their specific role to efficiently muster and direct the party's faithful. They would build a party presence in each county, enlist workers, build platforms, recruit candidates, and bring out voters to elect them.

Browning did not give Douglas much time to think about all that. Just two days after the Democratic convention, Browning launched a two-hour attack on Douglas at Pittsfield, a larger Whig town only an hour's ride south of Griggsville. The organ for Browning's campaign was the *Quincy Whig*, which immediately after Browning's nomination and tirade against Douglas, attacked Douglas as well on a charge that he had used the bench at Quincy only as a stepping-stone to his next public post. Unlike Browning who was making a personal sacrifice as a candidate, the *Whig* said, Douglas was a "striving politician" interested only in collecting political support to serve his own ambitions. Although his judicial district was in Quincy, the newspaper once again claimed Douglas did not even live in Quincy, did not support it, and maintained his official home in Jacksonville. The *Whig* doubted Douglas had any friends in the community except for political cronies. His goal in the campaign, the newspaper added, was "to live off the people."[32] History had shown Douglas, the *Whig* informed its readers, to be "unsettled and migratory ... carrying him wherever he can get an office, and keeping him there no longer than a better and more valuable one is within his reach in some other section of the State." Douglas had no loyalty to Western Illinois, the newspaper added, charging that he was not now a resident of the district and would not be if he were elected. If the people did not elect Douglas to the job, the *Whig* said, Douglas would simply "impose [more] bad laws on the people, leave you and go where he can get some other and a better grab at the 'spoils.'"[33]

Contestants Browning and Douglas agreed to a series of joint debates in July, a decision that would lead to other forensics during a tour of the district together for forty days, Sundays excluded—from that day until the day before the August 7 election. The usually dandified Browning for this campaign to the hinterlands dispensed with ruffled shirts and suits for uncharacteristic Kentucky jeans. He and Douglas launched what observers were calling the "hottest contest for a seat in Congress that ever was fought in Illinois."[34] At the start of their campaign, however, the two men agreed that their demeanor should provide an example of a political contest in which the opponents would fight hard from the platform but would stand above personal rancor.

"Before entering upon the canvass," as Browning years afterward described their agreement, "we came to the mutual understanding not to violate with each other the courtesies and proprieties of life; not to permit the excitement of debate to betray us into personalities."[35]

Their debate throughout the largest congressional district in the state—Browning believed it was among the largest in the country—was strenuous.[36] In a form that Douglas would suggest to Lincoln, when Lincoln opposed Douglas for his U.S. Senate in 1858, the first speaker took an hour, the second spoke for one and a half hours and the third concluded in the last half hour. On occasions when that convention was not used, Douglas usually spoke about two hours and Browning for about half that time. Browning acknowledged the hard-fought campaign, calling it "one of the most excited, arduous, and earnest political campaigns that was ever made in the State."[37]

Browning believed the district's constituents were as fiscally conservative as he was and he exploited Douglas's vote in 1836 for internal improvements, whose costs still burdened and embarrassed the state. Browning considered Douglas vulnerable for his vote for it. Douglas resented the charge and continued to point out he had fought to subdue the surge for public works. His vote, he said, was a service to his constituents, who had instructed him to vote for internal improvements.[38] Browning continued to ignore Douglas's explanation.

The two also battled over national issues, mainly protectionism, federal land sale proceeds, and banking. In high Whig spirit, Browning argued that Clay's tariff already was stimulating manufacturing in the country and that credit available through national banks would make capital available for an even stronger industrial economy. Their debate over the tariff put Browning and Douglas squarely at opposite ends on the key issue between the Whigs and Democrats. Browning charged in a three-hour debate with Douglas in Payson, just south of Quincy, on July 5 that the Democracy's candidates "were willing to sacrifice white labor and industry of the country, to gratify the rich slave holders and nabobs of the south."[39]

His voice and hands rising in great exertions, Douglas replied that the tariff had benefited the rich at the expense of the poor and the working class and had worked against the agricultural interests of farmers like those of Payson. And further reflecting his Jacksonian bent, he said he believed in a hard money system.[40]

Douglas's campaign style surprised the Whigs. In each town, he visited with the people, patting the back of a farmer here, congratulating, commiserating, and sympathizing there. Browning had none of this gentler political art of courting a common voter. Although he could dress as they dressed, he was not comfortable in the kinds of back-slapping, kid-kissing, slobberish appeals that came so easily to Douglas. Douglas would roll up his sleeves, have a keg of cider opened, and attack. If idiotic bluster worked as well as substance, so much the better. There were few concerns among the electorate about the tactic: "I admit what he said he said well and with much energy of manner," said one debate attendee who found little to chew on, "but there was no argument, no reason, no patriotism; it was all bold and vague assertion, without proof, intended to work on the passions and prejudices of his party."[41]

The observation was prescient, Douglas provoking similar comments throughout the rest of his political career. Browning, however, praised Douglas for never betraying their agreement for courtesy and propriety during the campaign. "I am proud to say that the compact was well and faithfully kept on both sides. During the entire campaign not one unkind word or discourteous act passed between us; and we closed the canvass with the friendly relations which had previously subsisted undisturbed, and maintained them, without interruption, to the day of his death."[42]

The rigors of the campaign took Browning and Douglas to towns like Carrollton, White Hall, Scottville, and Carlinville. They would finish up with debates in Liberty, Clayton, Houston, and Marcelline, close to their Quincy homes, in the last week of the contest.[43] By the day of the election both men were exhausted, Browning admitting that he had tired earlier than Douglas.

By the last days of the campaign, Browning in fact was confined to bed and dangerously ill.[44] The *Quincy Daily Whig* complained that the "locofocos" were so bent on taking advantage of any opportunity that they had circulated a rumor "*that Browning was actually dead*. They [the Democrats] were not content, said the newspaper, with defaming the Whig candidate, in that sewer of filth and falsehood—the *Quincy Herald*—but they must, to fill the measure of their infamy, take advantage of his illness, to circulate the falsehood that he is dead."[45]

The election results demonstrated the effectiveness of the Democratic legislature's reapportionment effort. Douglas and his party's candidates in five other districts—Robert Smith in the First, John A. McClernand the Second, Orlando B. Ficklin in the Third, John Wentworth in the Fourth, and Joseph P. Hoge in the Sixth—had won election to seats in the 28th Congress. The Democrats' only loss was in the Seventh Congressional District, where John J. Hardin, against whom Douglas had waged and won his first political contest, easily won the seat his fellow Whig Lincoln had too quietly desired. The blustering Douglas won his election by 461 votes, 8,641 to 8,180, the narrowest margin in any Illinois congressional contest that year. Browning had carried Adams County, in which Quincy was the county seat and Judge Douglas had presided, by a sizable margin.[46]

Quincy's Whig newspaper called the margin of Douglas's victory a cause for rejoicing. Just the year before, the *Quincy Daily Whig* noted, "The locofoco candidate for Governor received a majority of near eight hundred votes in this district ... and the foreign population, which usually votes on that side of the question, has been materially increased in the district since the election for Governor." That the Democrats ran the most popular man of their party, as the newspaper called Douglas, in a district drawn to send him to Congress and found their candidate barely eking out a win was reason for hope that he could be beaten in the next election.[47]

Democratic Governor Ford, on the other hand, was convinced Douglas lost the Mormon vote, that Mormons in Adams County had been directed to vote the Whig ticket.[48] And, in fact, despite Mormon leader Joseph Smith's professed liking for him, Douglas did not get the Mormon vote in the church's Quincy District. Because they considered Governor Ford a threat[49]—in June 1843 he was considering yet another request to extradite Smith to Missouri—Mormon leaders had instructed their followers to vote for Whigs. Jacob B. Backenstos, a Douglas friend who had left Springfield to establish a mercantile store in Hancock County, had become influential among the Mormons. At their request, he went to Springfield to determine whether Ford intended to send the state militia against them. Backenstos reported to the Mormons "that he had the most ample assurances of favor to the Mormons so long as they voted the democratic ticket."[50] Ford, who said he knew nothing of the promise until three years later, denied any such assurances, and in fact would later send the militia to order the Mormons to leave Illinois. Douglas would serve in that militia as a major under the command of Colonel John J. Hardin. The Backenstos report had been enough to convince the Mormons to change their votes in Hancock County, providing a large plurality of nearly seventy-four percent for the election of Democrat Joseph P. Hoge over Cyrus Walker, who was Joseph Smith's lawyer and for whom Smith said he would vote. Word of the change did not reach the Mormons of northern Adams County, however, who voted for Browning.[51] The help of friend Gustave Koerner of Belleville, who stumped the Fifth District at Douglas's request to appeal to the district's large population of German settlers, helped give Douglas enough votes to win his slim majority. Koerner was admired among the Germans as an established lawyer in Belleville and active in Democratic politics. He had won election to the Illinois House in 1842. Himself a German émigré, Koerner was the right man to appeal to the many Germans who had immigrated into Central Illinois seeking to escape reprisals for their liberalism.

This latest Mormon circumstance caused a significant repercussion in both Whig and Democratic camps. With the church's reversal that swept Hoge into office, Whig newspapers renewed their crusades against the Mormons and charged Democratic leaders with championing false claims to gain the Mormon vote. Although Democrats generally appreciated the vote that helped Hoge win election, Douglas's friends were not happy that the Quincy church's members had voted for Browning. Democrats joined Whigs in calling for Mormons to leave the state.

17. Natural Phenomena

In the six years Douglas lived in Quincy, first at John Tillson's Quincy House, then in a small boarding house he rented just southwest of John's Square, the city's politics had shifted Democratic. Orville Browning made sure that Whigs were not pushed too far into the background. But Douglas's ceaseless political energies had switched the electoral majority from Browning's party to his that year. In the spring elections, Democrats won every seat on the Quincy City Council.[1]

On January 4, 1843, the heaviest earthquake residents could recall rocked Quincy. Although there was little damage, it was the first of many rumblings and shakings that soon were to upset the delicate balance on several matters—slavery among them—that had been achieved in the Mississippi River town.

To the consternation of the region's farmers who traded in Quincy, the city council that year decided to fence in John's Square. The teams of horses and oxen that had been allowed to graze on the open lot on the square now would have to be sheltered and fed at additional cost. But most farmers and stockmen did not vote in Quincy municipal elections. The city's elected officials ignored the complaints, and the fence stayed.

The Council that year dedicated the city's new, most prominent thoroughfare, which physically divided the town north and south. They named it Maine Street. No meaning was intended with the name—although there were those who thought it might be considered provocative by their Missouri neighbors. Maine was the free state brought into the Union with the slave state of Missouri to maintain the free-and-slave-state balance in accordance with the Union's unwritten rule for statehood development. Although that so-called Missouri Compromise eased growing tensions over efforts to extend slavery in 1820, Southerners in the more recent decade were finding the compromise a bad deal. It was true that Southern congressmen had agreed to limit the expansion of slavery to territory below Missouri's southern border, the 36° 30' line of latitude. But more recently, statesmen of the south were arguing persuasively that the constitution had not given congress power to regulate slavery. If codified, that would render the Northwest Ordinance and the Missouri Compromise unconstitutional.

So there was no provocation intended in naming Maine Street. Planners, in fact, had determined to name several streets on the south side of town for northern and southern states. Maine Street was opened from the plateau of the limestone bluff, which rose nearly one hundred feet above the river, to the waterfront. There, the city council had obtained permission from several property owners to create a new landing for steamboats. Councilmen ignored the objections of some owners whose property they declared within the landing area, although they had no easement to do so. The new waterfront enterprise struggled that winter, however, when ice closed the river from December 2, 1842, until January 24, 1843. It was reopened, but only briefly before winter's ice jams closed it again until April 6.[2] In a tribute to one statesman

Orville Hickman Browning (above) and Stephen Douglas were opponents for the new Fifth congressional seat in Western Illinois in 1843. The men travelled, ate, slept, and debated each other for 40 days, excluding Sundays, in their contest. Both were exhausted by the time the vote was counted. Although redistricting cost Douglas the Mormon votes he had expected, he beat Browning by 461 votes out of 17,069 cast (Library of Congress).

they decided more important to the country's history than John Quincy Adams, city fathers also that year changed the name of the square from John's Square to Washington Square.[3]

On June 28, 1843, Douglas resigned as judge and justice of his state's Fifth Judicial Circuit courts. And although the majority of Quincy's voters cast their ballots for Whig Orville Hickman Browning in the August congressional election, voters in the Fifth District overall provided enough votes to give him Douglas a 461-vote win to become a representative in the U.S. Congress.

Douglas's departure from the bench brought an irony with Governor Ford's appointment of Jesse B. Thomas, Jr., as Douglas's successor on the bench. Thomas was the son of the U.S. senator from Illinois, Jesse B. Thomas, who assisted in drafting the amendment achieving the Missouri Compromise, limiting slavery in the Louisiana Territory. Ford's choice was a mistake. A number of Fifth District residents thought little of Judge Thomas. His portly appearance was not helpful. The problem was that before Douglas, who was wise enough to ingratiate himself with most citizens around the circuit, judges were "home men." Locals were generally unfriendly to Thomas, who was transferred.[4]

By November, Douglas received from Illinois Secretary of State Thompson Campbell the certification of his election to Congress. Early the following month he left Quincy for Washington, D.C. It would be an unusual Illinois congressional delegation, and it would work to Douglas's advantage. The number of Illinois seats had increased from three to seven. Douglas need only remember the achievements of his friend Lincoln and the Long Nine to understand the power possible with such a larger delegation. There had been fourteen candidates in Illinois for those seven seats, and only one, Zadok Casey, had served in Congress. Casey, who in 1843 was seeking his sixth term, had changed his party affiliation in the fifth. Voters remembered that and in August ejected him from office. Douglas's Democratic friends took every other congressional seat but one. His Morgan County friend, the Whig John J. Hardin, succeeded John Todd Stuart in the First District.

1843 would be the last year in which congressional elections were held in odd-numbered years. Douglas would stand for re-election in 1844, a presidential election year. The timing would not be more appropriate. It was an election during which his growing desire to expand the nation matched the nation's own desire to grow. He was about to become a full player in the congressional debates that would follow on the Missouri Compromise. Within little more than a decade, he would take center stage in national controversies over territories and states. In seeking to expand the nation, Douglas in every measure he proposed came face to face with the nation's most lasting controversy. Slavery.

Stephen A. Douglas had had no destination in mind when he started west in June 1833. By the time he reached Jacksonville, Illinois—the community that beckoned him because it had been named for his hero—that November, Douglas had spent all but $1.25 of the $300 his mother had given him when he started, and the additional $200 she had sent to pay his medical expenses during a four-month illness in Cleveland. Douglas had cut his previous life's ties. He had been near death. His months of illness in Cleveland had been a life-changing experience. Moving on, and within only weeks after discovering Jacksonville, he declared himself a "Western man." Having cheated death, Douglas believed that whatever life might put in front of him, he would meet any challenge and doing so feel fulfilled. On his journey to this spot ten years after his arrival in Illinois, Douglas had been an auction clerk, schoolteacher, law student, licensed attorney, Illinois state's attorney, state representative, register of a federal land office at Springfield, founder and chairman of the Illinois Democratic Party, Illinois secretary of state and the youngest-ever Illinois Supreme Court justice, a record unlikely to be broken.[5] The offices were not a matter of fortune but the advancements of a young man who took full advantage of the opportunities that came to him—and made opportunities where they had not existed. Douglas summarized the reasons for his early advancements by saying he owed his position to "the *Lord*, the *Legislature*, and *General Jackson*."[6]

Douglas's rise had been meteoric. Although he had his critics, even the most vituperative spirit respected his capabilities and achievements. The able Whig lawyer Justin Butterfield, who had battled with Douglas in 1840 in the so-called Alien Case, believed Douglas "the very best and most acute Judge in all this democratic state."[7]

One of his school friends was flabbergasted by the moves Douglas had orchestrated for himself in Illinois.

"Douglas's ascent amazed me," said Canandaigua Academy classmate George C. Bates, who also studied law with Douglas in the offices of Canandaigua attorney John C. Spencer. "Although I knew he was a man of talent and industry, yet, when he was elected Judge, I was sure he would fail there."[8]

John M. Palmer, the young man Douglas helped certify for the bar in 1839, recalled Douglas's ability to analyze the strengths and weaknesses of an opposing lawyer's case, then ignore everything if there was another tack he could take to win.

"He approached the strong with caution, but assailed the weak ones with irresistible force," Palmer wrote. "Nor was he mistaken in the strength of his own positions. He invited attack upon those that were impregnable, but covered the weak with marvelous ingenuity."[9]

Another lawyer who had migrated into Illinois saw something more than talent and industry in the young jurist. In a letter that appeared in the fourth volume of the Boston *Law Reporter* in 1842, he described Douglas: "The judge of our circuit is SA Douglas, a youth of 28, who was the democratic candidate for Congress in 1838 in opposition to JT Stuart, the late member. He is a Vermonter, a man of considerable talent and in the way of despatching [*sic*] business is a perfect steam engine in breeches.... He is the most democratic judge I ever knew. While a case is going on he leaves the bench and goes among the people and among the members of the bar, takes a cigar and has a social smoke with them or often sitting in their laps being in person, say, five feet nothing or thereabouts and probably weighing about 100 pounds, I have often thought we should cut a queer figure if one of our Suffolk bar should accidentally drop in."[10]

Abraham Lincoln's law partner William Herndon recalled Douglas with respect. Douglas, Herndon said, was not well read but was blessed with a love and honest practice of law that placed him among the most formidable at the bar.

"Mr. Douglas was then, as afterwards, aggressive, bold and defiant. Douglas at the bar was a broad liberal-minded gentleman, a good lawyer, courteous, was not very well read in the law but his great good common senses carried him along with the best of the bar." Herndon had known Douglas since 1837, the year he and Lincoln moved to Springfield. "In law Douglas was generous, courteous, fair, and as I remember it, he never stooped to gain his case.... In politics Douglas did stoop a little to conquer much, but in law never. I did not worship Douglas but am willing to do him justice; he was naturally a great man, a good lawyer, a gentleman, and a patriot."[11]

By the end of 1840, Douglas's law practice was receding into the shadows of a brighter spotlight he enjoyed as a political leader. He was not regarded as a technically adept attorney, spent little time studying and preparing for cases, but had an intuitive sense about the law. He was good at recognizing the winning points of a case and presenting them to juries with the same fire he might present a political point to an awe-struck crowd. If winning was not everything, it was the main thing.

"Douglas made use of all his privileged make-shifts to win his case," wrote one observer. "He would bluff. He might distort evidence, motive, manner, law; everything was regarded fair that tended to win the jury."[12]

Opposing lawyers occasionally found his pleadings so flawed that Douglas would have to amend them or to file new ones altogether. Yet, his peers considered Douglas's work as an attorney, taken all together, highly successful. Douglas argued thirteen cases before the Illinois Supreme Court between 1835 and 1840. He won all but three of them.[13]

From the time of his appointment as secretary of state in 1840, however, it was politics that drove Douglas, satisfied his aspirations. Douglas's advancements from one public office to another and the related moves from place to place demonstrated his unquenchable ambition. It didn't stop at the boundary of the state he now represented. Not long after taking his seat in Congress Douglas was pondering his next move. He made it his work to broaden the boundaries of his country. Douglas envisioned "ocean-bound republic.

"I would blot out the lines on the map which now mark our national boundaries on this continent, and make the area of liberty as broad as the continent itself," Douglas would say. "I would not suffer rival petty republics to grow up here, engendering jealousy at each other, and interfering with each other's domestic affairs, and continually endangering their peace."[14]

Douglas so earned the trust and respect of his House colleagues, most of them part of a growing group of expansionists who believed Americans had a "Manifest Destiny" to promote democracy throughout the world, that they made him chairman of the Committee on the Territories, considered equal to the Ways and Means as the House's most powerful committees. Responsible for organizing the western territories at a time in the country's history when Americans saw their destiny as filling every crevice of the unsettled northern continent (and some wanted even more, including even Cuba, Mexico, and Central and South America), Douglas sought even higher office. He would find it across the rotunda of the capitol building in the U.S. Senate. Douglas was a man of "no ordinary ambition," observed the *Peoria Register* in clear understatement shortly after Douglas's first election to Congress in 1843.[15]

Douglas would say he was never as happy as when he was in making cabinets as a boy of fifteen. For ten years in Illinois he had devoted himself to mastering the business of designing and building political advantage for his beloved Democratic Party— and for himself. With a scruffy newspaper editor and fellow adherent of Andrew Jackson in Jacksonville, Douglas had built Illinois' first political apparatus, which immediately acquired the power to place Democrats in elective and appointed offices throughout the state. But there was more to Douglas than party fealty that appealed to his supporters. Douglas's power was built on understanding the power of relationships. His power never came between him and the lowliest Democrat:

> Scarcely a man, woman or child ... escaped his attention, or passed by unspoken to. At one moment he talks with the old, stern-visaged politician who had been soured by a thousand defeats and disappointments; in the next, to that well formed and genial Kentuckian, who has just sought a free State; now he sits down with the little girl approaching her teens, and asks of her school studies; and he pats the little boy on the head, and in the presence of his mother and proud father says a word of his mild eyes and glossy locks.[16]

Making his way toward the nation's capital on a chilly day in November 1843, Douglas stopped in Cleveland to visit his cousin Daniel P. Rhodes, who was building wealth as an industrialist. Douglas could speak to his cousin about the foundations of a political sovereignty for the Democracy he had built. His work had by this time extended the reign for his party throughout the State of Illinois. And he could describe how he had made it work for him and for those who believed, as did he and his hero Andrew Jackson, in the wisdom of the people.

Vox populi, vox Dei.

From Cleveland, Douglas continued on to Canandaigua, New York. There, he called on his frail mother Sarah to keep the promise he had made ten years before. Now, thirty years old and still driven by ambition and impatience and the Jacksonian love for the people and Democracy, Stephen A. Douglas, his certificate of election in hand, evidence of fulfillment of his ten-year political apprenticeship in Illinois, was on his way to Congress.

The tensions of his first ten years in Illinois had changed Congressman Stephen A. Douglas's appearance considerably. Though more furrowed and portly, Douglas could look back on his political apprenticeship as the springboard by which he would become the most powerful Democrat in the nation (Library of Congress).

Epilogue

On December 4, 1843, the day before he was to take his seat in the U.S. House of Representatives, thirty-year-old Stephen A. Douglas arrived in Washington City. Hogs rooted along the boulevards, a scene not unusual to his eyes. Quincy, Illinois, the town of his residence, had used hogs, a particularly long-snouted variety found along the Mississippi River bottom north of the city, for the same purpose—to clean the streets. What was unusual to Douglas's eyes was an occasional oddity of a black woman tagging a few steps behind a white woman or a black man idling alongside some horses. There were barred pens that held black-skinned property within eyesight of the nation's capitol building. No one sought to hide them or to take notice of them. As easily as they could ignore the porkers in the streets, a good share of the country's citizens took for granted, didn't care, or were not aware that the U.S. constitution had formulated a way for slavery to exist in the nation's capital. Never mind that here was the nation's "Temple of Liberty,"[1] where brilliant men sought answers to growing questions about the balance between the sovereignty of men and their government. Few held any anxiety about the incongruity that the foundation for their freedoms had been negotiated in secret in a hall in Philadelphia during the summer of 1787. The important factor was that the crowning document that established a subservient government for a free people was created by compromise. That compromise produced a constitution achieved a nation at the expense of a class of human being whose pigment alone made them property instead of persons.

In a letter to Patrick Henry after the Constitutional Convention completed its work, George Washington, who chaired the convention, wrote that the constitution was not a perfect document because of significant disagreements among the delegates.

"Your own judgment," he wrote, "will at once discover the good and the exceptionable parts of it, and your experience of the difficulties which have ever arisen when attempts have been made to reconcile such variety of interests and local prejudices as pervade the several states will render explanation unnecessary. I wish the Constitution which is offered had been made more perfect, but I sincerely believe it is the best that could be obtained at this time; and, as a constitutional door is open to amendment hereafter, the adoption of it under the present circumstances of the Union is in my opinion, desirable."[2]

It was the best constitution the Founders could create at the time if they were to get past the day's unsolvable problems. Compromise provided the way to unite these thirteen divergent states into a national union. By agreement, the Founders left open a door that would permit amendments thereafter. Until Lincoln, who recognized this dialectic, his "standard maxim," Stephen A. Douglas assumed his place in the tradition of Clay, Calhoun, and Webster to seek the compromises that advanced the union toward the day when the unsolvable problems were solved.

Freshman Congressman Douglas visited the capital building, which would be his workplace for the next eighteen years, the day before the Twenty-Eighth Congress convened. As his eyes swept across the expanse of the great rotunda—96 feet in diameter and designed to be 96 feet from floor to its oculus apex, Douglas could see passing moments in the heroic history of the United States depicted in paintings framed in raised-oak panels set around the circular walls. Here, too, were heroic statues of George Washington and Lady Justice. The sculptor had placed drapery over Justice in a concession that followed warnings that public sentiment would not admit nudity. There was no such need to accord discretion in the statue of Washington, whose slaves did not have to be shorn from around him.

At precisely 11 a.m. on Tuesday, December 5, 1843, Senate president pro tempore Willie Mangum, U.S. senator from North Carolina, called the Upper House of the Twenty-Eighth Congress to order. Mangum advised his colleagues that he would steer the Senate on a straight and orderly course. He announced the rules of the upper house, dictated a dress code for admittance to the Chamber, introduced the new members of the Senate—among them Sidney Breese of Illinois, and David Atchison of Missouri—and instructed senators about the use of their allowance for newspapers. Mangum then adjourned the Senate to await the organization of the U.S. House of Representatives.

In the House of Representatives on the second story of the capitol's south wing there was none of the dignity or decorum on which Mangum had insisted on the other side of the rotunda. All Hell was breaking loose. Twenty-two representatives had been elected in four states in apparent violation of a Whig law, passed two years earlier, which had ended general elections of congressmen. The law replaced the old method for electing their representatives statewide with elections in districts in proportion to population. In the minority at the time the law was passed, Democrats knew that the new system could be gerrymandered to work against Democrats in the future.

It took more than four days to calm the passions in the U.S. House of Representatives. In a moment of quiet, Ohio Democrat John Weller called for a voice vote to elect Representative John W. Jones of Virginia Speaker. The jam broken, Jones restored order and began the business of the House. Among Jones's first appointments was Illinois' Stephen A. Douglas to the Committee on Elections. It would leave to Douglas the most serious task of finding an answer to the dispute over seating the twenty-two congressmen from the four states that had ignored the law. In the Douglas appointment the Speaker recognized the experience of the thirty-year-old freshman congressman who had been a Supreme Court justice in his state of Illinois. Douglas arrived at a satisfactory solution, which won him approbation for ending what easily could have become a constitutional crisis.

Chapter Notes

Epigraph

1. Herman E. Von Holst, *John C. Calhoun* (Boston: Houghton Mifflin, 1882), 73.

Preface

1. Dr. James M. Cornelius, telephone interview, July 29, 2014, with author to update Cornelius's "How Many 'Books on Lincoln' Are There?" *For the People: A Newsletter of the Abraham Lincoln Association* 12.2 (Summer 2010), 7.
2. Hardin's widowed mother was married to Henry Clay's brother, Porter Clay.
3. In three more years the National Republicans would adopt the name Whig (Theodore Calvin Pease, *Illinois Election Returns, 1818–1848* [Springfield: Illinois State Historical Society, 1923], 101).

Introduction

1. "Extreme Weather Conditions during Lincoln's Residence in Rural Illinois," *Lincoln Lore*, Dr. Gerald McMurtry, ed. (January 1962), 2.
2. Tolbert Chisum, "A Message from the Chairman and Chief Executive Officer," *Four Score and Seven* (Winter 2009), 2.
3. Until October 1846, Douglas spelled his surname Douglass. This book uses the spelling Douglas chose to use for his last name.
4. Abraham Lincoln to Albert G. Hodges, *Collected Works of Abraham Lincoln*, Roy Basler, ed. (New Brunswick: Rutgers University Press, 1953), 7: 282. Hereafter cited as *CWL*.
5. Carlin had wanted to appoint Isaac Newton Morris, who, like Carlin, was a Quincy Democrat.
6. Appointed when he was twenty-seven years old, Douglas still holds the distinction of being the youngest justice ever to serve on the state's highest court, a record unlikely to be broken (interview with Chief Justice Ann Burke, Springfield, Illinois, April 4, 2013).
7. Lincoln, for example, was not Douglas's only opponent in his 1858 campaign for re-election to the U.S. Senate. President Buchanan worked for Douglas's defeat, firing Douglas-sponsored Illinois patronage workers who would have expected to work in Douglas's behalf. Among them was Austin Brooks, Quincy, Illinois, postmaster and editor of the Democratically oriented *Quincy Herald*. Douglas earned Buchanan's wrath by refusing the president's instructions that he accept the Lecompton constitution, which would have imposed slavery in Kansas.
8. AL, Fragment on Stephen A. Douglas, December 1856 (?), *CWL*, 2:382–383.
9. Joseph H. Barrett, *Life of Abraham Lincoln* (Cincinnati: Moore, Wilstach and Baldwin, 1864), 54.
10. Albert Beveridge, *Abraham Lincoln, 1809–1858* (Cambridge, MA: Riverside Press, 1928), 1:297.
11. Michael Burlingame, *Abraham Lincoln: A Life* (Baltimore: Johns Hopkins University Press, 2008), 1:166; Earl S. Miers, *Lincoln Day by Day* (Washington: Lincoln Sesquicentennial Institute, 1960), 1:171; and *Sangamo Journal*, November 12, 1841.
12. The Logan-Lincoln partnership was dissolved in 1847. Lincoln partnered with Herndon in December that year.

Chapter 1

1. When Vandalia in 1819 was selected the site of the state capital, legislators recognized that the growing population was shifting northward. For that reason, lawmakers wrote into the bill that the capital could be moved in 1839.
2. John Drury, *Old Illinois Houses* (Chicago: University of Chicago Press, 1977), 16.
3. T.A. Post, *Truman Marcellus Post, D.D.: A Biography, Personal and Literary* (Boston: Congregational Sunday-School and Publishing Company, 1891), 90.
4. Don Harrison Doyle, *The Social Order of a Frontier Community: Jacksonville, Illinois, 1825–1870* (Urbana: University of Illinois Press, 1983), 146.
5. Ibid., 145.
6. Frank J. Heinl, "Jacksonville and Morgan County," *Journal of the Illinois State Historical Society* (April 1925), 6.
7. Ibid., 8–9.
8. John Henry, "The Memoirs of John Henry," C.H. Rammelkamp, ed., *Journal of the Illinois State Historical Society* (April 1925), 46.
9. Illinois College continues to use the building.
10. James Stuart, *Three Years in North America*

(Edinburgh: Robert Cadell and Whittaker and Company, 1833), 2:377.
 11. Ibid., 372.
 12. Heinl, "Jacksonville and Morgan County," *JISHS*, 7.
 13. Robert Rogers Hubach, *Early Travel Narratives: An Annotated Bibliography, 1634–1850* (Detroit: Wayne State University Press, 1998), 75.
 14. Coined from William Cullen Bryant, "The Prairies," accessed at http://www.vcu.edu/engweb/webtexts/Bryant/prairies.html.
 15. William Cullen Bryant, *The Letters of William Cullen Bryant, Vol. I: 1809–1836*, William Cullen Bryant II and Thomas G. Voss, eds. (New York: Fordham University Press, 1975), 1:342.
 16. Frank J. Heinl, "The Bryants of Jacksonville," *JISHS* (April 1925), 218–220.
 17. Ibid.
 18. Ibid., 218.
 19. Frank E. Stevens, "Autobiography of Stephen A. Douglas," *JISHS* (April 1912), 324.
 20. Heinl, "Jacksonville and Morgan County," *JISHS*, 6.
 21. Martin H. Quitt, *Stephen A. Douglas and Antebellum Democracy* (New York: Cambridge University Press, 2012), 37.
 22. Theodore Calvin Pease, ed., *Illinois Election Returns, 1818–1848* (Springfield: Illinois State Historical Library, 1923), 58 and 80.
 23. Frank J. Heinl, "Newspapers and Periodicals in the Lincoln-Douglas Country, 1831–1832," *JISHS* (1930), 374.
 24. Pease, 14–15.
 25. Katherine Wheeler, "Edward Coles Second Governor of Illinois," *Transactions of the Illinois State Historical Society* (Springfield: Trustees of the Illinois State Historical Library, 1904), 103.
 26. Elizabeth Duncan Putnam, "The Life and Services of Joseph Duncan, Governor of Illinois, 1834–1838," *Transactions of the Illinois Historical Society for the Year 1919* (Springfield: Trustees of the Illinois State Historical Library, 1920), 183. This is discussed further in Gerald Leonard, *The Invention of Party Politics*, 241.
 27. Ibid., 142. This is discussed further in Gerald Leonard, *The Invention of Party Politics*, 241.
 28. John J. Hardin to Robert W. Scott, September 24, 1830. Katherine Helm, *The True Story of Mary, Wife of Lincoln* (New York: Harper & Brothers, 1928), 67–68.
 29. John D. Barnhart, "The Southern Influence in Early Illinois," *Journal of the Illinois State Historical Society* (Springfield: The Illinois State Historical Society, 1939), 361.
 30. Frederick Jackson Turner, *The Rise of the New West, 1819–1829* (New York: Harper and Brothers, 1906), 53–54.
 31. Pease, *Illinois Election Returns, 1818–1848*, 28.
 32. Doyle, *The Social Order of a Frontier Community*, 51.
 33. Ibid., 371.
 34. James Davis, *Frontier Illinois* (Bloomington: Indiana University Press, 1998), 186, 265–266. The fear was that the Jesuit university established in St. Louis in 1818 had a head start on evangelization of the West. Protestants had to catch up or risk a Roman Catholic West. Institutions like Illinois College, McKendree College at Lebanon, and others were established for that purpose.
 35. Heinl, "Jacksonville and Morgan County," *JISHS*, 11.
 36. Ibid., 14.
 37. Pease, *Illinois Election Returns, 1818–1848*, 371.
 38. Heinl, "Jacksonville and Morgan County," *JISHS*, 12–13.
 39. Frederick Jackson Turner, *The Frontier in American History* (Tucson: University of Arizona Press, 1997), 153.
 40. Doyle, *Social Order of a Frontier Community*, 2.
 41. Helm, *The True Story of Mary, Wife of Lincoln*, 70.
 42. Ibid., 69.
 43. "An Epitome to 1975," compiled by Frank J. Heinl for the Centennial Commission, Committee on History and Historical Publications, at Schewe Library, Illinois College, Jacksonville.
 44. This book uses a single l in the spelling of the McConnel surname, the way the McConnel family spelled it on the Jacksonville attorney's tombstone. My thanks to Greg Olson of the *Jacksonville Journal-Courier*, who verified the spelling by visiting the McConnel gravesite.
 45. George Murray McConnel, "Some Reminiscences of My Father, Murray McConnel," *Journal of the Illinois State Historical Society* (April 1925), 94.
 46. An important discussion of this distinction in political culture is in Kenneth S. Greenberg's *Masters and Statesmen: The Political Culture of American Slavery* (Baltimore: Johns Hopkins University Press, 1985), 4–22.
 47. "Henry, John (1800–1882)," *Biographical Directory of the United States Congress*, http://bioguide.congress.gov/scripts/biodisplay.pl?index=H000507.
 48. Stevens, "Autobiography of Stephen A. Douglas," *JISHS*, 324.
 49. Georgia L. Osborne, "Pioneer Women of Morgan County," *Journal of the Illinois State Historical Society* (April 1925), 235.
 50. Ray A. Billington, "The Frontier in Illinois History," *An Illinois Reader*, Clyde C. Walton, ed. (DeKalb: Northern Illinois University Press, 1970), 91.
 51. Heinl, "Jacksonville and Morgan County," *JISHS*, 11.
 52. Arvareh E. Strickland, "The Illinois Background of Lincoln's Attitude Toward Slavery and the

Negro," *Journal of the Illinois State Historical Society* (Autumn 1963), 476.

53. Clark E. Carr, "Annual Address," *Transactions of the Illinois Historical Society for the Year 1911* (Springfield: Illinois State Journal Co. State Printers, 1913), 22.

54. Helm, *The True Story of Mary, Wife of Lincoln*, 68.

55. Joseph Gillespie, *Recollections of Early Illinois and Her Noted Men*, read before the Chicago Historical Society, March 16, 1880 (Chicago: Fergus Printing Company, 1880), 37; Burlingame, 214.

56. Gillespie, *Recollections of Early Illinois and Her Noted Men*, 38.

57. Porter Clay to John J. Hardin, August 20, 1833, in Richard Lawrence Miller, *Lincoln and His World: The Early Years* (Mechanicsburg, PA: Stackpole Books, 2006), 192.

58. Ibid., 197.

59. Heinl, "Jacksonville and Morgan County," *JISHS*, 18.

60. Doyle, *The Social Order of a Frontier Community*, 54, and *Jacksonville Journal-Courier*, November 7, 2009.

61. Julian M. Sturtevant, *Julian M. Sturtevant: An Autobiography* (New York: Fleming H. Revell Co., 1896; reprint, Jacksonville: Trustees of Illinois College), 215.

62. J. B. Turner, *The Three Great Races: Their Origin, Character, History and Destiny* (Springfield: Bailhache and Baker, Printers, 1861), 37.

63. Theodore Calvin Pease, *The Frontier State: 1818–1843* (Springfield: Illinois Centennial Commission, 1918; reprint, Urbana: University of Illinois Press, 1987), 89.

64. Davis, *Frontier Illinois*, 365.

65. Jos. C.G. Kennedy, Superintendent, *Preliminary Report on the Eighth Census. 1860* (Washington, D.C.: Government Printing Office, 1862), 126–127. Davis, *Frontier Illinois*, 362. The author notes that Judge Thomas's Negro property holdings were an example of the growth of slavery in Illinois. Thomas had two slaves in 1810, three in 1818 and five in 1820, which was after Illinois entered the Union as a free state.

66. Doyle, *The Social Order of a Frontier Community*, 148.

67. Ibid., 151.

68. Osborne, "Pioneer Women of Morgan County," *JISHS*, 241.

Chapter 2

1. Frank E. Stevens, "Life of Stephen A. Douglas" *JISHS* XVI (October 1923–January 1924), 257.

2. Ibid., 18.

3. Edward S. Marsh, ed., *Stephen A. Douglas: A Memorial* (Brandon, VT: Committee of Arrangements, 1914), 36.

4. SD, "Autobiographical Sketch, September 1, 1838," in Robert W. Johannsen, ed., *The Letters of Stephen A. Douglas* (Urbana: University of Illinois Press, 1961), 57.

5. "Col. John Brown's Expedition Against Ticonderoga and Diamond Island, 1777," *The New England Historical and Genealogical Register 1920* 74, 284–292.

6. Ron Chernow, *Washington: A Life* (New York: Penguin, 2010), 184.

7. Abner Y. Ellis to William H. Herndon, January 23, 1866, *Herndon's Informants: Letters, Interviews, and Statements about Abraham Lincoln*, eds. Douglas L. Wilson and Rodney O. Davis (Urbana: University of Illinois Press, 1998), 174.

8. Alexander Davidson and Bernard Stuvé, *A Complete History of Illinois from 1673 to 1884* (Springfield, IL: H.W. Rokker, Publisher, 1884), 697.

9. *Brandon, Vermont: A History of the Town, 1761–1961* (Brandon, VT: The Selectmen of Brandon, 1962), 166–168.

10. Robert Taft, "The Appearance and Personality of Stephen A. Douglas," Address to the Kansas State Historical Society Annual Meeting, October 20, 1953, *The Kansas Historical Quarterly* (Spring 1954), 10.

11. Davidson and Stuvé, *A Complete History of Illinois from 1673 to 1884*, 702.

12. Taft, "The Appearance and Personality of Stephen A. Douglas," 10.

13. Ibid.

14. Allen Johnson, *Stephen A. Douglas: A Study in American Politics* (New York: Macmillan, 1908), 5.

15. *Brandon, Vermont: A History of the Town, 1761–1961*, 106.

16. Richard Ellis, *The Jeffersonian Crisis: Courts and Politics in the Young Republic* (New York: W.W. Norton, 1974), 269.

17. Jackson Turner Main, *The Anti-Federalists: Critics of the Constitution, 1781–1788* (New York: W.W. Norton, 1961), 15–16.

18. The first constitution outlawed slavery for men over twenty-one and women over eighteen and did not prohibit indentured servitude.

19. Kennedy, *Preliminary Report on the Eighth Census. 1860*, 124–131.

20. "Stephen A. Douglas," *Brandon, Vermont: A History of the Town, 1761–1961* (Brandon, VT: The Selectmen of Brandon, 1961), 179.

21. Ibid., 180.

22. SD, "Autobiographical Sketch," *Letters*, 57.

23. *Brandon, Vermont: A History of the Town, 1761–1961*, 179.

24. Ibid., 180.

25. Stephen A. Douglas, "By a Cashmarian Indian," Copy Book, Brandon District School, Vermont (1829). Stephen A. Douglas Papers, Abraham Lincoln Presidential Library, Springfield, Illinois.

26. Ibid.

27. SD, "Autobiographical Sketch," *Letters*, 57.

28. Ibid.
29. Quitt, *Stephen A. Douglas and Antebellum Democracy*, 19.
30. *Brandon, Vermont: A History of the Town, 1761–1961*, 181.
31. Stevens, "The Autobiography of Stephen A. Douglas," *JISHS*, 329.
32. Stevens, *Life of Douglas*, 261.
33. SD, "Autobiographical Sketch," *Letters*, 58.
34. John Lauritz Larson, "Congress, Internal Improvement, and the Problem of Governance," *The American Congress*, Julian E. Zelizer, ed. (Boston: Houghton Mifflin, 2006), 120.
35. James W. Sheahan, *The Life of Stephen A. Douglas* (New York: Harper and Brothers, 1860; (reprint, Whitefish, MT: Kessinger, 2004) 6, and Robert V. Remini, *John Quincy Adams* (New York: Times Books, Henry Holt, 2002), 124. The Adams campaign contended General Jackson had executed six of his own soldiers for misdemeanor-level misdeeds.
36. SD, "Autobiographical Sketch," *Letters*, 58.
37. Ibid.
38. Sean Wilentz, *The Rise of American Democracy: Jefferson to Lincoln* (New York: W.W. Norton, 2005), 306.
39. SD, "Autobiographical Sketch," *Letters*, 58.
40. *Brandon, Vermont: A History of the Town, 1761–1961*, 53.
41. Ibid., 181.
42. Stevens, "Autobiography of Stephen A. Douglas," *IJSHS*, 329.
43. Sheahan, *The Life of Stephen A. Douglas*, 6.
44. SD, "Autobiographical Sketch," *Letters*, 59.
45. Johannsen, *Stephen A. Douglas*, 14.
46. George Fort Milton, *Eve of Conflict: Stephen A. Douglas and the Needless War* (Boston: Houghton Mifflin, 1934), 16.
47. Quitt, *Stephen A. Douglas and Antebellum Democracy*, 46.
48. SD, "Autobiographical Sketch," *Letters*, 59.
49. Ibid.
50. Milton, *Eve of Conflict*, 16.
51. Elroy McKendree Avery, *A History of Cleveland and Its Environs: The Heart of New Connecticut* (Chicago: The Lewis Publishing Company, 1918), 148.
52. Stevens, "Autobiography of Steven A. Douglas," *IJSHS*, 331.
53. SD to Julius N. Granger, September 20, 1833, *Letters*, 1.
54. Harvey Rice, *Sketches of Western Reserve Life* (Whitefish, MT: Kessinger, 2005), 119.
55. SD to Julius N. Granger, December 15, 1833, *Letters*, 2.
56. Sheahan, The *Life of Stephen A. Douglas*, 7; Stevens, "Autobiography of Stephen A. Douglas," *JISHS*, 331.
57. Quitt, *Stephen A. Douglas and Antebellum Democracy*, 37.
58. Sheahan, *The Life of Stephen A. Douglas*, 6.
59. SD, "Autobiographical Sketch," *Letters*, 59.
60. Dr. Robley Dungison, *Medical Lexicon: A Dictionary of Medical Science* (Philadelphia: Lea and Blanchard, 1829), 263.
61. SD, "Autobiographical Sketch," *Letters*, 60.
62. SD to Julius N. Granger, September 20, 1833, *Letters*, 1.
63. SD, "Autobiographical Sketch," *Letters*, 59. Ruminations about his loneliness, likely a result of the effects of the illness, contradict his confirmation in the letter of September 20, 1833, to his brother-in-law that he saw Canandaigua friends nearly every day.
64. Ibid., 60.
65. Ibid.
66. Ibid.
67. William Garrott Brown, *Stephen Arnold Douglas* (Boston: Houghton Mifflin, 1902), 8.
68. Stevens, *Life of Douglas*, 270. Also on the boat was David Atchison, who would succeed Linn as U.S. senator from Missouri and become a U.S. Senate colleague of Douglas when Douglas arrived in 1846.
69. Ibid.
70. SD to Samuel Wolcott, April 26, 1854, *Letters*, 324.
71. Ibid.
72. Marsh, *Stephen A. Douglas: A Memorial*, 63.
73. Greg Olson, "A Historic Spot: Heslep Tavern Catered to Stephen A. Douglas," *Jacksonville Journal-Courier*, February 2, 2004.
74. Ensley Moore, "The Place of Jacksonville, Illinois, in the History of the Northwest," *Proceedings of the Mississippi Valley Historical Association for the Year 1913-1914* (Cedar Rapids: The Torch Press, 1914), 275.
75. McConnel, 92.
76. Ibid., 100.
77. SD, "Autobiographical Sketch," *Letters*, 61.
78. Sheahan, *The Life of Stephen A. Douglas*, 16.
79. Henry Asbury, *Reminiscences of Quincy, Illinois: Containing Historical Events, Anecdotes, Matters Concerning Old Settlers, Old Times, Etc.* (Quincy, IL: D. Wilcox and Sons, 1882), 50.
80. SD, "Autobiographical Sketch," *Letters*, 61.
81. Stevens, *Life of Douglas*, 274. In his "Recollection of Stephen A. Douglas," George Murray McConnel, whose father, Jacksonville lawyer Murray McConnel, provided letters of introduction for Douglas, does not believe Douglas walked to Winchester. McConnel said it was too easy to find a ride with someone enroute to Winchester. He said his father often provided transportation to the teacher (*Transactions of the Illinois Historical Society for the Year 1900* [Springfield, IL: Phillips Brothers, State Printers, 1900], 40).
82. "Knock Family Genealogy," RootsWeb.com, http://wc.rootsweb.ancestry.com/cgi-bin/igm.cgi?op=AHN&db=knock&id=I287614.
83. Samuel B. Orth, *Five American Politicians: A*

Study in the Evolution of American Politics (Cleveland: The Burrows Brothers Company, 1906), 301.
84. Stevens, *Life of Douglas*, 274.
85. SD to Julius N. Granger, December 15, 1833, *Letters*, 3 (emphasis mine).
86. Stephen A. Douglas and Abraham Lincoln, *The Lincoln-Douglas Debates of 1858*, ed. Robert W. Johannsen (New York: Oxford University Press, 1965), 158.
87. Allan Nevins, "Stephen A. Douglas," *An Illinois Reader*, ed. Clyde C. Walton (DeKalb: Northern Illinois University Press, 1970), 267.
88. Johnson, *Stephen A. Douglas: A Study in American Politics*, 16; Milton, *Eve of Conflict*, 18.
89. William Henry Millburn, *Ten Years of Preacher-Life: Chapters from an Autobiography* (New York: Derby & Jackson, 1860), 133.
90. Ibid., 134.
91. McConnel, "Recollection of Stephen A. Douglas," *Transactions of the Illinois Historical Society for the Year 1900*, 41.
92. Ibid.
93. Sheahan, *The Life of Stephen A. Douglas*, 16.
94. In his "Autobiographical Sketch," written five years afterward, Douglas remembered him as "Josiah Lambert" (*Letters*, 62).
95. "Josiah Lamborn," *Historical Encyclopedia of Illinois*, Newton Bateman and Paul Selby, eds. (Chicago: Munsell Publishing Company, 1903), 327.
96. Cyrus Epler, "History of the Morgan County Bar," *JISHS* (October 1926–January 1927), 170.
97. Pease, *Illinois Election Results, 1818–1848*, 80.
98. Sheahan, *The Life of Stephen A. Douglas*, 17.
99. SD, "Autobiographical Sketch," *Letters*, 62–63.
100. Johnson, *Stephen A. Douglas: A Study in American Politics*, 16.
101. SD, "Autobiographical Sketch," *Letters*, 62–63.
102. McConnel, "Some Reminiscences of My Father," *JISHS*, 41.
103. Post, *Truman Marcellus Post, D.D.: A Biography, Personal and Literary*, 51.
104. Charles M. Eames, *Historic Morgan and Classic Jacksonville* (Jacksonville, IL: The Daily Journal Steam Job Printing Office, 1885), 88.
105. Ensley Moore, "A Notable Illinois Family," *Transactions of the Illinois State Historical Society* (Springfield, IL: Philips Bros., State Printers, 1908), 315.
106. Sheahan, *The Life of Stephen A. Douglas*, 16–17.
107. Ibid., 17.
108. SD, "Autobiographical Sketch," *Letters*, 62.
109. Milton, *The Eve of Conflict*, 18.
110. Sheahan, *The Life of Stephen A. Douglas*, 421.
111. SD to Julius N. Granger, March 11, 1834, *Letters*, 5.
112. Ibid.
113. SD to Julius N. Granger, July 13, 1834, *Letters*, 8.
114. SD to Julius N. Granger, December 15, 1833, *Letters*, 3.
115. SD to Julius N. Granger, March 11, 1834, *Letters*, 5.
116. SD to Henry Howe, January 14, 1836, *Letters*, 33.
117. Ibid., italics Douglas's.
118. Ibid.
119. Hall's *Letters from the West* appeared in 1828 to describe "the geography, people, manners, and life of the frontier country."
120. SD to Henry Howe, January 14, 1836, *Letters*, 34.
121. Ibid. The Jacksonville Female Academy, to which Douglas referred, was established on May 22, 1833, six months before Douglas's arrival. It was the first institution in Illinois established for the education of women (Osborne, 246).

Chapter 3

1. Pease, *Frontier State*, xxiv.
2. Nathan O. Hatch, *The Democratization of American Christianity* (New Haven: Yale University Press, 1989), 173.
3. Peter Cartwright, *Autobiography of Peter Cartwright* (Nashville, Abingdon Press, 1984), 44.
4. R. Carlyle Buley, *The Old Northwest: Pioneer Period 1815–1840* (Bloomington: Indiana University Press, 1951), 2:421.
5. "Cane Ridge, KY, and the Great 'Revival,'" *The Disciples of Christ Magazine*, Isaac and Russell Errett, eds. (January 1985), 20.
6. Johannsen, *The Lincoln-Douglas Debates of 1858*, 158.
7. Davidson and Stuvé, *History of Illinois*, 697.
8. Mason H. Newell, "The Attorneys-General of Illinois," *Transactions of the Illinois State Historical Society for the Year 1903* (Springfield, IL: Phillips Bros., State Printers, 1904), 214.
9. Christiana Holmes Tillson, *A Woman's Story of Pioneer Illinois*. (Chicago: Lakeside Press Company, 1929), 8n.
10. Wheeler, "Edward Coles Second Governor of Illinois," *TISHS*, 101.
11. Newell, "The Attorneys-General of Illinois," *TISHS*, 214.
12. Milton, *Eve of Conflict*, 18.
13. Epler, "History of the Morgan County Bar," *JISHS*, 165.
14. At this time, associate justices also served as circuit judges. Douglas soon would change that.
15. McConnel, "Recollection of Stephen A. Douglas," *Transactions of the Illinois Historical Society for the Year 1900*, 42.
16. Davidson and Stuvé, *History of Illinois*, 702.
17. SD to Gehazi Granger, November 9, 1835, *Letters*, 23.

18. SD to Julius N. Granger, July 13, 1834, *Letters*, 7.
19. Ibid.
20. Ibid., 8.
21. SD to Julius N. Granger, May 9, 1835, *Letters*, 15.
22. Marsh, *Stephen A. Douglas: A Memorial*, 43.
23. SD to Julius N. Granger, May 9, 1835, *Letters*, 16.
24. Frank J. Heinl, "Jacksonville and Morgan County," *JISHS*, 26.
25. Ibid., 7.
26. Hubbart, *The Older Middle West*, 5. Shawneetown is among the oldest towns in Illinois and with Washington, D.C., one of only two federally chartered towns.
27. SD, "Autobiographical Notes, April 17, 1859," *Letters*, 445.
28. Post, *Truman Marcellus Post, D.D.: A Biography, Personal and Literary*, 50.
29. Millburn, *Ten Years of Preacher-Life*, 132.
30. Stevens, *Life of Douglas*, 288. Roberts was the law partner of Murray McConnel.
31. SD, "Autobiographical Sketch," *Letters*, 16.
32. Ibid., 15.
33. Stevens, *Life of Douglas*, 283.
34. Ibid., 282.
35. Walter W. Wright, "The Life and Character of Stephen A. Douglas," lecture, Iroquois Club, Chicago, IL, April 23, 1945.
36. SD, "Autobiographical Sketch," *Letters*, 63.
37. Ibid.
38. Gerald Leonard, *The Invention of Party Politics*, 114–115.
39. Henry Parker Willis, *Stephen A. Douglas* (Philadelphia: George W. Jacobs and Company Publishers, 1910), 24.
40. Douglas, "Autobiographical Sketch," *Letters*, 63.
41. SD to Julius N. Granger, May 9, 1835, *Letters*, 16.
42. SD, "Autobiographical Sketch," *Letters*, 64.
43. Ibid.

Chapter 4

1. Roberts, "A Reminiscence of Stephen A. Douglas," *Harpers Monthly Magazine* 87 (November 1893), 957. Roberts was the law partner of Douglas's Jacksonville Democratic friend and mentor Murray McConnel.
2. Julia Duncan Kirby, *Biographical Sketch of Joseph Duncan, Fifth Governor of Illinois* (Chicago: Fergus Printing Company, 1888), 55.
3. *The Black Hawk War, 1831–1832*, vol. 2, edited by Ellen M. Whitney (Springfield: Illinois State Historical Society, 1973), 64.
4. Thomas Ford, *A History of Illinois from its Commencement as a State in 1818 to 1847*, ed. Milo Milton Quaife (Chicago: The Lakeside Press, 1945), 2:340–34.
5. Gordon S. Wood, *Empire of Liberty: A History of the Early Republic, 1789–1815* (New York: Oxford University Press, 2009), 446.
6. SD to Julius N. Granger, May 9, 1835, *Letters*, 16.
7. Ibid.
8. Ibid., 15.
9. Isaac N. Arnold, "The Early Illinois Bar Forty Years Ago," *Fergus Historical Series, Issue 14* (Chicago: Fergus Printing Company, 1881), 158.
10. Henry Clyde Hubbart, *The Older Middle West, 1840–1880* (New York: Russell and Russell, Inc., 1963), 4.
11. *Vandalia Illinois Advocate and State Register*, September 3, 1834.
12. Richard Lawrence Miller, *Lincoln and his World: Prairie Politician, 1834–1842* (Mechanicsburg, PA: Stackpole Books, 2008), 109.
13. AL to Mary S. Owens, Vandalia, December 13, 1836, *CWL*, 1:54.
14. Usher F. Linder, *Reminiscences of the Early Bench and Bar of Illinois* (Chicago: The Chicago Legal News Company, 1879), 280.
15. John Francis Snyder, *Adam W. Snyder and His Period in Illinois History, 1817–1842* (Ann Arbor: University Microfilms, 1968), 177.
16. *An Oral History of Abraham Lincoln: John G. Nicolay's Interviews and Essays*, ed. Michael Burlingame (Carbondale: Southern Illinois University Press, 1996), 13.
17. William E. Baringer, *Lincoln's Vandalia: A Pioneer Portrait* (New Brunswick: Rutgers University Press, 1949), 32–34.
18. Beveridge, *Abraham Lincoln, 1809–1858*, 1:162.
19. Mary Burtschi, *Vandalia: Wilderness Capital of Lincoln's Land* (Vandalia, IL: The Little Brick House, 1972), 42–43.
20. *An Oral History of Abraham Lincoln: John G. Nicolay's Interviews and Essays*, 13.
21. Ibid., 3, 127n.
22. Ibid., 13.
23. Ibid.
24. Ibid., 135n.
25. Illinois General Assembly, *Journal of the House of Representatives of the Ninth General Assembly of the State of Illinois, at Their First Session, Begun and Held in the Town of Vandalia, December1, 1834*, 9:1, 7.
26. Ewing served as governor from November 17 to December 3.
27. Nicholas Gordon, *The Man Who Freed His Slaves: A Narrative of the Life of Edward Coles*, http://poemsforfree.com/edwardcoles.html.
28. Pease, *History of Illinois*, 74; Paul E. Stroble, Jr., *High on the Okaw's Western Bank: Vandalia, Illinois, 1819–39* (Urbana: University of Illinois Press, 1992), 76.

29. W. T. Norton, *Edward Coles: Second Governor of Illinois* (Philadelphia: J. B. Lippincott Company, 1911), 18.
30. James Simeone, *Democracy and Slavery in Frontier Illinois: The Bottomland Republic* (DeKalb: Northern Illinois University Press, 2000), 4.
31. Simon, *Lincoln's Preparation for Greatness*, 107.
32. Illinois General Assembly, *JHR*, 9:1, 5.
33. Ibid., 20–22.
34. Marsh, *Stephen A. Douglas: A Memorial*, 44.
35. Johnson, *Stephen A. Douglas: A Study in American Politics*, 22.
36. Blatchford, 17.
37. Illinois General Assembly. *JHR*, 9:1, 37.
38. Ibid., 39.
39. Ibid., 118.
40. Baringer, *Lincoln's Vandalia: A Pioneer Portrait*, 43.
41. *Journal of the Senate of the Ninth General Assembly of the State of Illinois* 9, Issue 1 (Vandalia: J. Y. Sawyer, Public Printer, 1835), 168.
42. Stevens, *Life of Douglas*, 289.
43. Ibid., 325.
44. Linder, *Reminiscences of the Early Bench and Bar of Illinois*, 78.
45. Illinois General Assembly. *JHR*, 9:1, 522.
46. Illinois General Assembly, *Journal of the Senate of the General Assembly of the State of Illinois* (Vandalia: J.Y. Sawyer, Public Printer, 1835), 480.
47. SD to Julius Granger, April 25, 1835, *Letters*, 13n. Douglas served under Hardin when appointed to negotiate removal of the Mormons from Illinois.
48. Forquer was the older half brother of Thomas Ford, Illinois governor from 1842 to 1846.
49. *An Oral History of Abraham Lincoln: John G. Nicolay's Interviews and Essays*, 14.
50. SD to Julius N. Granger, February 22, 1835, *Letters*, 12. Douglas italicized the title of his new position.
51. SD to Julius N. Granger, May 9, 1835, *Letters*, 17.
52. Johannsen, *Steven A. Douglas*, 31.
53. Roberts, "Reminiscence," 957.
54. Stevens, *Life of Douglas*, 291.
55. Joseph Hartwell Barrett, *Life of Abraham Lincoln* (New York: Moore, Wilstach & Baldwin, 1865), 820.
56. *Life and Works of Abraham Lincoln*, 2d ed., ed. Marion Mills Miller (Rahway, NJ: The Quinn & Boden Co. Press, 1907), 1:125.
57. Ford, *History of Illinois*, 1:263.
58. *An Oral History of Abraham Lincoln: John G. Nicolay's Interviews and Essays*, 13.
59. SD, "Autobiographical Sketch," *Letters*, 65.
60. SD to Julius N. Granger, May 9, 1835, *Letters*, 19. Italics and parenthetical sentences are Douglas's.
61. Ibid.
62. Ibid.

Chapter 5

1. Marsh, *Stephen A. Douglas: A Memorial*, 44; Roberts, 959. In his description of Douglas's departure, Roberts says it was he who had lent Douglas the single book, on criminal law, Douglas took with him. Douglas's recollection was that he had taken with him all the standard criminal law books, including Archibold, Chitty, Roscoe, McNally and Hales *Pleas of the Crown* (SD, "Autobiographical Sketch," *Letters*, 65).
2. SD to Julius N. Granger, February 22, 1835, *Letters*, 12.
3. Ibid. Italics are Douglas's.
4. Ibid.
5. *History of Sangamon County, Illinois* (Chicago: Inter-State Publishing Company, 1881), 183.
6. *History of Pike County, Illinois* (Chicago: Chas. Chapman & Co., 1880), 394.
7. *People of the State of Illinois ex rel Charles R. Matheny v. Mordecai Mobley*, I Scammon (2 Ill), 215 in T. Walter Johnson, "Charles Reynolds Matheny: Pioneer Settler of Illinois (1786–1839)," *JISHS* (December 1940), 456–457.
8. Ibid., 395.
9. Ibid., 395–401.
10. Ibid.
11. SD, "Autobiographical Sketch," *Letters*, 66.
12. Sheahan, *The Life of Stephen A. Douglas*, 24.
13. SD, "Autobiographical Sketch," *Letters*, 66.
14. Sheahan, *The Life of Stephen A. Douglas*, 24–25.
15. SD, "Autobiographical Sketch,," *Letters*, 66–67.
16. Stevens, *Life of Douglas*, 353.
17. Ibid. Italics mine.
18. Stevens, *Life of Douglas*, 353.
19. John McAuley Palmer, *The Bench and Bar of Illinois, Historical and Reminiscent* (Chicago: The Lewis Publishing Company, 1890), 1:176.
20. Albert A. Woldman, *Lawyer Lincoln* (New York: Carroll & Graf, 1994), 89.
21. James C. Conkling, "Recollections of the Bench and Bar of Central Illinois," *Early-Chicago Reminiscences*, 52–53.
22. SD to Julius N. Granger, May 9, 1835, *Letters*, 17–18.
23. SD to Julius N. Granger, April 25, 1835, *Letters*, 13.
24. SD to Julius N. Granger, January 7, 1835 [1836], *Letters*, 31.
25. Ibid.
26. Stevens, *Life of Stephen A. Douglas*, 292.
27. SD to Gehazi Granger, November 9, 1835, *Letters*, 21.
28. Ibid.
29. Ford, *A History of Illinois*, 1:122.
30. Dr. James C. Finley, "Letter to Representative Duncan, May 27, 1834," in Elizabeth Duncan Putnam,

"The Life and Services of Joseph Duncan, Governor of Illinois, 1834–1838," *TISHS*, 145n.
31. Ford, *A History of Illinois*, 1:41.
32. Baringer, *Lincoln's Vandalia: A Pioneer Portrait*, 38.
33. Sheahan, *The Life of Stephen A. Douglas*, 26.
34. Ibid.
35. Ford, *A History of Illinois*, 1:97.
36. Putnam, "The Life and Services of Joseph Duncan, Governor of Illinois, 1834–1838," *TISHS*, 144.
37. Pease, *Illinois Election Returns*, 100.
38. Paul Angle, *Here I Have Lived: A History of Lincoln's Springfield* (Springfield, IL: Abraham Lincoln Association, 1935), 60–61.
39. Miller, *Lincoln and His World: The Early Years, Birth to Illinois Legislature*, 287.
40. Ibid.
41. Angle, *Here I Have Lived: A History of Lincoln's Springfield*, 61.
42. Miller, *Lincoln and His World: The Early Years, Birth to Illinois Legislature*, 293.
43. Ibid., 294.
44. Richard Brookhiser, *Alexander Hamilton, American* (New York: Touchstone Books, 1999), 97–100.
45. Pease, *Illinois Election Returns*, 100. Morgan County gave May 513 votes and Mills 116 and Sangamon elected May 480 to 48 votes.
46. Ibid., 86–89: Duncan, 17,330 votes; Kinney, 10,224; Robert K. McLaughlin, 4,315; and James Adams, 887.
47. SD to Julius N. Granger, February 22, 1835, *Letters*, 12.
48. SD to Julius N. Granger, September 21, 1834, *Letters*, 9. Elected with May were Zadoc Casey and John Reynolds.

Chapter 6

1. Janet Covert Nolan, *The Story of Stephen A. Douglas and Abraham Lincoln* (New York: J. Messner, Incorporated, 1942), 98.
2. McConnel, "Some Reminiscences of My Father," *JISHS*, 41.
3. Miller, *Lincoln and his World: Prairie Politician, 1834–1842*, 28.
4. Stevens, "Autobiography of Stephen A. Douglas," *JISHS*, 287–298.
5. Milton, *Eve of Conflict*, 21.
6. "Going to Bed Before a Young Lady: A Story Attributed to the Hon. Stephen A. Douglas," *The Library of Wit and Humor, Prose and Poetry*, A.R. Spofford and Rufus E. Shapley, eds. (Philadelphia: Gebbie and Company, Publishers, 1894), 398–399.
7. John T. Stuart, interview by William H. Herndon, July 21, 1865, *Herndon's Informants*, 77.
8. Johnson, *Stephen A. Douglas: A Study in American Politics*, 10.
9. Pease, *The Frontier State: 1818–1843*, 253.
10. Ford, *A History of Illinois*, 1:314–315.
11. Pease, *The Frontier State: 1818–1843*, 254.
12. Leonard, *The Invention of Party Politics*, 31.
13. SD, "To the Democratic Republicans of Illinois," December 31, 1835, *Letters*, 42.
14. Buley, *The Old Northwest*, II:216.
15. Pease, *The Frontier State: 1818–1843*, 254.
16. Illinois General Assembly, *JHR*, 9:2, 27. http://lincoln.lib.niu.edu/cgi-bin/philologic/getobject.pl?c.82:3.lincoln.
17. Illinois General Assembly, *JHR*, 9:2, 234.
18. Ibid., 256–277.
19. Miller, *Lincoln and His World: Prairie Politician*, 54–55.
20. SD, "To the Democratic Republicans of Illinois," December 31, 1835, *Letters*, 25.
21. Sheahan, *The Life of Stephen A. Douglas*, 26.
22. *An Oral History of Abraham Lincoln: John G. Nicolay's Interviews and Essays*, 10.
23. Stevens, "Autobiography of Steven A. Douglas," *JISHS*, 296; Sheahan, *The Life of Stephen A. Douglas*, 26.
24. Greenberg in his *Masters and Statesmen* at pages 51–55 provides an excellent discussion of this issue.
25. Ibid., 351.
26. SD to Julius N. Granger, April 8, 1836, *Letters*, 36.
27. Ford, *A History of Illinois*, 1:315. See also Ward Hill Lamon, *The Life of Abraham Lincoln from His Birth to His Inauguration as President* (Boston: James R. Osgood and Company, 1872), 191.
28. Simon, *Lincoln's Preparation for Greatness*, 34.
29. Pease, *The Frontier State: 1818–1843*, 259.
30. SD to the Democratic Republicans of Illinois, December 31, 1835, *Letters*, 24.
31. Pease, *Illinois Election Returns*, 298.
32. *An Oral History of Abraham Lincoln: John G. Nicolay's Interviews and Essays*, 14.
33. Pease, *Illinois Election Returns*, 289–303.
34. Stevens, *Life of Stephen A. Douglas*, 292.
35. Ibid., 295.
36. Johannsen, *Stephen A. Douglas*, 42.
37. "White, Hugh Lawson, (1773–1840)," *Biographical Directory of the United States Congress* at http://bioguide.congress.gov/scripts/biodisplay.pl?index=W000376.
38. SD to Julius N. Granger, April 25, 1835, *Letters*, 14n.
39. SD to Julius N. Granger, January 7, 1835 [1836], *Letters*, 32.
40. AL to the editor of the *Sangamo Journal*, New Salem, June 13, 1836, *CWL*, 1:48.
41. Heidler and Heidler, 182; "Election of 1824," *The American Presidency Project*, http://www.Presidency.ucsb.edu/showelection.php?year=1824.
42. William Coffin, *Life and Times of Hon. Samuel*

D. *Lockwood* (Chicago: Knight & Leonard Co., Printers, 1889), 39.
43. SD to Julius N. Granger, April 25, 1835, *Letters*, 14.
44. *Quincy Daily Whig*, June 30, 1838, 2.
45. Greenberg, *Masters and Statesmen: The Political Culture of American Slavery*, 53.
46. Ibid., 52.
47. Pease, *Frontier Illinois*, 143.
48. Putnam, *Life and Services of Joseph Duncan*, 144–145.
49. Pease, *Frontier Illinois*, 145.
50. Pease, *Illinois Election Returns, 1818–1848*, 86–89. The 5,217 votes cast for the three other gubernatorial candidates in the 1834 election would not have changed the outcome.
51. Douglas, *Letters*, 27.
52. Miller, *Lincoln and His World: Prairie Politician, 1834–1842*, 53.
53. Douglas, *Letters*, 31n.
54. Elected president, Van Buren in Illinois received 18,359 votes, or 55 percent, and the state's five electoral votes. Whig candidate William Henry Harrison received 15,220 votes. White ended up winning the popular and electoral votes of Georgia and Tennessee. Danial Webster won both in his state of Massachusetts.
55. Lincoln, Abraham; Nicolay and John Hay, eds. "Resolutions at a Whig Meeting at Springfield, Illinois, March 1, 1843" in *The Complete works of Abraham Lincoln*, Vol 1. New York: Francis D. Tandy Company, 1894.

Chapter 7

1. Baringer, *Lincoln's Vandalia: A Pioneer Portrait*, 79–80.
2. Beveridge, *Abraham Lincoln, 1809–1858*, 1: 177.
3. Baringer, *Lincoln's Vandalia: A Pioneer Portrait*, 26.
4. Stroble, *High on the Okaw's Western Bank: Vandalia, Illinois, 1819–39*, 114.
5. Burlingame, *Abraham Lincoln: A Life*, 1:93.
6. Edmund Flagg, *The Far West: or, a Tour Beyond the Mountains* (New York: Harper & Brothers, 1838), 1:229.
7. Ford, *A History of Illinois*, 2:269.
8. Baringer, *Lincoln's Vandalia: A Pioneer Portrait*, 14.
9. Ibid., 40.
10. Ibid., 85.
11. AL to Mary Owens, December 13, 1836, *CWL*, 1:54.
12. Baringer, *Lincoln's Vandalia: A Pioneer Portrait*, 46.
13. Stroble, *High on the Okaw's Western Bank: Vandalia, Illinois, 1819–39*, 49.

14. Ninian W. Edwards, *History of Illinois from 1778 to 1833; and Life and Times of Ninian Edwards* (Springfield: Illinois State Journal Company, 1870), 30–32.
15. Pease, *Illinois Election Returns*, xix.
16. Ford, *A History of Illinois*, 1:77–80.
17. Leonard, *The Invention of Party Politics*, 70.
18. Pease, *Illinois Election Returns*, 36.
19. Edward F. Dunne, *Illinois: the Heart of the Nation* (Chicago: The Lewis Publishing Company, 1938), 1:299.
20. "Joseph Duncan," *Biographical Directory of the United States Congress, 1774 to Present*, http://bioguide.congress.gov/scripts/biodisplay.pl?index=D000535.
21. Kirby, "The Life and Services of Joseph Duncan, Governor of Illinois, 1834–1838," 124.
22. Baringer, *Lincoln's Vandalia: A Pioneer Portrait*, 42.
23. Ibid., 155.
24. Blatchford, "Biographical Sketch of Hon. Joseph Duncan, Fifth Governor of Illinois," 8.
25. Dunne, *Illinois: the Heart of the Nation*, 1:344.
26. Blatchford, "Biographical Sketch of Hon. Joseph Duncan, Fifth Governor of Illinois," 9.
27. Dunne, *Illinois: the Heart of the Nation*, 1:346.
28. The slipperiest of oils with which political operators were said to grease the hands of politicians for the operator's purposes (Ford, *A History of Illinois*, 1:120).
29. Davidson and Stuvé, *History of Illinois*, 418.
30. Miller, *Lincoln and His World: Prairie Politician*, 16.
31. Ford, *A History of Illinois*, 1:263.
32. Miller, *Lincoln and His World: Prairie Politician*, 16.
33. Ford, *A History of Illinois*, 1:263.
34. *An Oral History of Abraham Lincoln: John G. Nicolay's Interviews and Essays*, 13.
35. SD to Julius N. Granger, April 25, 1835, *Letters*, 13.
36. Ibid., 13–14. "Bentonian Shiners" was a reference to the hard money U.S. Senator Thomas Hart Benton of Missouri advocated instead of paper money.
37. Davidson and Stuvé, *History of Illinois*, 420.
38. Park, "Land Speculation in Western Illinois Pike County, 1821–1835," *JISHS*, 123–124.
39. Ford, *A History of Illinois*, 1:149–150.
40. Davidson and Stuvé, *History of Illinois*, 307.
41. Ibid.
42. Davidson and Stuvé, *History of Illinois*, 419–420.
43. Ford, *A History of Illinois*, 1:271.
44. Dunne, *Illinois: The Heart of the Nation*, 1:347.
45. Stroble, *High on the Okaw's Western Bank: Vandalia, Illinois, 1819–39*, 52.
46. Pease, *Illinois Election Returns*, 268–277 and 289–303.

47. Baringer, *Lincoln's Vandalia: A Pioneer Portrait*, 87.
48. Illinois General Assembly, *JHR*, 10:1, 15–19.
49. Illinois General Assembly, *JHR*, 10:1, 15–19.
50. SD to Julius N. Granger, February 22, 1835, *Letters*, 12.
51. Ibid.
52. SD, "Autobiographical Sketch," *Letters*, 67.

Chapter 8

1. Milton, *Eve of Conflict*, 7; SD to Gehazi Granger, November 9, 1835, *Letters*, 23.
2. SD to Julius N. Granger, November 14, 1834, *Letters*, 11–12; SD to Julius N. Granger, May 24, 1835, *Letters*, 18.
3. Carl Sandburg, *Abraham Lincoln: The Prairie Years and the War Years* (Boston: Houghton Mifflin Harcourt, 2002), 36.
4. SD to Julius Granger, February 22, 1835, *Letters*, 10.
5. This was the same John Wood who was active in Governor Coles's anti-slavery movement in 1824 and called his leadership of the successful opposition in the Illinois Military Tract his life's greatest achievement (Reg Ankrom, "John Wood Fights Slavery in Illinois," *Quincy Herald-Whig*, August 20, 2012). Elected lieutenant governor on the first Republican ticket in 1856, Wood became governor in March 1860 when Governor William Bissell died in office. With the legislature's session adjourned, Wood stayed in Quincy, where he spent his time reorganizing the Illinois militia, which had languished since the end of the Mexican War (Reg Ankrom, "John Wood Raises Regiment for War," *Quincy Herald-Whig*, May 14, 2014).
6. Gen. John Tillson, *History of Quincy*, in William H. Collins and Cicero F. Perry, *Past and Present of the City of Quincy and Adams County, Illinois* (Chicago: S.J. Clarke, 1905), 19.
7. William A. Richardson, Jr., "Many Contests for the County Seat of Adams County, Ill.," *Journal of the Illinois State Historical Society* (October 1924), 370.
8. Library of Congress, "Chronicling America: Illinois State Gazette and Jacksonville News," http://chroniclingamerica.loc.gov/lccn/sn82015301/; Gen. John Tillson, *History of Quincy*, 53–54.
9. Richardson, "Many Contests for the County Seat of Adams County, Ill.," *JISHS*, 372–373.
10. "Illinois Public Domain Land Tract Sales," *Illinois State Archives*, http://www.cyberdriveillinois.com/departments/archives/data_lan.html.
11. Ford, *A History of Illinois*, 1:261.
12. Kay J. Carr, *Belleville, Ottawa, and Galesburg: Community and Democracy on the Illinois Frontier* (Carbondale: Southern Illinois University Press, 1996), 70–71.
13. Leonard, *Empire of Liberty: A History of the Early Republic, 1789–1815*, 97–98.
14. Buley, *The Old Northwest: Pioneer Period 1815–1840*, 1:260.
15. Theodore L. Carlson, *The Illinois Military Tract: A Study of Land Occupation, Utilization and Tenure* (Urbana: University of Illinois Press, 1951), 6.
16. Richard Taylor Stevenson, *The Growth of the Nation, 1809–1837* (Philadelphia: George Barrie and Sons, 1905), 346. Emphasis mine.
17. *An Oral History of Abraham Lincoln: John G. Nicolay's Interviews and Essays*, 12; Bateman and Selby, *Historical Encyclopedia of Illinois*, 2.
18. Gurdon Saltonstall Hubbard, *The Autobiography of Gurdon Saltonstall Hubbard* (Chicago: The Lakeside Press, 1921), xx.
19. William K. Ackerman, "Early Illinois Railroads," paper read before the Chicago Historical Society, February 20, 1883 (Chicago: Fergus Printing Company, 1884), 19.
20. *An Oral History of Abraham Lincoln: John G. Nicolay's Interviews and Essays*, 12–13.
21. Hubbard, *The Autobiography of Gurdon Saltonstall Hubbard*, xv–xvi.
22. Snyder, *Adam W. Snyder and His Period in Illinois History, 1817–1842*, 199.
23. Sheahan, *The Life of Stephen A. Douglas*, 11.
24. *Sangamo Journal*, December 3, 1836; Lamon, *The Life of Abraham Lincoln from His Birth to His Inauguration as President*, 196.
25. Sheahan, *The Life of Stephen A. Douglas*, 27.
26. Miller, *Lincoln and His World: Prairie Politician*, 103.
27. AL to the editor of the *Sangamo Journal*, June 13, 1836, *CWL*, 1:48.
28. Robert L. Wilson to William H. Herndon, February 10, 1866, *Herndon's Informants: Letters, Interviews, and Statements about Abraham Lincoln*, 203.
29. William Herndon and Jesse Weik, *Abraham Lincoln: The True Story of a Great Life* (New York: Appleton and Company, 1892), 1:166.
30. Baringer, *Lincoln's Vandalia: A Pioneer Portrait*, 87.
31. Willard King, *Lincoln's Manager: David Davis* (Cambridge: Harvard University Press, 1960), 22.
32. Sheahan, *The Life of Stephen A. Douglas*, 67.
33. SD, "Autobiographical Sketch," *Letters*, 67.
34. John Reynolds, *My Own Times, Embracing also the History of My Life* (Chicago: Fergus Printing Company, 1879), 324.
35. Simon, *Lincoln's Preparation for Greatness*, 112.
36. Snyder, *Adam W. Snyder and His Period in Illinois History, 1817–1842*, 365.
37. Herndon and Weik, *Abraham Lincoln: The True Story of a Great Life*, 156.
38. Joshua F. Speed, interview by William H. Herndon, 1865–66, *Herndon's Informants*, 474.
39. Illinois General Assembly, *JHR*, 10:1, 34.
40. Illinois General Assembly, *JHR*, 10:1, 202–203.

41. Ibid., 208–210.
42. Baringer, *Lincoln's Vandalia*, 101.
43. John Dawson, William F. Elkin, Ninian W. Edwards, Job Fletcher, Archer G. Herndon, Abraham Lincoln, Andrew McCormick, Daniel Stone, and Robert L. Wilson.
44. John Carroll Power, *History of Sangamon County, Illinois* (Chicago: Interstate Publishing Company, 1881), 919–920.
45. *An Oral History of Abraham Lincoln: John G. Nicolay's Interviews and Essays*, 21.
46. Miller, *Lincoln and His World: The Early Years*, 229.
47. Snyder, *Adam W. Snyder*, 221.
48. Pease, *Illinois Election Returns*, 94–97.
49. Ibid., 86.
50. Ibid., 94.
51. Ibid., 96–97.
52. Ibid., 94–97.
53. Ibid., 96–97.
54. Snyder, *Adam W. Snyder*, 57, 155.

Chapter 9

1. Pease, *Illinois Election Results: 1818–1848*, 283–303.
2. Ibid., 279–285.
3. Oscar and Lillian Handlin, *Abraham Lincoln and the Union* (Boston: Little, Brown, 1980), 32.
4. Ford, *A History of Illinois*, 1:288–289.
5. Pease, *The Frontier State: 1818–1843*, 205.
6. Robert Howard, *Mostly Good and Competent Men: Illinois Governors 1818 to 1988* (Springfield: Illinois Issues, Sangamon State University, Illinois State Historical Society, 1988), 82.
7. Ford, *A History of Illinois*, 2:289.
8. Illinois General Assembly, *JHR*, 10:1, 36.
9. Pease, *The Frontier State: 1818–1843*, 213.
10. Handlin, *Abraham Lincoln and the Union*, 44.
11. *An Oral History of Abraham Lincoln: John G. Nicolay's Interviews and Essays*, 11.
12. Lamon, *The Life of Abraham Lincoln from His Birth to His Inauguration as President*, 134.
13. Harry E. Pratt, "The Division of Sangamon County," *Journal of the Illinois State Historical Society* (Winter 1954), 403.
14. Ibid., 401.
15. Illinois General Assembly, *JHR*, 10:1, 83–84.
16. Ibid.
17. Ibid.
18. Baringer, *Lincoln's Vandalia: A Pioneer Portrait*, 95.
19. AL, "Discussion in the Illinois Legislature Concerning the Division of Sangamon County," December 21, 1836, *CWL*, 1:56.
20. Baringer, *Lincoln's Vandalia*, 96; Pratt, "The Division of Sangamon County," *JISHS*, 403.
21. SD, "Autobiographical Sketch," *Letters*, 68.
22. Stevens, *Life of Stephen A. Douglas*, 303n.
23. SD, "Autobiographical Sketch," *Letters*, 68.
24. Ibid., xxv.
25. Ibid.
26. Lamon, *The Life of Abraham Lincoln from His Birth to His Inauguration as President*, 196–197.
27. Howard, *Illinois: A History of the Prairie State*, 228.
28. "Report of the Auditor of the State of Illinois to the General Assembly, December 13, 1838," *Reports Made to the Senate and House of Representative of the State of Illinois at Their Session Begun and Held in Vandalia, December 4, 1838* (Vandalia, IL: William Walters, Public Printer, 1839), 12–13. Illinois General Assembly, *HJR*, 11:65.
29. Bateman, *Historical Encyclopedia of Illinois*, 187.
30. David Herbert Donald, *Lincoln* (New York: Simon & Schuster, 1995), 76.
31. Illinois General Assembly, *JHR*, 11:1, 224–225.
32. SD, "Autobiographical Sketch," *Letters*, 68.
33. *An Oral History of Abraham Lincoln: John G. Nicolay's Interviews and Essays*, 37.
34. Ibid.
35. Ford, *A History of Illinois*, 1:300.
36. Buley, 264.
37. Ford, *A History of Illinois*, 29.
38. Dunne, *Illinois: The Heart of the Nation*, 1:294.
39. Stevens, *Life of Douglas*, 394.
40. Bateman and Selby, *Historical Encyclopedia of Illinois*, 590.
41. AL to Mary S. Owens, December 13, 1836, *CWL*, 1:54.
42. Illinois General Assembly, *JHR*, 10:1, 50; Dr. J.F. Snyder, "Forgotten Statesmen of Illinois: Richard M. Young," *Transactions of the Illinois State Historical Society for the Year 1906*, 317.
43. Beveridge, *Abraham Lincoln, 1809–1858*, 1:183.
44. Johnson, *Stephen A. Douglas*, 33.
45. Illinois General Assembly, *JHR*, 10:61.
46. Beveridge, *Abraham Lincoln, 1809–1858*, 1:184.
47. Illinois General Assembly, *JHR*, 10:1, 29.
48. Illinois General Assembly, *HJR*, 10:1, 102–114.
49. Ibid.
50. Ibid., 115–116.
51. Stevens, *The Life of Stephen Arnold Douglas*, 301.
52. Ibid.
53. Ibid.
54. Gordon, http://poemsforfree.com/cc14.html.
55. Clarence Walworth Alvord, ed., *Governor Edward Coles* (Springfield, Illinois State Historical Society, 1920), 341.
56. Illinois General Assembly, *HJR*, 10:1, 134.
57. Illinois General Assembly, *HJR*, 10:1, 242.
58. Illinois General Assembly, *HJR*, 10:1, 241–245.
59. Both the joint committee's resolutions and the

language of the Lincoln-Stone protest are from *Collected Works of Lincoln*, 1:74–75.
  60. Illinois General Assembly, *Journal of the Senate of the Tenth General Assembly of the State of Illinois*, 198.

Chapter 10

  1. Illinois General Assembly, *JHR*, 10:1, 752–758.
  2. SD to the editor of the *Illinois Patriot*, *Letters*, 37.
  3. Ibid.
  4. Illinois General Assembly, *JHR*, 10:1, 752–759.
  5. Illinois General Assembly, *JHR*, 10:1, 760–767.
  6. Snyder, *Adam W. Snyder and His Period in Illinois History, 1817–1842*, 221n.
  7. U.S. Department of State, *The Biennial Register of All Officers and Agents in the Service of the United States* (Washington, D.C.: Blair & Rives, 1838), 82. The report incorrectly shows the initial for Douglas's middle name as R. instead of A.
  8. Illinois Secretary of State, http://www.sos.state.il.us/departments/archives/i&mpack/i&mintro.html.
  9. Peter Temin, *The Jacksonian Economy* (New York: W.W. Norton, 1969), 70–112.
  10. Ibid., 80.
  11. Ibid., 80–81.
  12. "Removal of the Deposits," *Illinois Patriot*, Jacksonville, Illinois, October 12, 1833, 3.
  13. Dunne, *Illinois: The Heart of the Nation*, 351.
  14. Putnam, "The Life and Services of Joseph Duncan, Governor of Illinois, 1834–1838," *TISHS*, 159.
  15. Ford, *A History of Illinois*, 1:297.
  16. "Abraham Lincoln, Banking and the Panic of 1837 in Illinois," http://abrahamlincolnsclassroom.org/abraham-lincoln-in-depth/abraham-lincoln-banking-and-the-panic-of-1837-in-illinois.
  17. Ibid., 268.
  18. *Biographical Directory of the United States Congress*, http://bioguide.congress.gov/biosearch/biosearch1.asp.
  19. Louis Howland, *Stephen A. Douglas* (New York: Charles Scribner's Sons, 1920), 20.
  20. Johannsen, *Stephen A. Douglas*, 59.
  21. "To the Democratic Republicans of Illinois," November 1837, *Letters*, 42.
  22. Johannsen, *Letters*, 40n.
  23. SD to Levi Woodbury, October 6, 1837 *Letters*, 41.
  24. Ibid.
  25. Ibid.
  26. Pease, *The Frontier State*, 246–247.
  27. Johnson, *Stephen A. Douglas*, 40.
  28. SD to Lewis W. Ross, August 12, 1837, *Letters*, 39.
  29. Ibid. Italics added.
  30. Ibid. The emphasis was Douglas's.
  31. Angle, *Here I Have Lived: A History of Lincoln's Springfield*, 64.
  32. Robert W. Johannsen, "John Calhoun: The Villain of Territorial Kansas," *The Trail Guide* 3 (September 1958), 4.
  33. SD to George R. Weber, January 20, 1838, *Letters*, 51.
  34. SD, "Autobiographical Sketch," *Letters*, 62; Johnson, 40.
  35. Johannsen, *Stephen A. Douglas*, 62.
  36. Pease, *The Frontier State*, 246.
  37. Ibid., 247.
  38. Gerald Leonard, *The Invention of Party Politics*, 161–162.
  39. Johnson, 41.
  40. Snyder, *Adam Snyder and His Period in History, 1817–1842*, 264.
  41. Ibid.
  42. Ibid., 250.
  43. Leonard, *The Invention of Party Politics*, 173.
  44. AL to William Minshall, December 7, 1837, *CWL*, 1:107.
  45. Burlingame, *Abraham Lincoln: A Life*, 139.
  46. SD to S. Francis, Esq., Springfield, Jan. 26, 1838, *Letters*, 53.
  47. SD to George R. Weber, January 30, 1838, *Letters*, 53.
  48. Ibid.
  49. King, *Lincoln's Manager: David Davis*, 31.
  50. Stevens, *Life of Douglas*, 317.
  51. Sheahan, *The Life of Stephen A. Douglas*, 36.
  52. Stevens, *Life of Douglas*, 328.
  53. Ibid., 319.
  54. John M. Palmer, *Personal Recollections of John M. Palmer: The Story of an Earnest Life* (Cincinnati: The Robert Clarke Company, 1901), 1:24.
  55. Jeremiah Bonham, *Fifty Years' Recollections: With Observations and Recollections on Historical Events* (Peoria: J.W. Franks & Sons, Printers and Publishers, 1883), 189.
  56. Stevens, *Life of Douglas*, 316.
  57. Ibid., 190.
  58. See Pease, *Illinois Election Results*, 106.
  59. Pease, *Illinois Election Returns*, 109.
  60. Sturtevant, *Julian M. Sturtevant: An Autobiography*, 289.
  61. *Bloomington Pantagraph*, March 12, 1898, in *Lincoln Log*, Thursday, May 10, 1838, Bloomington.
  62. John W. Forney, *Anecdotes of Public Men* (New York: Harper and Brothers, 1881), 2:180.
  63. James Gourley, interview by William H. Herndon, 1865–66, Herndon's *Informants*, 451; John J. Nicolay and John Hay, *Abraham Lincoln: A History* (New York: The Century Company, 1909), 1:182.
  64. Miller, *Lincoln and His World: Prairie Politician, 1834–1842*, 246.
  65. Pease, *Illinois Election Returns*, 109.

66. SD to Francis Preston Blair, November 2, 1838, *Letters*, 69.
67. *History of Sangamon County*, 283.
68. Linder, *Reminiscences of the Early Bench and Bar of Illinois*, 347.
69. "STEWART [sic] AND DOUGLAS," *Quincy Whig*, January 8, 1838, 1.
70. Stevens, *Life of Douglas*, 319.
71. SD to George R. Weber, March 12, 1839, *Letters*, 72.
72. AL to the editor of the *Chicago American*, June 24, 1839, *CWL*, 1:151.
73. SD to Francis Preston Blair, November 2, 1838, *Letters*, 69.
74. Stephens, "Autobiography of Stephen A. Douglas," *JISHS*, 321.
75. AL to John T. Stuart, November 14, 1839, *CWL*, 1:154.
76. Douglas contended the certificate had been issued after the time for its issuance as set by law had expired (Ibid.).
77. This was a reference to the Democratic *Spirit* newspaper of Jacksonville, which colorfully lamented Douglas's loss.
78. "Horrible!—Horrible!" *The Quincy Daily Whig*, September 29, 1838, 3.
79. SD to George R. Weber, March 12, 1839, *Letters*, 72n.
80. AL to John T. Stuart, December 23, 1839, *CWL*, 1:159.
81. Johannsen, *Stephen Douglas*, 90.
82. Lincoln Legal Papers Curriculum, "Material Culture on the Prairie," p. 8, http://www.papersof abrahamlincoln.org/curriculum/MaterialCultureon thePrairie.pdf.
83. Milton, *Eve of Conflict*, 23.
84. Palmer, *The Bench and Bar of Illinois*, 1:177.
85. Bateman and Selby, *Historical Encyclopedia of Illinois*, 467.
86. Palmer, *Personal Recollections*, III:30.
87. AL to John Bennett, August 5, 1837, *CWL*, 1:93.
88. Francis was the editor of the *Illinois Journal*, Springfield's Whig newspaper.
89. AL to John T. Stuart, November 14, 1839, *CWL*, 1:154.
90. Johannsen, *Stephen A. Douglas*, 74.

Chapter 11

1. Mary Todd Lincoln, interview with William H. Herndon, September 1866, *Herndon's Informants: Letters, Interviews, and Statements about Abraham Lincoln*, 357.
2. Thomas F. Schwartz, "Mary Todd's 1835 Visit to Springfield, Illinois," *Journal of the Abraham Lincoln Association* (Winter 2005), http://www.history cooperative.org/journals/jala/26.1/schwartz1.html.
3. William H. Townsend, *Lincoln and His Wife's Hometown* (Indianapolis: Bobbs-Merrill, 1929), 78.
4. Ibid., 51.
5. Beveridge, *Abraham Lincoln, 1809–1858*, 1: 308.
6. Floyd Mansberger and Christopher Stratton, *The Architectural Resources of Aristocracy Hill Neighborhood, Springfield, Illinois* (Springfield, IL: Historic Sites Commission of the City of Springfield, 2003), 15–16.
7. Townsend, 59.
8. Charles J. Bauer, *The Lincoln-Douglas Triangle* (Silver Springs, MD: The Silver Springs Press, 1980), 1.
9. William Jayne to William H. Herndon, August 17, 1887, *Herndon's Informants: Letters, Interviews, and Statements about Abraham Lincoln*, 624.
10. John T. Morse, Jr., *Abraham Lincoln* (Boston: Houghton, Mifflin, 1893), 1:62.
11. Jean H. Baker, *Mary Todd Lincoln, A Biography* (New York: W.W. Norton, 1987), 79.
12. Edward J. Kempf, *Abraham Lincoln's Philosophy of Common Sense: An Analytical Biography of a Great Mind* (New York: The New York Academy of Sciences, 1965), 1:210.
13. Beveridge, *Abraham Lincoln, 1809–1858*, 1:309.
14. David S. and Jeanne T. Heidler, *Henry Clay: The Essential American* (New York: Random House, 2010), 282.
15. Daniel Mark Epstein, *The Lincolns: Portrait of a Marriage* (New York: Ballantine, 2008), 13.
16. Helm, *The True Story of Mary, Wife of Lincoln*, 32.
17. Townsend, 78.
18. Evarts Boutell Greene and Charles Manfred Thompson, eds., *Governor's Letter Books 1840–1853* (Springfield: Illinois State Historical Society, 1911), 106; Stevens, *Life of Douglas*, 323.
19. John Burt's *Lincoln's Tragic Pragmatism: Lincoln, Douglas, and Moral Conflict* (Cambridge: The Belknap Press of Harvard University Press, 2013) provides an important and thorough discussion of Douglas's and Lincoln's entirely different perceptions of the effectiveness of positive law as the people see it on such issues as slavery. See particularly Chapter 7, "The Dred Scott Case," 449–554.
20. In 1856 Bissell would be elected the first Republican governor of Illinois.
21. Abraham Lincoln to Jesse Olds Norton, February 16, 1855, at *The Lincoln Log*.
22. William H. Herndon and Jesse W. Weik, *Herndon's Life of Lincoln* (Cleveland: The World Publishing Company, 1965), 306.
23. Epstein, *The Lincolns: Portrait of a Marriage*, 13.
24. Beveridge, *Abraham Lincoln, 1809–1858*, 1: 305n.
25. Miller, *Lincoln and His World: Prairie Politician*, 441.

26. Beveridge, *Abraham Lincoln, 1809–1858*, 1: 308, 310.
27. Ibid., 310.
28. Stevens, *Life of Stephen A. Douglas*, 323.
29. Elizabeth Crawford to William H. Herndon, January 4, 1866, *Herndon's Informants: Letters, Interviews, and Statements about Abraham Lincoln*, 151; Herndon and Weik, *Herndon's Life of Lincoln*, 167.
30. Herndon, *Herndon's Life of Lincoln*, 167.
31. Wallace was married to Frances Todd, the second in line of Mary Todd's four sisters (Beveridge, *Abraham Lincoln, 1809–1858*, 1:307).
32. Kempf, *Abraham Lincoln's Philosophy of Common Sense*, 1:221.
33. Harriett A. Chapman, interview by William H. Herndon, 1886–87, *Herndon's Informants: Letters, Interviews, and Statements about Abraham Lincoln*, 646. The story is also told without comment in Jesse William Weik, *The Real Lincoln: A Portrait*, Michael Burlingame, ed. (Lincoln: University of Nebraska Press, 2002), 408n. Douglas biographers Stevens and Johannsen deny that Douglas sought the hand of Mary Todd in marriage (Stevens, *Life of Douglas*, 323; Johannsen, *Stephen A. Douglas*, 73). Lincoln friend and biographer Ward Hill Lamon says Todd refused Douglas's advances "on account of his bad morals" (Lamon, *The Life of Abraham Lincoln from His Birth to His Inauguration as President*, 238).
34. Herndon and Weik, *Herndon's Life of Lincoln*, 167. Herndon denied ever thinking Todd wanted to marry Douglas. It was Douglas, he added, who wanted to marry Todd, for which Herndon praised her "keen insight into men and things" (Emanuel Hertz, *The Hidden Lincoln from the Letters and Papers of William H. Herndon* [New York: Viking, 1938], 136).
35. Baker, *Mary Todd Lincoln, A Biography*, 85.
36. Ibid., 106.
37. Wilson, *Herndon's Informants*, 623.
38. Hertz, *The Hidden Lincoln*, 136.
39. Lamon, *The Life of Abraham Lincoln from His Birth to His Inauguration as President*, 238.
40. Johannsen, *Stephen A. Douglas*, 73. Todd's emphasis.
41. Milton, *Eve of Conflict*, 24n. The emphasis of the italics was Todd's.
42. Joshua Wolfe Shenk, *Lincoln's Melancholy: How Depression Challenged a President and Fueled His Greatness* (New York: Houghton Mifflin, 2005), 54.
43. *An Oral History of Abraham Lincoln: John G. Nicolay's Interviews and Essays*, 2.
44. "Ancestors of Joseph Caldwell and Jane McGrew: Eighth Generation," http://caldwellgenealogy.com/anc/ancg09.htm.
45. *An Oral History of Abraham Lincoln: John G. Nicolay's Interviews and Essays*, 1.
46. H. Donald Winkler, *The Women in Lincoln's Life* (Nashville: Rutledge Hill Press, 2001), 114.
47. Elizabeth and Ninian W. Edwards, interview by William H. Herndon, July 27, 1887, *Herndon's Informants*, 623.
48. *An Oral History of Abraham Lincoln: John G. Nicolay's Interviews and Essays*, 3.
49. Elizabeth and Ninian W. Edwards, interview with William H. Herndon, July 27, 1887, *Herndon's Informants*, 623.
50. *An Oral History of Abraham Lincoln: John G. Nicolay's Interviews and Essays*, 2.
51. Todd would write her friend Mercy Levering that her "*heart can never be his* [Webb's]," particularly—and speaking here of Webb's daughters—"with his two *sweet little objections*." In Justin G. Turner and Linda Levitt Turner, eds., "To Mercy Ann Levering, Springfield June 1841," *Mary Todd Lincoln: Her Life and Letters* (New York: Fromm International, 1987), 26.
52. Kempf, *Abraham Lincoln's Philosophy of Common Sense*, 1:225.
53. Joshua F. Speed, interview with William H. Herndon, 1865–66, *Herndon's Informants*, 474.
54. *Lincoln Day by Day: A Chronology, 1809–1865*, Earl Schenk Miers, ed. (Washington: Lincoln Sesquicentennial Commission, 1960), 1:134–144. AL to Mary Speed, September 27, 1841, *CWL*, 1:259.
55. Turner, *Mary Todd Lincoln: Her Life and Letters*, 16.
56. Ibid.
57. Ibid., 221.
58. Miller, *Lincoln and His World: Prairie Politician*, 448–449.
59. Douglas L. Wilson, *Honor's Voice: The Transformation of Abraham Lincoln* (New York: Alfred A. Knopf, 1998), 221; Miller, *Lincoln and His World: Prairie Politician*, 442.
60. Wilson, *Honor's Voice: The Transformation of Abraham Lincoln*, 149.
61. AL to Mrs. Orville H. Browning, April 1, 1838, *CWL*, 1:117.
62. Wilson, *Honor's Voice*, 225.
63. AL to John T. Stuart, January 20, 1841, *CWL*, 1:229n. Basler incorrectly refers to the correspondent as Martin McKee.
64. Herndon and Weik, *Herndon's Life of Lincoln*, 170.
65. Wilson, *Honor's Voice*, 221.
66. Kempf, *Abraham Lincoln's Philosophy of Common Sense*, 1:207; Miller, *Lincoln and His World: Prairie Politician*, 450.
67. Herndon and Weik, *Herndon's Life of Lincoln*, 183.
68. Epstein, *The Lincolns: Portrait of a Marriage*, 27.
69. *An Oral History of Abraham Lincoln: John G. Nicolay's Interviews and Essays*, 4.
70. Wilson, *Herndon's Informants*, 133.
71. Ibid., 444.
72. Ibid., 443–444.

73. Herndon and Weik, *Herndon's Life of Lincoln*, 169.
74. Ibid., 475.
75. Kempf, *Abraham Lincoln's Philosophy of Common Sense*, 1:229.
76. Herndon and Weik, *Herndon's Life of Lincoln*, 169.
77. Ibid.

Chapter 12

1. SD to Julius N. Granger, December 18, 1837, *Letters*, 50.
2. SD to Julius N. Granger et al., April 3, 1841, *Letters*, 99.
3. SD to Julius N. Granger, April 3, 1841, *Letters*, 98.
4. Quitt, *Stephen A. Douglas and Antebellum Democracy*, 50.
5. Ibid., 23.
6. Speed, *Reminiscences of Abraham Lincoln*, 23.
7. Ibid., 21.
8. Herndon and Weik, *Herndon's Life of Lincoln*, 151.
9. Ibid. and Speed, *Reminiscences of Abraham Lincoln*, 23.
10. David Herbert Donald, *Herndon's Lincoln* (New York: Knopf, 1948), 14.
11. Woldman, 31, and Speed, *Reminiscences of Abraham Lincoln*, 4, 23.
12. Ibid., 49, and Beveridge, I, 317n. Hurst bought the store when Speed moved back to Kentucky (Beveridge, 317).
13. Stevens, *Life of Douglas*, 324.
14. Herndon and Weik, *Herndon's Life of Lincoln*, 153.
15. Speed, *Reminiscences of Abraham Lincoln*, 23.
16. Burlingame, *Abraham Lincoln: A Life*, 1:148.
17. Speed, *Reminiscences of Abraham Lincoln*, 35–36.
18. *An Oral History of Abraham Lincoln: John G. Nicolay's Interviews and Essays*, 28.
19. Stephens, 325.
20. In Wilson, *Honor's Voice*, 199.
21. Wilson and Davis, *Herndon's Informants*, 181.
22. Stevens, *Life of Douglas*, 325.
23. AL Speech on the Sub-Treasury, December [26], 1839, *CWL*, 1:177–178.
24. Ibid., I:177.
25. Wilson and Davis, *Herndon's Informants*, 181.
26. AL to John T. Stuart, January 20, 1840, *CWL*, 1:184.
27. Speed, *Reminiscences of Abraham Lincoln*, 24–25.
28. Snyder, *Adam W. Snyder and His Period in Illinois History*, 292.
29. King, *Lincoln's Manager, David Davis*, 37.
30. Maurice Baxter, *Orville H. Browning* (Bloomington: Indiana University Press, 1957), 34; Buley, *The Old Northwest*, I:248–249.
31. Snyder, *Adam Snyder and His Period in Illinois History*, 293.
32. Ibid., 292–293.
33. AL to John T. Stuart, January 20, 1840, *CWL*, 1:184.
34. Thomas C. Browne to Henry Eddy, February 25, 1840, Illinois State Historical Society, Eddy Mss., Transcripts.
35. Saturday, February 1, 1840, Springfield, IL, *The Lincoln Log*, http://www.thelincolnlog.org/.
36. Angle, *Here I Have Lived*, 115.
37. AL to John T. Stuart, January 20, 1840, *CWL*, 1:184.
38. Johannsen, *Stephen A. Douglas*, 80.
39. SD to Lewis W. Ross, June 27, 1837, *Letters*, 93.
40. Ibid.
41. Davidson and Stuvé, *A Complete History of Illinois from 1673 to 1884*, 698.
42. Johnson, *Stephen A. Douglas*, 50.
43. James H. Matheny, interview by William H. Herndon, *Herndon's Informants: Letters, Interviews, and Statements about Abraham Lincoln*, 471.
44. William M. Holland, *The Life and Political Opinions of Martin Van Buren, Vice President of the United States* (Hartford, CT: Belknap & Hamersley, 1836), 182–183.
45. AL Speech at Tremont, Illinois, May 2, 1840, *CWL*, 1:210.
46. Scott G.G. Reed, "Once Upon a Time: From Ireland to Adams County, One Man Leaves His Mark," *Quincy Herald-Whig*, February 3, 2012.
47. The Rev. Landry Genosky, ed. *The People's History of Quincy and Adams County, Illinois: A Sesquicentennial History* (Quincy, IL: Jost & Kiefer Printing Co., [n.d.]), 275.
48. October 22, 1836; Pease, *Illinois Election Returns*, 103.
49. Miller, *Lincoln and His World: Prairie Politician*, 89.
50. "Foreign Voters," *Quincy Whig*, September 8, 1838, 2. Carlin was gubernatorial candidate Thomas Carlin of Quincy. Carlin was the federal land agent there.
51. Ibid.
52. AL to John T. Stuart, January 1, 1840, *CWL*, 1:181. Emphasis mine.
53. Ford, *A History of Illinois*, 1:332.
54. Charles Manfred Thompson, *The Illinois Whigs Before 1846* (Urbana: University of Illinois, 1915), 79. See also Pease, *Illinois Election Returns*, 109–110.
55. Bateman and Selby, *Historic Encyclopedia of Illinois*, 238.
56. *The Life of Stephen A. Douglas*, 44.
57. Qui Tam Info Center, http://www.quitaminfocenter.com/.
58. Ford, *A History of Illinois*, 1:332.

59. "Thomas Spraggins appellant, vs. Horace H. Houghton, appellee," *Reports of Cases Argued and Determined in the Supreme Court of the State of Illinois*, Vol. III (Chicago: Stephen F. Gale & Company, 1843), 211–214; Sheahan, *The Life of Stephen A. Douglas*, 45.

60. James Conkling, "Recollections of the Bench and Bar of Central Illinois," lecture to the Chicago Bar Association, Wednesday, January 12, 1881, 49.

61. Stevens, *Life of Douglas*, 333.

62. Ford, *A History of Illinois*, 1:332.

63. Sheahan, *The Life of Stephen A. Douglas*, 44.

64. Ibid.

65. Johannsen, *Stephen A. Douglas*, 83; Sheahan, *The Life of Stephen A. Douglas*, 45.

66. Ford, *A History of Illinois*, 1:333.

67. Spraggins v. Houghton, 3 Illinois Reports, 2 Scammon, 380–382.

68. Sheahan, *The Life of Stephen A. Douglas*, 45.

69. Ibid., 40.

70. Stevens, *Life of Douglas*, 334.

71. E.B. Washburne, *Sketch of Edward Coles, Second Governor of Illinois and the Slavery Struggle of 1823-4, Prepared for the Chicago Historical Society* (New York: Negro University Press, 1969), 121.

72. Ford, *A History of Illinois*, 1:340–341.

73. Sheahan, *The Life of Stephen A. Douglas*, 45.

Chapter 13

1. Letter of Joseph J. Kelly, DeWitt County Circuit Clerk, to W.H. Herndon, April 24, 1866, http://www.lawpracticeofabrahamlincoln.org/Results.aspx.

2. *People v. Turner, The Law Practice of Abraham Lincoln*, http://www.lawpracticeofabrahamlincoln.org/Results.aspx; Miers, *Lincoln Day by Day*, 1:137.

3. Ibid.

4. Johannsen, *Stephen A. Douglas*, 90.

5. Ford, *A History of Illinois*, 1:318.

6. Angle, *Here I Have Lived*, 110. John Todd Stuart, Abraham Lincoln, Edward D. Baker, Stephen T. Logan and Anson G. Henry.

7. Johannsen, *Stephen A. Douglas*, 83.

8. Howard, *Illinois: A History of the Prairie State*, 212.

9. Tuesday, June 3, 1840, Springfield, IL, *The Lincoln Log*, http://www.thelincolnlog.org/.

10. SD to the people of Illinois, June 4, 1840, *Letters*, 85–87.

11. Ibid., 88.

12. "Friday, June 5, 1840."

13. Ibid., 91. Typical Douglas misstatement, Douglas took license regarding his information about King George's birthday. George III was born on June 4, 1738.

14. Ford, *A History of Illinois*, 1:340.

15. Stevens, *Life of Douglas*, 334.

16. Ford, *A History of Illinois*, 1:342. Sheahan, *The Life of Stephen A. Douglas*, 46.

17. SD to John A. McClernand, January 29, 1841, *Letters*, 95.

18. Ibid., 95–96.

19. SD, "Autobiographical Sketch," *Letters*, 66–67.

20. Johannsen, *Stephen A. Douglas*, 83.

21. Stevens, "Autobiography of Stephen A. Douglas," *JISHS*, 334.

22. SD to John A. McClernand, January 29, 1841, *Letters*, 96n.

23. Pease, *Illinois Election Returns, 1818–1848*, 117.

24. Ibid., 117–119.

25. Baxter, *Orville H. Browning*, 39.

26. Ibid., 117–119.

27. Stevens, *Life of Stephen A. Douglas*, 334.

28. "Thomas Spragins, appellant, *v.* Horace H. Houghton, appellee," *Reports of Cases Argued and Determined in the Supreme Court of the State of Illinois*, Vol. III (Chicago: Stephen F. Gale & Company, 1843), 377–417. Note that the court spelled Spragins's name differently from the earlier hearing.

29. Ford, *A History of Illinois*, 1:340–341.

30. Sheahan, *The Life of Stephen A. Douglas*, 47.

31. John Carroll Power, "Early Settlers of Sangamon County—1876," http://sangamon.ilgenweb.net/1876/allen.htm.

32. SD to Robert Allen, April 23, 1840, *Letters*, 81.

33. Pope managed to revise the northern boundary of Illinois to 42° 30' north, acquiring additional, important frontage along the western border of Lake Michigan and much of the future city of Chicago.

34. Pease, *The Frontier State: 1818–1843*, 278.

35. Ibid.

36. Miller, *Prairie Politician*, 305.

37. Greene and Thompson, *Governor's Letter Books 1840–1853*, 80.

38. Johannsen, *Stephen A. Douglas*, 85.

39. "McClernand vs. Robert Irwin & Co," *The Law Practice of Abraham Lincoln, Second Edition*, http://www.lawpracticeofabrahamlincoln.org/Details.aspx?case=139788.

40. Johannsen, *Stephen A. Douglas*, 86.

41. Greene and Thompson, *Governor's Letter Books 1840–1853*, 81.

42. Conkling, "Recollections of the Bench and Bar of Central Illinois," *Early-Chicago Reminiscences*, 48.

43. Miller, *Prairie Politician*, 308.

44. *Illinois State Register*, July 26, 1839.

45. SD, "Autobiographical Sketch," *Letters*, 445.

46. Stevens, *Life of Douglas*, 337.

47. See Ford, *A History of Illinois*, 2:131.

48. Illinois General Assembly, *Journal of the Senate*, 11:2, 236–237.

49. Illinois General Assembly, *Journal of the Senate*, 12:1, 31. Two Whigs and two Conservatives voted for Douglas while two Democrats voted against him.

50. Palmer, *Personal Recollections of John M. Palmer: The Story of an Earnest Life*, III:31.

51. Bateman and Selby, *Historical Encyclopedia of Illinois*, 165.

Chapter 14

1. Greene and Thompson, *Governor's Letter Books 1840–1853*, 83.
2. Herndon and Weik, *Herndon's Life of Lincoln*, 161.
3. Gillespie, *Recollections of Early Illinois and Her Noted Men*, 25.
4. Ibid.
5. Ibid.
6. Pease, *Frontier Illinois*, 311.
7. AL Remarks in Illinois Legislature Concerning Commemoration of the Battle of New Orleans, January 8, 1841, *CWL*, 1:226.
8. AL to John T. Stuart, January 20, 1841, *CWL*, 1:228.
9. King, *Lincoln's Manager: David Davis*, 40.
10. Shenk, *Lincoln's Melancholy*, 45.
11. Wilson, *Herndon's Informants*, 480.
12. Burlingame, *Abraham Lincoln: A Life*, 1:166.
13. Michael Holt, *The Rise and Fall of the American Whig Party* (New York: Oxford University Press, 1999), 214–215.
14. Herndon and Weik, *Herndon's Life of Lincoln*, 304.
15. Shenk, *Lincoln's Melancholy*, 28.
16. Ford, *A History of Illinois*, 336–337.
17. SD, "Autobiographical Sketch," *Letters*, 65.
18. The cases were *Field vs. The People, ex rel. John A. McClernand*, 3, Ill. 79 and *Spragins vs. Houghton*, 3 Ill. 377.
19. Jeffry H. Morrison, *The Political Philosophy of George Washington* (Baltimore: Johns Hopkins University Press, 2009), 129.
20. Gustav Koerner, *Memoirs of Gustave Koerner, 1809–1896*, Thomas J. McCormack, ed. (Cedar Rapids: The Torch Press, Publishers, 1909), 1:449.
21. Ford, *A History of Illinois*, 1:336.
22. Lamon, *The Life of Abraham Lincoln*, 216.
23. Ibid., 300. With Senator Baker, the protesters were senators Jonathan Hamlin, George W. Harrison, W. Fithian, John Henry and William L. Sargent.
24. April 2, April 9 and May 21, 1841.
25. Beveridge, *Abraham Lincoln, 1809–1858*, 1:296.
26. Ford, *History of Illinois*, 1:336.
27. *House Journal*, Sess 1840-I, 311.
28. James L. Huston, *Stephen A. Douglas and the Dilemmas of Democratic Equality* (Lanham, MD: Rowman & Littlefield, 2007), 29.
29. Ibid., 312.
30. Ward Hill Lamon, *The Life of Abraham Lincoln from His Birth to His Inauguration as President*, 220.
31. Simon, *Lincoln's Preparation for Greatness*, 250.
32. Ibid., 251.
33. Ford, *History of Illinois*, 1:337.
34. *Chicago American*, February 18, 1841, reported in Johnson, *Stephen A. Douglas: A Study in American Politics*, 56.
35. Simon, *Lincoln's Preparation for Greatness*, 252.
36. Johannsen, *Stephen A. Douglas*, 96.
37. Burlingame, *Abraham Lincoln: A Life*, 1:164.

Chapter 15

1. Willis, *Stephen A. Douglas*, 44, and Sheahan, *The Life of Stephen A. Douglas*, 53.
2. Stevens, *Life of Douglas*, 343.
3. "Quincy Historical Papers of 1912," 141, *Quincy Daily Whig*, June 23, 1909, 162.
4. Johanssen, *Stephen A. Douglas*, 97.
5. Thad W. Ward, *Quincy and Adams County Illinois* (Quincy, IL: Thad Ward, 1936), 21. Davis, *Frontier Illinois*, 205.
6. Davis, *Frontier Illinois*, 208.
7. Richard Lyman Bushman, *Joseph Smith: Rough Stone Rolling* (New York: Alfred A. Knopf, 2006), 412.
8. Howard, *Illinois: A History of the Prairie State*, 215. The city charter provided that any public official who attempted an arrest in Nauvoo without the mayor's approval was subject to life imprisonment. Even the governor, the charter said, could not pardon the offender without the mayor's permission. Stevens, *Life of Douglas*, 341.
9. Ford, *A History of Illinois*, 2:64.
10. Johannsen, *Stephen A. Douglas*, 105.
11. Bonham, *Fifty Years' Recollections: With Observations and Recollections on Historical Events*, 191.
12. SD to Thomas Carlin, February 16, 1841, *Letters*, 97.
13. "Stephen A. Douglas, Oath of Office, March 1, 1841," Illinois State Historical Library.
14. Willis, *Stephen A. Douglas*, 45n.
15. At least one Democrat believed the appointment also represented payback for Peck's assistance in the organization of the Democratic Party in Illinois (Ford, *History of Illinois*, 1:316).
16. Tillson, *History of Quincy*, 51.
17. *Quincy Daily Whig*, June 23, 1909, 3.
18. Tillson, *History of the City of Quincy, Illinois*, 81.
19. Johnson, *Stephen A. Douglas: A Study in American Politics*, 64.
20. Eugene Morrow Violette, *A History of Missouri* (Boston: D.C. Heath, 1918), 225.
21. *Quincy Daily Whig*, March 2, 1839.
22. The Smiths, Lyman Wight, Alexander McRae, Caleb Baldwin, and Sidney Rigdon were detained in Liberty Jail in December 1838. Rigdon was released following a habeas corpus hearing and before the change of venue (Jeffrey N. Walker, "Habeas Corpus in Early Nineteenth-Century Mormonism: Joseph Smith's Legal Bulwark for Personal Freedom," *BYU Studies Quarterly* 32, no. 1. [2013], 24–34).

23. *History, 1838–56*, Vol. C-1, http://josephsmith papers.org/paperSummary/history-1838-1856-volume-c-1?p=376.
24. Sheahan, *The Life of Stephen A. Douglas*, 49–50.
25. Ibid.
26. Walker, "Habeas Corpus in Early Nineteenth Century Mormonism: Joseph Smith's Legal Bulwark to Personal Freedom," 38.
27. Ibid., 39.
28. *Times and Seasons*, January 1, 1842.
29. *Alton Telegraph and Democratic Review*, May 14, 1842. Actually, only two of the Mission Institute subjects, James E. Burr and George Thompson, were students. Alanson Work was an instructor at the institute. Lynn Snyder, "Crusaders and Songwriters," pamphlet for *Douglas Chautauqua* conducted June 22, 2013, at the Historical Society of Quincy and Adams County, Quincy, Illinois.
30. *Vandalia Standard*, June 18, 1842, and "Apostasy of John C. Bennett," http://www.ldsces.org/inst_manuals/chft/chft-21-25.htm#24-e-14.
31. Sheahan credits Douglas with single-handedly negotiating the Mormon departure from Illinois in 1846. Douglas at the time was a major serving under old political foe but personal friend John J. Hardin, who was in charge of a company of 450 Illinois militiamen. Governor Ford had ordered Hardin and the troops to stop the belligerence of the Mormons and their neighbors in the region (Ford, *A History of Illinois*, 2:51).
32. Walker, *Habeas Corpus in Early Nineteenth Century Mormonism: Joseph Smith's Legal Bulwark for Persona Freedom*, 68.
33. Ibid., 58.
34. Ibid., 63.
35. SD to James Shields, April 2, 1841, *Letters*, 98.
36. Check issued by James Shields. In collection of Mr. George Arthur Buss, Freeport, Illinois.
37. John C. Waugh, *One Man Great Enough: Abraham Lincoln's Road to Civil War* (New York: Harcourt Brace, 2007), 123.
38. Johnson, *Stephen A. Douglas: A Study in American Politics*, 63.
39. Ibid.
40. Clark Carr, *Stephen A. Douglas: His Life, Public Services, Patriotism, and Speeches* (Chicago: A.C. McClurg & Company, 1909), 42.
41. Willis, *Stephen A. Douglas*, 47.
42. Asbury, *Reminiscences of Quincy, Illinois*, 140.
43. J. Young Scammon, "HORACE WOODWARD plaintiff in error, v. GILBERT TURN BULL Treasurer of Warren County defendant in error," *Reports of Cases Argued and Determined in the Supreme Court of the State of Illinois* (Chicago: Stephen F. Gale & Company, 1843), III:2.
44. Ibid., "GEORGE GARDNER plaintiff in error, v. THE PEOPLE defendants in error," III:83–90.
45. Elizabeth Duncan Putnam, "Diary of Mrs. Joseph Duncan," *Journal of the Illinois State Historical Society* (April 1928), 47.
46. Eames, *Historic Morgan and Classic Jacksonville*, 102.
47. Park, "Land Speculation in Western Illinois Pike County, 1821–1835" *JISHS*, 122n.
48. Scammon, "Calvin A. Warren, plaintiff in error, v. Edward A. Nexsen, *et al*, defendants in error," III:41.
49. Angle, *Here I Have Lived*, 83.
50. John Carroll Power, Sarah Power, *History of the Early Settlers of Sangamon County, Illinois* (Springfield, IL: Edwin A. Wilson & Co., 1876), 47.
51. Ibid., 48.
52. "Note for the Completion of the State Capitol," March 22, 1838, *CWL*, 1:116–117.
53. AL note for the completion of the State Capitol, *CWL*, 1:116; Patrick A. Pospisek, "Springfield's Acquisition of the Illinois Seat of Government," *Journal of the Illinois State Historical Society* (2006), 16.
54. "Milton Carpenter, Treasurer of the State of Illinois, plaintiff in error, v. Thomas Mather, defendants in error," *Reports of Cases Argued and Determined in the Supreme Court of the State of Illinois* IV:376–377.
55. Milton, *Eve of Conflict*, 25.
56. "DAVID BAILEY, appellant, *v.* WILLIAM CROMWELL et al., administrators of *Nathan Cromwell, deceased, appellees*," 3 Scammon 73 (July 1841).
57. *Preamble and Constitution of the Adams County Anti-Slavery Society*, August 1835. File MCA, Historical Society of Quincy and Adams County.
58. Merton L. Dillon, *Elijah P. Lovejoy, Abolitionist Editor* (Urbana: University of Illinois Press, 1961), 107.
59. "Proceedings of the Ill. Anti-Slavery Convention Held at Upper Alton." *Alton Observer* extra (Alton, Illinois: Parks and Breath, 1838). File D397, Historical Society of Quincy and Adams County.
60. James Blackwood, *Quincyans and the Crusade Against Slavery: The First Two Decades, 1824–1844* (Quincy, IL: Blackwood Enterprises, 1972), 51.
61. Howland, *Stephen A. Douglas*, 15.
62. Others were at Alton and Chester.
63. Tillson, *History of the City of Quincy, Illinois*, 82.
64. Reg Ankrom, "Asa Turner Builds a Church in Quincy," *Quincy Herald-Whig*, March 24, 2013.
65. George F. Magoun, *Asa Turner, a Home Missionary and His Times* (Boston: Congregational Sunday-School and Publishing Society, 1889), 164.
66. Paul Simon, *Freedom's Champion, Elijah Lovejoy* (Carbondale: Southern Illinois University Press, 1994), 19–21.
67. The Eells story is told in Asbury, *Reminiscences of Quincy*, 71; "The Trial," *Quincy Whig*, April 26, 1843, 2; Eells v. People of State of Illinois, 5 Ill. 498 (1843).

68. Quitt, *Stephen A. Douglas and Antebellum Democracy*, 183.
69. Landry, *The People's History of Quincy and Adams County, Illinois: A Sesquicentennial History*, 773.
70. Baxter, *Orville H. Browning*, 66–68.
71. Tillson, *History of the City of Quincy, Illinois*, 88.
72. *Governors' Letter Books, 1840–1853*, 70.
73. Earl M. Maltz, *Slavery and the Supreme Court, 1825–1861* (Lawrence: University Press of Kansas, 2006), 159–161.
74. Johannsen, *Stephen A. Douglas*, 103.
75. *Quincy Whig*, April 26, 1843, 2.
76. Ibid.
77. Jacksonville *Illinoisan*, May 6, 1843.

Chapter 16

1. Dr. J.F. Snyder, "Forgotten Statesmen of Illinois: Richard M. Young," *Transactions of the Illinois State Historical Society for the Year 1906*, 319. Young was entirely unqualified for the arena of finance. He and three fellow commissioners deposited $1 million in Illinois bonds with the London firm John Wright & Co. without security. The placement ended in a loss to the state of more than $500,000.
2. SD to Harry Wilton, March 27, 1842, *Letters*, 100–101.
3. *Springfield Journal*, September 2, 1842.
4. November 4, 1842, as cited by Johnson, *Stephen A. Douglas: A Study in American Politics*, 61.
5. SD to Harry Wilon, March 27, 1842, *Letters*, 101.
6. Milton, *Eve of Conflict*, 26.
7. Sheahan, *The Life of Stephen A. Douglas*, 54, although biographer Stevens said the meeting occurred on December 9.
8. Snyder, "Forgotten Statesmen of Illinois. Richard M. Young," 320.
9. Stevens, *Life of Douglas*, 358.
10. Angle, *Here I Have Lived*, 99.
11. Sheahan, *The Life of Stephen A. Douglas*, 55.
12. Baxter, *Orville H. Browning*, 42.
13. Carr, *Stephen A. Douglas: His Life, Public Services, Patriotism, and Speeches*, 43n.
14. AL to Alden Hull, February 14, 1843, *CWL*, 1:306.
15. Ibid., 307.
16. Ibid., 308.
17. Ibid., 319.
18. AL to Martin S. Morris, April 14, 1843, *CWL*, 1:321. Neither Lincoln nor Baker won the nomination. It went to Hardin of Jacksonville.
19. *Sangamo Journal*, April 13, 1843.
20. Johnson, *Stephen A. Douglas: A Study in American Politics*, 66.
21. *Quincy Daily Whig*, June 11, 1843, 2.
22. *Quincy Daily Whig*, May 3, 1843, 2. Douglas to Messrs. Samuel Holmes, E. Conyors, W.H. Taylor, and others, Quincy, April 29, 1813.
23. Ibid.
24. *Quincy Daily Whig*, August 2, 1843.
25. Ibid., June 13.
26. Ibid., June 28, 1843, 2.
27. "A Toast Volunteered at a Public Dinner at Athens, Illinois, August 3, 1837," *CWL*, 1:88.
28. Herndon and Weik, *Herndon's Life of Lincoln*, 155.
29. Paul Simon, *Lincoln's Preparation for Greatness*, 90.
30. Baxter, *Orville H. Browning*, 51.
31. It included the counties of Adams, Brown, Calhoun, Fulton, Greene, Jersey, Macoupin, Marquette, Peoria, Pike and Schuyler in Western Illinois.
32. Baxter, *Orville H. Browning*, 43.
33. *Quincy Daily Whig*, July 19, 1843, 2.
34. Stevens, *Life of Douglas*, 359.
35. Baxter, *Orville H. Browning*, 43. See also Orville Hickman Browning, "Address of Mr. Browning of Illinois," *Addresses on the Death of Hon. Stephen A. Douglas, Delivered in the Senate and House of Representatives on Tuesday, July 9, 1861* (Washington: U.S. Government Printing Office, 1861), 27.
36. Ibid., 26.
37. "Campaign in 1843," Orville Hickman Browning, *Stephen A. Douglas: A Memorial*, 45.
38. Baxter, *Orville H. Browning*, 44.
39. "Discussion at Payson," *Quincy Daily Whig*, July 19, 1843.
40. Ibid.
41. Huston, *Stephen A. Douglas and the Dilemmas of Democratic Equality*, 34.
42. *Stephen A. Douglas: A Memorial*, p. 45.
43. *Quincy Daily Whig*, August 2, 1843.
44. Ibid., and August 9, 1843.
45. *Quincy Daily Whig*, August 9, 1843, 2.
46. Pease, *Illinois Election Returns, 1818–1848*, 135–141.
47. "The Election," *Quincy Daily Whig*, August 16, 1843, 2.
48. Ford, *History of Illinois*, 2:154.
49. In June 1843, Ford acted on another Missouri warrant for Smith's arrest. A municipal court dismissed Smith and Missouri asked Ford to renew the warrant. Walker appealed to Ford in Smith's behalf, but Ford saw in the request—Whig Walker having announced for Congress—a self-serving political motive. Feeling he had done his duty in acting on the first warrant, Ford refused to revitalize the warrant. Nonetheless, without Ford's knowledge, Democrats spread the rumor in Nauvoo that Ford would send the militia unless Mormons voted democratic (Ford, *A History of Illinois*, 2:150).
50. Ford, *A History of Illinois*, 2:151.
51. Pease, *Illinois Election Returns*, 140.

Chapter 17

1. Tillson, *History of Quincy*, 91.
2. Ibid., 91–92.
3. Asbury, *Reminiscences of Quincy, Illinois*, 80.
4. Ibid.
5. Conversation with Chief Justice Ann Burke of the Illinois Supreme Court by the author, September 22, 2013.
6. Milton, *Eve of Conflict*, 20.
7. Stevens, *Life of Stephen A. Douglas*, *JISHS*, 349.
8. Ibid.
9. Palmer, *Personal Recollections of John M. Palmer: The Story of an Earnest Life*, III:605.
10. Davidson and Stuvé, *History of Illinois*, 698.
11. Emanuel Hertz, *The Hidden Lincoln*, 218.
12. Stevens, *Life of Douglas*, 351–355.
13. Ibid.
14. *Cong. Globe*, 28th Congress, 2nd Ses, 227 (1845).
15. Johannsen, *Stephen A. Douglas*, 120; *Peoria Register and North-Western Gazetteer*, quoted in *Quincy Whig*, June 28, 1843.
16. Stevens, *Life of Douglas*, 297.

Epilogue

1. This phrase was borrowed from Garry Wills' *Negro President: Jefferson and the Slave Power* (Boston: Houghton Mifflin, 2003), 2.
2. George Washington, "To Patrick Henry, September 24, 1787," *The Writings of George Washington, Being His Correspondence, Addresses, Messages, and Other Papers, Official and Private, Selected and Published from the Original Manuscripts, With a Life of the Author, Notes and Illustrations*, vol. 9, Jared Sparks, ed. (Washington, D.C.: United States Government Printing Office, 1835), 266.

Bibliography

Unpublished Sources

Angle, Paul. "Stephen Arnold Douglas, Chicagoan and Patriot." Address delivered at the Chicago Historical Society, June 2, 1961.

Governor Duncan Mansion & Duncan Park: Historic Structure Report: History. Chicago: Johnson-Lasky Architects. Vertical Files, Jacksonville Public Library, Jacksonville, Illinois.

Stephen A. Douglas. "By a Cashmarian Indian." *Brandon, Vermont, District School Copy Book.* Springfield: Archives of the Illinois State Historical Library (SC415).

——. "Ellen Channing Douglass." *Brandon, Vermont, District School Copy Book.* Springfield: Archives of the Illinois State Historical Library (SC415).

——. "Oath of Office, S A Douglass, Associate Justice Supreme court, March 1, 1841." (Handwritten.) Springfield: Archives of the Illinois State Historical Library (SC415).

Published Primary Sources

Alton Telegraph and Democratic Review, June 1842.

Bancroft, Hubert H. *The Works of Hubert Howe Bancroft: History of Nevada, Colorado and Wyoming*, Vol. XXV. San Francisco: The History Company Publishers, 1890.

Biographical Directory of the United States Congress. http://bioguide.congress.gov.

Browne, Thomas C., to Henry Eddy, February 25, 1840, Illinois State Historical Society, Eddy Mss.

Browning, Orville H. *Addresses on the Death of Hon. Stephen A. Douglas, Delivered in the Senate and House of Representatives on Tuesday, July 9, 1861.* Report. Washington, D.C.: U.S. Government Printing Office, 1861.

Bryant, William Cullen. *The Letters of William Cullen Bryant*, Vol. I. Edited by William Cullen Bryant II and Thomas G. Voss. New York: Fordham University Press, 1975.

Carlson, Theodore L. *The Illinois Military Tract: A Study of Land Occupation, Utilization and Tenure.* Urbana: University of Illinois Press, 1951.

Douglas, Stephen A. *The Letters of Stephen A. Douglas.* Edited by Robert W. Johannsen. Urbana: University of Illinois Press, 1961.

——. "Speech to the U.S. House of Representatives." *Congressional Globe*, 28th Congress, 2nd Session. Washington, D.C., 1845.

Governor's Letter Books 1840–1853. Edited by Evarts Boutell Greene and Charles Manfred Thompson. Springfield: Illinois State Historical Society, 1911.

History, 1838–1856 (Manuscript History of the [Mormon] Church). The Joseph Smith Papers at http://josephsmithpapers.org/the-papers.

Illinois General Assembly. *Journal of the House of Representatives of the Ninth General Assembly of the State of Illinois, at Their First Session, Begun and Held in the Town of Vandalia, December 1, 1834.* Journal of Proceedings. Vandalia: J.Y. Sawyer, Public Printer, 1834.

——. *Journal of the House of Representatives of the Ninth General Assembly of the State of Illinois, at Their Second Session, Begun and Held in theTown of Vandalia, December 7, 1835.* Journal of Proceedings. Vandalia: J.Y. Sawyer, Public Printer, 1835.

——. *Journal of the House of Representatives of the Tenth General Assembly of the State of Illinois, at Their First Session, Begun and Held in the Town of Vandalia, December 5, 1836.* Journal of Proceedings. Vandalia: J.Y. Sawyer, Public Printer, 1836.

——. *Journal of the House of Representatives of the Tenth General Assembly of the State of Illinois at a Special Session of the General Assembly, Begun and Held in the Town of Vandalia, July 10, 1837.* Journal of Proceedings. Vandalia: J.Y. Sawyer, Public Printer, 1837.

——. *Journal of the Senate, of the Ninth General Assembly of the State of Illinois, At Their First Session, Begun and Held in the Town of Vandalia, December 1, 1834.* Vandalia: J.Y. Sawyer, Public Printer, 1835.

——. *Reports Made to the Senate and House of Representatives of the State of Illinois at Their Session Begun and Held in Vandalia, December 4, 1838.* Vandalia: William Walters, Public Printer, 1839.

Illinois Patriot, October 1833.

Illinois State Register, April 9, 1841.

Illinois Supreme Court. *Report of Cases Argued and Determined in the Supreme Court of the State of Illinois.* Chicago: Stephen F. Gale & Company, 1843.

The Illinoisan, May 1843.
Jacksonville Journal-Courier. November 7, 2009.
Life and Works of Abraham Lincoln. Edited by Marion Mills Miller. Rahway, NJ: The Quinn & Boden Co., 1907.
The Lincoln-Douglas Debates of 1858. Edited by Robert W. Johannsen. New York: Oxford University Press, 1965.
"Lincoln Legal Papers Curriculum." *Papers of Abraham Lincoln*. http://www.papersofabrahamlincoln.org/curriculum/MaterialCultureonthePrairie.pdf.
National Party Platforms, 1840–1972. Compiled by Donald Bruce Johnson and Kirk H. Porter. Urbana: University of Illinois Press, 1975.
An Oral History of Abraham Lincoln: John G. Nicolay's Interview and Essays. Edited by Michael Burlingame. Carbondale: Southern Illinois University Press, 1996.
Quincy Daily Whig, September 29, 1838.
Randolph, Thomas Jefferson. *Memoirs, Correspondence, and Private Papers of Thomas Jefferson, Late President of the United States*, vol. 4. London: Henry Colburn and Richard Bentley, 1829.
"Research on the John Wood Mansion, 425 South Twelfth Street, Owned by the Historical Society of Quincy and Adams County, By the Research and Restoration Committees." File MS WOO, "Research," Historical Society of Quincy and Adams County.
Sangamo Journal, May 21, 1841.
Vandalia Illinois Advocate and State Register, September 3, 1834.
Vandalia Standard, June 18, 1842.
"Election of 1824." *The American Presidency Project*. http://www.Presidency.ucsb.edu/showelection.php?year=1824.
The Lincoln Log. http://www.thelincolnlog.org.
Turner, Justin G., and Linda Levitt Turner, eds. *Mary Todd Lincoln: Her Life and Letters*. New York: Fromm International, 1987.
U.S. Department of State. *The Biennial Register of all Officers and Agents in the Service of the United States*. Washington D.C.: Blair & Rives, 1838.
Washington, George. *The Writings of George Washington, Being His Correspondence, Addresses, Messages, and Other Papers, Official and Private, Selected and Published from the Original Manuscripts, With a Life of the Author, Notes and Illustrations*, Vol 9, Jared Sparks, ed. Washington: D.C.: United States Government Printing Office, 1835.

Published Secondary Sources

Alvord, Clarence Walworth, ed. *Governor Edward Coles*. Springfield: Illinois State Historical Society, 1920.
Asbury, Henry. *Reminiscences of Quincy, Illinois: Containing Historical Events, Anecdotes, Matters Concerning Old Settlers, Old Times, Etc*. Quincy, IL: D. Wilcox and Sons, 1882.
Arnold, Isaac N. "The Early Illinois Bar Forty Years Ago." *Fergus Historical Series* 14, 1881.
Barnhart, John D. "The Southern Influence in Early Illinois." *Journal of the Illinois State Historical Society* XXXII, no. 3 (1939).
The Black Hawk War, 1831–1832, Vol. 2. Edited by Ellen M. Whitney. Springfield: Illinois State Historical Society, 1973.
Bonham, Jeremiah. *Fifty Years' Recollections: With Observations and Recollections on Historical Events*. Peoria, IL: J.W. Franks & Sons, Publishers and Printers, 1883.
Edwards, Ninian W. *History of Illinois, from 1778 to 1833; and Life and Times of Ninian Edwards*. Springfield: Illinois State Journal Company, 1870.
History of Sangamon County, Illinois. Chicago: Interstate Publishing Company, 1881.
Herndon's Informants: Letters, Interview, and Statements about Abraham Lincoln. Edited by Douglas L. Wilson and Rodney O. Davis. Urbana: University of Illinois Press, 1998.
Hubbard, Gurdon Saltonstall. *The Autobiography of Gurdon Saltonstall Hubbard*. Chicago: The Lakeside Press, 1921.
Kelly, Joseph J. Letter of Joseph J. Kelly, DeWitt County Circuit Clerk, to W.H. Herndon, April 24, 1866. http://www.lawpracticeofabrahamlincoln.org.
Koerner, Gustav. *Memoirs of Gustave Koerner, 1809–1896*. Edited by Thomas J. McCormack. vol. 1 of 2. Cedar Rapids: The Torch Press, Publishers, 1909.
Lovejoy, Joseph C., and Owen. *Memoir of Rev. Elijah P. Lovejoy*. Reprint, Freeport, NY: Books for Libraries Press, 1970.
Millburn, William Henry. *Ten Years of Preacher-Life: Chapters from an Autobiography*. New York: Derby & Jackson, 1860.
Palmer, John M. *The Bench and Bar of Illinois, Historical and Reminiscent*. Chicago: The Lewis Publishing Company, 1890.
_____. *Personal Recollections of John M. Palmer: The Story of an Earnest Life*. Cincinnati: The Robert Clarke Company, 1901.
Pease, Theodore Calvin. *The Frontier State: 1818–1843*. Urbana: University of Illinois Press, 1987.
_____. *Illinois Election Returns, 1818–1848*. Edited by Theodore Calvin Pease. Statistical Series, I. Springfield: Illinois State Historical Society, 1923.
Power, John Carroll. *Early Settlers of Sangamon County—1876*. http://sangamon.ilgenweb.net/1876/allen.htm.
_____. *History of Sangamon County, Illinois*. Chicago: Interstate Publishing Company, 1881.
Reynolds, John. *My Own Times, Embracing also the History of My Life*. Chicago: Fergus Printing Company, 1879.

Sturtevant, Julian M. *Julian M. Sturtevant: An Autobiography*. Edited by J.M. Sturtevant, Jr. Jacksonville, Illinois: The Trustees of Illinois College, 2005.
Stuve, Alexander and Bernard Davidson. *A Complete History of Illinois from 1673 to 1884*. Springfield, IL: H.W. Rokker, Publisher, 1884.
Tillson, General John. *History of the City of Quincy, Illinois*. Edited by William H. Collins. Quincy, IL: S.J. Clarke, 1905.
Townsend, Water A. *Illinois Democracy: A History of the Party and Its Representative Members—Past and Present*. Edited by Charles Boeschenstein. Springfield, IL: Democratic Historical Association, Inc., 1935.

General

"Abraham Lincoln, Banking and the Panic of 1837 in Illinois." http://abrahamlincolnsclassroom.org/abraham-lincoln-in-depth/abraham-lincoln-banking-and-the-panic-of-1837-in-illinois.
Ackerman, William K. *Early Illinois Railroads*. Paper, Chicago Historical Society. Chicago: Fergus Printing Company, 1884.
Adams, Carl M. "The First Slave Freed by Abraham Lincoln: A Biographical Sketch of Nance Legins (Cox-Cromwell) Costley, circa 1813–1873." *For the People: A Newsletter of the Abraham Lincoln Association*. Springfield, IL: Abraham Lincoln Association, Autumn 1999.
Angle, Paul. *Here I Have Lived: A History of Lincoln's Springfield*. Springfield, IL: Abraham Lincoln Association, 1935.
Ankrom, Reg. "Asa Turner Builds a Church in Quincy." *Quincy Herald-Whig*, March 24, 2013.
_____. "John Wood Fights Slavery in Illinois." *Quincy Herald-Whig*. August 20, 2012.
_____. "John Wood Raises Regiment for War." *Quincy Herald-Whig*. May 18, 2014.
_____. "Quincy Outmaneuvers Columbus for County Seat." *Quincy Herald-Whig*. March 23, 2012.
Avery, Elroy McKendree. *A History of Cleveland and Its Environs: The Heart of New Connecticut*. Chicago: The Lewis Publishing Company, 1918.
Baker, Jean H. *Mary Todd Lincoln, A Biography*. New York: W.W. Norton, 1987.
Barrett, Joseph Hartwell. *Life of Abraham Lincoln*. New York: Moore, Wistach & Baldwin, 1865.
Bauer, Charles J. *The Lincoln-Douglas Triangle*. Silver Springs, MD: The Silver Springs Press, 1980.
Baxter, Maurice. *Orville H. Browning*. Bloomington: Indiana University Press, 1957.
Billington, Ray A. "The Frontier in Illinois History." *An Illinois Reader*. Edited by Clyde C. Walton. DeKalb: Northern Illinois University Press, 1970.
Blackwood, James. *Quincyans and the Crusade Against Slavery: The First Two Decades, 1824–1844*. Quincy, IL: Blackwood Enterprises, 1972.
Blatchford, E.W., LLD. "Biographical Sketch of Hon. Joseph Duncan, Fifth Governor of Illinois." *Address to the Chicago Historical Society*. Chicago, December 5, 1905.
Brandon, Vermont: A History of the Town, 1761–1961. Brandon, VT: The Selectmen of Brandon, 1962.
Brookhiser, Richard, *Alexander Hamilton, American*. New York: Touchstone Books, 1999.
Brown, William Garrott. *Stephen Arnold Douglas*. Boston: Houghton Mifflin, 1902.
Buley, R. Carlyle. *The Old Northwest: Pioneer Period 1815–1840*. Vol. 1 of 2. Bloomington: Indiana University Press, 1951.
Burt, John. *Lincoln's Tragic Pragmatism: Lincoln, Douglas, and Moral Conflict*. Cambridge: The Belknap Press of Harvard University Press, 2013.
Burtschi, Mary. *Vandalia: Wilderness Capital of Lincoln's Land*. Vandalia, IL: The Little Brick House, 1972.
Bushman, Richard Lyman. *Joseph Smith: Rough Stone Rolling*. New York: Alfred A. Knopf, 2006.
Carr, Clark E. "Annual Address." *Transactions of the Illinois State Historical Society for the Year 1911* (Trustees of the Illinois State Historical Library) XVI (1913).
_____. *Stephen A. Douglas: His Life, Public Services, Patriotism, and Speeches*. Chicago: A.C. McClurg & Company, 1909.
Carr, Kay J. *Belleville, Ottawa, and Galesburg: Community and Democracy on the Illinois Frontier*. Carbondale: Southern Illinois University Press, 1996.
Cartwright, Peter. *Autobiography of Peter Cartwright*. Nashville: Abingdon Press, 1984.
Chernow, Ron. *Washington: A Life*. New York: Penguin, 2010.
Coffin, William. "Col. John Brown's Expedition Against Ticonderoga and Diamond Island, 1777." *The New England Historical and Genealogical Register, 1920* (New England Historic Genealocical Society), 1920.
_____. *The Life and Times of Hon. Samuel D. Lockwood*. Chicago: Knight & Leonard Co., Printers, 1889.
Converse, Henry A. "The House of the House Divided." Address to the Lincoln Centennial Association, Springfield, February, 12, 1924.
Davis, James. *Frontier Illinois*. Bloomington: Indiana University Press, 1998.
De Tocqueville, Alexis. *Democracy in America*. Translated by Henry Reeve. New York: D. Appleton, 1904.
Deters, Mrs. Ruth. "The Underground Railroad." *People's History of Quincy and Adams County: A Sesquicentennial History*. Edited by OFM Rev. Landry Genosky. Quincy, IL: Jost & Kiefer Printing Co., n.d.
Dickens, Charles. *American Notes for General Circulation*. New York: Appleton and Company, 1868.
Dillon, Merton L. *Elijah P. Lovejoy, Abolitionist Editor*. Urbana: University of Illinois Press, 1961.

Donald, David Herbert. *Lincoln*. New York: Simon & Schuster, 1995.

Doyle, Don Harrison. *The Social Order of a Frontier Community: Jacksonville, Illinois, 1825–1870*. Urbana: University of Illinois Press, 1983.

Dungison, Dr. Robley. *Medical Lexicon: A Dictionary of Medical Science*. Philadelphia: Lea and Blanchard, 1829.

Dunne, Edward F. *Illinois: the Heart of the Nation*. Vol. 1 of 5. Chicago: The Lewis Publishing Company, 1938.

Eames, Charles M. *Historic Morgan and Classic Jacksonville*. Jacksonville, IL: The Daily Journal Steam Job Printing Office, 1885.

Ellis, Richard. *The Jeffersonian Crisis: Courts and Politics in the Young Republic*. New York: W.W. Norton, 1974.

Epler, Cyrus. "History of the Morgan County Bar." *Journal of the Illinois State Historical Society* (Illinois State Historical Society) XIX, no. 3–4 (October–January 1926–1927).

Epstein, Daniel Mark. *The Lincolns: Portrait of a Marriage*. New York: Ballantine, 2008.

Ernst, Ferdinand. "Travels in Illinois in 1819." *Transactions of the Illinois State Historical Society for 1903* (Trustees of the Illinois State Historical Library) VIII (1904).

Errett, Isaac, and Russell, eds. "Cane Ridge, KY, and the Great 'Revival.'" *The Disciples of Christ Magazine* (Standard Publishing Co.), January 1985.

Findley, Paul. *A. Lincoln: The Crucible of Congress*. New York: Crown, 1979.

Flagg, Edmund. *The Far West: or, A Tour Beyond the Mountains*, vol. I. New York: Harper & Brothers, 1838.

Ford, Thomas. *A History of Illinois from Its Commencement as a State in 1818 to 1847*. Edited by Milo Milton Quaife. 2 vols. Chicago: The Lakeside Press, 1945.

Forney, John W. *Anecdotes of Public Men*. New York: Harper and Brothers, 1881.

Gillespie, Joseph. *Recollections of Early Illinois and Her Noted Men*. Chicago: Fergus Printing Company, 1880.

"Going to Bed Before a Young Lady: Story Attributed to the Hon. Stephen A. Douglas." *The Library of Wit and Humor, Prose and Poetry*, edited by A.R. Spofford and Rufus E. Shapley. Philadelphia: Gebbie and Company, Publishers, 1894.

Greenberg, Kenneth S. *Masters and Statesmen: The Political Culture of American Slavery*. Baltimore: Johns Hopkins University Press, 1985.

Greene, Evarts B. "Sectional Forces in the History of Illinois." *Transactions of the Illinois State Historical Society* (Trustees of the Illinois State Historical Library) IX (1904).

Handlin, Oscar, and Lillian. *Abraham Lincoln and the Union*. Boston: Little, Brown, Company, 1980.

Hardin, John J. *The Illinoisan*, May 1843.

———. "John J. Hardin to Robert W. Scott." In *The True Story of Mary, Wife of Lincoln* by Katherine Helm. New York: Harper & Brothers, 1928.

Hatch, Nathan O. *The Democratization of American Christianity*. New Haven: Yale University Press, 1989.

Heidler, David S., and Jeanne T. *Henry Clay: The Essential American*. New York: Random House, 2010.

Heinl, Frank J. "The Bryants of Jacksonville." *Journal of the Illinois State Historical Society* (The Blakely Printing Co.) XVIII, no. 1 (April 1925).

———. "Jacksonville and Morgan County." *Journal of the Illinois State Historical Society* (The Blakely Printing Co.) XVIII, no. 1 (April 1925).

———. "Newspapers and Periodicals in the Lincoln-Douglas Country, 1831–1832." *Journal of the Illinois State Historical Society* (The Illinois State Historical Society) XXIII, no. 3 (1930).

Henry, John. "Captain Henry's Account of the First Printers and Book Binders in Morgan County." *Journal of the Illinois State Historical Society* (Illinois State Historical Society) XVIII, no. 1 (April 1925).

———. "The Memoirs of John Henry." Edited by C.H. Rammelkamp. *Journal of the Illinois State Historical Society* (The Blakely Printing Co.) XVIII, no. 1 (April 1925).

Herndon, William Herndon, and Jesse Weik. *Abraham Lincoln: The True Story of a Great Life*. New York: Appleton and Company, 1892.

———. *Herndon's Life of Lincoln*. Cleveland: The World Publishing Company, 1965.

Hertz, Emanuel. *The Hidden Lincoln from the Letters and Papers of William H. Herndon*. New York: Viking, 1938.

"History and Architecture: Pasfield House Inn." http://www.pasfieldhouse.com/history/community_capital.php.

Holland, William M. *The Life and Political Opinions of Martin Van Buren, Vice resident of the United States*. Hartford, CT: Belknap & Hamersley, 1836.

Holt, Michael. *The Rise and Fall of the American Whig Party*. New York: Oxford University Press, 1999.

Howard, Robert. *Illinois: A History of the Prairie State*. Grand Rapids: William B. Eerdmans, 1972.

———. *Mostly Good and Competent Men: Illinois Governors 1818 to 1988*. Springfield: Illlinois Issues, Sangamon State University, Illinois State Historical Society, 1988.

Howland, Louis. *Stephen A. Douglas*. New York: Charles Scribner's Sons, 1920.

Hubach, Robert Rogers. *Early Travel Narratives: An Annotated Bibliography, 1634–1850*. Detroit: Wayne State University Press, 1998.

Huston, James L. *Stephen A. Douglas and the Dilemmas of Democratic Equality*. Lanham, MD: Rowman & Littlefield, 2007.

Johannsen, Robert W. *Stephen A. Douglas*. New York: Oxford University Press, 1973.

———. *The Letters of Stephen A. Douglas*. Urbana: University of Illinois Press, 1961.

John T. Morse, Jr. *Abraham Lincoln*. vol. 1 of 2. Boston: Houghton Mifflin, 1893.

Johnson, Allen. *Stephen A. Douglas: A Study in American Politics*. New York: Macmillan, 1908.

Johnson, T. Walter. "Charles Reynolds Matheny: Pioneer Settler of Illinois (1786–1839)." *Journal of the Illinois State Historical Society*, December 1940.

"Josiah Lamborn." *Historical Encyclopedia of Illinois*. Edited by Newton Bateman and Paul Selby. Chicago: Munsell, 1903.

Kempf, Edward J. *Abraham Lincoln's Philosophy of Common Sense: An Analytical Biography of a Great Mind*. vol. 1 of 3. New York: The New York Academy of Sciences, 1965.

Kennedy, Jos. C.G. *Preliminary Report on The Eighth Census. 1860*. Washington, D.C.: Government Printing Office, 1862.

King, Willard. *Lincoln's Manager: David Davis*. Cambridge: Harvard University Press, 1960.

Knock Family Genealogy. Roots Web. http://wc.rootsweb.ancesry.com/cgi-bin/igm.cgi?op=AHN&d=knockk&id=I287614.

Lamon, Ward Hill. *The Life of Abraham Lincoln from His Birth to His Inauguration as President*. Boston: James R. Osgood and Company, 1872.

Larson, John Lauritz. "Congress, Internal Improvement, and the Problem of Governance." *The American Congress*. Edited by Julian E. Zelizer. Boston: Houghton Mifflin, 2006.

Leonard, Gerald. *The Invention of Party Politics: Federalism, Popular Sovereignty, and Constitutional Development in Jacksonian Illinois*. Chapel Hill: University of North Carolina Press, 2002.

Lincoln Day by Day: A Chronology, 1809–1865. Edited by Earl Schenck Miers. vol. 1 of 3. Washington: Lincoln Sesquicentennial Commission, 1960.

Linder, Usher F. *Reminiscences of the Early Bench and Bar of Illinois*. Chicago: The Chicago Legal News Company, 1879.

Lindsey, David. *Democracy and Enterprise*. Cleveland: Howard Allen, Inc., Publishers, 1962.

Mahoney, Timothy R. *Provincial Lives*. New York: Cambridge University Press, 1999.

Main, Jackson Turner. *The Anti-Federalists: Critics of the Constitution, 1781–1788*. New York: W.W. Norton, 1961.

Maltz, Earl M. *Slavery and the Supreme Court, 1835–1861*. Lawrence: University Press of Kansas, 2006.

Mansberger, Floyd, and Christopher Stratton. *The Architectural Resources of Aristocracy Hill Neighborhood, Springfield, Illinois*. Springfield, IL: Historic Sites Commission of the City of Springfield, 2003.

Marsh, Edward S., ed. *Stephen A. Douglas: A Memorial*. Brandon, VT: Committee of Arrangements, 1914.

McConnel, George Murray. "Recollection of Stephen A. Douglas." *Transactions of the Illinois State Historical Society* (Trustees of the Illinois State Historical Library) V (1900).

———. "Some Reminiscences of My Father, Murray McConnel." *Journal of the Illinois State Historical Society* (Illinois State Historical Society) XVIII, no. 1 (April 1925).

McCormick, Richard P. *The Second American Party System: Party Formation in the Jacksonian Era*. New York: W.W. Norton, 1966.

Miller, Richard Lawrence. *Lincoln and His World: The Early Years*. Mechanicsburg, PA: Stackpole Books, 2006.

———. *Lincoln and His World: Prairie Politician, 1834–1842*. Mechanicsburg, PA: Stackpole Books, 2008.

Milton, George Fort. *Eve of Conflict: Stephen A. Douglas and the Needless War*. Boston: Houghton Mifflin, 1934.

Moore, Ensley. "A Notable Illinois Family." *Journal of the Illinois State Historical Society* (Trustees of the Illinois State Historical Library), 1908.

Morrison, Jeffry H. *The Political Philosophy of George Washington*. Baltimore: Johns Hopkins University Press, 2009.

Nevins, Allan. "Stephen A. Douglas." In *An Illinois Reader*, edited by Clyde C. Walton. DeKalb: Northern Illinois University Press, 1970.

Newell, Mason H. "The Attorneys-General of Illinois." *Transactions of the Illinois State Historical Society for the Year 1903* (Trustees of the Illinois State Historical Library), 1904.

Nicholas, Gordon. *The Man Who Freed His Slaves: A Narrative of the Life of Edward Coles*. http://poemsforfree.com/edwardcoles.html.

Norton, W.T. *Edward Coles: Second Governor of Illinois*. Philadelphia: J.P. Lippincott, 1911.

Orth, Samuel B. *Five American Politicians: A Study in the Evolution of American Politics*. Cleveland: The Burrows Brothers Company, 1906.

Osborne, Georgia L. "Pioneer Women of Morgan County." *Journal of the Illinois State Historical Society* (Illinois State Historical Society) XVIII, no. 1 (April 1925).

Park, Syoung. "Illinois Land Speculation in Western Illinois: Pike County, 1821–1835." *Journal of the Illinois State Historical Society* (Illinois State Historical Society) LXXVII, no. 2 (Summer 1984).

Pospisek, Patrick. "Springfield's Acquisition of the Illinois Seat of Government." *Journal of the Illinois State Historical Society* (Illinois State Historical Society) IXC, no. 1 (Spring-Summer 2006).

Pratt, Harry E. "The Division of Sangamon County." *Journal of the Illinois State Historical Society* XLVII, no. 4 (Winter 1954).

Putnam, Elizabeth Duncan. "Diary of Mrs. Joseph Duncan." *Journal of the Illinois State Historical So-*

ciety (Illinois State HIstorical Society) XXI, no. 1 (April 1928).

———. "The Life and Services of Joseph Duncan, Governor of Illinois, 1834–1838." *Transactions of the Illinois Historical Soceity for the Year 1919* (Trustees of the Illinois State Historical Library) XXVI (1920).

Qui Tam InfoCenter. http://quitaminfocenter.com.

Quincy Whig. "STEWART AND DOUGLAS." January 8, 1838.

Quitt, Martin H. *Stephen A. Douglas and Antebellum Democracy.* New York: Cambridge University Press, 2012.

Rammelkamp, Charles Henry. *Illinois College, A Centennial History.* New Haven: Yale University Press, 1928.

Randall, Henry Stephens. *The Life of Thomas Jefferson.* Philadelphia: J.B. Lippincott, 1871.

Reed, Scott G.G. "From Ireland to Adams County, One Man Leaves His Mark." Mss., Historical Society of Quincy and Adams County, 2012.

Remini, Robert V. *John Quincy Adams.* New York: Times Books, Henry Holt and Company, 2002.

Rennick, P.G. "Courts and Lawyers in Northern and Western Illinois." *Journal of the Illinois State Historical Society* (Illinois State Historical Society) XXX, no. 3 (October 1937).

Rice, Harvey. *Sketches of Western Reserve Life.* Kila, Montana: Kessinger, 2005.

Roberts, Daniel. "A Reminiscence of Stephen A. Douglas." *Harper's Monthly Magazine* LXXXVII (November 1893).

Roske, Ralph J. *His Own Counsel: The Life and Times of Lyman Trumbull.* Reno: University of Nevada Press, 1979.

Sandburg, Carl. *Abraham Lincoln: The Prairie Years and the War Years.* Boston: Houghton Mifflin Harcourt, 2002.

Schwartz, Thomas F. "Mary Todd's 1835 Visit to Springfield, Illinois." Edited by Bryon Andreason. *Journal of the Abraham Lincoln Association* (Abraham Lincoln Association) XXVI, no. 1 (Winter 2005).

Sheahan, James W. *The Life of Stephen A. Douglas.* New York: Harper and Brothers, 1860.

Shenk, Joshua Wolfe. *Lincoln's Melancholy: How Depression Challenged a President and Fueled His Greatness.* New York: Houghton Mifflin, 2005.

Simeone, James. *Democracy and Slavery in Frontier Illinois: The Bottomland Republic.* DeKalb: Northern Illinois University Press, 2000.

Simon, Paul. *Freedom's Champion, Elijah Lovejoy.* Carbondale: Southern Illinois University Press, 1994.

Snyder, Dr. J.F. "Forgotten Statesmen of Illinois: Richard M. Young." *Transactions of the Illinois State Historical Society for the Year 1906.* Springfield: Trustees of the Illinois State Historical Society, 1906.

———. *Adam W. Snyder and His Period in Illinois History, 1817–1842.* Ann Arbor, Michigan: Michigan University Microfilms, 1969.

Snyder, Lynn. "Crusaders and Songwriters" (pamphlet), Historical Society of Quincy and Adams County, June 22, 2013.

Speed, Joshua Fry. *Reminiscences of Abraham Lincoln and Notes of a Visit to California.* Louisville: John P. Morton and Company, 1884.

Stephen A. Douglas: A Memorial, edited by Edward S. Brandon, Vermont: Committee of Arrangements, 1914.

"Stephen Arnold Douglas." encyclopedia.com. http://www.encyclopedia.com/topic/Stephen_Arnold_Douglas.aspx.

Stevens, Frank E. "Autobiography of Stephen A. Douglas." *Journal of the Illinois State Historical Society* (The Illinois Printing Co.), April 1912.

———. "Life of Stephen A. Douglas." *Journal of the Illinois State Historical Society.* Springfield, Illinois: Illinois State Historical Society, XVI, no. 3–4, October–January 1923–1924.

Stevenson, Richard Taylor. *The Growth of the Nation, 1809–1837.* Philadelphia: George Barrie and Sons, 1905.

Strickland, Arvareh E. "The Illinois Background of Lincoln's Attitude Toward Slavery and the Negro." *Journal of the Illinois State Historical Society* (Illinois State Historical Society) LVI, no. 3 (Autumn 1963).

Stroble, Jr., Paul E. *High on the Okaw's Western Bank: Vandalia, Illinois.* Urbana: University of Illinois Press, 1992.

Stuart, James. *Three Years in North America.* vol. 2 of 3. Edinburgh: Robert Cadell and Whittaker and Company, 1833.

Sturtevant, Julian M. "Sectional Forces in the History of Illinois." *Transactions of the Illinois State Historical Society* (Trustees of the Illinois State Historical Library) VIII (1896).

Sylla, Richard, "Review Essay" of *The Jacksonian Economy* at http://eh.net/book_reviews/the-jacksonian-economy/.

Taft, Robert. "The Appearance and Personality of Stephen A. Douglas: Address to the Kansas State Historical Society Annual Meeting, October 20, 1953." *The Kansas Historical Quarterly* (Kansas State Historical Society), Spring 1954.

Tarbell, Ida M. *Abraham Lincoln and His Ancestors.* New York: Harper & Brothers, 1924.

Temin, Peter. *The Jacksonian Economy.* New York: W.W. Norton, 1969.

Temple, Wayne C. *Stephen A. Douglas, Freemason.* Bloomington: The Masonic Book Club, The Illinois Lodge of Research, 1982.

Thompson, Charles Manfred. *The Illinois Whigs Before 1846.* Urbana: University of Illinois, 1915.

Tillson, Christiana Holmes. *A Woman's Story of Pioneer Illinois.* Chicago: Lakeside Press Company, 1929.

Tillson, General John. *History of the City of Quincy, Illinois.* Edited by William H. Collins. Quincy, IL: S.J. Clarke, 1905.

Turner, Frederick Jackson, *The Frontier in American History.* Tucson: University of Arizona Press, 1997.

———. *The Rise of the New West, 1819–1829.* New York: Harper and Brothers, 1906.

Turner, J.B. *The Three Great Races: Their Origin, Character, History and Destiny.* Springfield, IL: Bailhache and Baker, Printers, 1861.

Violette, Eugene Morrow. *A History of Missouri.* Boston: D.C. Heath, 1918.

Walker, Jeffrey N. "Habeas Corpus in Early Nineteenth-Century Mormonism: Joseph Smith's Legal Bulwark for Personal Freedom." *BYU Studies Quarterly* 32, no. 1, 2013.

Washburne, E.B. *Sketch of Edward Coles, Second Governor of Illinois and of the Slavery Struggle of 1823-4, Prepared for the Chicago Historical Society.* New York: Negro Universities Press, 1969.

Waugh, John C. *One Man Great Enough: Abraham Lincoln's Road to Civil War.* New York: Harcourt Brace, 2007.

Weik, Jesse William. *The Real Lincoln: A Portrait.* Edited by Michael Burlingame. Lincoln: University of Nebraska Press, 2002.

Weld, Theodore D. *Slavery and the International Slave Trade in the United States of North America.* London: Thomas Ward, Publisher, 1841.

Wheeler, Katherine F.E. "Eward Coles, Second Governor of Illinois." *Transactions of the Illinois State Historical Society for the Year 1903* (Trustees of the Illinois State Historical Library) VIII (1904).

Wiebe, Robert H. *Self-Rule: A Cultural History of American Democracy.* Chicago: University of Chicago Press, 1995.

Wilentz, Sean. *The Rise of American Democracy: Jefferson to Lincoln.* New York: W.W. Norton, 2005.

Willard, Samuel. "Personal Reminiscences of Life in Illinois: 1830 to 1850." *Transactions of the Illinois State Historical Society for the Year 1906* (Trustees of the Illinois State Historical Library) XI (1906).

Willis, Henry Parker. *Stephen A. Douglas.* Philadelphia: George W. Jacobs and Company Publishers, 1910.

Wilson, Douglas L. *Honor's Voice: The Transformation of Abraham Lincoln.* New York: Alfred A. Knopf, 1998.

Winkler, H. Donald. *The Women in Lincoln's Life.* Nashville: Rutledge Hill Press, 2001.

Woldman, Albert A. *Lawyer Lincoln.* New York: Carroll & Graf, 1994.

Wood, Gordon S. *Empire of Liberty: A History of the Early Republic, 1789–1815.* New York: Oxford University Press, 2009.

Wright, Hon. Walter W. "The Life and Character of Stephen A. Douglas." Lecture delivered before the Iroquois Club, Chicago, Illinois, April 23, 1945.

Index

Adams, John Quincy 7, 21; wins 1824 presidential election 70
Adams County 83–84, 164; county seat dispute 181
Alien Case 117, 142–143, 146, 149; impact of vote by foreign residents 141; *Spraggins vs. Houghton* 143; Supreme Court hearing in 147
Alien Vote: Lincoln disturbed by 119
Allen, Robert (Douglas friend) 150
Alton, Illinois (anti-slavery convention) 10–11
Alton Observer 173
"American System" 41
Andrews, Sherlock J. (prominent Cleveland lawyer) 24
Archer, William B. (Illinois-Michigan Canal commissioner) 86
"Aristocracy Hill," Springfield 123
Asbury, Henry (Quincy justice of the peace) 174
Atchison, David 192

Backenstos, Jacob B. 185
Baker, Edward D. 14, 46, 53, 56, 135, 136, 140; nominated to Congress 180
Barnet, Berryman (Quincy underground railroad conductor) 173
Bates, Edward (St. Louis attorney) 26
Beecher, Dr. Edward (Illinois College president) 5
Bell & Company general store, Springfield 135
Bennett, John Cook 122, 163, 166; Mormon excommunication 168
Bissell, William Harrison (first Illinois Republican governor) 126
Blair, Francis Preston (St. Louis anti-slavery supporter) 119
Blankenship, Eli (state capital relocation conspirator) 90
Boggs, Missouri Governor Lilburn W. 162
Bond, Shadrach (first governor of Illinois) 76
Bounty Land Register (Quincy newspaper) 84
Brandon, Vermont (Douglas birthplace) 5
Breed, Sands 116
Breese, Sidney 7, 44, 45, 151, 178; elected U.S. senator, 1842 178; elected Supreme Court associate justice, 1840 161
"Brigham House" (Douglas residence in Quincy) 164
Brooks, Samuel S. 32–33, 41, 64, 67, 111; suggests convention system 60
Browne, Justice Thomas C. 121
Browning, Eliza Caldwell 46, 129, 131
Browning, Orville Hickman 5, 46, 50, 56, 102, 129, 136, 138, 166; appearance, demeanor of 182; before Judge Douglas 170; bill makes capital site permanent 105; criticizes abolitionists 174–175; nominated for Congress, 1843 179
Bryant, Henry L. (Douglas Canandaigua friend) 34
Bunkum (first Illinois trial site) 44
Bushnell, Nehemiah (land speculator) 182
Butler, William (Lincoln Springfield benefactor) 135
Butterfield, Justin (Alien Case attorney) 143; defends Joseph Smith 168, 170; praises Douglas courtroom acumen 172

Calhoun, John 111, 112, 136, 139; hired Lincoln as land surveyor 83
Calhoun, John Caldwell 129; introduced "equal footing" concept 102; Springfield first named for 123
Campbell, H.B.: Douglas opposes in murder case 145
Canandaigua, New York 7
Carlin, Thomas 152, 166, 179; defeats Cyrus Edward for governor 128; federal land register, Quincy 107; fires Secretary of State Field 151; replaces Stephenson as governor nominee 113
Carrollton, Carlinville (1838 campaign town) 184
Cartwright, Reverend Peter (popular Methodist circuit riding preacher) 66
Catfish Hotel (Douglas stop in Meredosia) 28
Cavarly, Alfred V. (first judicial circuit lawyer) 61, 66, 179
Casey, Zadoc: switches parties 187
Channing, Ellen: Douglas affection for 21
Chapman, Harriett: reveals Douglas-Todd betrothal 127
Charlie (subject of Douglas's fugitive slave trial) 173
Chase, Salmon Portland: represents abolitionist Dr. Richard Eells 175
Chinn, Marcus A. (Jacksonville slave owners) 14
Clay, Elizabeth Hardin: inherits Hardin slave plantation 13
Clay, Henry 21, 102, 123; and "corrupt bargain" 70
Clay, Porter: ignored Illinois anti-slavery laws 40
Cloud, Newton: in Democratic landslide wins 68
Coles, Edward (Illinois anti-slavery governor) 7, 47; calls for end of slavery in Illinois 107
Columbus Village: Douglas rules in Adams County dispute 84
Conant, John Adams: claims to save baby boy Douglas's life 16
Conkling, James C. (Springfield lawyer, Lincoln friend) 131

Cook, Daniel Pope: 1824 vote costs seat in Congress 70; Illinois-Michigan canal sponsor 76
Council on Revision: vetoes Douglas measures 43, 44, 150
Cutts, Adele (second Douglas wife) 20

Davis, David 88, 138, 149; despondent over Whig chances 156; Douglas critic 115; Eighth Judicial Circuit lawyer 57
Davis, Levi: warns state near bankruptcy 98
Dawson, John (Springfield lawyer; Lincoln friend) 65
DeForrest, Ann (nurse) 16
Democratic Party Convention, 1838: criticizes "land office convention" 113; Douglas controls 112; first convention attracts converts 66
Democrats 68
Demont, John: colludes in states attorney bill 49
"Doctrine of Instruction" 87
Douglas, Benajah (Douglas's paternal grandfather) 18, 19
Douglas, Martha Martin (Douglas's first wife) 19
Douglas, Sally (sister): marries Julius N. Granger 22
Douglas, Sarah Fisk (mother): marries Gahazi Granger 22
Douglas, Stephen A. 5, 20, 23, 28, 47, 68, 136, 147, 150, 179; accused of self-serving votes 105; active in General Assembly 89; admired Lincoln's abilities 135; "admit nothing; require adversary to prove everthing" 57, 146; admitted to practice law 37; advises Mormon leader Joseph Smith 168; against agitation over slavery 103; another woman 128; answers electioneering charges 111; applies for law license 28; appointed secretary of state 152–153; attracted to Jacksonville 9; begs recount in 1838 race 119; and bill to reorganize circuit court system 91; blames Hardin, Lockwood for attacks 42; 1838 campaign turns violent 118; campaigns for U.S. Senate 177–178; casts "vote of my constituents" for internal improvements 97; chairs Illinois Van Buren campaign 130–136, 139; congressional campaign of 1843 181–187; considered slavery an abstraction 39; resolves constitutional crisis 192; court reform bill passed 50; court reorganization 156, 157, 159, 161; courtroom demeanor, administration 169–170; deathly ill 24; debates Lincoln at Speed's store 135; decides to stay in Jacksonville 34; denied education 20; denies McConnel appeal 170; devastates anti–Jackson arguments 32; earns sobriquet, "Little Giant" 42; at ease with people 38; at ease with young ladies 125; *Eells vs. People of Illinois* 173–176; effort to stop Lincoln, internal improvement plan 95; elected senator December 13, 1846 99; elected state's attorney 50; elected Supreme Court associate justice 161; embellishes success 39; engagement to Mary Todd told 127; enters Canandaigua Academy 22; estranges self from family 134; explains his bank vote 79; favors limited internal improvements 82; first run for Congress, 1838 113–124; frequent ill health of 20; gains a position in Cleveland 24; gains favor of Mormon leader Joseph Smith 163; growing power in Congress 189; influenced by the West 11; "I have become a Western man" 29; joins the cause of Democracy 21; joint debates with Stuart 117; journeys west 24; judge and justice 168; as justice reverses own ruling 171; law partnerships of 121; Lincoln trial partner 145; marriage proposal 129; move to Quincy 164; moves divorce cases from legislature 100; named federal land register, 1837 107; nominated to legislature 67; nominated to Congress 179; opens school in Winchester 30; organizes Illinois Democratic Party 109; panders to Mormons 166; passes convention bill 66; physical description 17–18; plans to win Supreme Court seat 150; plots against Hardin, Lockwood 43; popular sovereignty, calls for 96; on his popularity 63; power of relationships 190; proclaims himself a "Western man" 29; Quincy quarters 164; relationship with Mary Ann Todd 127–128; resigns as state's attorney 73; respect for jurisprudence 188–189; rules on Springfield debt 171; runs out of money, quits recount appeal 121; seeks to control Internal Improvements 88; sees need to organize party 62; and slavery 172; slavery, witnesses 191; speculates in land 83, 84; sworn in as Supreme Court justice 164; takes seat in Illinois House 74; tests early political skills 31; thwarts governor's anti–Jackson attack 100; tries misdemeanor and murder cases 170; turns table on Governor Duncan 101; Twenty-Eighth Congress, attends 192; value of friends 34; wanted capital relocated in Jacksonville 92; wins appeal against judge 55
Douglas, Stephen Arnold, Sr. (father) 16
Duncan, Joseph 43, 45, 49, 75, 76, 140, 151, 168; apostate Democrat 9; attacks convention system 67; attacks Jackson in address 82; bails out state banks 109; calls special session on economy 108; defeats "Edwards Dynasty" 77; denied re-election over veto of works 99; drifts away from Jackson 77; elected governor 48; secret plan to relocate capital 90; speculates on Mormons 171
Dunlap, Sarah (Mary Todd Jacksonville friend) 125
Durkee, Chauncey (Missouri slave owner) 174

Eddy, Henry 113
Edwards, Benjamin (Springfield lawyer for Joseph Smith) 168
Edwards, Elizabeth Todd (Mary Todd sister) 132
Edwards, James E. (anti–Douglas newspaper publisher) 42
Edwards, Ninian W. (third governor of Illinois; Mary Todd brother-in-law) 14, 53, 75, 76, 123, 150; pays for Springfield celebration 106; represents Emily Logan 14; resigns office to avoid Vandalia 45
"Edwards Dynasty" 77
Eells, Dr. Richard (Quincy abolitionist) 164, 172; U.S. Supreme Court upholds conviction 175
Evans, James (jilted by John Hardin) 43
Ewing, William L.D. (Illinois shortest-serving governor) 151, 154
Exeter (first Morgan County town) 12

Ficklin, Orlando B. (elected to Congress in Democratic sweep) 184
Field, Alexander Pope (resigns as secretary of state) 55, 113, 119, 150, 153
Fisk, Edward (Douglas's uncle) 19
Fithian, Dr. William: alleges Van Buren supported black vote 140

Flack, Mathilda (Vandalia hotelier) 45
Flack, Milton (Vandalia hotelier) 45
Ford, Thomas 44, 59, 66, 93, 111, 144, 168, 178; elected governor, 1842 177; election to Supreme Court 161; on power of public opinion 99; torn by slave controversy 175
Forquer, George (Ford stepbrother; Douglas law partner) 50, 53, 66, 123
Francis, Newton (debate participant) 135
Francis, Simeon 122; manhandles Douglas 139; refuses to reveal identity of "Conservative" 114

Gillespie, Joseph 13, 135, 138, 154
Godfrey Gilman & Company 80
Goudy, Robert (*Jacksonville News* publisher) 32
Granger, Emily 134
Granger, Francis: writes recommendation for Douglas 23
Granger, Gehazi 58, 134
Granger, Julius N. 134; makes trip to Jacksonville 39
Gridley, Asahel 138
Griggsville (site of Democratic nominating convention) 179, 182–183

Hall, James (*Illinois Monthly Magazine* publisher) 73
Happy, William W. (winner in 1836 Illinois Democratic landslide) 68
Hardin, John J. 5, 45, 50, 53, 56, 58, 68, 96, 101, 125, 140, 154, 160, 180; background of 39–40; Clay, Elizabeth Hardin 7; Clay, Henry, shirttail relative 7; Hardin, Martin D., father 7; lauds Douglas's Eells decision 175; lone Whig congressional winner, 1836 185; loses eye in gun misfire 13; refuses help to Democrats 43; sells slaves 13
Harlan, Justin (circuit judge appointee) 44
Hay, Milton (Springfield lawyer; Lincoln friend) 12
Henry, John 12, 65, 68
Herndon, Archer 96
Herndon, Billy (William) 10, 132, 135; critiques Douglas 189; Illinois College riot participant 11
Heslep, Thomas (Jacksonville innkeeper) 26
Hoge, Joseph P. (1843 congressional winner) 184
Howe, Henry (Canandaigua Academy principal) 34
Hubbard, Gurdon S. (Internal Improvements promoter, beneficiary) 86
Hubbell, Walter (Canandaigua lawyer) 23

Illinois College 5, 6, 10, 20, 32; abolitionism at 10; funding controversy 62
Illinois Military Tract 84, 162
Illinois Republican 112
Illinois, slavery in 30, 46–47
Illinois State Bank 78, 79–80
Illinois State Capital: 1834 referendum indecisive 91; logrolling by "Long Nine" for 90; rumors of move 75
Illinois State Register (pro–Douglas newspaper) 147, 150, 151, 177
Illinois Supreme Court 73, 152
Illiopolis: in state capital speculation 30
Internal Improvements: convention piles on public works 87; Douglas favors "reasonable" works 88; petitions for flood Vandalia 85; state edges toward bankruptcy 93; statewide frenzy for 87

Irish canal builders: role in "Alien Case" 116
Irwin, John (Springfield Whig operative) 151
Irwin, Robert (Springfield Whig operative) 151

Jackson, Andrew (Douglas hero) 5, 21, 70
Jacksonville 5, 38, 140, 180; "Africa," blacks segregated in 6; Bryant, William Cullen, visits 6; commerce 6; education 6; politics in 12; religion 6; slavery in 9, 11
Jacksonville News (pro–Jackson newspaper) 32
Jacksonville Patriot (anti–Jackson newspaper) 42
Jayne, Julia (Mary Todd Lincoln rejects friendship) 125
Jefferson, Thomas 65

Kane, Elias Kent (Illinois' first secretary) 76, 99
Kansas-Nebraska Act 126
Kellogg, Colonel Seymour: hoodwinked by Quincy founders 83
Kelly, Captain Timothy 141
Keyes, Willard (Quincy co-founder) 162
Kinney, William (perennial gubernatorial candidate) 62
Knapp, Samuel B. (Winchester emigrant from Canandaigua) 39
Knowlton, Deacon Caleb (Brandon cabinetmaker) 22
Koerner, Gustav 182; wins German vote for Douglas 185

Lamborn, Josiah 31, 53, 56, 136; complains Douglas loose with facts 42; doubts Douglas's ability 33; prosecutor in Joseph Smith trial 168
Levering, Marcy (Mary Todd confidante) 128
Lincoln, Abraham 5, 45, 50, 53, 56, 65, 68, 89, 101, 111, 135, 136, 141, 151, 154; amorousness of 131; announces for internal improvements 87; aspirations for Congress 179–180; attacks Douglas under pseudonym 114; concerned about Stuart victory margin 119; dissents on slave resolutions 103; encourages Whig Party organization 138; fills in for exhausted Stuart 117; forestalls loss of state bank charter 108–109; love for Matilda Edwards 129; party shuns 180; personal strains 156; promotes Internal Improvements 89; proposes marriage to another 131; rejects offer to run for governor 155; Sangamon delegation leader 74; says beware of Douglas 120; second Mary Todd engagement 133; yields 1855 Senate bid to Trumbull 126
Linder, Usher 49, 96, 118
Little, Sidney H.: sponsors Mormon bill 163
lobby: Douglas's self-serving "third house" 78, 166
Lockwood, Samuel Drake (Illinois Supreme Court associate justice) 5, 28, 50, 56, 73
Logan, Stephen Trigg 50, 53, 55, 125, 136
Long Nine 68, 92, 105, 146; scheme to relocate capital to Springfield 93, 96–97
Lovejoy, Reverend Elijah P. 172

Mangum, Willie (U.S. Senate president pro tem) 192
Manley, Uri 65
Marquette County proposal 181
Matheny, Charles 55, 126
Matheny, James 127, 135

Mather, Thomas 123, 171; switches opinion in conflict of interest 78
Matteson, Joel (participant in Douglas Senate plan) 126
May, William 60, 66, 106, 141; admits adultery, wins election 62; critical of Douglas 110
McClernand, John A. 100, 125, 178; succeeds Douglas in legislature 151, 184
McConnel, Murray 12, 26, 53, 56, 143, 161; advises Douglas 28; avoids Jackson controversies 41; comments on Douglas personality 31
McLean, John: loses congressional bid 76
McLean County controversy 56–57
Meredosia (Illinois River community) 28
Middlebury, Vermont 21
Millburn, William (fan of Douglas from childhood) 40
Mills, Benjamin: challenges William May for congress 61
Miner, Edward Griffith: batched with Douglas in Winchester 30
Missouri Compromise 102, 126
Morgan County: politics in 7; rejects slavery-related referendum 10
Morganian Society 10
Mormons: exchange favors with Douglas 163; leaders held for treason 167; order of extermination against 162; political parties vie for votes of 149

Nance, Thomas J. 122
Nauvoo: city charter grants broad power 163
Nelson, Dr. David (abolitionist): converted Elijah P. Lovejoy 173, 174
Ninth Illinois General Assembly 90
Northwest Ordinance of 1787 15

O'Rear, William 68
Owen, Mary 131

Palmer, John McAuley: appreciation for Douglas's skills 121
Panic of 1837 107
Parker, Nahum (Middlebury cabinetmaker) 21
Peck, Ebenezer: reverses vote to pass Douglas bill 164
Pettit, J.H. (land speculator) 84
Pittsfield 182
Pope, Nathaniel (secretary, Illinois Territory) 135, 150
Presidential Campaign of 1836 69
Presidential Campaign of 1840 69–72, 130, 136, 146
Prigg v. Pennsylvania 175

Quincy: county seat agitation 83-84; federal land office at 161; headquarters for Fifth Judicial Circuit 163; Northern Cross Railroad terminus 141; provides refuge to exiled Latter Day Saints 162
Quincy anti-slavery movement 172; Anti-Slavery Society of Adams County 172, 174; division in over slavery 174; earthquakes, natural and political 186; Mission Institute 168, 174; representatives oppose abolition 102; underground railroad in 173
Quincy Daily Whig: opposition to Douglas 70, 180, 181
Quincy House Hotel 164
Quincy Whig: criticizes "alien vote" 141; lauds Douglas's Eells decision 175

Ralston, James 43, 55, 88, 102, 116, 151
Reynolds, Thomas (Missouri governor) 40, 175
Rhodes, Daniel (Douglas cousin) 24
Richardson, William Alexander (close Douglas colleague) 50, 56, 153, 179
Rickard, Noah (Whig debate participant) 131, 135
Roberts, Daniel (Jacksonville Democratic attorney) 27, 40, 50
Rockwell, Dennis (land speculator) 84
Ross, Lewis (Fulton County Democratic leader) 140
Rowan, Ira (Winchester tavern keeper; postmaster) 28
Rushville 91

Sangamo Journal (anti–Douglas newspaper) 61, 89, 138, 159; sarcasm over Douglas nomination 112–114
Scates, Walter B. (associate justice of Supreme Court) 161
Second Presbyterian Church (Douglas-Lincoln debates) 136
Semple, James (Illinois house speaker) 45; appointed U.S. senator in 1843 99; elected speaker with Douglas help 74
Seward, William Henry: defends Quincy abolitionist Richard Eells 175
Shields, James 135, 169; resigns from U.S. Senate 126
Shurtleff, Dr. Benjamin (Illinois land speculator) 47, 80, 101–104, 188
Smith, Joseph (Founder, Church of Latter Day Saints): trial in Judge Douglas's court 167–168
Smith, Robert (Democratic landslide congressional winner) 184
Smith, Theophilus Washington (associate justice, Illinois Supreme Court) 80, 121; studied law under Aaron Burr 144, 184
Snow, Henry H. (Adams County justice of the peace) 173
Snyder, Adam 139, 157; proposes referendum to relocate capital 90
Speed, Joshua 126, 128, 132, 138, 180; Bell & Company general store 135; "Douglas-Lincoln Debates" 135; introduces Lincoln to Todd 127
Spraggins v. Houghton 142
Springfield 105, 106; "Aristocracy Hill" 45, 123, 133
Springfield Republican (Whig newspaper, Springfield) 151
State Bank failure 154
Stephenson, James 113
Stone, Dr. Barton W. (leader in religious "Great Awakening") 36
Stone, Dan 53; protests anti-abolition resolutions 102; trial judge in "Alien Case" 142
Strong, Schuyler ("Alien Case" attorney) 143–144
Stuart, James (Scot author, *Three Years on the Continent*) 6
Stuart, John Todd 53, 56, 65, 125, 140, 141; Douglas opponent for Congress 113; internal improvements trading by 86; Lincoln assists congressional campaign 114; state representative 45, 73
Stuart, Robert (Lincoln voice for internal improvements) 95

Sturtevant, Julian Monson (Illinois college president; abolitionist) 14

Temin, Peter: contra-theory of Panic of 1837 107–108
Tenth General Assembly 73; governor's message to 77
Thomas, Jesse B.: crafted Missouri Compromise amendment 102
Thomas, Jesse B., Jr.: succeeds Douglas as circuit judge 136, 187
Thornton, William F. (Illinois-Michigan Canal commissioner) 86
Tillson, John: (Illinois land speculator) 80, 164
Todd, David (Missouri judge; Mary Todd uncle) 130
Todd, Dr. John (Mary Todd uncle) 130
Todd, Mary Ann: attracts numerous beaus 124; concerned about weight 131; descriptions of 124–126; failed in ploy to attract Lincoln 129; flirtations 125, 129; left at the altar by Lincoln 128; Lincoln amorousness upsets 131; reveals continuing Douglas interest 130; suitors 127; summer 1940 in Columbia, Missouri 130
Treat, Samuel H. 14, 58; election to Supreme Court 161
Trumbull, Lyman: defeats Lincoln for U.S. Senate 125–126
Turner, Reverend Asa 173
Turner, Jonathan Baldwin (Illinois College professor; author) 14

Van Buren, President Martin: appoints Douglas land register 109, 123
Vandalia (second Illinois state capital) 45, 73–74, 80
Vermont 18
Vox populi, vox dei 190

Walker, Cyrus 143, 185
Walker, Richard S. 68
Warren, Calvin A. 171
Washington, George: defends compromise on slavery 191
Weatherford, William: jilted by John Hardin 68
Webb, Edwin "Bat": seeks to lure Democrats from convention 66
Weber, George (editor, *Illinois Republican*) 115
Webster, Daniel (Whig congressman visits Jacksonville) 5
Wentworth, John: elected in 1843 Democratic landslide 184
White, Hugh Lawson: Whig candidate for president 69
Whiteside, John D. (Illinois Treasurer) 97; examiner in Douglas 1838 vote challenge 119
Whitney, J.W. 56, 164; "Lord Coke" 78
Wiggins, Samuel: involved in Illinois finances 80
Williams, Archibald (Quincy lawyer; Lincoln friend) 99
Willson, Marcius (Douglas's school friend) 24
Winchester: influences on school teacher Douglas 27–41
Wood, John (Quincy co-founder) 43, 162
Wyatt, John: blames Douglas for House loss 68; conspires with Douglas 43; elected House speaker 47; no gain from supporting Douglas 50

Yale Band (Illinois College founders) 10
Yates, Richard (first judicial circuit lawyer; Lincoln friend) 56
Young, Richard M.: appointed circuit judge 44; beats Lincoln's candidate for U.S. Senate 100; malfeasance dooms re-election 177; pays political debt to Douglas 106; turns against May on Douglas's word

www.ingramcontent.com/pod-product-compliance
Lightning Source LLC
Chambersburg PA
CBHW081552300426
44116CB00015B/2855